SECRETS & LIES

SECRETS & LIES

A History of CIA Mind Control & Germ Warfare

GORDON THOMAS

JR BOOKS

First published in Great Britain in 2008 by
JR Books, 10 Greenland Street, London NW1 0ND
www.jrbooks.com

A catalogue record for this book is
available from the British Library.

ISBN 978-1-906217-72-3

1 3 5 7 9 10 8 6 4 2

Printed by The Cromwell Press, Trowbridge, Wiltshire

TABLE OF CONTENTS

In Memory of

William Buckley,
soldier, spy and friend:
the bravest of the brave.

and

Frank Olson, who was murdered
not knowing that through his
death the truth would
finally emerge.

"I swear by Apollo Physician and Asclepius and Hygeia and Panacea and all the gods and goddesses, making them my witnesses, that I will fulfill according to my ability and judgment this oath and this covenant. To hold him who has taught me this art as equal to my parents and to live my life in partnership, and if he is in need of money to give him a share of mine, and to regard his offspring as equal to my brother in male lineage and to teach them this art if they desire to learn it without fee and covenant; to give a share of the precepts and oral instruction and all the other learning to my sons and to the sons of him who has instructed me and to pupils who have signed the covenant and have taken an oath according to the medical law, but to no one else. I will apply dietetic measures for the benefit of the sick according to my ability and judgment; I will keep them from harm and injustice. I will neither give a deadly drug to anybody if asked for it; nor will I make a suggestion to this effect. Similarly I will not give to a woman an abortive remedy. In purity and holiness I will guard my life and my art. I will not use the knife, not even on sufferers from stone, but will withdraw in favor of such men as are engaged in this work. Whatever houses I may visit, I will come for the benefit of the sick, remaining free of all internal injustice, of all mischief and in particular of sexual relation with both female and male persons, be they free or slaves. What I may see or hear in the course of the treatment or even outside the treatment in regard to the life of men, which on no account one must spread abroad, I will keep to myself holding such things shameful to be spoken about. If I fulfill this oath and do not violate it, may it be granted to me to enjoy life and art, being honored with fame among all men for all time to come; if I transgress it and swear falsely, may the opposite of all this be my lot."

— **The Oath of Hippocrates**

"I solemnly swear to devote all my knowledge and strength to the preservation and improvement of the health of man, to the curing and prevention of diseases, to work conscientiously wherever the interests of society demand; to be ever ready to render material aid, to be attentive and thoughtful of the patient, to maintain medical confidence; constantly to perfect my medical knowledge and physician's skills; to further by work the development of medical science and practice; to turn, if the patient's interest demand it, for advice to my professional colleagues and that I myself will never refuse advice and help to them; to preserve and further the noble traditions of our native medicine, and that I will in all my actions be guided by the principles of Communist morality, ever to bear in mind the high calling of the Soviet physician, and of my responsibility to the people of the Soviet state. I swear that I will be faithful to this oath throughout the rest of my life."

— The Russian Physician's Oath

"I swear by God, the Great; to regard God in carrying out my profession; to protect human life in all stages and under all circumstances, doing my utmost to rescue it from death, malady, pain and anxiety; to keep people's dignity, cover their privacies and lock up their secrets; to be all the way an instrument of God's mercy, extending my medical care to near and far, virtuous and friend and enemy; to strive in the pursuit of knowledge and harnessing it for the benefit but not the harm of mankind; to revere my teacher, teach my junior, and be brothers to members of the medical profession joined in piety and charity; to live my Faith in private and in public, avoiding whatever blemishes me in the eyes of God, His Apostles and my fellow Faithful. And may God be witness to this Oath."

— The Islamic Physician's Oath

"Torture remains an essential instrument of many governments. They use psychiatrists, surgeons and the whole range of associated disciplines to pressure people to confess. There is no sign of it ending; there is ample evidence it will only get worse in the twenty-first century."

Albert Joyce, Professor of Ethics in Medicine, UCLA, San Francisco.

"There is often no real distinction between what is done in the name of lawful government and terrorist organizations in the way they use doctors for their purposes."

William Buckley, CIA officer, in conversation with the author shortly before he was taken hostage in Beirut, Lebanon.

"People have said I played God. That is nonsense. I was merely making use of the gifts the Almighty had given me to try and defend what I believed in then, and do so now: the right of the United States to defend itself by all means possible."

Sidney Gottlieb, CIA scientist, in conversation with the author shortly before his death.

CHAPTER ONE

On January 4, 2006, winter cold gripped Washington D.C. President George W. Bush informed the White House press corps, and through them the world, that the United States had not engaged in, and would not condone, torture. He was responding to charges that the United States armed forces or its intelligence agencies, especially the CIA, had routinely used torture to obtain information to pursue the War on Terror that the president had declared five years previously, following the attacks on the Twin Towers and the Pentagon by al-Qaeda.

The president's words were accompanied by the same occasional hand-chopping gestures, eye swiveling and the little rictus smile that had become the physical hallmarks of his second term in office. But there was no mistaking his message. No American had been allowed to commit torture — and none ever would be allowed to do so. That was not the American way. Tough interrogation — yes. Torture? No. Manifestly — no.

Bush spoke with fervor and seemed surprised to be finally called upon to deal with such an issue in public. His words had been written by his speech-writers. Every syllable bore the mark of having been agonized over, every sentence scrutinized for the correct nuance. The president's denial was his first real comment on a subject that been garnering increasing attention in the press: the U.S. practice of extraordinary rendition. *Rendition* is CIA-speak for secretly flying suspected terrorists to interrogation centers far beyond the protection of American justice. These centers were located in the Balkans, Morocco, Egypt and various Central Asian nations. They had been identified by Alvaro Gil-Robles, Commissioner for Human Rights at the Council of Europe. The day before Bush's press conference, Alvaro had stated: "A regular gulag appears to have been created, places where the CIA is given access to the prisoners at all times." The commissioner feared that the most high value prisoners — senior members of the Taliban and al-Qaeda — were moved "like an invisible caravan from one of the so-called black sites to another." Outrage over such revelations had led to the Council appointing a Swiss lawyer, Dick Marty, to discover what went on at the interrogation centers and to determine which European countries may have helped the CIA by allowing "torture flights" to overfly or refuel.

Even as President Bush delivered his carefully couched denial, he knew that in 2002 his own Department of Justice had set down legal guidelines — classified "Secret, Hold Close" — on how terrorists could be questioned. Identified as "enhanced interrogation techniques" in a still-secret document seen by the author, the guidelines permitted the "belly slap" to the stomach. No mention was made that — depending on the force applied — this can cause damage to the spleen and other organs. Another technique the guidelines condoned without equivocation was described as "long time standing," in which prisoners "can be made to stand, handcuffed and with their feet shackled to a bolt in the floor, for up to 40 hours." "Water boarding" in which a prisoner was strapped to a board and held underwater to mimic the experience of drowning was also deemed permissible. Sleep deprivation, verbal intimidation and threats of further violence all were allowed under the guidelines.

These interrogation methods are based on two CIA manuals. One is titled "Coercive Questioning," the other "Human Resource Exploitation." This latter document contains the reminder that "when planning an interrogation room, the electric current should be known in advance so that transformers or

2

other modifying devices will be on hand when applying electric shocks."

The 104 pages of "Coercive Questioning" give detailed instructions on inducing fear. "The threat to inflict pain can trigger fears more damaging than the immediate sensation of pain. Threats delivered coldly are more effective than those shouted in rage." Caution is urged about "delivering the threat of death against hard-headed types who realize that silencing them forever would defeat the interrogator's purpose. They must be broken by other procedures."

The section on pain warns that inflicting "intense pain is quite likely to produce false confessions as a means of escaping from distress." It goes on to say: "If an interrogatee is caused to suffer pain rather late in the interrogation and after other tactics have failed, he is almost certain to conclude that the interrogator is becoming desperate. If pain is going to be inflicted, it should be used at an early stage and carefully calculated in its intensity."

The manual is equally specific on how to attack the mind. "Hypnosis offers one advantage over other interrogation techniques or aids: the posthypnotic suggestion. It should be possible to administer a drug to a resistant source in food or drink and persuade him, as a drug takes effect and he is slipping into a hypnotic trance, to shift his frame of reference so that his reasons for resistance become reasons for cooperating. Interrogate him, and conclude the session by implanting the suggestion that when he emerges from his trance he will not remember anything about what has happened." In 2006, the CIA had a number of its staff of doctors on retainers in various countries who could be called upon to attend such sessions to supervise attempts to induce a reluctant subject to talk and to administer drugs. The CIA manual states, "Drugs can be effective in overcoming resistance not dissolved by other techniques. The judicious use of a drug, matching the subject's personality, careful gauging of dosage and a sense of timing make its administration a hard-to-equal ally for the interrogator. One of the most important of the interrogator's functions is providing the doctor with a full and accurate description of the psychological make-up of the interrogatee. Persons burdened with feelings of shame or guilt are more likely to unburden themselves when drugged, especially if these feelings have been reinforced by the interrogator."

Both manuals were the work of two distinguished psychiatrists: Dr. Louis Jolyon "Jolly" West, a former chairman of the Department of Psychiatry at the University of Los Angeles, and Dr. William Sargant, the founder and director of the Department of Psychological Medicine at St.Thomas's Hospital in London. Both maintained a close working relationship with the CIA and Britain's MI6 until their deaths. Sargant was the author of *Battle for the Mind*, a book still widely read by the interrogators in the intelligence world. Both advocates for using drugs to break the will of a suspect, Sargant and West were deeply involved in unethical research concerning hypnosis, psychosurgery, electroshock and the whole gamut of techniques of behavioral control. Time and again both broke their medical oath to harm no person; more shocking still is that the methods they created have only changed in one respect: the mind-bending drugs and pain-inducing gadgets have become more sophisticated.

It is equally disturbing that in 2006 Amnesty International reported that these methods were being used in Iraq, Afghanistan and Guantanamo Bay. Suspected terrorists who showed they could resist the techniques laid down in the manuals and in the U.S. Department of Justice guidelines were put on a CIA rendition flight to one of the black sites, where President George Bush insisted no torture was carried out in the name of the United States. He issued his denial shortly after Amnesty International announced there were currently 90 countries that routinely used torture. A month before, on December 5, 2005, a U.S. Air Force transport plane landed at Guantanamo Bay in Cuba. On board were five "emergency restraint chairs," each costing $1,150. Twenty more would be flown in within days of the president's denial. The chairs were designed by the CIA Research and Development Department for a specific purpose: to end hunger strikes by the inmates of Guantanamo Bay, or in any other CIA-linked interrogation center. Strapped to a chair, an inmate was force-fed by tubes inserted in the nose, throat and veins. These tubes were often removed so violently that some prisoners bled or fainted. It was another way to induce pain.

Confronted with these allegations, the White House spokesman said on February 15, 2006, "Claims of abuse or torture are nonsense. It is well known that al-Qaeda detainees are trained in the dissemination of false allegations. The methods used are consistent with those employed in federal prisons in the United States." It should be pointed out, however, that inmates of federal prisons have been tried before a court and found guilty of specific crimes by a jury of their peers. No such right has been afforded the detainees of Guantanamo Bay. Like the black sites, Guantanamo is outside the jurisdiction of U.S. courts. Guantanamo was specifically chosen because legal constraints do not apply.

Many of the inmates of Guantanamo Bay were caught by accident in the American trawl for suspects in Afghanistan and Pakistan; sometimes they were handed over by rivals for reasons that had more to do with bounty collection than the War on Terror. Human rights lawyers say that only 8 percent of prisoners have been classified as al-Qaeda fighters and that less than half of those, according to Pentagon documents seen by the author, have committed a "hostile act" against the United States. But they cannot be released, insisted a Pentagon spokesman, "because they will revert to doing bad things against America."

Far from acceding to the demands of the United Nations and Bush administration allies – let alone its many enemies – that Guantanamo Bay be closed, the U.S. Department of Justice announced in February, 2006, that a "new and permanent facility" was to be built on site. The White House has continued to refuse to offer a full account of what goes on at Guantanamo Bay and the other black sites that have been accused of contravening the 1984 United Nations Convention banning torture, to which the United States is a signatory. The convention defines torture as: "Any act by which severe pain or suffering, either physical or mental, is intentionally inflicted on a person for coercing him or a third person, or for any reason based on discrimination of any kind, when such pain or suffering is inflicted by or at the instigation of or with the consent or acquiescence of a public official or other person acting in an official capacity."

The convention specifically forbids sending suspects to countries where there are substantial grounds for believing they will be tortured. In Britain, a month before President Bush issued his blanket denial, the House of Lords ruled that English courts could not use evidence that "may have been obtained by torture."

Two hours flying time from where President Bush gave his solemn assurances that America abided by the United Nations Convention, his undertaking was routinely being broken at Guantanamo Bay. There were still 460 Muslim suspects who had been brought there in the same secrecy which continued to surround the rendition flights. America has always had a tradition of treating its most dangerous *convicted* prisoners in a tough, no-nonsense manner. On the whole, law-abiding Americans still like to see criminals who are found guilty of serious crimes treated harshly. So it should be no surprise that recent polls across the United States showed support for the way the prisoners of Guantanamo Bay were treated.

But there is one significant difference in the status of the Guantanamo prisoners. By the time of this writing many still have not been charged, let alone convicted of any crime. There may indeed be strong suspicions against them. Some very likely could turn out to be guilty of barbaric crimes in Afghanistan for the Taliban, and in Iraq for Saddam Hussein. Certainly, the majority are fanatical Islamic fundamentalists. But they have not yet been found guilty of any offense. Until very recently prisoners in Guantanamo Bay have had no right to choose their own lawyers, to have a jury trial, or be allowed any access to any appeal system. When tried, they will face a military tribunal. Their attorneys must be U.S. citizens vetted by the U.S. Defense Department. And, though court cases are pending at present, the only appeal allowed to a prisoner is to the Secretary of Defense. It would be surprising if he were to do anything but ratify the sentences handed down by the tribunal's presiding judge. The prisoners of Guantanamo are mostly in their twenties. One was only thirteen when he was grabbed by U.S. Special Forces in Afghanistan. Another is barely fifteen. The prisoners come from 43 countries. Most are Arabs, with Saudi Arabia accounting for over 100 of the detainees. Eighty-five are from Yemen. Not one has been categorized as a prisoner of war, entitled to the protection of the Geneva Convention, of which the United States is a signatory. But President Bush, in the full flush of launching his War on Terror, pronounced the prisoners were not entitled to the Convention's protection, "because they were non-uniformed combatants."

Officially, Guantanamo is known as Camp Delta, the name that the U.S. Defense Department publicists prefer to use. To facilitate the work of journalists, there is a "media observation post." It is about 250 meters from the nearest cell block. Close enough to need sunglasses to combat the glare off the metal roofs of the guard posts and the chain-link fences which surround the camp. Not close enough to see what goes on inside the fence. By night, the compound is lit by powerful white lights mounted on poles. The perimeter, all the way back to the media lookout, is sown with ground sensors. The nearby beach – the prison sits on a bluff above the Caribbean ocean – is patrolled day and night by U.S. soldiers. At sea, U.S. Coast Guard boats cruise back and forth, ready to thwart any attempt to rescue prisoners. All the guards have orders to shoot to kill.

The Pentagon proudly points to the fact that the prison cells have floor-level toilets — to conform with Muslim requirements to be able to squat — as "evidence of our understanding of their cultural needs." Detainees sleep on metal frames covered with thin mattresses. Again, the Pentagon insists these are the same as used in U.S. prisons. Each prisoner on Guantanamo receives one hour's exercise and a shower a day. By the time he returns from his ablutions, he may have been moved to another cell. This is to avoid the risk of what the American guards call "clique making." Detainees are taken, shuffling in their restrictive ankle chains, to interrogation at any time of the day — or night. Prisoners who protest at being awakened are placed in isolation cells. Prisoners are questioned for hours at a time by a succession of CIA — and sometimes MI6 — officers.

It is what happens during these interrogations that has raised most concern among human rights organizations. Prisoners who have finally been released without charge have all described being subjected to physical and mental attacks that amount to torture. "The torture is shocking because of the skilled way it is applied. Inducing fear and outright terror are standard methods," said Steve Ballinger, a director of Amnesty International.

In between interrogations life — of a sort — goes on at Guantanamo. A recorded call to prayer comes over the compound loudspeakers five times a day. Arrows point in the direction of Mecca. All meals are prepared according to the *halal* diet. There is a copy of the Koran in each cell. These are the only signs that America recognizes the needs — and basic rights — of their prisoners. When a protest came from within the prison from the prisoners' American Muslim imam, a U.S. naval officer Lt. Mohammed Saiful-Islam, that conditions were increasingly affecting the emotional and psychological stability of many of the prisoners, Lt. Saiful-Islam was promptly shipped out to California. He told the author in December 2005 that he is no longer allowed to speak publicly about what he witnessed. The CIA-sponsored rendition flights have continued, not only to Guantanamo Bay, but to secret black sites in Egypt, Morocco, Uzbekistan and other countries. Dick Marty, the lawyer appointed to investigate the rendition process, reported in late January 2006 that "at least 100 people had undergone the process since 2004." He had not been allowed to visit the interrogation centers and had to rely in his report on the testimony of independent witnesses like Craig Murray, the former British Ambassador to Uzbekistan. Murray has alleged, using supportive evidence, that the CIA station chief in that country had told him at least one prisoner had been "boiled alive" when his interrogation had yielded no further information. Murray finally managed to publish his memoirs in 2007, after overcoming legal threats from the British government. Murray believes the threats were reinforced by demands from Washington to ensure that what he knows about rendition would not surface in the public domain.

Rendition goes to the heart of the long history of the CIA in developing a whole program of torture. At the same time, in equal secrecy, the agency was carrying out biological warfare experiments. This book makes the case that agencies of the United States government have engaged in a systematic assault on the human psyche, seeking to find a way to control human behavior, and at the same time they have created and tested weapons for germ warfare — weapons that were later given to Saddam Hussein when he was in favor in Washington. These sinister activities highlight the lack of accountability in the most powerful democratic nation on earth, a nation whose system of laws its president is under oath to protect. Many powerful interests believe it essential that the full and untold story of the secret history of the CIA and its germ warfare programs be kept secret.

September 11, 2001, was one of those balmy days Americans like to call God-given — but which many of them would forever remember as their day of infamy. It was the start of what President George Bush called "the first World War of the twenty-first century," following the total destruction of the World Trade Center and part of the Pentagon. The question uppermost in everyone's minds was what would follow next. The answer was not long in coming. In October a wave of anthrax cases appeared across an already stunned and terrified nation. Anthrax is easy to spread and has a mortality rate of almost 100 percent unless it is discovered sufficiently early to be treated with antibiotics. Was it a follow-up attack by al-Qaeda? No one knew. Fear swiftly spread across the globe; here was a silent, invisible plague that could be disseminated by equipment readily obtained on the Internet. Stories multiplied of how untold billions of anthrax microns could drift through the air and settle on streets, gardens, trees, window ledges and even drift down chimneys into homes. Thirty thousand of those microns could fit on a large pinhead — more than enough to wipe out a household, perhaps a street of households. The harder various government agencies tried to still the panic, the greater the fear grew. All the investigative skills of the FBI and CIA could not discover where the anthrax came from. A consensus emerged that it had to be al-Qaeda. The dissemination of the anthrax virus dramatically illustrated one of the essential aims and techniques of terrorism. The precept was formulated by Sun Tzu, the Chinese philosopher, 2,500 years ago in *The Art of War:* "Kill one, frighten ten thousand."

As of the publication date of this book, who distributed the anthrax remains unknown. Scores of suspects have been interviewed. None were charged. Not one of them had any links to al-Qaeda or any other terrorist groups. In 2004, the U.S. armory of weaponized biological agents consisted of 19 bacteria, 43 viruses, 14 toxins and 4 rickettsiae. Their use remains outlawed under the Geneva Protocol of 1925. Within five years of the protocol's creation Italy, Belgium, Canada, France, Britain, the Netherlands, Poland and the Soviet Union had all signed. The United States did not sign until 1975. By then the U.S. had developed a massive biochemical arsenal. Shortly before the September 11 attack, the Pentagon admitted that at Nellis Air Force base, one of the most secret in America, it had established the world's largest stockpile of biological and chemical weapons. It had been created largely by CIA scientists. One of these scientists had been an obsessive biochemist whose work pioneered the research which eventually led to the stockpile. His name was Frank Olson.

On that terrible September day in 2001, Olson's son, Eric, was living in the family home in Frederick, Maryland, a short distance from Fort Detrick, where his father had worked for the CIA. That establishment then — and now — remains a restricted place, guarded by a variety of electronic defenses and armed guards. As the television set in Eric's living room endlessly replayed the 9/11 scenes of destruction from New York and Washington, he typed into his computer — on which he had stored so many astonishing matters relating to the death of his father — the most astounding claim of all:

"My father was murdered because the CIA feared he would reveal the biggest American secret of the Cold War, perhaps of all time. It is the secret of how the CIA was involved in biological warfare as well as mind control. My father had a key part in both programs."

On November 28, 1953, shortly after 2:00 A.M., Armand Pastore, the night manager at the Statler Hotel, opposite Penn Station in Manhattan, New York, ran out of the hotel's front door into Seventh Avenue. Lying on the sidewalk in his undershirt and shorts was a man.

Pastore later told the author: "The man was flat on his back, his legs all smashed up and bent at a terrible angle. I don't know why but I looked up to see where he had come from. I saw a blind pushed up in a window on the tenth floor of the hotel. I thought to myself, 'Jeez, how'd he get up sufficient speed to crash through the double-glazing in the window?' He was trying to mumble something but I couldn't make it out. It was all garbled. I knelt beside him, close to his face, asking him who he was.".

The man was Frank Olson, Eric's father, the husband of Alice Olson. A priest appeared, followed moments later by an ambulance and a police car. Frank Olson died while the priest administered the Last Rites. Pastore took two policemen up to the room on the tenth floor. They found a man sitting on the toilet seat in the bathroom of Room 1018A, which Frank Olson had occupied. He was Dr. Robert Lashbrook. Apart from giving the policeman his name, he declined to provide any details except to say he worked "for the government." Lashbrook, a withdrawn and diffident man, was a biochemist who worked, like Olson, in the CIA's chemical-biological program at the cutting edge of its innovative and lethal research.

Eric Olson was nine years old and asleep in the family home when his mother woke him with the news his father was dead. She led him into the living room. Waiting was a man Eric vaguely recognized, Lieutenant-Colonel Vincent Ruwet, his father's superior. He told Eric "something bad" had happened. To discover how and why his father had died became a quest that would take Eric through adulthood and ever deeper into the darkest corners of America's secret history. In that journey he came to see himself as "the Hamlet of the CIA," the son who would do anything to avenge his father's death.

Frank Olson died just as the Korean War ended and the Cold War was starting. It was also a time, Eric later discovered, that his father had begun to express to his wife Alice and some of his colleagues moral doubts about the CIA's highly secret, and illegal, experiments to test the efficacy of certain bacterial strains on human beings. In one instance live bacteria had been released by aerosols over San Francisco. People developed flu-like symptoms. Many were hospitalized; later a number of deaths were laid at the door of the test. These cases formed the basis of a lawsuit against the government, but the case never went to court. The delivery system used in San Francisco had been developed by Frank Olson.

Frank Olson was buried on a cold November day in 1953. The man who had approved the experiments, dressed in a sober dark suit and limping slightly, stood behind the family mourners and watched Frank Olson's coffin lowered into its grave. Alice and Eric had no idea then that he was one of the most calculating employees of the Central Intelligence Agency. His name was Sidney Gottlieb.

For over twenty years Gottlieb remained no more than a vague name to Eric Olson. Then, on June 11, 1975, the *Washington Post* published a story headlined "Suicide Revealed." The story described how "a civilian employee of the Army jumped to his death from a New York hotel window after being drugged with LSD during a CIA meeting." Eric recognized that the article was referring to his father. By now a successful clinical psychologist, Eric gave up his practice to unearth the reason for his father's death — and who was responsible. The more obstacles he met on that journey of painful discovery, the more obsessive he became. In 1994 he had his father's coffin exhumed. Forty-one years before, the Olson family had been told by the CIA that Frank Olson's body could not be viewed for them to say their farewells because "it was broken up and there were extreme cuts and lacerations on my father's face caused by his fall. In fact the body had been embalmed and was in near perfect condition. Another plank in the web of lies that had been created around my father's death had been exposed," Eric would recall to the author.

To conduct the autopsy, Eric assembled a forensic team led by Professor James Starrs of George Washington University, a respected criminologist with a colorful resume. Over the years Starrs had dug up various notables including Jesse James. Starrs concluded: "The death of Frank Olson is suggestive of homicide." There were no cuts on Frank Olson's head or neck to indicate he had jumped to his death. But there was a large bruise over Olson's left eye which suggested "he had been hit on the head with a blunt object before going out of the window. That blunt object could have included a blow from a closed fist." Such a means of killing was described in the CIA's Assassination Manual that Eric had obtained.

The eight-page document was titled "Assassination Methods." It contained sufficient material for a dozen thrillers or Hollywood movies. Excerpts from this extraordinary document are published here for the first time.

"Assassination is a term thought to be derived from "Hashish," a drug similar to marijuana, said to have been used by

Hasan-i-Sabah to induce motivation in his followers who were assigned to carry out political and other murders, usually at the cost of their lives. It is here used to describe the planned killing of a person who is not under the legal jurisdiction of the killer, who is not physically in the hands of the killer, who has been selected by an organization for death, and whose death provides positive advantages to that organization. No assassination instructions should ever be written or recorded. Decisions and instructions should be confined to an absolute minimum of persons. Ideally only one person will be involved.

"It is possible to kill a man with bare hands, but very few are skillful enough to do it well. However, a hammer, axe, wrench, screwdriver, fire poker, kitchen knife, lamp stand, or anything hard, heavy and handy will suffice. A length of rope or wire or a belt will do, if the assassin is strong and agile. All such improvised weapons have the important advantage of availability and apparent innocence.

"The contrived accident is the most effective technique. When successfully executed, it causes little excitement and is only casually investigated. Falls into the sea or swiftly-flowing rivers may suffice if the subject cannot swim. It will be more reliable if the assassin can arrange to attempt rescue, as he can thus be sure of the subject's death and at the same time establish a workable alibi. If the subject's personal habits make it feasible, alcohol may be used to prepare him for a contrived accident of any kind. Falls before trains or subway cars are usually effective, but require exact timing and can seldom be free from unexpected observation. Automobile accidents are a less satisfactory means of assassination. If the subject is deliberately run down, very exact timing is necessary and investigation is likely to be thorough. If the subject's car is tampered with, reliability is very low. The subject may be stunned or drugged and then placed in the car, but this is only reliable when the car can be run off a high cliff or into deep water without observation.

"Arson can cause accidental death if the subject is drugged and left in a burning building. Reliability is not satisfactory unless the building is highly combustible. Drugs can be very effective. An overdose of morphine administered as a sedative will cause death without disturbance and is difficult to detect. The size of the dose will depend upon whether the subject has been using narcotics regularly. If not, two grains will suffice. If the subject drinks heavily, morphine or a similar narcotic can be injected at the passing out stage and the cause of death will often be held to be acute alcoholism. Firearms are often used in assassination, often very ineffectively. Firearms should be used which can provide destructive power at least 100% in excess of that thought to be necessary and range should be half that considered practical for the weapon. Bombs or grenades should never be thrown at a subject. It is sloppy, unreliable and bad propaganda. Placing the charge surreptitiously permits a charge of proper size to be employed, but requires accurate prediction of the subject's movements.

"The ideal explosive is of fragmentation material. Metal or rock fragments should be walnut-size rather than pea-size. Military or commercial high explosives are practical for use in assassination. Home-made or improvised explosives should be avoided. They tend to be dangerous and unreliable. Anti-personnel explosive missiles are excellent, provided the assassin has sufficient technical knowledge to fuse them properly. The charge should be so placed that the victim is not ever less than six feet from it at the moment of detonation."

One instruction drew Eric Olson back time and again.

"Blows should be directed to the temple, the area just below and behind the ear, and the lower rear portion of the skull. Of course, if the blow is very heavy, any portion of the upper skull will do. The lower frontal portion of the head, from the eyes to the throat, can withstand enormous blows without fatal consequences. The most efficient assassination is a fall of 75 feet or more onto a hard surface. Elevator shafts, stairwells, unscreened windows and bridges will serve. The act may be executed by sudden, vigorous shaking of the ankles, tipping the subject over the edge."

The manual described what had befallen Frank Olson. Eric learned that at the time his father died every field agent had a copy of the manual. The author of the CIA's Assassination Manual was the man he had seen standing at the back of the church at Frank's funeral: Dr. Sidney Gottlieb. It would be some years before Eric discovered who he was and what role he had played in Frank Olson's death.

On Saturday, May 19, 2001, Eric sat with a former colleague of Frank Olson, a man with whom he had been in contact for some time. Eric had finally persuaded the man, now in his eighty-first year, to see him though he was reluctant to talk at first. Their previous telephone talks were all neatly filed in what was growing into a small library that contained Eric's ever-widening investigation into the death of his father. He was building a case history that he hoped would eventually bring his father's murderer or murderers to justice. The day before they met, the old man had finally agreed to talk to Eric and reveal all he knew under the guarantee his identity would be protected. It was not the first time such a request had been made to Eric. Each time he had honored it. He did so again with the old man. They sat in his living room, and Eric, with all his clinical skills for drawing out a person, listened attentively and — he later admitted — with "incredible astonishment" at what he heard.

"My host told me about secret trips my father made to Britain and Germany in the 1950s. These involved various experiments my father had created in what my host called 'information retrieval'. This involved getting people to reveal information they wanted to keep secret. My father returned to the CIA after his last trip in the late summer of 1953. My host said he was visibly upset. My father had witnessed some of the experiments, which had ended in the deaths of the subjects. They had been 'terminated', killed by the CIA officers. By then my father had also become aware that his work had also led to biological weapons being used in the Korean War by the United States. My host said, 'Korea is the key to your father's death. It was where the two secret CIA programs — mind control experiments and the use of biological weapons — came together'. My host told me my father was killed because the concern had developed within the top echelon of the CIA that he was on the verge of going public, becoming a whistleblower. So he was murdered."

But, tantalizingly, the old man said he could not be certain how the crime had been planned or who had ordered it. "Because he was not certain, he would not name names," Eric later recalled to the author. Nevertheless the information spurred Eric on. Desperately short of cash, living a hand-to-mouth existence in the by now run-down family home, he devoted every penny he had to trying to bring the jigsaw of events into place. He was unaware that his father's death had become a case study for a number of intelligence services. They included the Russian KGB and the East German Stasi. Papers found in their files when Soviet Communism collapsed, seen by the author, show that Frank Olson's death was also closely analyzed by MI6. A Stasi file called it "the perfect murder by suicide." But the most significant use of the death was made by Mossad, the Israeli secret service. Since 1976, when President Gerald Ford stopped all CIA assassinations, the role of eliminating America's enemies had discreetly passed to Mossad. Since then, Mossad is estimated to have killed over 1,000 enemies of the United

States and Israel. One of the methods used is identical to the fake suicide of Frank Olson. How to carry it out remains part of the technique used by the Mossad *kidon*, its state-approved assassination unit.

Interwoven into the murder of Frank Olson were the career and death of a long-serving CIA officer who also knew of the secret experiments the scientists had conducted. Like Olson, he too had become alarmed about them. His name was William "Bill" Buckley. Buckley would recall his "immense sense of pride on joining the CIA. I immediately felt a sense of belonging. I was given an internal telephone directory, for which I signed, and cautioned to never leave my office unlocked. It was my first taste of the bureaucracy that permeated the Agency; every action I took had to be reported to a superior. After several months of 'kicking my heels', I found myself transferred to work for the Department of Science and Technology on a project called MK-ULTRA. It was designed to study methods of human mind-control and was under the overall control of Dr. Sidney Gottlieb," Buckley recalled to the author.

It was at about the same time that Buckley also discovered the other great fixation in Dr. Gottlieb's life — germ warfare.

Bill Buckley was an important and totally reliable source for me in the intelligence world. He also became a good and trusted friend. Bill was highly educated, articulate and a gifted host. He could easily have found himself a secure place on Wall Street or at a high level in government. He chose to work for the Central Intelligence Agency because "the United States had never before had a peacetime intelligence agency of such breadth and concept." He saw it as a real opportunity to satisfy two powerful driving forces in his psyche: his desire to serve his country and his need for a life of excitement. He was hooked on the sense of danger that permeated so much of what he did.

In the beginning, the relationship between Buckley and me was a little awkward. He knew that as a foreign correspondent it was inevitable that I would come into conflict with the way government and the military like to control the news. I had encountered this in half a dozen wars from the Suez Crisis in 1956 down to the First Gulf War. Along the way there had been Vietnam and lesser conflicts in Asia and Africa. My own, perhaps over-passionate, dislike of spin doctors acted as an ice-breaker with Buckley. He said the reporter who lost his independence became a mere propagandist, and he had his fill of them in Vietnam with its gung-ho reports on Vietnamese body counts and Saigon briefings that had no bearing on what was really going on. As simple as that, our friendship had begun. One of the first things we did was to dispense with the fiction that Bill was only a protocol officer attached to the local United States embassy in whichever country we happened to meet. Playing the role of a State Department flunkey is a familiar cover for many agents, but Buckley admitted that doing so could be irritating.

Our first meeting was in Rome. Part of my daily duties was doing the "embassy circuit," getting the various diplomatic spins on what was happening or about to happen around the western Mediterranean basin. Over lunch with Bill one day, I mentioned that my father-in-law had been an MI6 officer running a spy network in post-World War II Germany. Bill smiled and said he already knew that. Bill was not exactly handsome. The angles of his face did not quite coalesce to produce a striking whole. His chin would jut out at unexpected moments and his eyes were a little too close-set, giving him a look of theatrical menace. To really appreciate his best physical side you had to catch him in motion, crumbling a roll for his soup or using his finger to make a point. In those early meetings we explored the similarities between journalism and the intelligence profession. Both survive on information and sources ranging from the noble to the base. Each depends on confidentiality. Without it, sources would evaporate and almost certainly would not be re-placed by new ones. In both our jobs we collected information in response to orders; mine came from an assignment editor, Bill's from some desk man in Langley. Over a bottle of Frascati near the Pantheon in Rome one night, Bill said we both had to be persuasive and be prepared to tell lies in pursuit of the truth. I couldn't think of a better description for our work. We both agreed that sometimes we got things wrong; in my profession it probably didn't matter in the long run. In Bill's, it could trigger one of those nasty little wars.

As I came to know him, I realized that Bill cultivated his lit-tle eccentricities and displayed them like badges of honor. He wore ties whose patterns never seemed to match his shirt or jacket. There was the long leather topcoat he wore for a while so that he looked like an extra in a wartime movie. His greatest concern was to ensure his shoes always gleamed. He could not pass a shoe-shine stand without stopping for an application of further gloss.

In Rome, we began to meet on a regular basis. Usually Bill would turn up with two or three staff from the embassy. The conversation was as good as the food. One night he arrived with William Colby, a quiet and self-contained man with the inquisitorial manner of a foot soldier in the Society of Jesus. Later Bill told me that Colby had parachuted into German-occupied France in 1944. At the age of twenty-four he was already a full-blown major in the OSS, the forerunner of the CIA. After the war he had gone on fighting the Fascists in Italy as an early member of the CIA. That night, Bill chose as his dinner topic the great spy scandals of the Cold War: the be-trayal of America's atomic bomb secrets by Klaus Fuchs and the compromising of agents of MI5 and MI6 by Guy Burgess and Donald MacLean. I said that each had made treachery and duplicity a byword. Buckley had smiled at the observation. I would come to know that smile.

I had also formed other impressions by now. Bill had a waspish way with words. He once said the only real way to write about intelligence matters was to listen for "the murmurs in the mush." It was his shorthand description for learning to seize the salient fact from within the clouds of deliberate obfuscation. As we came to know one another better, he gradually convinced me that secret intelligence is the key to fully understanding international relations, global politics and terrorism.

Later, over dinners in Beirut or his other postings where I was assigned, Buckley began to speak to me with increasing frankness about past times; describing the personalities involved. He told me about the mind control experiments and his time in Korea. Buckley did not see himself as a whistleblower. He simply wanted me to "understand." It was a word he used often to try and rationalize what he had seen and participated in.

I later had occasion to speak at length about Buckley with William Casey, the Director of the CIA under President Reagan. Casey was impressed from the outset by Buckley's recognition that action cannot wait for certainty. What had begun as mutual respect developed into genuine friendship between them. Buckley became Casey's special assistant, regularly accompanying him on trips to CIA outposts, mostly in the Middle East. Those visits kindled an old fire in Bill Buckley: the desire to get back into the field.

In June 1981 he was posted as deputy chief of the CIA station in Cairo. It was there I met him once more. The conversation turned to what I was writing next. I told him. He looked at me for a long moment, then asked: "You mean about what happened in Montreal with Dr. Cameron?"

"Among others, yes."

Buckley nodded. "It's the dream of any intelligence service to be able to control someone's mind."

"Tell me," I said. "Tell me more about Dr. Gottlieb."

We spoke over several days and we arranged to meet at the Semeris Hotel in Cairo later. But when I called the United States embassy in the city, I was told he was "abroad."

It would be a year before I would see him again. On a hot summer day in 1982, we both stood among a crowd of U.S. Marines on Beirut's waterfront watching the PLO fighters leaving the city, driven out by Israeli fighter bombers, which had turned entire areas of Beirut into rubble. The new president in the White House, Ronald Reagan, had given Yasir Arafat a guarantee of safe passage, and Buckley was there to observe that the Israelis did not attack the PLO as they set sail for Tunisia. I told him that in his linen suit, chukka boots and with his deep-tanned face, he looked the quintessential CIA man on the spot. He grinned and said: "Beirut is the best place I've been in for a long time." His sojourn in Lebanon ended when Casey recalled him to Langley to assume responsibility for the CIA's countermeasures against terrorists.

In March, 1983, I was in Washington, continuing my preliminary research into mind control when I again met Buckley in his apartment. We had hardly begun to catch up on what had happened since our last meeting when the early evening news broke the story that an Islamic terrorist group had exploded a huge bomb outside the United States embassy in Beirut. Among the sixteen Americans killed had been a number of CIA officers, including the agency's Near East division chief, Robert Ames. He had only been in the country for twenty-four hours. Within days Buckley was back in Beirut, but before he left Washington, he took time to call me. He wanted to know how my mind control project was shaping up. I said it was still too early to say. There was a pause, and then he said: "Listen, this may interest you. The Israelis are saying that the Hezbollah are getting sophisticated. They've recruited a doctor who's been trained by the Soviets in mind control. If I hear any more I'll let you know." They were the last words William Buckley spoke to me.

Between Bill Buckley and Frank Olson, I have unraveled a story that is more shocking than many others I have investigated throughout my career.

CHAPTER TWO

The mourners making their way into the auditorium of the clapboard building were glad to be out of the raw wind tugging at their topcoats and hats on that grey, overcast afternoon in late March 1999.

They were an unusual mix: retired CIA spies who had never quite given up their habit of checking a room upon entering; members of a Zen group huddled together and softly singing an old spiritual; children from the local school, in their Sunday best, solemn faced and glancing at each other; patients from a nearby hospice, where the man to whom they had come to bid their farewells had worked as a speech therapist, even though he was a lifelong stutterer and — unknown to them — had spent a great part of his adult life trying to devise ways to kill.

The television news cameramen panned over the two-story high school building in Rappahannock, Virginia — a tiny township outside of Washington, sheltering in the lee of the Shenandoah Mountains — and the reporters copied down the words of the handwritten notice pinned to the auditorium door, announcing this was "A Memorial to Sid."

The widow and her four adult children walked slowly to their seats, their faces composed. Around them sat those whose lives had been touched in one way or another by the man to whom they had come to say their farewells, Dr. Sidney Gottlieb. Margaret Gottlieb, his widow, despite her advanced years still had steel in her sinewy frame; it was there in her ramrod back, her composed face devoid of makeup, the skin taut around her mouth. Her devotion to raising her children was at the core of her own character, just as her husband's devotion to work had been at his.

To some, Dr. Sidney Gottlieb was a misunderstood patriot. The reporters who had come to witness tribute his final called him the great survivor. To others he was the devil's apostle.

Gottlieb would pass from this world with none of the pomp and circumstance accorded to some for their service to the nation. Three weeks before, after a short illness, he had been cremated. Until this damp, grey Saturday afternoon, there had been nothing to mark his passing. No marching band, their drums beating the measured cadence of death. No guard of honor to walk in steady pace to the crematorium. As one mourner followed another to the auditorium microphone to praise the dead man, no one mentioned that a great part of Gottlieb's working life had been devoted to trying to find the means to control human minds. His obsession was to turn ordinary human beings into robotic figures whose value systems could be so altered that they would even kill on command — and then be programmed to forget who had given the order. He labored to make science fiction into science fact. No one would ever know how long the dream had been in Sidney Gottlieb's mind, but he never lost the belief that somewhere was the key that would give him the one great victory that would set him apart from all others.

Gottlieb had lived to be eighty years old, twenty-two of them spent in deep shadow. He had been the chief of the Central Intelligence Agency's Technical Services Branch. In his day it was affectionately known within the agency as "the department of potions and dirty tricks." In reality Gottlieb organized an unprecedented system of medical torture, conducted in the utmost secrecy during all the years he spent with the Agency. To do so he assembled a team of like-minded staff doctors who were supported by eminent physicians outside the CIA who lent their names and their patients for a series of monstrous experiments.

In return, Gottlieb rewarded them with considerable sums of money from the untraceable United States government funds he controlled.

Gottlieb had made his life in the Agency and spoke of the CIA with an affection that was almost boyish. He saw himself as part of an organization that ultimately served one client, the President of the United States. Greeting a newcomer to the Technical Services Branch, Gottlieb would remind him that he was now one of the President's men, there to serve him without question. He would point out the plaque inset on a wall in the CIA's entrance lobby that bore the words of the Apostle John: "And the truth shall set you free." That was to be their leitmotif. Then he would add, accompanied by one of his rare smiles, that there were many ways to reach that truth.

There were some in the auditorium of the old high school building who would testify to that. They had served Gottlieb, creating situations and experiments that contravened the most basic moral standards. Gottlieb had encouraged them to do so and to disregard the ethics of what he had ordered to be done.

Dr. Sidney Milton Gottlieb died on March 7, 1999. The cause of death was given as congenital heart failure resulting from pneumonia. Some of the reporters wondered if that was the only cause. His body had been taken from the University of Virginia hospital and cremated. Wasn't that a little convenient, one reporter asked another? But then, Dr. Gottlieb had attracted rumors and scandal for so long. Two weeks prior to his death, he was due in a New York courtroom to face civil charges that he had poisoned Stanley Glickman, a promising young painter. The plaintiffs intended to prove that in the autumn of 1952 on a balmy evening in an outdoor Paris café, Dr. Gottlieb had doctored Glickman's drink with a massive dose of LSD. Glickman had been arguing with some fellow Americans about the meaning of patriotism. Fed up with their views, Glickman had been about to walk away when one of the group — an "older man with a club foot and a cultured New York accent with a stutter," the court would have learned — offered to buy him a drink.

Glickman had been drinking coffee. But the man insisted on buying him a glass of Chartreuse. The man had gone inside to the bar and brought back the liqueur. The other Americans, according to an affidavit, had "fallen silent and leaned forward, fascinated." Soon after finishing the drink, Glickman began to complain he felt "strange and distorted." Fearing he had been poisoned, Glickman fled from the café.

Over the years Glickman continued to insist that he had been drugged. But his claim was rejected at every turn. Finally he met Dr. Lester Grinspoon, an associate professor of psychiatry at Harvard University. Grinspoon told Glickman that the description of the club-footed man fitted Dr. Gottlieb. Grinspoon told Glickman that in 1952, the CIA was conducting tests using LSD on unsuspecting victims in Europe. Glickman's lawyers intended to show that Gottlieb had been in Paris around the time their client's drink was spiked — an action expert medical witnesses would testify had eventually led to Glickman's death in December 1992. The CIA had been forced to hand over numerous documents; and while many were destroyed on the orders of CIA Director Richard Helms in 1973, a sufficient number survived to paint a disturbing picture of Dr. Gottlieb's methods.

Glickman's family and friends had gathered witnesses to support their claim that it was Dr. Gottlieb and a team of CIA agents who had chosen Stanley Glickman for one of their experiments. With Gottlieb's death, the case was closed. But not far from where the mourners assembled in the auditorium, Eric Olson continued his own search for the truth about what Dr. Gottlieb had done to his father. Eric believed, like the biblical inscription in the CIA lobby, the truth would finally set him free.

On a sunny day in 1984, in search of that release, Eric and Alice Olson had driven through the pleasant Virginia landscape to finally meet Dr. Gottlieb. Numerous references in Eric's files linked the scientist to his father. But none conclusively proved "that he was directly involved in his murder," Eric recalled. Nevertheless he decided the time had come to confront Dr. Gottlieb. The man who opened the door to them had changed little in the thirty years since Eric had glimpsed him among the mourners at his father's funeral. He was narrow-shouldered with his hair badly trimmed. His mismatched clothes still suggested a touch of the campus don. Eric had been told by those who had worked for him that at the CIA Dr. Gottlieb had set a punishing pace, invariably eating lunch at his desk, nibbling from neatly wrapped packages of raw carrots, cauliflower and home-baked bread, washed down by a bottle of goat's milk. He viewed money, clothes and other outward signs of success with something close to contempt. The abiding memory his old colleagues had was of a man who radiated a quiet confidence and certainty. Eric recalled his shock when Dr. Gottlieb stared at them from his doorway and spoke.

"Oh my God, so you actually came! Well, I'm so glad to see that you don't have guns," Dr. Gottlieb said. His voice was weak and wavering.

"We are only here to talk to you," replied Eric.

"Talk?" Dr. Gottlieb hesitated. "Let me tell you what I want to talk about. I had a dream last night. You had come with weapons to kill me."

He motioned them into the house. For a moment they sat in silence in the living room. Then Dr. Gottlieb asked: "What shall we talk about?"

"My father and how he died," said Eric. "He didn't commit suicide. He was murdered. I just want to know why. Just the truth."

Dr. Gottlieb had spread his hands. "I know nothing. I really cannot help you."

The brief meeting came to an end with Dr. Gottlieb still insisting he knew nothing about Frank Olson's murder.

Later Eric would tell the author, "the business about us turning up with guns was meant to unsettle us, putting my mother and myself in the position that I had to reassure the man whom I was already certain was responsible for my father's death that I meant him no harm. He wanted us to feel we were the guilty party. Not for nothing was he the master of mind control. But it also helped to confirm my growing certainty that Gottlieb had orchestrated the murder of my father."

Now, on that March afternoon in 1999 — fifteen years after his one and only meeting with Dr. Gottlieb — Eric continued to review his ever-expanding files on the death of his father. Meanwhile, on the other side of the Shenandoah Mountains, the memorial service for the man Eric had started to refer openly to as "my father's killer" proceeded.

Seated, with kid gloves worn against the cold, scarves knotted at the neck, Dr. Gottlieb's former colleagues might well have wondered how different things would have been if the memorial service had happened at an earlier time. Gottlieb had once been the darling of the upper echelons of the CIA. Allen Welsh Dulles — the fifth man to hold the post of Director of Central Intelligence — had admired Gottlieb and had been the first to say to him "go and find the answer to mind control." Dulles' successor, John Alex McCone, was another of Gottlieb's ardent supporters. The same could not be said of the seventh Director, William Francis Raborn. During his few months in office, Raborn had gone out of his way to avoid Gottlieb. But certainly the next director, Richard McGarrah Helms, would have been there if poor health had not kept him away. Helms, the former foreign correspondent whose early life read like something out of a Hemingway thriller, was the eighth Director to occupy the seventh floor suite in Langley. He had found in Gottlieb a ready listener — and for Gottlieb he was a powerful ally. Once he had settled in, Helms sent for Gottlieb and listened for hours. Then he nodded and said, "Sidney, whatever you want, you get. Whatever." None of the old spies who had come to the memorial would have doubted that Helms would have walked tall and proud to celebrate his friend.

But not William Colby. To a man, the mourners would have frozen him from their presence. CIA Director William Egan Colby was the whistleblower who had disclosed to Congress what Gottlieb had done, the only time the secret agency had revealed its own secrets. The undeniable truth was that Colby, having been a committed Cold War warrior, was a man dedicated to the facts and wary of speculation. He had become Director of Central Intelligence at a time when the agency was under fire from all quarters. Justified or not, those old men gathered at the funeral — spies, analysts, lawyers, men as far removed from the world of James Bond as it was possible to be — could not begin to forgive Colby. There were some, it was true, who would listen to the argument that Colby had no alternative but to break the code of *omerta*. But, for the majority of the CIA, he was the great betrayer.

There were some in the auditorium who had only known Dr. Gottlieb in his later years: as a man who had worked in a leprosy hospital in India and then returned to raise goats on a farm in northern Virginia. Somewhere along the way he had developed a passion for folk dancing. Despite his club foot he had cut a fine figure on the floor. Others remembered how Gottlieb liked to walk in the foothills of the nearby Blue Ridge Mountains during breaks from his voluntary work at the hospice. But the old spies, sitting together in a row at the back of the hall, had served alongside him in the glory days when

Gottlieb had presided over a CIA department that specialized in creating mind-changing drugs and lethal toxins. Between them they had developed wrist watches that could blow off a person's hand, dart guns that killed without trace, poisons which paralyzed muscles and induced what Gottlieb called "involuntary sleep."

In the twenty-two years he had been with the CIA, Dr. Gottlieb had hidden his work from his family and closest friends. To them he was vague about his responsibilities; his strength was in concealment, and he took pride in obscurity. He never let on what he knew. And nearly everyone assumed he knew even more. It had helped him to survive the purges which from time to time swept through Langley.

Some of those in the auditorium had themselves been victims of the corrosive rumors, the discreet whispers that ended careers during the long days of suspicion. They remembered Gottlieb as a methodical, careful scientist with a readiness to experiment far beyond the limits of any ethical code. In one instance he had ordered his men to travel north to Canada, to the prairie city of Winnipeg. There they repeated a test Frank Olson had developed with "harmless bacteria." The results were compared with similar tests being conducted in equal secrecy at Porton Down, Britain's biological warfare center. Clouds of similar bacteria had been released over the medieval English town of Salisbury and the port of Southampton.

In the early '50s when the Cold War had Washington in its grip, the Secretary of Defense received a memo Dr. Gottlieb had helped to draft: "The United States is highly vulnerable to germ warfare attacks. There is a need to produce more effective weapons than we hold at present in this area. We need to be in a position to retaliate." The argument was persuasive. Congress secretly voted $90 million to renovate a World War II arsenal near the small town of Pine Bluff, Arkansas. Within its ten stories were fermenters for the mass production of bacteria. The site became part of Dr. Gottlieb's ever-expanding empire.

The Pentagon informed Gottlieb that North Korea might be the first target for a biological attack after it invaded its neighbor to start the Korean War. There was a fear, based on CIA intelligence, that the North Koreans and the People's Liberation Army of China could unleash germ war against the South Koreans and their allies. Sidney Gottlieb was also given a further $10 million to improve the CIA laboratory facilities. On Gottlieb's team was Frank Olson; they began to create a battery of new weapons that included fountain pens filled with bacteria-infested ink; anthrax-laden turkey feathers, and fleas, lice and mosquitoes carrying bubonic plague and yellow fever. Some days Dr. Gottlieb was so delighted at what he saw that he would dance an impromptu jig as he walked from one lab to another.

In his work for the CIA, Gottlieb practiced a perversion of science, one that made the world a darker place. During those twenty-two years, he conducted inhuman experiments on a scale that came close to those of the Nazi doctors; of Soviet psychiatrists who diagnosed dissenters as mentally ill; of Japanese doctors during the Second World War who performed vivisection on live prisoners. In the end there was little difference between their actions and what Dr. Gottlieb had done or authorized, for there is nothing darker or more menacing or harder to accept than the participation of any physician in such work. Some of Dr. Gottlieb's victims died. Others went mad. Many more suffered irreversible psychological damage. The experiments he performed or ordered others to carry out mocked and subverted the very idea of the ethical physician. He and his colleagues had been turned from healers to abusers by a common belief: that what they did was to protect the United States — and ultimately the free world — against Communism. This belief replaced moral judgment. They were fitting examples of what Hannah Arendt called the "banality of evil," her term for the German creators of the Holocaust. Perhaps most shocking was that to the very end Sidney Gottlieb and his fellow doctors saw no wrong in what they did. Many were devoted family men who were convinced they were doing God's work to combat the godlessness of Communism.

Sidney Gottlieb, the son of Jewish immigrants from Hungary, had early on rejected the faith of his parents, preferring to experiment with "everything from agnosticism to Zen Buddhism." At the City College of New York he had flirted with Catholicism. By the time he graduated magna cum laude from the University of Wisconsin with a chemistry degree in 1940, he had become a Lutheran. Later, having earned a doctorate in biochemistry from the California Institute of Technology, he listed his faith as Protestant when he married Margaret Moore.

In his teen years, Sidney Gottlieb had flirted with Communism, though he had never been a card-carrying member of the Party. When he applied to join the CIA, he told the recruiting board about his beliefs. It made no difference. It was a period in the CIA's history when it found it hard to attract people of the right caliber: highfliers could find more rewarding careers in academia or business both in terms of remuneration and public prestige. What appealed to Dr. Gottlieb was the call of patriotism and the mystique that would surround his work. He felt he would always know more than his peers on the outside. And so it had proven to be. The Agency allowed him to work within the framework of his own ethic that the end justified the means.

The old men in the school auditorium recalled what he had been like in his prime. He had shown unusual physical stamina and assertiveness which more than compensated for his clubfoot. His constitution was extraordinary. He required only five hours of sleep in normal times and could function effectively with two-hour catnaps for extended periods. He solved problems with a stunning speed because of his instinct for spotting and exploiting the talents, motivations and limitations of all those who worked for him. Detail fascinated him. He prized facts. He stored huge quantities of them in his head and was always ready to absorb more. Yet he would be totally consumed by the immediate task at hand. It made him perfectly equipped to be the CIA's resident murderer-by-any-means-possible. The old spies remembered how skillfully he negotiated the deep waters of the intelligence community. He made enemies, sometimes quite deliberately, and relished bettering them. In his friends he inspired total loyalty. Their memories were still fresh of those times they had made trips with him to the rain forests of Latin America and Africa. Then he always insisted they did what he did: live and eat with the locals. He had shown a childlike pleasure, one not always shared by his companions, at being served frogs boiled in their skins and snakes and lizards of all kinds roasted on a spit. In Nicaragua he had carved slices from a monkey's broiled thigh and drank banana beer fermented with human saliva. In the highlands of East Africa he used a knife to scoop out ants from their hills and snacked on them the way a child scoffs jellybeans. He had slept at night in the fork of a tree and enjoyed a breakfast of wild pig. And all the time he searched for botanicals, the poisons and narcotic fungi he believed could help him in his search for a means to brainwash. He spoke to *sangomas*, the witch doctors of Africa, to Mexican Indians, to the Incas and the tribesmen who lived in the jungles near Ciudad Perdida in Colombia. From them he learned about the drugs used, to prepare virgins for human sacrifice a thousand years before Christ. He brought his samples back to Langley: a leaf that killed cattle quicker than a sten gun, a plant deadly to fish, another which caused human hair to fall out overnight. His collection of botanicals became legendary.

Later, when the war in Vietnam was winding down, what Dr. Gottlieb had done there began to emerge. He was in Istanbul when a letter came from the Department of Justice, ordering him to return to Washington to testify before Congress to answer to the revelations Colby had made. To the old spies in the auditorium it had been Dr. Gottlieb's shining hour. He could have disappeared again. But two days later he was back in Washington. It was an act of courage beyond what should be expected of anyone, his colleagues said, the finest example of that slogan carved on the lobby wall of the CIA, the truth shall set you free. Providing it was not the whole truth. Dr. Gottlieb was granted immunity from prosecution and allowed to testify in private sessions. Much of what he said never became public. But the old spies listening to the plaudits being delivered on that Saturday afternoon knew he had not betrayed them. That had been left to Colby.

As the light outside the auditorium began to fade, a man in a rain parka stepped up to the microphone. He was in his late thirties, but his slight stoop made him appear older. He smiled politely towards Margaret Gottlieb and asked if he could say a few words. She nodded politely back. She did not know who he was, but assumed he was someone her husband had met; "Sidney always had a way of attracting people," she later told the author. The man cleared his throat and began to speak in a low precise voice.

"Anyone who knew Sid knew he was haunted by something."

There was an intake of breath in the room. The man raised and lowered one hand, almost a gesture of benediction. He asked them all to join him in a prayer to "get rid of this something so that Margaret and the family can live in peace."

After leading them in the Lord's Prayer, he walked quickly out of the room. The old spies followed him out into the wintry cold, but he was gone. As they made their way to their cars, questions from reporters were met with dismissive headshakes. Over the years these men had remained among the empty spaces on the organization charts newspapers liked to piece together and publish. They still took their anonymity seriously. They knew Dr. Gottlieb would have expected no less. Margaret had asked the Clore English Funeral Home not to disclose details of the final disposition of Sidney's ashes. The local paper, *The Rappahannock News*, was persuaded to restrict notice of his passing to one terse paragraph that ended with the sentence: "Services will be private." But even as the last of the carefully chosen list of people were making their way out of the auditorium, old memories had been rekindled with an anger that the passing years had not diminished. The *Times* of London observed: "When Churchill spoke of a world 'made darker by the dark lights of perverted science' he was referring to the revolting experiments conducted on human beings by Nazi doctors in the concentration camps. But his remarks might with equal justice have been applied to the activities of the CIA's Sidney Gottlieb."

Gottlieb left others to continue his work — physicians who had studied his methods; who believed that where Dr. Gottlieb had failed they could succeed; who sought to control the mind of a subject and bend his or her will to their wishes. They often worked within the framework of state-sponsored torture and sometimes for terror groups. While the torture chambers of Syria, Iraq, Iran and the repressive regimes of Latin America continued to echo with the screams of victims, both men and women, the doctors who were part of that program were searching for new means that would subject their victims to their control. In 2006, Amnesty International asserted that there were hundreds of doctors engaged in this research.

CHAPTER THREE

In October 2001 America was staggering in the aftermath of the destruction of the Twin Towers. Further anthrax attacks had led the government to keep the CIA and FBI on Delta Alert, the highest level of warning. For his part, Eric Olson had assembled most of the evidence about his father's work, the work that had ended with his murder. The information was contained in black covered folders, each impeccably catalogued. Together, they formed a small library that traced the minutiae of both Eric and Frank Olson's lives, and how they became entwined in Eric's search to know what happened.

One of Eric's files contained details of how the family was invited to meet President Gerald Ford in the White House to discuss the elder Olson's death. Ford had been gracious, displaying concern and contrition over what had happened to Frank Olson. "It should never have happened; it must never happen again," Eric recalled the President's words. Alice, in her best frock, had stood beside the president while he shook her hand for the photographer. The children appear solemn faced, perhaps intimidated by their surroundings. Ford's last words were that he was recommending that Congress approve compensation of $750,000 for the family.

A week later, Eric and Alice were shown into the seventh floor suite of CIA Director William Colby in Langley. Colby had asked for the meeting. Eric had taken the precaution of bringing along two lawyers. Eric prepared himself for the meeting, reviewing in his mind all the questions he wanted answers to, sharpening them and putting them in order. In the end, they came down to the one that had been there for twenty-two years:

"'Why was my father murdered? Colby must know the answer,' I kept telling myself," Eric later recalled to the author.

Eric's first impression of Colby did not change during what became a hostile encounter. At first, Eric later wrote, "Colby's manner was cold and controlled and he seemed tense and awkward." The two lawyers sat silent and watchful, both taking notes. If Colby objected, he did not say so. Colby would say afterwards: "This was one of the most difficult assignments I have ever had." The director led them to the dining room reserved for senior staff. The meal became increasingly acrimonious, with Eric challenging Colby about the justification for the Vietnam War. Colby had served as chief of the war's most notorious project, code-named Phoenix, which was allegedly responsible for the deaths of twenty thousand Vietnamese.

"The whole thing was obscene and immoral," Eric said.

Colby bridled. "We could have won. With more weapons, we would have won."

Eric wondered if Colby was referring to the weapons Frank Olson had worked on. He already knew a little about them. But any chance of exploring the question further was abruptly stopped by Colby. He said he had something to give them. Together they and their lawyers followed the director back to his office. On the desk was an inch-thick file that Eric had noticed there before. Colby picked it up and looked at Alice before deciding who to hand it to. He finally thrust the file at Eric.

"This is a copy of the documents relating to your father's death. It will show you everything," Colby said.

Eric leafed through the folder. The documents were photocopies of the agency's in-house investigation of his father's death. There were unexplained terms, like "Artichoke" and "Bluebird."

Colby watched him. "It's all there. The full story. Take it away and read it. Take your time. There is nothing more to hide," he finally said.

He thanked them for coming and led the family to the door. He had not told them — and the folder did not reveal — that Frank Olson had not been a civilian employee of the Department of the Army but a department head working at Fort Detrick for the CIA.

On the night of August 4, 1975, having written up the account of the visit to Colby, Eric settled down to read the file. "Artichoke" and "Bluebird" were the precursors of the project that would become known as MK-ULTRA, which had started at the outset of the Korean War. It was clear from the documents that the project was to explore the use of drugs, such as LSD and truth serums, as well as botulism and anthrax, for covert assassinations. But had his father also been working on something even more fearful — biological and chemical weapons — to be used as weapons of mass destruction? With that question uppermost in his mind, Eric Olson began a journey of discovery, one that he carefully chronicled.

The starting point of a long and tortuous road was April 16, 1943. Professor Albert Hoffman, the director of research at the Sandoz drug and chemical conglomerate in Basel, Switzerland, had been working with a substance he had first discovered in 1938. He called it d-lysergic acid diethylamide, LSD. Professor Hoffman looked like a scientist. He peered owlishly from behind rimless glasses and kept his hair cropped close to his scalp. His long white coat was a symbol of his senior position at Sandoz; junior scientists wore short white jackets. His one known pleasure was bicycling to and from his home near his laboratory complex. At thirty-seven years old, Professor Hoffman was regarded as a *wunderkind* by Sandoz management.

On that warm April afternoon, while across the border German cities were being bombed around the clock, Professor Hoffman's laboratory was an oasis of calm. For some weeks he had been working to create a drug to improve blood circulation, and once more he had gone back to his small store of LSD. This time he decided he would mix it with another substance, ergot. The history of ergot had always fascinated him. In China and parts of the Middle East, the fungus was held to have curative power for a number of ailments. But throughout Europe, it was remembered as the scourge that had swept the continent in the Middle Ages, leaving a trail of death like the Plague. The symptoms were strikingly similar: fingers and toes reduced to blackened stumps and bellies distended. A German cardinal had named it St. Anthony's Fire, claiming it mainly attacked those who had offended one of the saints of the Church.

Professor Hoffman had planned to mix an extract of ergot with LSD. He took the LSD from a bottle and measured out 250 micrograms (under 1/100,000 of an ounce). A few micrograms touched his fingers. He rubbed them together to remove the specks of powder. Within forty minutes he became restless, pacing up and down in his laboratory. Unable to concentrate, he became increasingly disorientated and stumbled from the laboratory. By the time he cycled home, his white coat flapping behind him like a sail, he was shivering and dizzy. The last time he had felt like this was on his graduation night when he had imbibed too much schnapps. His mind was racing, and he could not remain still. A clinician would have noticed his dilated pupils and rapid pulse. Later when he had recovered, Professor Hoffman set down his experiences. "I saw an uninterrupted stream of fantastic images in my mind. They were in kaleidoscope-like colors, coming and going. I was afraid. I feared I was going crazy. I had the idea that I was out of my body. I thought I had died."

Eric read Hoffman's description several times. Was that what his father had experienced? The file Colby provided indicated that Olson had been given LSD surreptitiously. Had his father swallowed, not a carefully measured quantity like Professor

Hoffman had used, but a substantially larger amount, one that had driven him, through a haze of those kaleidoscope colors Hoffman had seen, to jump from the hotel window?

While Professor Hoffman had been gripped by his mind-blowing experience, there were other scientists conducting similar experiments. Two hundred miles from the Sandoz laboratories in the labs of the Dachau concentration camp, Nazi doctors were experimenting on their prisoners with mescaline. One of them, Walter Neff, told his U.S. interrogators later that "the intention was to eliminate the will of persons. In other words, to take control of their minds." The Nazi doctors fed the mescaline to prisoners by spiking their coffee. Neff noted the subjects soon displayed "sentiments of hatred and revenge" and became "alternately melancholy and gay."

Eric remembered that Alice had spoken of similar mood changes in his father. He discovered that at the time the Dachau experiments started, the Office of Strategic Services — the OSS — had set up a "truth drug" committee under Dr. Winfred Overholster, the director of St. Elizabeth's Hospital in Washington. It was at this time that Frank Olson arrived at Fort Detrick. With his Ph.D. in biochemistry, Olson was invited to join the staff at Fort Detrick by Dr. Ira L. Baldwin, the head of his university department. In one of his files, Eric wrote: "Pressurized by evidence the German war machine was vigorously pursing a CBW (Chemical and Biological Weapons) program, Detrick became the top-secret center for America's chemical-biological research. My father became one of the first civilian scientists to work there." Apart from his undoubted scientific qualifications, why else had he been chosen, Eric wondered? Was it because the nature of the work at Fort Detrick did not permit those engaged in it the luxury of moral doubt? In 1948, Dr. Baldwin had written a secret paper that set down the ground rules for that research. "It is to use CBW by all means possible."

Eric's investigation also took him back to that dark period in America's post-war history when McCarthyism aroused the country's paranoia and led to disgrace and ruin for many good people. Senator Joseph R. McCarthy was an unsavory politician looking for a cause with which he could make his name. He found one in the Cold War. He said there were "205 known Communists" in the State Department. Their loyalty was to Moscow, he thundered in a speech in the little town of Wheeling, West Virginia. McCarthy waved a piece of paper at his audience, implying he had the names, as a result of his own "intense investigation." No one saw the list close-up and when approached later by reporters McCarthy said he had lost the paper. His career took off overnight. Forgotten was the time he had taken bribes from a Washington lobbyist for Coca Cola and gambled away the money, or that he always had a bottle of whiskey in his tan briefcase. This shifty-eyed man, with his high-pitched voice, snickering laugh and bull-necked body, became a national figure, the nation's champion against "the Red Menace," the senator who knew how to captivate the media, a master of the sound bite, able to destroy a man's career with a few poisonous words. Figures and statistics — no matter how improbable they seemed — were his weapons. Soon he had identified "twelve diplomats who took the Moscow ruble at the U.S. mission at the United Nations;" there "could be as many as thirty-four Commies in the Department of Agriculture." "They are everywhere: at the Voice of America studios; in Hollywood. Everywhere, everywhere."

His voice rasped across the nation, lighting a fuse; soon the bonfire was out of control. The witch hunt occupied prime time television and radio; small forests of newsprint were devoted to McCarthy's accusations. Tens of millions of Americans came to regard the Wisconsin junior senator as the great crusader against Communism. Those who did not support him were looked upon as fellow travelers. What united the masses was McCarthy's demand that Communism be rooted out and stopped by any means.

Thinking about that time, Eric wondered whether that was why his father — ironically another son of Wisconsin — had been among the scientists given the go-ahead to produce weapons that could destroy the Soviet Union by wiping out its population with a whole range of deadly germs. During the long months of suspicion generated by McCarthy, Frank Olson's loyalty had never been in doubt. Others working on secret research had suddenly found their security clearance withdrawn. Frank Olson had continued to sustain his reputation as a methodical scientist totally committed to what he was doing, helping to build what would become the world's largest arsenal of toxic weapons.

In the CIA file Colby had passed along to Eric, Sidney Gottlieb was often no more than a signature on a memo, approving financing for one project or signing off on another. But his presence was there, sharpening Eric's suspicions that the documents did not contain the whole truth. "It was like I was being told to put up or shut up," Eric later told the author.

McCarthy's monstrous claims had led to huge sums of money being secretly provided for the funding and security of Fort Detrick, on a par with that provided to the Manhattan Project, which produced the atomic bomb. But here even greater devastation was being contemplated. There were no moral qualms among the scientists at Fort Detrick who worked for the newly formed CIA Special Operations Division (SOD), the most secret of all the agency's secret units. Its laboratories were patrolled by armed guards with orders to shoot any intruder. Inside, protected by air locks, the scientists grew lethal cells and cultured deadly viruses.

It was when Eric began to probe into the seminal events of the 1950s that his journey of personal discovery took a new turn.

On the last weekend of June 1950, America was enjoying the first heat wave of the summer, with temperatures in Washington over the hundred-degree mark. President Harry Truman had been driven in air-conditioned comfort to open Baltimore's new Friendship International Airport. He dedicated it to "the cause of peace," then flew to spend the weekend with his brother Vivian in Kansas. Other senior members of the administration were also away from the capital. Secretary of Defense Louis Johnson, and Omar Bradley, the World War II hero who was now Chairman of the Joint Chiefs of Staff, were on a military plane high over the Pacific, returning from Tokyo. Secretary of State Dean Acheson was gardening at home in Maryland. Beyond his fence line armed guards patrolled to protect him against intruders who might be driven to attack Acheson for "harboring" Communists in his department. Dean Rusk, the Assistant Secretary of State was also out of Washington.

In Fort Detrick it was another working day. Frank Olson and his colleagues at SOD were running more tests on a range of bacteria they hoped to weaponize. Outside the fort, the corn stalks had begun to ripen among the stands of brown hickory and yellow ash. White painted farmhouses dotted the landscape, all the way to the Appalachians, the distant range of mountains. At noon, Frank Olson took his customary lunch break. On the other side of the world it was 4:00 A.M. along the 38th Parallel. It was at that moment, as General Douglas McArthur, commander-in-chief of all U.S. forces in the Pacific, later said, "North Korea struck like a cobra."

On June 25, 1950, the fifth anniversary of the formation of the United Nations, 38,000 North Korean troops, supported by squadrons of Soviet tanks, swept across the 38th Parallel. Their objective was to unite the two Koreas.

After the country had been liberated from a harsh Japanese occupation in 1945, the United States and the Soviet Union agreed that Korea should be run by a single national government. But the question of who would serve in such an administration and where it would be sited had resulted in increasing friction. This gave rise to guerrilla warfare and had finally resulted in North Korea crossing the imaginary line on the map that divided it from South Korea.

The UN Security Council called upon its member states to condemn the invasion. Fifty-three nations did; twenty-six offered to send military aid to South Korea; sixteen ultimately committed troops. A land area smaller than the state of Oregon became a battlefield for almost three million combatants.

Two months after the outbreak of war, on August 21, 1950, President Truman appointed General Walter Bedell Smith to head the CIA. The former U.S. ambassador to the Soviet Union was convinced the Russians and Chinese were intent on a global confrontation with the United States. One of Smith's first acts was to visit Fort Detrick. He met Dr. Gottlieb and both men agreed the war in Korea was the ideal opportunity for the Office of Policy Coordination (OPC) to display its mandate for covert warfare. The OPC was known as the "dirty tricks money man" within the Washington intelligence community. Smith told Dr. Gottlieb that Fort Detrick would have no problem obtaining the funding to field-test biological weapons.

After Labor Day 1950, Dr. Gottlieb flew to Tokyo. From there the 24th Infantry and 25th Infantry divisions of the United States Army had sailed to South Korea to repel the North Korean advance. With little battle experience and equipped with outdated weapons, they were no match for the mighty T-34 Soviet tanks. Both divisions had been driven back, suffering heavy casualties; U.S. prisoners, with their hands tied behind their backs, were bayoneted by the North Koreans. Only

MacArthur's military skills prevented a total rout. He created a 120-mile defense perimeter around Pusan; the bridgehead arced from the Sea of Japan in the east to the Korean Strait in the south. President Truman had authorized a draft of 600,000 men, but Dr. Gottlieb believed the secret biological weapons being developed by his team would have a greater effect on the outcome of the war than all the young men being called up.

In Japan, Gottlieb went to the secret base the CIA operated at the Atsugi Naval Air station near Yokohama. From its fifty-acre compound, the CIA had started to run covert operations into North Korea. These were under the control of Hans Tofte, an OSS veteran. He boasted that he knew "every inch of the countryside" from his days hunting big game in the region. During World War II he had waged a successful guerrilla campaign against the Japanese. Now his experience was available to the CIA. "I am, I suppose, the classic gun for hire," he once said. Dr. Gottlieb instructed Tofte to obtain a selection of Korea's insect life and small field animals, like jungle rats and voles. Dr. Gottlieb then flew to Pusan to meet U.S. Army Captain Henry Alderholt. Alderholt's pilots were part of a group nicknamed the "Kyushu Gypsies" because of their ability to drop into jungle clearings in the dead of night and create havoc behind enemy lines. With his six C-47 aircraft, Alderholt ran his own outfit without outside interference. That appealed to Dr. Gottlieb — along with Alderholt's swashbuckling manner and can-do mentality. Dr. Gottlieb gave him the same shopping list he had told Tofte to fill.

By mid-October, Dr. Gottlieb was back in Fort Detrick with his precious collection of insect and animal life and vegetation.

Frank Olson and his fellow researchers set to work with the bugs and animals. Each scientist had signed a waiver: in the event of his death from a disease contracted through their work, he bequeathed his corpse to the United States government. Each man was vaccinated to protect against the germs they would use to infect the bugs and animals brought from Korea. Like the others, each morning before starting work, Frank Olson swallowed a range of antibiotics and showered in a powerful sterile solution. Dressed in a protective hood, suit and boots, he breathed purified air once he entered the labs, which were bathed in ultra violet light, the wavelength best suited for killing any germs that might escape from the "hot boxes." To reach inside a box, Olson used the attached rubber gloves to manipulate the microbes swarming on pieces of glassware. One by one the groups of various grubs and animals were judged on their suitability to form the basis for biological weapons.

It was slow and deadly dangerous work. The infected bugs from Korea were tested on guinea pigs, rabbits, rhesus monkeys and pigs, in a windowless structure rising through eight floors, a skyscraper among the low buildings of Camp Detrick. This was Building 527; inside its walls was a metal sphere, some forty feet in diameter. It was there that biological weapons were dispersed on the animals to determine their suitability as vectors for such diseases as encephalitis, the brain disease which rapidly produces seizures and comas, and which often ends in death.

Over the coming months, Frank Olson and his colleagues confirmed the suitability of Dr. Gottlieb's collection from Korea for spreading a variety of viruses for germ warfare.

On December 5, 1950, a secret memo from the Department of Defense Committee on Biological Weapons arrived in Dr. Gottlieb's office. It asked for "guidance in the search for evidence of the immunity against disease from biological weapons by enemy deserters and prisoners of war." A week later came a second memo, from the Far East Command in Tokyo that asked how "work is progressing from the biological warfare point of view." The memo was signed by Colonel Richard P. Mason, Commanding Officer of Unit 406.

Dr. Gottlieb decided it was time to return to Tokyo to visit Unit 406. This time he took Frank Olson with him. They arrived in early January, 1951. The Far East Command's Unit 406 Medical General Laboratory had been established in 1946 and was now headquartered in the Mitsubishi Higashi Building in Tokyo's downtown area. Its original purpose had been to provide various public health services for the American occupiers and the civilian population. That work still played an important role, and the center was staffed with some of the best public health doctors from the United States. But there was another side to Unit 406, known only to Colonel Mason and a few of his senior staff. In a restricted laboratory complex, researchers were working with plague, anthrax, undulant fever and cholera to discover their potential for weaponizing. Every month some twenty thousand mice along with hundreds of guinea pigs and other small animals were sacrificed in experiments. The American researchers were assisted by some of the Japanese scientists who had been brought to Fort Detrick in 1945. Promised immunity for their war crimes, they had revealed details of their own experiments with biological weapons on U.S. prisoners during World War II.

Under Colonel Mason's energetic leadership, Unit 406 had expanded its links to scores of Japanese public laboratories to keep track of research that could be adapted for biological weapons work. Into Unit 406 came reports of surveys of birds as carriers of encephalitis and equine encephalitis, a survey of Tokyo's rat population, a study of salmonella.

Gottlieb and Olson had arrived at a time when Unit 406 was about to expand even further into the sinister world of biological warfare. An ultra high-security unit, known only as 8003, had been set up on a separate floor. It was still in the development stage. Frank Olson's first job in Japan was to develop the new unit's capability to work alongside the CIA's Fort Detrick's laboratories, the very core of America's secret biological warfare program.

By April, 1951, America and its allied forces had launched fierce counterattacks, which resulted in the capture of large numbers of North Korean prisoners. They were held in a camp on Koje Island in South Korea. That month, a U.S. Navy landing craft fitted out as a laboratory by Unit 406 arrived offshore. Dr. Gottlieb was on board. The ship was reportedly there to deal with an outbreak of amoebic dysentery among the prisoners. Three thousand oral and rectal cultures were taken.

In the following months, almost 20,000 prisoners were afflicted with the illness; 1,800 died. Throughout Asia, reports began to circulate that the prisoners had been used to test a bug for germ warfare. *Newsweek* summarized the allegations as "North Korea and China allege numbers of Chinese Reds tested on Bubonic Plague ship." The Associated Press ran a similar follow-up story. Finally, the respected *Journal of Tropical Medicine and Hygiene,* the organ of American Society of Tropical Medicine, reported the "most unusual feature of the epidemic was its size."

Suddenly all further comment on the incident stopped. Years later, when William Colby appeared before Congressional hearings, he said the CIA records for its biological warfare program for the period were "very incomplete" because many had been destroyed in 1972-1973. He could not recall why. It was possible they included the full details of the mysterious dysentery outbreak among Korean prisoners.

Now, over half a century later, in October 2001, the pieces in the jigsaw of Frank Olson's life that his son Eric had patiently assembled were finally coming together. He now knew about the other secret trips his father had made to South Korea. He also had learned of the confessions of U.S. Air Force officers shot down during the Korean War that they had dropped biological weapons. Most of the depositions had come from flyers of the Fifth Air Force: two colonels, two captains and twenty lieutenants. They described how the germ bombs were loaded only minutes before they took off to avoid the danger of a mishap that could have wiped out an air base. Each airman confessed, independently, that the aim of the attacks was to create a contamination belt across central North Korea so as to stop the movement of soldiers and supplies south to the 38th Parallel. They revealed they were each told that the ultimate aim of their mission was "to shorten the war and save American lives." One briefing had ended with the reminder of "how the atomic bomb ended the last war." Each pilot said he had been given a detailed explanation of how the germ-laden bombs would "create epidemics among the enemy." At the end of the war, in 1953, when they were repatriated, the fliers had withdrawn their confessions. But those retractions did not have the same conviction as their original statements to their captors. In those, they had all stated they would have faced U.S. court-martial if they had not carried out their missions.

Eric had learned of eyewitness accounts of Korean and Chinese survivors of the biological weapons. Like the confessions of the pilots, their claims had been denied by the United States.

Eric had come to realize that his father, for all his loyalty to his country and his readiness to perform his duty as an apostle of the biology of doom, had finally allowed his strong sense of morality to get the better of him. As a result, he had become another "expendable" in the sinister world that Dr. Gottlieb had created.

Many of the details surrounding Olson's life and death would be discovered by another dedicated member of the CIA, a genuine American hero of the Korean War. His name was William Buckley. His life would become inextricably linked to Sidney Gottlieb's work and his fate tied to Frank Olson's murder.

CHAPTER FOUR

Bill Buckley was born on May 31, 1928, in Medford, Massachusetts. His father was a stockbroker; his mother had raised him and his two sisters to respect authority, earn good grades and love their country. The family was religious but not devout; they were Roman Catholic, attending church for Sunday Mass and holidays.

Bill grew up during a turbulent time. He was barely four and still learning to read the headlines of his father's *New York Times* when, in the summer of 1932, he was told that Washington D.C. was under siege — not from some invading force but from its own war veterans. The Great Depression was destroying the nation as no enemy had; millions were without work and close to starvation. The veterans had come to the capital asking for assistance for their families; over 100,000 camped out around the White House clamoring for help. President Herbert Hoover's response was to send in armed troops against the vets under the command of Major George Patton, who later found fame in World War II. Washington D.C. became his first battlefield.

In their middle-class security Bill's parents were shocked by what had happened; but they also believed that the poor were somehow responsible for their fate. They felt that they had little in common with those reduced to selling their jewelry, pawning their furniture and borrowing money, let alone with anyone begging on the streets.

Slowly but surely America pulled its way back up the ladder to solvency. Bill was eleven when World War II broke out in Europe. Then came Pearl Harbor, and Europe's war became

America's. For the teenage Bill these were stirring times; he followed every battle with avid interest. Years later he could still accurately recall some of the headlines — *9th Army 57 miles from Berlin* or *Marines Gain on Okinawa*. And, of course, *Roosevelt Dead — Truman New President*. Followed by: *Jap Cities Destroyed by New Bombs*, and finally the headline that mattered the most: *V-J Day*. The post-war years included the Marshall Plan, the New Look in fashion, the first reports of flying saucers, and the day China became the Communist People's Republic of China. Bill had countless other personal memories: his first date and kiss; the first time he got drunk; his first fistfight with the local bully, which he won by a knock-out — all familiar stepping stones for any teenage boy growing up in the first peacetime decade. But in some ways, however, Bill's experience was not so typical.

Early on, Bill's father had mapped out a future for his son. It was modeled on his own good, clean life instilled with a New Englander's sense of self-sacrifice and an abiding belief that success could only be achieved through hard work and strict probity. In this planned future Bill would go to college, study the liberal arts and go on to get a sound grounding in business. Afterward he would join his father's brokerage firm. At some point he would meet a girl, marry, raise a family and continue the process his own father had begun. This would ensure a succession of Buckleys who would vote Republican and proudly display their patriotism and their belief in the United States.

Bill had other ideas. Even as a child he had shown a taste for intrigue; he avidly read comics, newspapers, magazines and books, anything that would deepen his knowledge of war. By his early teens he could lecture his classmates on the intricacies of the great battles of the First World War; by fifteen he knew more about the philosophy of Napoleon and Wellington than his teachers. At home he played endless war games on the floor of his bedroom, spending hours grouping his armies of lead soldiers. The metal men in smart, straight rows were mown down by the cannons concealed behind the legs of his bed and bureau. His obsession with war and politics was a personal one; no one else in the family had even a remote interest in either subject.

In June 1945, Buckley enlisted in the United States Army as a buck private. He saw it as his patriotic duty. His only disappointment was that he was too late to see action; Japan surrendered just two months after he entered boot camp. Four years later the Korean War began. Buckley, now a commissioned officer, was among the first to lead his troops onto the battlefields of Asia. Within months he won his first Silver Star, the army's medal for gallantry, for single-handedly destroying a North Korean machine-gun nest. Shortly afterwards he was promoted to captain. Two Purple Hearts for wounds received in battle quickly followed. The first medal was for destroying another North Korean machine-gun post despite being shot in the arm. The second came when he led his platoon to safety from the battlefield. Once he was satisfied his men were secure, he returned to the fighting and, clutching a machine-gun with belts of bullets strapped around his body, he had charged the enemy. Many died under his onslaught. That night he had gone to a brothel, gotten drunk and danced until dawn. From then on he was known as the "Steel Man."

In Korea Buckley had read in U.S. newspapers a story he believed at the time, he later recalled, to be "frankly bullshit." "The North Koreans had put out they had captured some of our fly-boys who had confessed to dropping 'germ bombs,'" he recalled. "They said they even had photographs of some of these bombs that had failed to explode. Now everybody knew that some of our armaments didn't explode. But a dud 'germ bomb.' I thought, 'Jesus, they gotta be kidding.' I remember

MacArthur coming on the radio and saying it was nonsense." Buckley had no inkling that the Chinese claims had caused what he later found out was a "God-awful ruckus in Washington."

Controversy was inevitable once the accusation surfaced that the United States had waged biological warfare in Korea. "Most of it was experimental work. Experiments with 'vectors', insects like the yellow fever-carrying mosquito, capable of transmitting disease from one body to another." That unequivocal allegation was made by Dr. Joseph Needham, an expert on Oriental medicine, who later became Master of Gonville and Caius College in Oxford, one of the most prestigious pillars of the English establishment. He had traveled to North Korea in the company of leading scientists from the Soviet Union, Italy, France and Sweden. They concluded: "North Korea did actually serve as the target for bacteriological weapons."

Washington steadfastly denied the claim — let alone admitted that both Dr. Sidney Gottlieb and Frank Olson had been in Korea supervising the launch of those "germ bombs." By the time Buckley did discover this, he was working for Gottlieb.

After thirty-seven months of bloodshed had left two million dead, — among them thirty-seven thousand Americans — peace of a kind finally came to Korea. The South had gained 2,500 square miles of territory and the North 850 miles. Nothing else had really changed. No principles on either side had been vindicated. Negotiations begun by President Truman had been completed by his successor, Dwight Eisenhower. When he was asked how he felt, Ike's first comment was, "I just hope my boy is coming home soon." It was a sentiment felt by all parents whose children had served in Korea.

On July 27, 1953, at 10:01 A.M. in Panmunjon, on the 38th Parallel, (it was 08:01 A.M., July 26, in Washington), eighteen copies of the armistice were signed on a freshly lacquered table.

No words were exchanged between the opposing signatories. There were no handshakes.

Now a battle-hardened veteran, Bill Buckley returned from Korea the week after the ceremony. It was a very different world from the one he had left more than two years before. A new teen subculture had sprung up, with its own rites and fads: ducktail haircuts and sleeves rolled up to a certain length for boys, for girls poodle haircuts and waist-length necklaces. Those who didn't follow the style were labeled "squares." The "facts of life" were an endless topic; drive-in movie theaters were known as "passion pits." Only those with "wheels" could enter. A survey in the summer of 1953 showed that 75 percent of all high school juniors had driver's licenses and some 60 percent borrowed the family car for "social purposes." Television had established itself as the great consumer outlet; 94 percent of all mothers across the country said they were regularly asked by their children to buy goods advertised on television.

It was a world to which Bill Buckley found difficulty in adjusting. He was twenty-six years old, yet felt older. His experiences in Korea had changed him, but he didn't feel comfortable talking about them. With his crew-cropped hair and military uniform, he also sensed, even in Washington, that he was an outsider. Sometimes he asked himself if what was happening across America was a good reason for him to have gone to war.

He was reassigned to the Pentagon. But no one knew quite what to do with an authentic hero. They couldn't send him on tour to promote life in the Army. Many families who experienced losses in Korea were reluctant to encourage another son to sign on for a hitch in the armed forces. In the end Buckley had been posted to the Pentagon archives to help assemble the documentation from Korea. He was told it was a job for life if he wanted it.

What attracted him in the archives was the files still marked "Classified." He had seen classified reports in Korea: intelligence reports, casualty reports, reports on morale. But the reports he now came across were different. They dealt with the confessions of the U.S. Air Force pilots who had told their Chinese captors they had dropped biological bombs in North Korea. Many of the prisoners had been held in a compound close to the Yalu River. There were several prison camps there, but the one for officers was a little distance from the others, near a small settlement where the guards lived. By the end of the war there were some three hundred prisoners being held behind barbed wire. They came from the United States, Britain and Australia.

When the first confessions started to be broadcast, the U.S. government said the airmen had been brainwashed. The term had first been used in September, 1950, when a Miami newspaper published an article by Edward Hunter entitled "Brainwashing Tactics Force Chinese into Ranks of Communist Party." This became a stock phrase in stories about Russian and Soviet methods during the Cold War. Hunter was a CIA officer working undercover as an author who had written several books on the subject. In a memo attached to file copies of his writings, Buckley read how Hunter coined the word from the Mandarin, *hsi-nao*, "to cleanse the mind." The phrase had no political connotation in Mandarin. But it helped form American public opinion concerning the way the confessions had been obtained.

In other files Buckley read how, after being repatriated, the pilots were subjected to intense interrogation, including questioning by Army psychiatrists. The doctors' reports were marked: "Highly Classified. Not to be Released." The consensus was they had not been brainwashed nor were they victims of physical abuse or torture. That made the details in the confessions all the more remarkable. The fliers had described the various types of bombs they had carried to disperse germs and the varieties of vectors used. They had provided details of the U.S. Air Force bases from which they had flown, and the number of missions they had carried out before being shot down. One confession stated: "The most-used germ bomb was a 500-pounder. Each had several compartments to hold different kinds of germs. Insects like fleas and spiders were kept separate from rats and voles."

A confession by Colonel Frank H. Schwable, the most senior officer shot down, said some of his bombs were attached to parachutes. At a certain height, the chutes opened to disperse "germ powder." Buckley pulled Schwable's record. He was the son of a distinguished father who had fought in the Boxer Rebellion in Beijing in 1909. Schwable had joined the Marine Corps in 1929. During World War II, he collected four Distinguished Flying Crosses and in Korea had been awarded a Gold Star. So why had he confessed? All the pilots were combat veterans, trained not to reveal military secrets. Yet one by one, Schwable and the others had signed their detailed and highly damaging admissions. Why had they decided to break the code of ethics that had been instilled during their days at flying school?

Buckley turned to the sworn denials the pilots had all made upon returning to the United States. They all began with the same words: "I am making this retraction on my own free will and do so without any inducement and acknowledge this statement or any portion may be used in evidence against me in a court-martial." But there had been no trials. Schwable had faced only a court of inquiry. Afterwards he had been promoted a rank and allowed to retire to his home in Norfolk, Virginia.

Early in February 1954, William Buckley received a phone call from the CIA Personnel Office. He was to be one of the "stud detail" for a party Clover Dulles, the wife of CIA director Allen Welsh Dulles, was giving. Buckley had heard about these assignments. "You got dressed up in your best uniform and mingled with the guests, making sure no one was left unattached or was bored or in need of a drink." Those who worked the stud details were "glorified nannies." Buckley would have tried to wriggle out of the assignment, but the prospect of meeting the legendary Allen Welsh Dulles had a distinct appeal. He took extra care he would cut a dashing figure, pressing knife-edge creases into his trousers and giving his shoes an extra shine. By early afternoon he was waiting for the car to convey him and other members of the detail to the Dulles home in the Washington suburbs.

Clover greeted each man with a handshake and positioned them in various rooms. Each was given a drink and the instruction to greet and mingle. In his immaculate dress uniform, Buckley was a fine example of a can-do military hero. With his easy manner, polite smile and a willingness to downplay his achievements in Korea, he was an instant success with the guests.

Allen Dulles moved among the crowd, pausing to greet here a senator, there an admiral and, over by the fireplace, a group of Foreign Service officials. He was the epitome of the attentive host, emitting that soft laugh some people said was not really a sign of amusement but merely a way diffuse the tension he often felt. Sometimes he squeezed the elbow of a beautiful woman. No party was complete for the middle-aged spy-master without its quota of models, television starlets and the most elegant of the long-legged secretaries working on Capitol Hill. There was endless speculation on the city's embassy party circuit over who would be the next girl he would seduce. No one could be certain. He was, in every sense, a man of secrets.

Buckley had watched Dulles' behavior with an amusement that he took care not to show. For his part, he had been propositioned by several women already. He had tactfully made his excuses and moved on, joining one group, then another, waving away the waiters whenever they approached with a tray of cocktails. He hoped the party could lead to a job with the CIA. Meantime, he continued to circulate among the guests, smiling shyly when they pointed to his medal ribbons and saying, "really, a lot of guys got these," or "I was just doing my job."

One group consisted of lawyers, sober-faced and suited, older men with fob chains across their vests and with what Clover had called "courtroom eyes." Her husband always insisted that his parties have a quota of attorneys. They knew how to reach out and connect all kinds of people: the rich and powerful, the clever, the reckless, those who lived on the fringe of the law, and even beyond it. The lawyers knew most of the skeletons in Washington's closets, keeping Dulles as well-informed as J. Edgar Hoover.

Leonard W. Hall was probably the wealthiest attorney at the party. He was also chairman of the Republican National Committee. Every time he came to a party, he brought with him a different associate, a lawyer Hall felt was a rising star in the profession and could benefit from rubbing shoulders with the elite of Washington. Hall's companion on this night had not looked his hostess in the eye and mumbled his name so badly that Hall had to say, "This is Bill Casey. You ever got a problem with investments; he's the one to sort it out."

Clover smiled politely, mentally reminding herself she knew a hundred lawyers she would consult before even thinking of going to this awkward, heavy-jowled man with fleshy lips and gaps between his teeth. Yet her husband had greeted Casey like an old friend, fetching him a drink, taking his arm, guiding him into a corner of the room where they had stood, heads close in deep conversation, oblivious to everyone else.

William Casey, like Dulles, was a World War II veteran of the Office of Strategic Services (OSS), the forerunner of the CIA. When Casey left the OSS to enter law practice, Dulles had predicted "you'll be back. Once this business is in your blood, there is no letting go."

Another of the party groups was dominated by Congressman Lyndon Johnson of Texas. He was discussing the latest move in the deepening crisis between the White House and the Republican leaders over taking a tougher line with Moscow. The Republican leadership wanted to renounce all wartime agreements made at Tehran, Yalta and Potsdam. President Eisenhower had procrastinated, finally agreeing to a draft resolution to go before Congress which fell short of what the Republicans demanded.

The document had been written by Allen's brother, Secretary of State John Foster Dulles and was based largely upon the analysis of their sister, Eleanor Lansing Dulles, who was in charge of the Berlin Desk at the State Department. This family triumvirate effectively created and controlled the foreign policy of the United States.

Johnson said he was going to tell the President that Democrats were equally unhappy about his conciliatory attitude toward the Soviets, but they would not embarrass the White House, and further divide the country, by voting against the draft. Johnson could be certain "that before sun-up Foster and Eleanor would know. Allen's parties were a conduit," Clover Dulles would later write.

Dulles moved to where Air Force General Curtis Le May was holding court. The chunky hard-muscled World War II veteran had been instrumental in the fire-bombing of Tokyo and the atomic missions to Hiroshima and Nagasaki. He was telling an attentive group of State Department officials that the only way to stop the Russians and Chinese was to use similar tactics. Like Johnson, Le May knew his views would be noted.

Allen Dulles had reached the peak of his own profession. As DCI (Director of Central Intelligence) he controlled, with the absolutism of a medieval monarch, an organization with an annual budget larger than some European countries: one with unrivalled technical facilities to gather intelligence and the manpower to conduct espionage operations. He had in excess of $100 million a year to spend, which he could disperse with only the most notional accounting. Neither Congress nor the President would have any real idea of how or where the money went. Without consulting anyone outside the Agency, he could dispatch agents against any nation, friend or foe.

Dulles continued to move gracefully among his guests, leaning slightly forward as he listened to a conversation, then straightening himself when he moved on. Those little movements were the only sign of the club foot he had been born with and which, in spite of corrective surgery, had left him with less than perfect balance. In quiet moments he still brooded over the deformity, and some people said it had affected his personality. He had insisted the family never discuss the matter with outsiders. Some said that marked Allen's entry into the world of secrets.

One of the guests had a similar affliction, Dr. Sidney Gottlieb. He dealt with it by radiating confidence and success. The intensity of his gaze was arresting. He was still in his mid-forties, yet everything about him was fatherly and reassuring. Only Dulles and a senior aide, Richard Helms, knew of a remarkable document Gottlieb had written. It proposed "a program for the covert control of human behavior that the Communists seem to have success with."

Guests kept arriving. Clover wore the satisfied look of a hostess who knew her party was a success. In her youth she had been a hauntingly beautiful woman, and the smile she wore as she greeted each guest was a reminder of that.

Clover recognized one of the guests, Dr. Ewen Cameron, and pointed him out to Buckley. In fact, she had once consulted Cameron about her difficulties coming to terms with her husband's philandering. But the doctor had left her feeling uneasy. Clover did not know that he was at the party for a very specific reason having to do with the Korean War.

The North Koreans had captured not only aircrews but also U.S. combat troops. In the months following their repatriation, many of the soldiers had praised life under Communism. The President had demanded an explanation. Had the enemy taken control of the minds of patriotic Americans? Why did they now sound like rabble-rousers? How could American soldiers allow themselves to become turncoats? There were many questions — but no answers. Finding them became a top priority within the CIA. The Agency had collected hundreds of articles that had appeared in the left-wing press in Europe, Africa and Asia by American ex-prisoners extolling Communism. The FBI had checked on the authors: Almost none had shown any previous aptitude for writing. Yet the articles were well-written. Upon their return to the United States, the veterans had made it clear they had no wish to live in America. There was uproar and violent clashes between the vets and bewildered citizens. The fear of brainwashing spread; some in the agency felt that this was the greatest threat the United States had faced. Finding a way to deal with it was the reason why Allen Dulles was so preoccupied on the night of his party. Hours earlier he had sat in the Oval Office reviewing for President Eisenhower what the CIA knew and what he had done so far to combat the threat.

By then, Fort Detrick had gone into overdrive to create a vast bacteriological arsenal. The United States had secretly abandoned the principle of using biochemical weapons only in retaliation. A classified document, "Armed Forces Doctrine for Chemical and Biological Weapons Employment and Defense," prepared by the Pentagon, said that "henceforth the decision for U.S. forces to use chemical and biological weapons must rest with the United States." The retaliation policy had been replaced with one of first-strike.

Dr. Gottlieb and his team of scientists began to create war games with China as the enemy. A memo he sent to the commander of Fort Detrick, Brigadier-General J. H. Rothschild, a distant relative of the banking family, stated: "Biological warfare could have an important role as a deterrent to stop China initiating a war. China is subject to polar outbreaks. From October to March, cold air flows down from Siberia over the populous areas of the Chinese coast. From May to August the summer monsoon air creates a layer some 10,000 feet deep from the South China Sea and the Pacific Ocean over those same areas. Either of these areas can be seeded with biological agents from the air or water. Anthrax or yellow fever would be suitable." Fort Detrick now had sufficient quantities to poison the entire coastal region of China. But for the moment there was the pressing matter of what had made prisoners of war become whistle-blowers revealing what America had already done in North Korea. Gottlieb had written the paper Dulles used in briefing the president.

Dulles started his briefing to eisenhower by describing the notorious show trials of the 1930s in Russia during which a succession of Communist leaders had confessed to crimes they clearly had not committed. The consensus among reporters covering the trials was that the accused had been given drugs. The same conclusion was drawn at the 1949 trial of the Hungarian leader of the Catholic Church, Cardinal Josef Mindszenty. He had sounded and moved like a robot before his Soviet judges as he delivered a monologue of the treasonable acts he admitted committing. That trial, Dulles told the President, had persuaded the CIA to study behavior control.

He omitted telling the president that in 1951, a team of CIA scientists, led by Dr. Gottlieb, flew to Tokyo. Four Japanese suspected of working for the Russians were secretly brought to a locations where the CIA doctors injected them with a variety of depressants and stimulants over a twenty-four hour period. Denied sleep, the men became disoriented. Under relentless questioning, they confessed to working for the Russians. They were taken out into Tokyo Bay, shot and dumped overboard. The CIA team flew to Seoul in South Korea and repeated the experiment on twenty-five North Korean prisoners-of-war. They were asked to denounce Communism. They refused and were executed.

Dr. Gottlieb was now Fort Detrick's acknowledged expert on poisons, the more esoteric the better. He had tramped the jungles of Africa, Central America and Asia to find new and better toxins. His view on killing was clear-cut. "Killing is usually wrong, but where it involves the safety of the United States it is permissible. The decision to kill is not one to take lightly. But once taken, it must be followed through. That is not the time to raise moral questions," he would later write.

In 1952, Dulles brought Dr. Gottlieb and his team to post-war Munich in southern Germany. They set up base in a safe house near a number of refugee camps in the area. Dr. Gottlieb and his doctors began to tour the camps. He told his team they were looking for "individuals of dubious loyalty or suspected Soviet double agents." Throughout the winter of 1952-1953 scores of "expendables" were brought to the safe house. They were given massive doses of drugs, some of which Frank Olson had prepared back at Fort Detrick, to see if their minds could be altered. Others were given electro-convulsive shocks. Each experiment failed. The "expendables" were killed and their bodies burned. Dr. Gottlieb and his team returned to Langley and began to experiment with a new drug that Gottlieb had obtained. It was LSD. The drug was tried out on members of the team. While it resulted in a number of them "behaving like madmen," the drug had shown no evidence of being able to permanently change the human mind.

Continuing his Oval Office briefing, Dulles explained how Dr. Gottlieb had consulted old almanacs and studied the records of the Inquisition. No clue had emerged to point to how the North Korean brainwashing had succeeded. Yet something had happened to the American prisoners during captivity in Korea and Gottlieb was sure that the only way to discover the answer was to duplicate everything the POWs had experienced. That would require clinical trials of a kind never conducted before, and that would mean access to a hospital and patients.

No doubt Dulles was reflecting on that meeting as he drifted through the party. He began to indicate to selected guests that he would like them to join him in his study at the rear of the house.

Clover Dulles watched with resignation as her husband led the retreat to his sanctum. Standing beneath a portrait of her husband's father in clerical garb — the Reverend Allen Macy Dulles had been a Presbyterian minister — she told Buckley it was the way all their parties ended: with Dulles holding a conclave in his den. Watching guests making their discreet way there, Clover provided Buckley with details about those selected. Dr. Gottlieb lived in an old slave cabin and liked goats. Walking beside him was Richard Helms. Clover called him "tres snob," adding that Helms' claim to fame was a remarkably frank interview he had with Hitler on the eve of Pearl Harbor. At the time

Helms had been a United Press correspondent in Berlin. The aloof man walking to the den was Dr. James Monroe. He also worked with her husband. He was followed by the tiny figure of Dr. Harold Wolff. Clover told Buckley that even when the neurologist was in another room "she could sense the power of his personality." Buckley asked about the tall, silver-haired man walking shoulder-to-shoulder beside Dr. Cameron. Clover explained that Dr. William Sargant was a distinguished English psychiatrist who frequently came to Washington. He had given her a proof copy of his forthcoming book, *Battle for the Mind*. From a bookshelf Clover fetched the copy. Buckley saw it was inscribed to "Clover Dulles, a gracious lady." Her own judgment on Sargant was that "he's such a sweet man."

Tall and muscular, with a toothy smile that never quite reached his eyes, Dr. William Sargant had an athlete's stride, a legacy of his days on Cambridge University's track team. Buckley had already noticed his clipped speech and penetrating stare. Dr. Sargant had a nission, bordering on messianic zeal, to lead psychiatry into a new world. His weapons would include epileptic convulsions, induced by electroshock; hypoglycemic coma produced with insulin; and pre-frontal leucotomy in a procedure called psychosurgery.

From early in the Cold War, MI5 and MI6 had been looking for new ways to understand, combat and overcome the medical manipulations of Soviet and Chinese psychiatrists. In Dr. Sargant they found a willing tutor. At military bases in Britain, including one at Maresfield, near the south coast resort of Brighton, he conducted experiments on so-called "military volunteers." Other experiments were performed at Britain's biochemical warfare establishment at Porton Down on Salisbury Plain. Again, "volunteers" from military mental hospitals and from military prisons were used. (In March 2005, MI6 finally settled £10,000 on three "volunteers" who had been experimented on.)

The CIA had sent Dr. Sidney Gottlieb and Frank Olson to monitor Dr. Sargant's tests. The three men became close friends. On each trip they studied Dr. Sargant's patient records and shared with him the latest research on mind-alteration being carried out at Fort Detrick.

Dr. Sargant ruled supreme over the Department of Psychological Medicine at St.Thomas's, one of London's great teaching hospitals. He had established the department after he left – "not without a degree of acrimony" – that other citadel of British psychiatry, the Maudsley Hospital, also in London. Arriving at St.Thomas's, Dr. Sargant found he had to create "my department virtually from scratch in a dark, dank, rat-infested basement, nicknamed Scatari," he later told the author. It had one ward, a fearful place of drugged screams and troubled mumblings. It was here that Dr. Sargant, the son of a wealthy and staunchly Methodist family, began to experiment with what he called "heroic doses of drugs used in different combinations."

There was a secret side to Dr. Sargant. He had a voracious sexual appetite that could not be satisfied in normal relationships. He solved the matter by attending "swinger" parties. Many guests were doctors, lawyers and pillars of their churches. In the seclusion of English country mansions, Dr. Sargant found physical relief for his fantasies.

He was one of those who had been discreetly beckoned to join Dulles in the study. By ten-thirty, the other guests had left. In Washington, government went to bed early and woke up early. But in the study, the gathering had settled down for a long night.

Dr. Sargant later remembered that he had started the discussion. He explained the principles of religious conversion and the lessons to be learned from using fasting, physical discomfort and pain; properly applied all could arouse powerful feelings of guilt, anxiety, distress and finally nervous exhaustion. These were the prerequisites to create the necessary state for conversion, or change from one faith to another. He described the technique used by the English evangelist, John Wesley. Wesley would single out someone in his audience and create a sympathetic contact with him or her. It was a simple, but very effective method of mind control. Sargant had explained that Catholicism's rite of confession was another effective way. Finally he had turned to his own area of expertise, the manipulative effects of voodoo. Through its rites voodoo could create a variety of visual stimuli. Properly managed, it was an effective way to take someone to the edge of madness.

Dr. Sargant had concluded his remarks with a reminder of the lessons to be learned from what was known as the Kentucky Revival of 1800. A Calvinist preacher, the Reverend James Mc-Gready, had produced stress in his congregation by the clever use of darkness, while his acolytes beat a continuous tattoo on their drums. Eventually strong men had been driven to collapse. Psychologically it could be seen as a striking example of the psychology of self-surrender; old values had been replaced by new ones.

Dr. Monroe was the next to speak. He delivered a concise review of the latest drugs available to deal with the mentally disturbed. Their effect had been limited, Dr. Monroe suggested, because they had not been used in conjunction with other techniques. One of those methods he had begun to develop was sensory deprivation. He had very recently written a paper describing how sensory deprivation could "change a person's goals, values and ideals of a lifetime."

Finally Dr. Cameron spoke. He said he had studied a large number of the confessions made by the prisoners of the North Koreans. There appeared to be a common factor in all of them. Those confessions had most likely been obtained by creating what Dr. Cameron called "a strong sense of inner conflict." Personality, he reminded his listeners, was not only linked to role behavior but was also dependent on self-perception. His Scottish burr emphasized the words. The critical factor was to distinguish between a person playing out a role and someone who accepted the reality of a situation. Such self-perception was vital to understand. In the case of those POWs who had confessed, their captors had probed long and hard for weaknesses in their personalities to discover the differences.

Dr. Cameron outlined what was known as "traumatic psychological infantilism" in which a person becomes "compelled to turn to the very person who was threatening or even endangering his life. In the case of the prisoners, they would have come to see their kidnappers as good people. This was known as pathological transference," he would later write.

The discussions in the den continued in this vein. Finally Allen Dulles spoke. All he had heard reinforced his belief that "the mystery of brain washing could be cracked." He would provide a further $300,000 to fund new research, and Dr. Gottlieb would be in charge. His brief was "to investigate all possible means to modify human behavior," using technology, applied science, medical and psychophysical research. "Executive Action," the Agency's in-house euphemism for killing, would be his decision. "MK-ULTRA," the codename for the program, would maintain the highest classification of secrecy. Unless it was absolutely essential, outside researchers must never know they were working for the CIA or the final use to be made of their research. In turn, the Agency would guarantee to protect all those it recruited for the project.

Dr. Wolff and his colleagues at the Cornell University Medical Center would have direct responsibility for evaluating the 7,190 files the CIA held on the American POWs. Dr. Monroe would assess what the CIA knew about the interrogation methods used by the Russians and Chinese and would also be responsible for creating a suitable foundation which would act as a cover for all the research. It would be called the Society for the Investigation of Human Ecology and would be headquartered in a town house on East 78 Street in New York. Dr. Wolff would be the foundation's president.

Dulles asked Dr. Sargant if he would continue to act as liaison between the foundation and similar research going on in Britain at Porton Down. Dr. Sargant said he would continue to do so. Dulles asked Dr. Cameron if there was any way he could help. Dr. Cameron replied he would give the matter his most careful consideration. On that note the meeting had broken up.

Buckley's evening ended by helping the caterers to clear away. Afterwards, Clover Dulles invited him to join her for coffee, along with other members of the stud detail. She questioned each in turn about their futures. Buckley said he wanted to make his career in the CIA. He remembered how Clover had smiled and said that was "a worthwhile ambition and I'll mention it to my husband."

A month after the party, Buckley was summoned to a CIA office in the Pentagon. After a recruiter had gone through his military records, Buckley was told that he would have to undergo a battery of tests and a tough course of "special training." He was posted to the CIA's field training school at Fayetteville, North Carolina. He would recall: "The whole set-up was designed to determine when a person would lie, and what it would take him to tell the truth. I learned all about dead letter boxes, how to tap into phone lines, how to send messages in invisible ink. There was a lot of physical stuff like being roused out of bed, taken off for interrogation, kept in solitary confinement. The sort of thing we would expect the Russians or Chinese to do if they caught us."

He was the only one in his class to pass. He was assigned to work for Dr. Gottlieb's department. Even though his work was "general duties," which translated as carrying sealed documents to various offices, he felt he "was going to be at the center of things."

Buckley looked back on 1953 as a seminal year in the twentieth century. Stalin had died. Che Guevara was running rampage in Guatemala. The Shah had been installed in Persia. The double helix structure of DNA had been discovered. So had the first link between smoking and cancer. Puerto Rico had become the first Commonwealth of the United States, and Aristotle Socrates Onassis had been charged with conspiring to defraud the United States in the purchase of surplus ships.

The threat from Moscow deepened by the day and people spoke of the possibility of a new and even more terrifying war. Bill Buckley knew he wanted to be a part of trying to stop that.

On November 30 that year, Buckley, along with the other staff of the Chemical Division, was summoned to a lecture hall in one of the larger buildings the CIA had in mid-town Washington. A serious-faced Dr. Gottlieb told them he had sad news. Some of those present may already have heard that one of the staff at Fort Detrick was dead. His name was Frank Olson.

CHAPTER FIVE

On March 7, 1954, Buckley was transferred to new duties. He was given an office in the building in which Dr. Gottlieb had broken the news about Frank Olson's death and where the CIA's Department of Operations was then housed. Despite his raised security clearance, Buckley still did not have access to the upper floors where the Agency's spies came and went. Dr. Gottlieb's suite was at the opposite end of the corridor from Buckley's office. Its metal desk, chair, lock-up filing cabinet, telephone and bookcase were standard Pentagon approved furnishings.

Dr. Gottlieb sent for Buckley; it was the first time they had met formally. Previously they had exchanged no more than quick glances in a corridor or when Buckley had walked past Dr. Gottlieb's open office door. Now the scientist smiled and made small talk as if to relax Buckley, all the while studying him carefully. Buckley said that he liked working for the CIA though he was still getting used to Washington. Suddenly, Dr. Gottlieb sat back in his high-backed chair.

"You know why you are here?" he asked.

"No, sir."

"Because I need you. From now on you will work for me, understood?"

"Yes, sir."

It was only later that Buckley discovered this was Sidney Gottlieb's opening gambit for all those who came to work for him. But there was more. Dr. Gottlieb told Buckley to remain still and silent. Behind the Gottlieb's high-backed chair was a small display cabinet filled with jars and bottles containing insects and pieces of fungi preserved in solutions. They were some of the specimens Dr. Gottlieb had collected on his expeditions into Central and South America to find lethal botanicals. Buckley felt he was being studied with the same care Dr. Gottlieb must have used when assembling his display. After a while Dr. Gottlieb began to nod. Buckley felt he had passed some sort of test. When Gottlieb spoke, his voice was slow as if he knew that was the best way to control his stammer. He told Buckley he was to inspect the Division's safe houses; details of where they were located would be provided by the Travel Office. To any outsider who asked, he was a realtor inspecting property. In the meantime, he was to begin to familiarize himself with MK-ULTRA's projects.

Once more Dr. Gottlieb had sat back in his chair and explained it was pronounced M-K — ULTRA. The letters "MK" identified it as a current project. ULTRA had been chosen by him as a reminder of one of World War II's most secret projects, the program which had broken the German codes to its U-Boats.

"You will find we are engaged on something even more important — trying to crack what the Chinese did to our prisoners in Korea," said Dr. Gottlieb.

Buckley had been surprised. In the Pentagon files, he had read the matter was closed.

"It is not only the Chinese, but the Soviets who are doing it now. We have to know how they do it so that we can find the means to counter them," Buckley remembered Dr. Gottlieb saying. He remembered thinking this was why he had joined the CIA: to be part of a secret war.

Files would be delivered to Buckley's office every morning by a messenger, "your replacement," Dr. Gottlieb had smiled. If Buckley had to leave his office during the day, he must first lock away the files in his cabinet and then lock the office door. At the end of the day, the files would be collected by the messenger and returned the following morning. Buckley was to make weekly reports on what he had read; his evaluations of work in progress would be welcomed. Each report was to be on Dr. Gottlieb's desk at 7:30 sharp every Monday morning.

Over the next three months, Buckley inspected over twenty safe houses, apartments in exclusive parts of various cities. In New York one was on Madison Avenue, in San Francisco another was high up on Nob Hill. In Washington two were within a short walk of the White House. There were safe houses in Chicago and Seattle, close to university campuses. Each apartment was well furnished and fitted with two-way mirrors and concealed microphones. Buckley wondered if the fittings were for CIA officers to debrief informers. Each safe house had a small area, hidden behind a piece of fitted furniture, for storing recording equipment and spare tapes. A sophisticated security system protected windows and entry doors.

Between his journeys, Buckley read the MK-ULTRA files. There were gaps in many of them, and he assumed material had been removed. His new security clearance still did not allow him full access to the contents. He began to learn about the Division's work with LSD and other drugs in the search to change a person's sense of reality. The experiments had, by 1954, expanded to include many important medical centers in the U.S. . At the University of Oklahoma, Dr. Louis Jolyon West was testing LSD on unwitting patients. Similar work was being conducted in Boston and at Columbia University's medical school in New York. In all, there were twenty-three campuses where scientists were doing secret research on patients and being paid from Dr. Gottlieb's equally secret funds.

These funds were distributed by the Geschickter Foundation for Medical Research in Washington. The private family institute was controlled by Dr. Charles Geschickter, a close friend of Dr. Gottlieb. Through the foundation, grants of $40,000 and upwards — large amounts in 1954 — were routinely dispensed to researchers to study the manipulation of human behavior.

In June, 1954, Buckley was ordered by Dr. Gottlieb to assume his first undercover role. He was to pose as a freelance writer preparing science-related articles. To help him sound like a genuine journalist, Buckley spent time with Richard Helms; the tall, elegant intelligence officer was the reporter who once interviewed Adolf Hitler. He was now an enthusiastic supporter of Dr. Gottlieb and his work. Buckley's task was to test the security of the various research projects by seeing how much he could discover. Dr. Gottlieb said if the Russians realized the strategic importance of the work going on at the American campuses, they would be able to develop countermeasures. Buckley visited all the facilities and interviewed psychiatrists, psychologists, physiologists and clinicians. He told them he was preparing a series of articles on the beneficial use of drugs. They provided him copies of their papers published in professional journals but gave no hint of their secret work. Dr. Gottlieb was satisfied that security remained watertight for what he was planning.

Sidney Gottlieb was now working on two broad fronts. One was to discover how the Chinese and Russians brainwashed people. The other was to continue developing a biological arsenal ready to confront the nation's Cold War enemies. Fort Detrick had considerably expanded since he first came to work at the agency. Construction crews built new labs for the scores of scientists and technicians who were recruited. Living accommodations for their families were erected within barbed wire fences posted with warnings forbidding photography. Armed guards patrolled the perimeters.

The Special Operations Division (SOD) was housed in a long, low concrete-block structure, painted an incongruous yellow, the color of ripening corn. It was there that Frank Olson had conducted his secret experiments. Building 470 was an altogether more imposing structure, faced in redbrick; here weapons and their contents had been tested for use by the Air Force in Korea.

There was a Device Branch, a successor to the unit that produced secret-agent hardware for OSS agents in World War II. The Branch created a range of delivery systems for CIA operatives to launch biological weapons. The Agent Branch was staffed with some of America's leading botanists. Each was an expert on fungi, including mushrooms, which for two thousand years had been common poisons. The Empress Agrippa had known the correct mushroom to use when she poisoned her husband, the Emperor Claudius, so that her son Nero could sit on the imperial throne. The scientists of Agent Branch were creating a similar poison, extracted from the fungi they collected in the jungles of Central America. Their stockpile of lotions and potions was unequalled. From time to time Dr. Gottlieb brought out a senior officer from Clandestine Operations, and they would sit with the scientists and discuss the suitability of a botanical for assassination.

Among those who had joined the staff at Detrick was William Capers Patrick, whose ancestors came from the distant bogs of Ireland and Scotland. Dr. Gottlieb had watched this young microbiologist's career develop. Bill Patrick had a strong sense of independence and a readiness to accept challenges to learn more about that invisible world where germs fight each other in microscopic wars. Dr. Gottlieb sent a discreet invitation to Dr. Patrick to join Fort Detrick. He promised unprecedented funding and a chance to do important work for the protection of the United States. Dr. Gottlieb often played the "patriotic card to convince someone to come to Detrick," Buckley later recalled.

Shortly after his twenty-fifth birthday, Dr. Patrick drove through Detrick's guarded gates and entered a world few knew existed. Within months, encouraged by Dr. Gottlieb and supervised by Frank Olson, the microbiologist had created miniscule biological bomblets. Each was no bigger than a speck of dust. They would float through the air for hours on the wind and were designed to penetrate deep into the human respiratory system, entering through the mouth and nose into the lungs. There, in the lungs' spongy moistness, each speck multiplied at astonishing speed, producing millions more poisonous cells.

To establish the efficacy of these biological bomblets, tests were conducted on hundreds of unsuspecting U.S. soldiers in sealed chambers at Fort Detrick and out on the Dugway Proving Ground, a military test site in the Utah wilderness. The troops, all volunteers, were told they were taking part in a research project to find a cure for the common cold. Prisoners in the Ohio State Penitentiary were also enlisted, having been promised remission of their sentences. Sputum samples confirmed the bomblets were an ideal means to transmit a wide range of germs. Dr. Patrick and Frank Olson then set about weaponizing anthrax. They calculated that a single gallon of the bacterium when aerosolized would provide eight billion doses, sufficient to kill every single person on earth, plus much of its animal life.

The risks for those involved in the research were considerable. When two women technicians working in a "hot" lab became pregnant, their babies were born with such gross birth defects that their deaths were undoubtedly a merciful release. Both infants were autopsied by Detrick pathologists before the remains were cremated. By 1953, the year Frank Olson died, there had been nearly 500 other deaths resulting among his fellow workers from being infected by anthrax or Bolivian hemorrhagic fever. The latter deadly pathogen dissolves all internal organs and turns blood into a near colorless sludge. Under the waiver they had all signed, the victims had agreed that their bodies could be turned over for post-mortem. The findings were never released to their families. Dr. Gottlieb called the dead "our unsung heroes."

Dr. Patrick became a victim of Q fever, named after the state of Queensland, Australia, where it was first discovered in 1935. Its flu-like symptoms also produce hallucinations. While the effects are debilitating and the recovery slow the mortality rate is low. After he recovered, Dr. Patrick provided Dr. Gottlieb with a professional assessment of his experience. Dr. Gottlieb decided Q fever was an ideal illness to infect an enemy: field troops would be incapacitated and would require considerable nursing. An army would be unable to fight.

To test the effect of Q fever, it was decided to use Seventh Day Adventists. Their beliefs are based on the Old Testament commandment: "Thou Shalt Not Kill." Adventists are conscientious objectors and refuse to bear arms. But they are willing to serve as stretcher bearers, nurses and in other non-combat roles. They are also allowed to take part in medical trials. Adventists are taught they must do everything possible to support the law of the land and the government of the day.

Dr. Gottlieb sent a carefully worded message to the Adventists asking for volunteers who would help test "military medicine which could also have a beneficial effect on public health." In all, 2,200 volunteered. The trials were code-named Project CD-22; Dr. Gottlieb's had his guinea pigs. If the tests for Q fever worked, the volunteers could be used to test other, more lethal pathogens. Groups of Adventists were flown into Andrews Air Force Base outside Washington. Buckley escorted them to Fort Detrick. Waiting for them were Dr. Gottlieb and other scientists of the Special Operations Division. Over the past weeks they had made up batches of low dosage Q fever.

The Adventists were escorted to the windowless structure which towered over the camp and housed the sphere where

Frank Olson first sacrificed the bugs Dr. Gottlieb brought back from Korea. The sphere now had a name: the 8-Ball. The Adventists rode up in an elevator to a work station. Each was given a long white lab coat and led into a glass walled enclosure and told to put on a face mask connected to a rubber pipe. The door closed with a gentle hiss, signifying a secure seal. In the adjoining control booth, a technician pushed a button on a panel and a measured amount of a batch of Q fever silently passed along the pipes into the face masks. After a minute the test was over. The volunteers were told to remove their face masks. The door opened and they were taken to an isolation ward in another area. The next group of Adventists was brought up and the process repeated. All thirty-four volunteers of the group displayed symptoms of Q fever in the following days. They quickly responded to oxytetracycline, a powerful antibiotic, and all recovered. The results of sputum tests revealed the pathogens had lodged in their respiratory systems. Q fever was an effective weapon for aerosol dissemination. All that was required was to increase the potency of the pathogens. Dr. Gottlieb gave the order for this to be done. Then he drove back to Washington for a meeting with Dr. Ewen Cameron.

It had been almost a year since Gottlieb and Cameron had met at the Dulles party. Dr. Cameron told Dr. Gottlieb he had concluded that a combination of drugs, possibly linked to sensory deprivation and hypnotism, had been used to manipulate the American POWs into making their confessions. He added that that possibility had encouraged him to continue reading and evaluating, but he was also a practical man. A project of this size would require "massive funding and a high level of security." He had to be assured of both. CIA director Dulles provided it.

Later, Dr. Cameron spent a day with Dr. Wolff at the offices of the new Society for the Investigation of Human Ecology in New York. The foundation was to become the front organization for Dr. Cameron's work, as it was essential to distance what was going to happen in Montreal from the CIA. MK-ULTRA would be operating outside the United States, inside the border of a friendly neighbor. The political repercussions following discovery would be immense. Nevertheless, Dr. Cameron continued to weigh the options. He was being offered a level of funding he had never before obtained. If he were successful, his reputation would be further enhanced. Handled properly, the risks could be minimized.

Cameron flew to London to meet Dr. Sargant. Together they discussed how they would combine their work, with Dr. Sargant duplicating the Montreal experiments in his department at St. Thomas's hospital. They drove down to a former RAF base at Maresfield, near the Sussex Downs, where drugs were being tested on British army volunteers. The program was being supervised by Dr. Sargant. As yet, he had little to show for the experiments. Returning to Montreal, Dr. Cameron authorized preparations to convert the basement of the Allan Memorial Institute into a replica of the North Korean interrogation center Dulles had described to him. MK-ULTRA had taken on a new urgency.

Having conducted two atomic bomb tests, the Soviet Union was about to perform a third. It would, however, still be short of the five atomic bomb tests the United States had carried out in the Nevada desert. On Dr. Cameron's last visit to Washington, Dulles told him about a CIA-sponsored experiment in Boston. Dr. Louis Lasagnar had given LSD to a number of volunteers. The effect had been dramatic. Dulles said that under the drug the volunteers made all kinds of admissions. The news was a defining moment in Dr. Cameron's decision to go ahead with work for the CIA.

Meantime Dr. Gottlieb had ordered Buckley to supervise the security for the second Q fever experiment; this test would use more potent germs.

This time the test took place at the Dugway Proving Ground in Utah. The U.S. Army had been testing weapons there since 1942. In 1944, the pilots of the United States Air Force 509th Squadron used it to practice their mission to Hiroshima with an atomic bomb. Frank Olson had made his field tests at Dugway after returning from his first visit to Korea. He had tested a number of bomb casings to see how effective they would be in producing airbursts for the germs, using a harmless powder as a substitute. The result had been satisfactory. Dr. Gottlieb had ordered the casings be shipped to Korea; they were filled with germs by scientists from Unit 8003 (a department attached to Fort Detrick for special duties including arming weapons with biological and chemical substances). No record exists that documents their use in combat.

A transport plane filled with Adventists landed at Dugway's airstrip in the early summer of 1954. It was, Buckley recalled, like being on the moon. "Just desert stretching as far as the eye could see to the Dugway Mountains." The test would take place after sunset when the swirling wind that sent sage grass spinning over the sands would settle. The fierce sunlight would also have killed the germs. As dusk fell, Buckley escorted the Adventists to the test area, a row of wooden platforms positioned in a half-mile line across the desert. The men had all taken a shower fed from a water tank on a truck and dressed in clean clothes. Well clear of the test area, military police stood guard. Buckley himself ran one final check to make sure no one had smuggled in a camera to record what was about to happen.

On each platform, along with an Adventist volunteer, was a cage containing a number of rhesus monkeys held in metal boxes so only their heads were visible. Some of the platforms also had boxed guinea pigs. Each platform had a variety of laboratory equipment to collect samples of the air before, during and after the test. Arms by their sides and staring calmly ahead, the night breeze softly rustling the brush, the Adventists looked as if they were taking part in some ancient ritual. The pale starlight heightened the sense of eeriness.

The silence was broken by a generator coughing into life to power the semi-circle of disseminators facing the platforms half a mile away across the desert. The microbes began to emerge from the mouths of the disseminators and, invisible to the eye, began to drift on the wind towards the platforms. A scientist clicked his stopwatch to time the start of the test. Another scientist, using a bull horn, sent a reminder to the Adventists. "Remember, just breathe normally." The disembodied voice repeated the instruction one more time across the dark sand. Two minutes after the first click, the scientist clicked his watch again. The test was over. Two trucks drove out to the platforms. The drivers wore rubber lab suits, goggles and face masks. They looked like aliens. One truck picked up the Adventists, the other collected the caged animals and the monitoring equipment. The Adventists were taken to the shower room and told to strip. Their clothes were taken to a closed incinerator and burnt while they showered in water that was tinged violet. They were told to put on the clothes in which they had arrived.

Buckley escorted them out to the airstrip. On the way to Dugway, he had sat with the Adventists, learning a little about their faith; how it was founded on the Second Coming of Christ and was one of the wealthiest religions in the United States, with its own campuses and medical schools where members were taught to serve God and country in time of war. But for the flight back to Washington, he was told to travel on a separate aircraft with the team from Fort Detrick. One of the scientists explained the Adventists had to be kept in isolation as much as possible to ensure the "purity of the test."

Later Buckley learned how successful the experiment had been. Mixed in with the Q fever germ was a small amount of LSD in powdered form. A few days later some of the Adventists displayed irrational behavior: one destroyed a favorite possession; another endlessly played the same record. These behavior patterns were closely observed by the Fort Detrick medical officers who visited the volunteers in their isolation chamber every day. Their case notes were sent to Dr. Gottlieb. He made copies and sent them to Dr. Cameron in Montreal.

In December, 1954, Buckley saw Dr. Gottlieb at work muffling allegations that had again started to surface in the Asian and European media, accusing the CIA of arranging for biological weapons to be used in the Korean War. Gottlieb put together a persuasive press pack that was distributed to the numerous journalists the CIA used to plant stories. Each pack contained a copy of the original article in the *New York Times* in March 1952, exposing Chinese germ warfare claims as "fakes." In the pack were two reports by "acknowledged independent experts" dismissing the Chinese claims as being on the level of "flying saucers have landed." Both the experts were scientists Dr. Gottlieb knew personally. The *Times* story was written by a journalist whose previous stories had been pro-CIA. A number of overseas newspapers ran versions of the press pack. Once more the truth about biological warfare in Korea was safely back in its box.

Early in January, 1955, Buckley attended a meeting between Dr. Gottlieb and Dr. Cameron in Washington. Their discussion focused on the question of obtaining sufficient subjects for the Montreal research. Dr. Cameron was reassuring; he had sufficient patients to meet all his requirements. Neither did he anticipate any ethical questions being raised by his staff, no matter how revolutionary the research would be.

He could well be confident he would win any confrontation. No other doctor had brought more prestige to McGill

University. Dr. Cameron was president of the all-powerful American Psychiatric Association, was soon to be president of the Canadian Psychiatric Association, and was also about to receive the supreme honor of his discipline, the first presidency of the World Association of Psychiatrists. He was the founder of the Canadian Mental Health Association and had served as chairman of the Canadian Scientific Planning Committee. No other psychiatrist on McGill's faculty had published so many scientific papers and so widely. No one had given so many lectures, was as well known in the medical world and had brought so many students to the campus.

Dr. Gottlieb explained that Buckley would be his personal liaison officer with Dr. Cameron. Buckley had already read the file which the CIA had developed on Dr. Cameron. The agency had similar files on all key personnel working on MK-ULTRA. In Dr. Gottlieb's world, knowledge was power.

Ewen Cameron was born on December 24, 1901, the son of the Reverend Duncan Cameron, minister to the parish of Bridge of Allan, a small town some twenty miles to the north of Glasgow, Scotland. He grew up hearing the bugle call and drum beat summoning his elders to the Great War. Some would return with medals, blind and maimed. He read about the German use of chlorine gas — the start of chemical warfare in World War I. Over 5,000 Canadian soldiers had died in one gas attack. Years later, he would still have in his private papers a copy of a post-mortem report detailing the effect of such an attack on a soldier: "The body showed definite discoloration of the face and neck and hands. On opening the chest, the two lungs bulged outwards. On removing the lungs there exuded a huge amount of frothy, light yellow fluid, evidently highly albuminous as slight beating was sufficient to solidify it like the white of eggs. The veins on the surface of the brain were found to be greatly congested, all the small vessels standing out prominently."

At the close of the Great War, Cameron studied medicine at the University of Glasgow and became fascinated by the brain. The newly graduated Dr. Cameron decided that the study of the complex problems of human behavior was to be his chosen career. After interning at the Glasgow Western Infirmary, he took a post-graduate course at the University of London. He received his diploma in psychological medicine, and in 1926 he left Britain to join the faculty of one of the most progressive hospitals in North America — Johns Hopkins in Baltimore. To the surprise of colleagues, he then made a career move that would take him beyond the medical horizon. He joined the staff of Manitoba's Brandon Mental Hospital. The prairie asylum was a repository for the rejects of Canadian society, a place of brutality, depersonalization and filth, a closed institution whose custodians made no distinction between the definition and categories of madness. Dr. Cameron had been promised a free hand in treating the institution's hundreds of acute patients.

Dr. Cameron brought a reformer's zeal and the conviction that the management of all kinds of mental illness depended on bold decisions. But the pharmacopoeia to support these actions consisted only of a few drugs. More advances in the field of psychopharmacology were still almost two full decades distant. At Brandon Cameron began to create the rationale that the end justified the means. Barely twenty-eight, he had a free hand to study the various schizoid mechanisms, psychotic fantasies and the strange world of the paranoid where inner and outer realities are continuously split. He had never been more content.

He read the work of Frederick Winslow Taylor, the founder of "scientific management" and the high priest of "human engineering." In 1911 Taylor had published a massive study that was primarily designed to show managers how to get more from their workers. Cameron realized it could be adapted to make patients function more efficiently. He began to carry out the first psychological tests at Brandon, using an amalgam of Taylor's teachings and U.S. Army tests from World War I. A set of questions was used to determine responses. Such diagnoses as "dangerous," "violent," "uncooperative" — common labels attached to the sick at Brandon — were quantified. It was Dr. Cameron's first plunge into behavioral science, and he became a convert. His search to bring a new order to Brandon brought another important discovery: the "science which could be applied to behavior made it respectable to manipulate my patients."

A disproportionate number of these patients were foreign-born, from Eastern Europe, human flotsam who had somehow ended up in Manitoba: Poles, Russians, Bulgarians, Lithuanians and Russians who had fled the Bolshevik Revolution. They had found life in the new world equally hard and had broken under the strain. Cameron believed the tests he designed and used could be extended to immigration screening, to keep out such people before they "infected" the community. He became fervent in his belief that psychiatry could be used to identify and remedy the problems of society: "The threat of impending race degeneration; the prospect of national mongrelization through lax eugenic practices; the growth of crime and immorality can all be changed by a radical approach to treatment," he wrote. Brandon was a good place to test his theories for creating his New Jerusalem. He began to publish medical papers which argued that mental health could be structured out of illness: "Brain cells are aroused to activity and restored to their normal freedom."

Cameron moved from Brandon back to the United States, to Worcester State Hospital in Massachusetts, where he was appointed director of research. Still restless and ambitious for more experience, in 1939 he became professor of psychiatry at the Albany Medical School in New York State. Here, he became an enthusiastic proponent of another radical form of treatment. Four years before — on November 12, 1935 — in a Lisbon hospital, Dr. Egaz Moniz, a neurosurgeon had drilled two holes one on each side of the forehead of a mental patient. He then injected the holes with pure alcohol, plunging the needle directly into the frontal lobes of the woman's brain in the hope of curing her violence. The result was only partly successful. He experimented on seven more patients. Then, for his eighth operation, the surgeon radically altered his intervention. Dr. Moniz inserted into each hole an instrument he had made. It resembled an apple corer. He used it to crush all the nerve fibers in its path. Dr. Moniz called his new technique pre-frontal leucotomy, from the Greek *leuco* for the white nerve fibers, and tome, knife. After twenty operations he called it lobotomy and, finally, psychosurgery. The technique became widely used. In 2006, it was still being used in Britain and several other countries.

Dr. Cameron began to refer his patients for the surgery. He would stand in the operating room and watch a neurosurgeon sever the frontal lobes around the ventromedial region, which regulated emotional experience. Destruction of this area produced marked changes. Violence gave way to stupor. Patients became forgetful, withdrawn and showed complete lack of spontaneity. With scar-tissue from the burr holes, vacant stares and monster-like gait, they often resembled Frankenstein's creature. But they were manageable and could be fitted into the general scheme of hospital society. In the end that was what mattered – not their impaired imagination, their diminished sexual responses, their displaced logic and inability to make judgments. Dr. Cameron rationalized that as institutional mental patients, they had no need for such responses. Another guiding principle had been laid down for his New Jerusalem.

Shortly before the Japanese attack on Pearl Harbor, Dr. Cameron became a member of the Military Mobilization Committee of the American Psychiatric Association. His appointment co-incided with developments that greatly alarmed the Roosevelt Administration. There were an increasing number of conscientious objectors who were prepared to endure the brutality of American mental hospitals rather than enlist. The second cause for concern was the high number of recruits discharged from military service for neuropsychiatric reasons. In all, two million of the 15 million inducted into the U.S. Armed Services would be rejected on such grounds. No other nation in World War II would have such a poor record.

At Albany, Dr. Cameron began a series of genetic, biochemical, intercultural and neurological studies designed to identify the electrochemical processes in the brain, which could have produced what he saw as lack of moral fiber in the conscientious objectors.

World War II heralded the Age of New Light in the medical profession. No ailment was too great or small to study or argue over in the learned journals. Nowhere were the battle lines more clearly drawn than in psychiatry. Endless attempts were made to define, specify and categorize mental illness. Dr. Cameron had little interest in such debates. The first years of war saw a significant increase in the manufacture of electroshock machines, restraint jackets, drugs and chemicals. The distinctions between voluntary and coerced treatments became blurred and often merged. Almost every month further syndromes, symptoms and mental illnesses entered the professional lexicon. There was little time for controlled studies into treatment methods. Psychiatry, like everything else, was subservient to the cry: "There's a war to be fought." If at all possible, mentally ill people had to be gotten back to the shop and factory floor and the front line. For Ewen Cameron the early 1940s were not only a time for bold decisions in handling patients, but also for deciding his own future. Albany was no longer enough. But in Montreal, there was an opportunity that he sensed, correctly, might never come again. McGill University was already developing a reputation under Wilder Penfield, the distinguished neurologist. There was a need for someone to chair its department of psychiatry. At Professor Penfield's suggestion, in 1943 the post was offered to Dr. Cameron. He immediately accepted. He had been given one assurance and offered two pieces of advice by his sponsor. He would have a free hand. In return he should try to learn French and take out Canadian citizenship.

The promise of independence was kept. But Dr. Cameron blithely ignored the suggestions to give up his American citizenship and to learn French. The CIA file noted that many of his French-speaking colleagues called him a "Wellmount Rhodesian," a disparaging reference to the English-speaking community who lived in a Montreal enclave, where sundowners were drunk and people wore English school ties and sang "The Eton Boating Song." As a Scot by birth, none of that appealed to Cameron. But then, he would sometimes say to his secretary, Dorothy Trainor, he found little to excite him apart from work in the grey limestone Italian Renaissance-style mansion which had become his citadel, the Allan Memorial Institute, an annex of McGill University.

On January 12, 1955, in the diary Buckley had begun to keep, he noted: "Met EC (Cameron). Pretended he could not remember meeting me at CDs (Clover Dulles) party. A cold fish. Dr. G (Gottlieb) made clear my job was to ensure acceptable deniability operates all times in Montreal."

On an icy January morning in 1955, Dr. Cameron drove his black Cadillac along Highway 87, heading north out of Lake Placid in upper New York State. Despite the treacherous road conditions, he drove fast, one gloved hand on the wheel, the other gripping a microphone attached to a portable recorder on the seat beside him. His words would be transcribed before nightfall by his team of secretaries. One would type his comments on the detailed case notes he had reviewed over the weekend at his home in Albany, while his wife, Jean, and the children, three boys and a girl, played chess. Another secretary handled administration. A third dealt with his publications: books, articles for scientific journals, lectures and statements to the press. He knew the value of publicity, but also when to avoid it. There would be no publicity about what he was dictating as he drove. Those words would be transcribed by the secretary who handled his most confidential work, the indefatigable Dorothy Trainor.

"We are requesting a grant to support studies upon the effects upon human behavior of the repetition of verbal signals. Our present interest is directed towards both the production of changes in behavior and changes in physiological function, the major emphasis to be upon the latter because of the greater ease of measurement."

It was his application for funding from the Society for the Investigation of Human Ecology . Long experience in applying for funding had taught Dr. Cameron how to immediately engage attention. During the past thirteen years he had raised more money than any other Canadian doctor, beginning with $40,000 in 1943 from the Rockefeller Foundation to create the Allan Memorial Institute. He had found further substantial sums to extend the Institute; no source was too great or small for him to overlook: government agencies, philanthropic foundations, wealthy businessmen, down to the proceeds of jumble sales and raffles. Even school collections were tapped. But the Society for the Investigation of Human Ecology could fund his secret dreams and pay him to find answers that had baffled psychiatry since it became a discipline. All his career he had been stirred by challenge. But the fame he craved, the fame of Freud, Jung and the other founding figures of analysis still evaded him. William Sargant was more famous than he was. If that rankled, it also spurred him on.

Dr. Cameron had taped a therapy session with a manic depressive, a woman of forty. He then edited the tape, selecting key passages. These had been assembled into a repetitive loop. He sat down with the woman and begun to play the tape with its endlessly repeated reminiscences from childhood when her mother had threatened to abandon her. Dr. Cameron was convinced the threat lay at the root of his patient's depression. All her life the woman was unable to cope with maternal rejection.

After he repeated the tape seven times, the woman asked him, "Do I have to listen?" He continued playing the tape. After eleven repetitions she cried out, "I hate listening!" He persisted. After four more repetitions she suddenly burst out, "It is the truth." When the tape had been played nineteen times, the woman began to tremble and cried out she hated the sound of her own voice. After thirty repetitions, she began to breathe rapidly and shake uncontrollably and moaned that she hated her mother. On the thirty-fifth repetition she chanted, "I hate! I hate!" After three more revolutions she begged for the tape to be stopped. The inexorable sound of her voice continued. She began to whimper and plead. On the forty-fifth repetition, Cameron stopped the recording. He noted how completely the woman's defense system had been penetrated. Was that what the Communists had done? Was that how they destroyed existing belief systems and replaced them with others? He called his discovery "psychic driving." It would become a cornerstone of his work for Dr. Gottlieb.

In Washington, Dr. Gottlieb was meeting with unexpected problems, summarized in a memo he circulated to his staff on March 4, 1955:

"As you know, one of the problems with an audio device in the wall or under a mat is that, like cameras, they take a picture of what *they* see and not what *you* see in their mind's eye. Human beings have a cochlea in our ears masking out noise so we can have conversations at a cocktail party. But if you tape a cocktail party, you get *all* the noise and you can't make out the conversation. We have been working on an audio device that has the ability to mask out noise. We have been using a real cochlea, a cat's cochlea. We wired up the cat so that he would mask out everything. We trained him to listen to conversations and not the background noise.

"We have spent a lot of money. We opened the cat, put batteries in him, then wired him up. We used his tail as an antenna. Then we tested and tested him. We found he would walk off the job when he got hungry so we took care of that by putting in another wire that stopped him feeling hungry. We then took him out to a park and said to the cat, 'Listen to those two guys. Don't listen to anything else — not the birds, no other cat or dog. Just those two guys!' As the cat was crossing the road, a taxi came along and ran him over. There we were, sitting in our van, ready to record the cat as he relayed back these two guy's conversation and the cat was dead!"

A different problem had been created by Dr. Richard Wendt, chairman of the Psychology Department at the University of Rochester. He had been given $30,000 to run his experiment. After several months, he claimed to have developed a powder that could make anyone talk. He insisted it was so potent it should only be tested on "expendables." Dulles ordered that Wendt be flown to Europe. He would be accompanied by Buckley. In his attaché case, Buckley packed his copy of Dr. Gottlieb's Assassination Manual. Every CIA operative going overseas on a mission had to carry one. Buckley did not expect to use it. His role had been clearly defined by Dr. Gottlieb. He was to write a report on Dr. Wendt's experiment. Arriving at the airport, Buckley was astonished to see Wendt was accompanied by an attractive young woman. He introduced her as his assistant. Buckley pointed out that she was not authorized to travel. Wendt was adamant: either she went or he was not going. Buckley called Dr. Gottlieb. Wendt insisted his assistant had helped to develop the powder and must go with him. Finally Dr. Gottlieb agreed.

Waiting for them at the USAF air base outside Frankfurt were two CIA officers. They drove the three to a safe house in a small village near the Black Forest. It had been fitted out exactly like the others Buckley had inspected, with hidden microphones and a two-way mirror that enabled Buckley and the other officers to watch Dr. Wendt at work.

His first subject was a man. For the next three days his food and drink was spiked with an increasing amount of Wendt's powder. When this showed no effect, Wendt announced, "The subject is unsuitable." The two officers took the man away. Only later did Buckley learn he had been shot and his body buried. Four more subjects were brought to the safe house. The first three were also rejected after a few hours of "treatment" and similarly executed. The fourth was a Soviet KGB officer. As well as the powder, the Russian was pumped full of drugs — an astonishing combination of 50 milligram shots of Dexedrine followed by 25 milligram injections of Seconal and equally large amounts of marijuana. He went into a dream-like trance, giggling happily to himself for hours on end. Wendt turned to the agent and tried a joke. "Guess it's back to the drawing board." The Russian was also executed.

In between his experiments, Wendt sat for hours playing his assistant the same lullaby on the safe house piano. These sessions ended when Wendt's wife abruptly arrived in Frankfurt. He had left his address in case of a family emergency. Mrs. Wendt was not amused to discover her husband's companion. Perhaps reacting to what had been a stressful time, Wendt ran from the safe house to a nearby church. He was overpowered by Buckley as he was on the point of jumping from the bell tower. Sedated with Seconal, Wendt and the two women in his life were secretly flown back to the United States. Wendt died a few years later, still convinced he had been shabbily treated.

Buckley arrived back in Washington on the day the CIA started its U2 spy plane surveillance over the Soviet Union. Among other things the U2 pilots were looking for, photographic evidence that the Russians had established a biological warfare base near the city of Novosbirsk in the remote vastness of Siberia. It would be many years before the CIA learned its name, the Virology and Biotechnology Research Center, and that its research had an acronym as meaningless to outsiders as MK-ULTRA: Biopreparat. Its deputy chief of research was Dr. Kanatjan Alibekov. Later, when he defected to the United States in 1992, his name was shortened to Ken Alibek. In Siberia, he had 32,000 scientists and technicians working for him developing weapons-grade anthrax and other lethal bio-weapons. All Buckley knew at the time, however, was that his report on what had happened in Frankfurt had aroused little interest in Dr. Gottlieb. On a Monday morning, a messenger delivered to Buckley's office another batch of files. They were copies of some of Dr. Cameron's case histories he would have to read before he made his first visit to Montreal.

CHAPTER SIX

Reading the case files, Buckley realized Dr. Cameron was far more radical than other psychiatrists he had met. Massive use of drugs was a cornerstone of treatment at the Institute. Patients' notes showed Dr. Cameron often found the side effects of a drug more interesting than its prescribed therapeutic use. A drug intended to facilitate anesthesia during surgery produced a "pharmacological lobotomy when given in larger doses. The patient became far more manageable," Dr. Cameron had written. It was clear from the notes that patients were never informed of the disturbing effects they could experience from the drugs.

In the file of a patient named Madeleine Lacroix there was a note of a brief conversation between her and the psychiatrist. "She asked why the nurses looked at her as if she was strange. I asked why did she think she was strange? "'I don't know,'" she responded. Later Madeleine said she felt "like a zombie must feel," Dr. Cameron had written.

The file indicated she had received a "sleep cocktail" three times a day, made from a combination of 100mg Thorazine, 100mg Nembutal, 100mg Seconal and 150mg Veronal. Taken by themselves, each drug was capable of producing confusion. Given the quantity being administered to Madeleine Lacroix, it was understandable that she felt like a zombie, Buckley thought. He made a note to visit Madeleine if she was still a patient at the Institute.

From Buckley's reading, it was clear Dr. Cameron was an enthusiastic user of what pharmaceutical companies marketed as the new "heroic drugs." One was chlorpromazine, sold under the brand name of Largactil. It was originally intended to cure the sea sickness of Allied troops as they prepared to invade Nazi Europe. The drug failed to alleviate the problem, but battle front anesthesiologists learned it could be successfully used to induce hypothermia and slow the heart rate, an important help in surgery in field hospitals. Dr. Cameron prescribed it as a powerful sedative on schizophrenic patients; he found they stopped hallucinating. For Dr. Cameron, it was further proof there was a chemical substratum to mental illness, that it was not just a psychological malady. "Therefore drugs were the answer and not merely the sympathetic ear of the psychoanalyst," he wrote in one of his growing number of medical papers. His willingness to prescribe large doses of available drugs in various combinations became unbounded. Many were used in combinations the manufacturers had not tested: Desoxyn was given with Largactil, Sodium Amytal was mixed with Prolixin. Patients came to develop what nurses at the Institute called "the Thorazine shuffle," noted in a case file as "only a temporary problem and to be expected."

A woman patient, diagnosed with post-partum depression after giving birth to twins, was listed as receiving five separate drugs three times daily. In another patient's file, Dr. Cameron observed "this man is showing good progress with increased dose of Meprobamate with his other drugs." A woman's case notes claimed "higher doses of Equanil are beneficial in resolving her insomnia." Time and again, there were references to the beneficial effects of combining drugs with electroshock therapy, ECT.

Electrodes were attached to a patient's temples and the current turned on for a half-second or second at a strength of 70-150 volts – the power needed to light a 100-watt bulb. The procedure induced an epileptic fit. The standard treatment was two or three shocks over a well-spaced period. Dr. Cameron used a higher voltage and gave more treatments over a shorter period. Patients included a 60 year-old man whose primary diagnosis was alcoholism; another was a 25 year-old woman with marital problems. Shock treatments were also given to a 50 year-old former track star who feared the onset of old age. A 30 year-old woman diagnosed as mentally subnormal, who had become a "management problem" at home, received a lengthy course of electroshocks.

Buckley wondered, whether like Madeleine Lacroix, those patients were now to be included in Dr. Cameron's experiments for MK-ULTRA. For his visit to Montreal, Buckley once more assumed the cover of a freelance science journalist preparing a series of articles on the latest therapeutic techniques. Cameron was the only member of the Institute staff to know who Buckley was really working for. He suggested that before coming that Buckley should talk to a number of companies that provided the medication which the Institute used.

Buckley learned there were drugs for treating the fifteen different types of schizophrenia, drugs to produce "adjustment reaction to adult life," for "social maladjustment," for "marital maladjustment" and drugs to combat "dissocial behavior." There seemed to be a drug available for every mental problem from anxiety and hysteria to full-blown psychosis. There was no common agreement among the doctors at the drug companies about the definitions of such terms as *psychosis* and *neurosis*. Even *syndrome* and *symptom* had different meanings. One company doctor spoke of a drug to treat "overriding compulsion." Another said his company was "working on a pill to help a depressed patient have an insight into his illness." Another claimed his drug house was on the verge of marketing a medicine to solve the depression many women experienced at menopause.

Buckley flew to Montreal and arrived at the Allan Memorial Institute early in June, 1955. He was shown into Dr. Cameron's office, where Cameron was waiting with his deputy, Dr. Robert Cleghorn, and his senior internist, Dr. Peter Roper. Buckley was impressed by both men. Introductions over, Dr. Cameron then took him on a tour of the Institute, explaining that the building once belonged to a shipping magnate who had built it to watch his steamers come and go along the St. Lawrence River, which flowed below Mount Royal. The mansion was a mismatch of Italian Renaissance and the limestone of northern Europe. Its original thirty-four bedrooms had been converted into wards or private rooms for paying patients. The ballroom was now used for staff meetings. The two drawing rooms were divided into treatment cubicles. The billiard room and the library had become a consulting room and a pharmacy. The former stables in the back were labs and research areas. In Queen Victoria's days, members of her family had stayed here on their Imperial visits to Canada. The greenhouse in the garden had been built to cultivate peaches. The conservatory and its adjoining vinery were erected for another royal guest, Prince Fushimi of Japan. Montreal society had attended summer tea parties on the grounds and concert recitals in the ballroom. Imposing doors through which grandees of old had once swept, now bore notices announcing "Electrophysiological Laboratory," or "Transcultural Studies Unit." One door led to "Experimental Therapeutics," another to "Vasulographic Studies." Closets, stairwells and even the old watchtower had been converted to house research units.

Buckley noticed that Dr. Cameron's own dynamic energy was infectious; everybody seemed to hurry, only pausing to nod politely at Dr. Cameron. When he acknowledged them, he called the nurses "lassie"; Buckley remembered he had addressed the women at the Dulles' party the same way. Dr. Cameron invariably called the doctors "doc," as if he wanted to keep personal contact to a minimum. The psychiatrist told Buckley he encouraged his staff to set their watches fifteen minutes ahead of the wall clocks so that their already long days would stretch a little further. "A new nurse told me she would have to have roller skates to keep up. Next day, I bought her a pair. She got the point," Dr. Cameron said.

"Run, don't walk," Buckley jotted in his notebook, "is a way of life with Cameron."

Buckley saw that the presence of another journalist was no surprise to the staff. They had become used to regular visits from reporters eager to amplify lectures they had heard Cameron give in Canada and the United States. He had, Buckley saw, a natural gift for communicating with staff. On a ward round, Dr. Cameron had posed a question to the doctor, "What do you do when other doctors elsewhere have given up?" He had answered his own question. "You go on! Your patients are desperate people! So you have to be bold! Find new ways! New combinations of treatments! There is always a drug there! You have to find it! Forget what the label says about dosage! Patients don't get better from labels! They get better because you are ready to make bold decisions."

As Cameron swept on, Buckley took notes. He could see why Dr. Gottlieb had chosen Dr. Cameron; they both had the same certainty that everything they said or did was correct. It was impressive and not a little unnerving. Yet Dr. Cameron, Buckley reminded himself, was dealing with patients who trusted him. As if the man had sensed what Buckley was thinking, the psychiatrist stopped in a corridor.

"For my patients, the choice is between still being able to have treatment or succumbing to a future of misery and incarceration in an institution where they are locked up day and night. Here we offer them hope. They may go back into the world different people. But that is better than what they were." These words went into Buckley's notebook.

Cameron led Buckley into a small darkened room where the only patient was asleep. "This is the lassie you asked to see." Buckley stared down at Madeleine Lacroix. Strapped to her head was a football player's helmet, in which two metal ear pieces had been inserted. Dr. Cameron motioned for Buckley to move closer. Through the ear pieces came the whispered voice of Dr. Cameron.

"We call it depatterning. She is now in the middle of her sleep therapy. She will only be awakened for her medication and to receive her electroshocks," explained Dr. Cameron.

Buckley stared down at the comatose woman, not knowing what to say. The thick case file he had read included minute details of the background to her illness, written in Dr. Cameron's bold handwriting. He had told Buckley "nothing is too small to be recorded." Buckley had seen interrogation reports that were less detailed.

The case file noted that a month earlier Madeleine Lacroix had awoken at home, her nightdress clinging to her body, perspiration chilling her skin. Madeleine had been a broadcaster at a local radio station in Montreal until one morning when she had refused to go into a studio "because what she called the Wise Men were sitting on the microphone. She had never returned to work," Dr. Cameron had written. Since then, the 27 year-old had often listened through the drug-induced fog for the voice of the newscaster who had replaced her. When he went to another station, she followed him on the radio dial.

"She doesn't know why, anymore than she can explain why something urges her to search through the apartment for the bottle of tablets her husband, Eddie, has hidden. She describes how she would rush from one room to another, clutching a floor mop, determined to find and drive out the Wise Men from her home. She says they were too smart, like Eddie, who had hidden her medicine in case she took an overdose," detailed the file.

Madeleine had told Dr. Cameron that when Eddie came home after his sales calls on all the hardware stores in and around Montreal, he would be exhausted and hungry. She had been too busy pacing and searching to have prepared dinner, but he would never complain. Instead, he held her tightly while she shook and tried to cry. The tears never came; they seemed to stop at some point just behind her eyes, just as something stopped her from telling Eddie about her feelings for her father. Trying to banish them, she would bury herself in Eddie's body. But when he tried to do more than hold her, she would draw away in panic. "Those were the moments she especially felt she was being unfaithful to her father," the case file recorded.

Eddie would cook dinner — mostly out of tins — and they ate on trays before the television. While he cleaned up, she tried to concentrate on the screen. But it was difficult, especially when the Wise Men suddenly appeared and danced back and forth across the top of the set. Once she laughed so loudly at their antics that Eddie came in from the kitchen and looked at her peculiarly because there was a murder mystery on. Every night by nine o'clock, drugged and drained, Madeleine would fall asleep, bringing to a close a day that had been just like the one before. "She had a recurring nightmare of being put in a baker's oven and slowly roasted alive. She always managed to kick open the door just as her skin started to drip fat," noted the file.

When Eddie kissed her goodbye in the morning he would leave her day-time tablets beside a glass of water in the kitchen. After Madeleine swallowed them, she would start to empty cupboards and drawers, searching for the bottle. She told Dr. Cameron how the Wise Men in their long grey robes with mist around their bare feet followed her, first balancing effortlessly on top of the coffee grinder and then, with a hop, skip and a jump, moving to the plate rack before dancing from one spice jar to another, all the time taunting her that she would never, ever, find the bottle. That drove her to tip out drawers onto the floor until the center of the kitchen was a pile of napkins, cutlery, crockery and old bills. With no sign of the bottle, Madeleine moved to the living room where the Wise Men sat on the large mirror over the mock fireplace. She started to walk towards the mirror, but the oldest of the Wise Men, the one with the beard which flowed from just below the large eye where his mouth should have been, waved her away. Their beards, she had decided, indicated their age: the youngest had a goatee and the beards of the others were increasingly longer. The oldest Wise Man, the one who had shooed her away, had a beard that reached his toes. The description confirmed Dr. Cameron's diagnosis "patient has deep-seated schizophrenia."

Attached to her case notes was a letter Madeleine had written shortly before she was admitted to the Institute. "Dear Eddie, I am happy you want…" The next sentence read, "Dear happy, you want to be Eddie." That was followed by: "You dear, I Eddie…"

Now, four weeks after her admission to the Institute, Buckley stared down at Madeleine for a moment longer, listening to her breathing, heavy from the drugs she had been given. He knew that the voice of Dr. Cameron in her ear was endlessly repeating the instruction that Madeleine must give up her sexual fantasies about her father.

Buckley followed Cameron out of the room. In the corridor, the psychiatrist explained that the treatment he had called "depatterning" was to break down Madeline's existing behavior, "both the normal and the schizophrenic." "The ultimate aim is first to clear her mind of all memory," Buckley noted. After further drug treatment Madeleine would experience a condition Dr. Cameron called "differential amnesia, in which her previous schizophrenic behavior would be forever re-moved." Buckley asked if she could look forward to complete remission. He noted Dr. Cameron's response.

"It will depend on how well she responds to 'psychic driv-ing.' That is what the helmet is for. Through the ear pieces I feed 'cue statements' to remove undesirable behavior traits."

Like all the others undergoing the treatment, Madeleine had been tape recorded over a number of sessions during which her relationship with her father had been explored. The tapes were then edited into loops. These were played back to her. This was "psychic driving." "The idea is to break down her natural defenses, in her case, her sexual fantasies about her father," explained Dr. Cameron.

Buckley asked what would have happened if Madeleine had refused to cooperate, or even had walked out of her session. Once more Dr. Cameron's response came as a surprise. She would have been given an injection of curare, which would have temporarily paralyzed her. "When her defenses are finally bro-ken down, she then begins her sleep therapy. The usual course runs for a month. But I am thinking of extending it to sixty days," Dr. Cameron said. The revelation also went into Buck-ley's notebook. He had one further question. Did Dr. Cameron think this was how the POWs in Korea had been manipulated into making their confessions? Dr. Cameron had said it was too early for him to come to a conclusion.

Buckley's visit ended when Dr. Cameron took him to the basement. Buckley's notes recalled: "I was astonished at what had been created. There was some sort of chamber that was pitch black inside and a whole range of equipment which I had seen in no other part of the hospital. Cameron said this was the core of his research. He refused to elaborate, saying "your people will know in good time."

*   *   *

Throughout the summer of 1955, the U2 spy planes continued to supply Dr. Gottlieb with further proof of how the Soviet Union was expanding its biological warfare capability. He received regular copies of high resolution photographs. The original complex among the larch and birch forests around Novosibirsk in Siberia had mushroomed to include a dozen more sites which photoanalysts said were clear evidence the buildings – with their squat smoke stacks – were engaged in the mass production of viruses and rickettsiae.

This doomsday scenario had led to further expansion of Fort Detrick. It officially became a "Fort" on February 3, 1956, marking its thirteen years in existence. Scores of new labs were established and hundreds of scientists and technicians hired to run them. Dr. Gottlieb was now a senior member of a secret empire that was proud, expansionist and in many ways sovereign. It answered to few people and had a secret budget of unrecorded millions of dollars. Among all his other duties, Dr. Gottlieb was also positioning himself to become special assistant to the Deputy Director of the CIA's Plans for Scientific Matters Department, which would place him in charge of all technical requirements for the agency's "termination" operations. He would become the scientist who made the choice of biological weapon to kill or incapacitate any person the CIA targeted.

Originally Frank Olson had been ordered to stockpile a selection of suitable biological agents that could kill or maim without leaving any suspicion. Ideally the germs should be indigenous to the area where they would be used: smallpox for Africa, anthrax for Asia, brucellosis for Europe. After Frank Olson's death, Dr. Gottlieb's killer germs had continued to be amassed at Fort Detrick and Olson's research continued to be fine-tuned.

Dr. Gottlieb had also supervised an increase in the output of Pine Bluff Arsenal, an army base the Chemical Division had taken over to begin a crash production of Brucella suspension that would be shipped to Europe inside cluster bombs. These would be dropped on Soviet targets should the Cold War escalate into military confrontation. Thousands of Brucella bombs had been sent to American air bases in West Germany and Britain. Each 500-pound bomb was designed to infect a four-hundred meter area. In the pantheon of biological weapons Dr. Gottlieb had at his disposal, Brucella was a relatively mild weapon, disabling rather than killing victims. However, it could still debilitate a person for up to a year, leaving permanent damage to the skeletal frame and the genito-urinary tract. In many ways, it is the perfect weapon to destroy the efficiency of an enemy's fighting force and leave its civilian population seriously impaired for a considerable time.

Back in Washington, Buckley wrote his report on his visit to the Institute, marking it as "Eyes Only" for Dr. Gottlieb. Afterwards he ate a solitary meal in a late-night restaurant. He was asleep by midnight.

Every morning, Buckley would get up promptly at six thirty. Over breakfast at a corner deli he would read the *Washington Post*, then, at the office, once more repeat the process of writing and reading. "It was as regular as night follows day," he would recall. He lived against a background that included Grace Kelly becoming a princess; the Davy Crockett craze giving way to the Beat Generation, and the emergence of Richard Nixon as a serious player on the political stage. On the television set in the apartment living room, *I Love Lucy*, continued to dominate the ratings. Buckley preferred the radio; he found TV too crude. Radio also gave him a chance to keep abreast of a story that had fascinated him, the accusation that Dr. J. Robert Oppenheimer, one of the men who had helped create the atomic bomb, had in fact subsequently worked hard to stop it being developed as a weapon of defense against the Soviet

Union. The allegation that the distinguished scientist had been a Soviet agent had been dismissed by the investigating tribunal. But Oppenheimer's career in government was over.

Shortly afterward the United States exploded its second hydrogen bomb on Bikini atoll in the Pacific. Monitoring equipment picked up traces of radioactive fallout as far away as Europe. The fallout was given a name, Strontium 90, with a half-life of 25 years. In humans it deposits itself in bones and causes cancer.

In his diary Bill Buckley noted: "Oh boy, what a world."

Dr. Gottlieb had traveled to Alaska to test germs in the Arctic to see how they would work when dropped in the steppes of Siberia. Missile sites in the mid-West were adapted to launch biological weapons against targets in the Soviet Union. Dr. Gottlieb attended Pentagon meetings where plans were dusted off, written and rewritten. Buckley supervised the security for tests in Okinawa, Panama and the Mariana Islands of the Pacific. In his diary he wrote: "My butt is being reshaped to match an airplane seat!"

After his return to Washington, he made further trips to Montreal to collect data on Dr. Cameron's search for the solution to brainwashing. Buckley helped Dr. Gottlieb to set up another test center in a disused army base outside Salt Lake City in Utah to evaluate the results of over one hundred different biological and chemical weapons tests MK-ULTRA had conducted around the world. For Dr. Gottlieb, the findings were satisfactory, the tests had been successful. "He was less happy about the lack of results from Montreal," Buckley would report. Once more, Buckley was ordered to go to the Institute as an observer to yet another experiment.

The key elements of this experiment were the Grid Room and the Chamber in the Institute's basement. The Grid Room had lines drawn across one wall and a hard-backed chair in front of them. At the opposite end of the room, a carefully concealed hole had been made in the wall to take the lens of a movie camera mounted on a platform on the other side. Anyone sitting in the chair would be unaware he or she was being filmed. Dr. Cameron explained the Grid Room was meant to measure "the angle of the trunk axis when sitting down," and to record on film how much "energy output" was used by a patient when moving. Each patient would be fitted with electrodes which he called "potentiometers," and which would "convert an analog signal and telemeter it to a receiving station" – a cubby-hole in a corner of the basement packed with electronic equipment. It included a large machine with dials and switches which Dr. Cameron called the "Body Movement Transducer." He claimed it would provide "up to 10,000 pieces of information per minute" from each patient. The Grid Room had also been fitted with concealed microphones to record any verbal sounds made.

The sound proofed Chamber resembled a prison cell with its heavy door and cladded walls. Dr. Cameron explained it "would help patients if they could be first isolated and then disoriented before he tried to restructure their attitudes." Even spending a short while in the chamber gave Buckley "a bad feeling."

Dr. Cameron told him that patients would remain incarcerated for weeks, even months. He had drawn up a list of patients with "something significant" to hide in their pasts; memories they were ashamed of and which made them feel guilty. He now believed the Chinese had selected only POWs whom they would be able to reduce to a state of dependency, and who would therefore be ready to accept their interrogators' views. "The Chinese had only dealt with healthy fighting men. I will have the infinitely harder task of brainwashing those who were disturbed. However, by successfully manipulating their psychological mechanisms, I am certain I will solve the mystery of mind control." Buckley noted Cameron's promise in his diary.

Buckley watched Madeleine Lacroix being brought into the basement on a bed by two nurses and wheeled into the Chamber. The door was closed and Madeleine was left in stygian darkness. Dr. Cameron said there would be no results to report for some weeks.

Mary Matilda Morrow had always wanted to be a doctor, to be respected, admired and loved like her father had been by his patients. Encouraged by him she had studied the medical history of the past century during which all the great advances of medicine were achieved, beginning in 1846 with the discovery of anesthesia, which led to painless surgery. Everything that went before, her father said, was part of the age of ignorance, of torture and a fruitless stumbling in the dark. She read about the first operation performed under gas in the Massachusetts General Hospital in Boston, how Louis Pasteur identified the microbic killers under his microscope, and how Joseph Lister used the first carbolic spray in the operating room, the harbinger of still higher surgical standards. Their heroic acts confirmed her belief that a career in medicine was the only one for her. Each of these pioneers had fought off bitter resistance as they pursued their ideas. The lesson was not lost on the fourteen-year-old.

She absorbed other lessons as she grew up. While surgery and the other disciplines of her father's profession were well served in Montreal, the city was no different from any other in Canada in its attitude toward the mentally ill. The two great custodial institutions in Montreal were Verdun Protestant Hospital and St.Jean de Dieu Hospital for Catholics, a place so large that it had its own private railway to transport its inmates from one monolithic depository to another. Morrow's father had told her there was almost no treatment provided and that the government allowed only seventy-five cents a day per patient for clothing, food and heat. This furthered her desire to be a doctor — even if that meant working in one of those grim, grey stone buildings. She was certain that, just as doctors had taken surgery out of the environment of the abattoir, so others would come along and do the same for psychiatry and its complementary disciplines of neurology and neuro-anatomy.

Morrow passed the entrance examination and entered McGill University in Montreal, the most prestigious medical school in Canada. When she graduated, qualified as a general practitioner, Dr. Morrow reflected that what her father had once said of Montreal was still true: "Next to Quebec it was the one Canadian city where a doctor, to get on, needed to know the rosary as well as how to read a blood pressure gauge." Not only did the Catholic Church physically dominate the city as the largest landowner, but it also reached deep into the minds of its people. Many of the patients she saw were filled with anxieties and guilt that came from being unable to live by their faith; for the most part they were people who had come from the rural world beyond Montreal, drawn into the city by the promise of high salaries. "They brought with them a lifetime of being taught by their priests to take baths in their undergarments to avoid the sin of exposing their own flesh," Dr. Morrow remembered.

The working of the human brain and the nervous system fascinated her. She hoped one day to make her own contribution to understanding it more fully. After holding a number of junior appointments in the United States, Morrow returned home to Montreal set up a private practice in the city. There was probably not a doctor in Montreal who worked as hard as she did. At times she could be brusque, but gradually she brought that tendency under control by adopting a rather impersonal coolness toward those she worked with. She also began to ask herself a question which increasingly troubled her: was lobotomy really the ultimate answer? Every year scores of Montreal's depressed, violent, schizophrenic and alcoholic patients had their frontal lobes severed. She was convinced there had to be a better treatment than hacking out the clusters of cells in the temporal lobes thought to control emotional responses, but she did not as yet have enough experience to begin to suggest an alternative.

To further her career, Dr. Morrow accepted a part-time post at the Montreal Neurological Institute. She was also doing highly specialized research on the blood vessels in the brain and still managed to find time to attend clinical conferences and keep abreast of the publications in her field. At times she began to wonder how she could continue to cope with such a workload. Dr. Morrow decided on another career move to study for her diploma in psychiatry under Dr. Cameron. She had recently re-read some of his clinical papers; they were fluent and persuasive and at times almost messianic. It was clear he saw psychiatry almost as the new religion of medicine.

By now Cameron was credited with turning the Allan Memorial Institute into one of the most renowned psychiatric teaching hospitals in North America — some said in the world. There was a behavioral laboratory which specialized in studying human responses by means of sound and visual recordings. The experimental therapeutics unit was under the direction of Dr. Robert Cleghorn, one of the most respected researchers in Canada. The electrophysiological laboratory was run by another renowned physician, Dr. Lloyd Hisey. There were departments for vasulographic studies, pharmacology and transcultural studies. From what she had heard, every nook and cranny of the old mansion on Mount Royal was occupied with research and treatment.

Morrow had heard some of the treatments at the institute were radical. Dr. Cameron prescribed large quantities of drugs, repeated courses of electroshock and the technique he had developed called "psychic driving." Upon arriving at the institute, Morrow had a pressing problem. In spite of all her hard work, she remained desperately short of money. It was not that she was extravagant; in many ways she lived a frugal, almost monastic life, not from choice, but because her schedule left her almost no time to relax and socialize. What little free time she had was given over to coaching students in her specialty, neuro-anatomy. Often she taught them without charge. At the end of a week she would feel, "so damned hungry and not have a dollar to satisfy it." She was close to forty years of age, a spinster, a dedicated doctor and ambitious. So where had her life gone so badly wrong, she would ask herself. But there was no time to consider the question. She forced the anxieties to the back of her mind.

In his office, Buckley was deeply immersed in trying to understand the complex physiological mechanisms which, either singly or in combination, Dr. Cameron had said must come into play to successfully brainwash a person. Comparing Cameron's papers to other data, there seemed to Buckley little difference between some of his methods and those which had been used to elicit confessions during the Spanish Inquisition and, more recently, by the Russians and Chinese. Indeed Dr. Cameron admitted as much. In the papers he had written, and which Gottlieb had passed on to Buckley, was one that contained the psychiatrist's evaluation of how the Chinese could have made their American prisoners-of-war confess during the Korean War.

"The Chinese, and I suspect the Soviets, have grasped the importance of inducing a sense of guilt and internal conflict in a prisoner. They would have achieved this by subjecting the man to a bombardment of accusations and continuous cross-examinations until his anxiety leaves him totally confused and he contradicts himself on some small point. This is then used as a psychological stick to beat him with; the end result is that his brain ceases to function normally. Eventually the prisoner mentally collapses. At that stage he is in a highly suggestible state. His previous thought patterns have been removed. He is ready, with little more prompting, to deliver the desired confession," Dr. Cameron wrote.

These techniques focused on fomenting anxiety in a person and feelings of real or imagined guilt, creating a conflict of loyalties. Again, the physiological mechanics that Cameron believed would produce the required results were strikingly similar to the behavior patterns implanted in their congregations by the Puritan preachers of New England and based on their Calvinist beliefs. They too made a practice of inducing guilt and acute apprehension as the first stage of conversion to their beliefs. Buckley later recalled: "I wondered how far Cameron was prepared to go. At times there was an element of the hell-fire preacher about him. He seemed to regard creating terror as one of the prerequisites to those whose minds he wished to control."

Buckley wondered whether Dr. Cameron was going to do this to his patients. Day after day Buckley ordered up more books from the library — William Sprague's *Lectures on Revivals of Religion*, George Orwell's *Nineteen Eighty-Four* and Aldous Huxley's *The Devils of Loudun*. One legal pad after another was filled with Buckley's handwriting. Commenting on St.Ignatius' famous book, *Spiritual Exercises*, used by Jesuits as a training manual, Buckley had written:

"Each exercise is devised to affect their object. The first ones are intended to reduce a neophyte to contrition, shame and fear. His mind is filled with frightening images. These are enhanced by his being physically weakened by lack of food and sleep. He has been reduced to a state of wretchedness. Then, suddenly, the first of a new set of exercises offers him salvation. He is shown that the way forward is to accept totally the ideal of Christ. He is encouraged to accept that all which he has endured before is no more than the road to accepting that ideal. The exercises are probably the most powerful method ever devised to gain control over the soul of a man. This is achieved through the previous use of constant mental terror and shame."

To Buckley this rang a familiar bell. He wondered if Dr. Cameron had adapted the *Spiritual Exercises* for his own use.

Buckley would read on well into the night, one night after another, until his was the only light burning in the office corridor. He was especially fascinated by Orwell's *Nineteen Eighty-Four* because he had noticed a copy of the novel on one of Dr. Cameron's bookshelves. Central to the book is the story of how the hero, while being indoctrinated, reveals he has an overwhelming fear of rats dating from his childhood. The revelation is used by his interrogator to procure the hero's acceptance of "Big Brother."

Buckley noted: "Orwell had created something that is very close to the methods used by Cameron. His papers indicate he is always on the lookout in a patient for something for which he or she is sensitive. He plays on these fears, ostensibly because he insists that he is trying to banish them. But by making a patient confront a fear, Cameron could also bring them more under his control. More ready to accept his suggestions."

The more he read, the more Buckley wondered whether the methods Dr. Cameron was using on his patients might actually destroy them.

Jeannine Huard was among the number of patients who found their way to the Institute, her fragile sense of peace stolen by feelings of dread and shame. No one — her husband, family or friends — really understood what it was like to be burdened with a depression so powerful that it affected her speech, her movements, kept her awake at night, filled her with self-recrimination, stopped her eating, took away her sexual desires, disrupted her menstrual cycle and physically stripped pounds from her already slight frame. Outsiders only saw a wan-faced young woman with a caring husband and a healthy baby daughter.

Recently, Jeannine had undergone an appendectomy in another hospital. Afterwards, her family doctor thought she was anemic and had prescribed a tonic. It did no good. She became apprehensive and finally alarmed when she lost five pounds in a week. She wondered whether she might have cancer. Because Jeannine could not afford private treatment, she went to a public clinic at the Royal Victoria Hospital in Montreal. The doctor referred her to the Allan Memorial Institute. A few days later she walked through its main door, beneath the word carved into its lintel, "*Spero*," the Latin for "I hope."

In the admissions room, a nurse filled out various forms and asked Jeannine to sign one headed "Consent for Examination and Treatment." Then she was escorted to her room. For days nothing happened. She lay in her bed, staring at the ceiling or trying to sleep, wondering why she had been asked to sign a form when no treatment had followed. Finally a doctor came and asked numerous questions about her life. She answered as best she could, even though she felt increasing anxiety under the probing. The doctor returned after a few days – this time with a tall, virtually bald man with unblinking eyes. He told her he was Dr. Cameron and called her "lassie." He asked if she sometimes felt her heart racing and wanted to faint or had throat spasms, if she became easily irritable, wanted to be left alone or became quickly upset. Jeannine felt increasingly frightened. The questions made her wonder if Dr. Cameron thought she really was crazy.

One day Cameron started to drug her. She would later say she had swallowed "up to forty pills a day." Semi-comatose from the side effects of the medication, her memory began to play tricks. She found herself unable to remember which day it was and then, which part of the day it was; morning, noon and night all became the same hazy blur. One morning she was taken to a treatment room. Dr. Cameron stood beside what looked like an electric chair. She was strapped in. A metal hat was placed on her head. Suddenly, a dazzling spotlight flashed into her eyes, so bright and powerful that she thought she had been blinded.

The next day, she was taken to another treatment room. This time she was ordered by a doctor to stand before him. He injected her in the arm. Next he fitted goggles with thick, hinged plastic lenses over her eyes. Jeannine felt fingers lift a hinge so that she could peer out with one eye. What she saw petrified her. In a later sworn affidavit (a copy of which is in the author's possession), Jeannine stated: "The physician was holding a gun close to my face. It had a tube running from its butt to a cylinder. Before I could beg him not to fire, he squeezed the trigger and a powerful blast of compressed air shot into my eye. I was about to slump to the floor when the doctor caught me, pulled me to my feet and commanded me to stand still. He lowered the lens, leaving me in trembling darkness. Then he lifted the other lens and, again at point-blank range, shot another jet of air into my eye."

Reeling from the shock and pain, her eyes inflamed, she was strapped in a chair with wires bedded in its arms and legs. The wires were taped to her fingers. Standing behind the chair, the doctor began to question her. She was spared nothing — from childhood fantasies to her wedding night; from schooldays to the birth of her baby. Had she always been a poor eater? Did her mother force her to eat? Did her father allow her not to clear her plate? Had she wet her bed? Did she love her father more than her mother? Or the other way round? Did she love her husband more than her child? Or her daughter more than her husband? Or equally? Did she love herself? Did she think she was a failure as a wife and mother? Did she get angry over little things? Did she like to keep her home immaculate? Or didn't she care about housework? Was she scared of being alone? Did she like being alone? Did she like making love? Did the prospect of sex sometimes frighten her? Had she enjoyed her wedding night? Did she have sexual dreams?

Jeannine thought the questions lasted "for hours and hours." Finally, her mind had reached the point where she was "so upset that I couldn't do anything." The wires were removed and she was taken back to her room — and given another injection that sent her into deep unconsciousness. She later knew what had caused that: insulin coma treatment, one she had found every bit as terrifying as being confronted by a gun and blasted in both eyes. No one, not the doctors or the nurses, ever explained the purpose of what had been done. After weeks of such treatment she left the hospital, feeling no better.

She had tried — "God, how I had tried" — to cope, to fend off a feeling of having failed her husband and her responsibilities. "Oh God," she would whisper. "Please help me. Please... please..."

Once again her depression returned, filling her with a crippling despondency, leaving her in torment that after all she would have to return to what she now thought of as "the house of horrors on the hill."

For Jeannine and the scores of other patients admitted to the Allan Memorial Institute since she had last been a patient, there had been many additions and changes to the treatment regime. Dr. Cameron's secret grants from the CIA had led to increased experimental research on those often too ill to know what was happening. A new wing had been added, increasing the bed capacity to one hundred.

As 1956 drew to a close and plans were being made for the annual staff Christmas party at which Dr. Cameron would make his usual brief appearance, the world had grown a little darker in the aftermath of the Suez Crisis and the Hungarian Uprising. Both the People's Republic of China and the Soviet Union looked somehow more menacing that winter. Despite the size of the vote which had returned President Eisenhower to the White House, the aging war hero seemed a poor defense against encroaching Communism.

Among the guests at the Institute party was William Buckley. Still playing the role of journalist, he told the staff he was back to check out the latest developments. Nobody questioned him; in truth nobody seemed overly surprised at his presence. Dr. Cameron had developed quite a reputation for cultivating reporters, though his senior staff did not always approve of this kind of publicity seeking. Among those Buckley spoke to was Dr. Morrow, who had recently joined the staff. He was struck by her enthusiasm and learned from some of her colleagues that Dr. Morrow was establishing something of a reputation for never being in a hurry to leave the Institute. She would often drop by on a weekend, even when she was not on call, to check on a patient. He formed the impression she was a woman whose life was totally dedicated to her work. There were plenty of people like that in the CIA.

Once more Dr. Cameron gave Buckley a package to be hand-couriered to Sidney Gottlieb, who later told him that the package contained the latest clinical evaluations of the mind-control experiments that Dr. Cameron was conducting. Dr. Gottlieb seemed so satisfied with them that he gave Buckley a Christmas gift. It was a bottle of goat's milk from his herd.

CHAPTER SEVEN

The results from Montreal were analyzed with a series of other MK-ULTRA programs that Dr. Gottlieb had categorized in a memo as "tests to administer specified drugs to unsuspecting persons with no clinical symptoms of mental instability." Originally there had been just two projects, which he had code-named *Bluebird* and *Artichoke*; the bird and vegetable were among his favorites. Later had come *Naomi*, the name of a distant cousin. But soon there were so many projects that he had resorted to simply numbering them. By now the total number of projects stood at over 100 (they would eventually reach 149). MK-Project 94 was to investigate "remote directional control of activities in specific brain centers." MK-Project 142 was to "study electrical brain stimulation."

In his never-ending search for information that could prove useful for the biological warfare program, Dr. Gottlieb had enlisted the support of the CIA archivists. They had turned up a box of documents which U.S. Army intelligence officers had recovered in Munich in 1945. The box was labeled: "German War Office Experiments 1934-39." The documents still bore the German classification "Secret." Among the experiments were those which had tracked air currents through the subway systems of Paris and London. "The tunnels would be prime targets in a future war when Londoners and Parisians sheltered in the tunnels during air raids. Using bacteria which were excellent biological tracers, the tunnels would be transformed into places for mass epidemics." The memo had been written in July 1934, after the Nazis had come to power.

Two months later on a hot summer's day, according to another document, German agents had sprayed "billions of microbes into the Paris Metro system from cars they had driven past the subway entrances. Exhaust gasses provided a satisfactory disguise for the release of the microbes from tanks linked to the car exhausts." A third document claimed that "six hours later, at the Place de la République Metro station, a mile and a half from the dispersal point, our agents discovered thousands of colonies of the germs." In Berlin the findings had been eagerly studied. A memo sent to Herman Goering, the head of the Luftwaffe, from the German War Office read: "It was possible to drop a suitable biological bomb and be highly certain that the bacteria would enter the subway system." Similar tests in London had been carried out by the Germans with "the same satisfying results."

Now, twenty years later, Dr. Gottlieb saw that what the Nazis had done in Europe could just as easily be replicated by the Russians on American citizens.

By the spring of 1957, Buckley had begun to develop mixed feelings about MK-ULTRA. While he liked the access that being involved gave him to the upper echelons of the CIA — he had regularly been invited to director Dulles' seventh floor office to sit in on highly secret meetings — he was becoming more convinced of Dr. Gottlieb's obsession with brainwashing than of the MK-ULTRA's chance of success. In a staff meeting on October 15 of that year, Dr. Gottlieb had said: "We are far too advanced with behavioral control to stop. We are bound to make further advances. And if we do not find the answers, then be sure the Soviets will. Then our people, all the peoples of the free world, will be their prisoners. So it is most important we find the antidote to what they are doing. To do that we have to discover all there is to be known about mind control."

Gottlieb told the meeting he was convinced that "successful brainwashing" was rooted in the use of drugs: LSD, mescaline, cocaine, or even nicotine. He did not yet know which one — "but it had to be something like that." He reminded them that all over the United States in research centers — Boston Psychiatric; the University of Illinois Medical School, Mount Sinai and Columbia University in New York, the University of Oklahoma, the Addiction Research Center at Lexington, Kentucky, the University of Chicago and the University of Rochester, among others — researchers were running projects funded by the CIA to try to prove his theory.

Part of Buckley's duties was to regularly visit the campuses where CIA research was conducted and to collect reports deemed to be too sensitive to mail. These trips had their compensations: he stayed in good hotels and ate in fine restaurants. Occasionally he picked up a girl, usually a student, and spent the night with her. At times there were moments of black comedy. In Boston, during an experiment with LSD, scientists had spiked each other's morning coffee. They were so stoned that Buckley had to wait several days before they recovered enough to hand him the documents he had come to collect. At the University of Oklahoma, a hallucinating scientist suddenly decided he was Fred Astaire and grabbed the nearest secretary, convinced she was Ginger Rogers. The typist had also eaten a doctored sandwich, and the pair spent an entire afternoon dancing on a conference room table. They were led away by anxious colleagues who sat with them throughout the night until the couple returned to normal. More worrying was the behavior of a Rochester doctor who drank a spiked coffee and ran from his office shouting he was going to kill himself. He was overpowered by his fellow physicians before he could jump off a parapet. Dr. Gottlieb told Buckley such incidents were the "usual hiccups in searching for the magic technique he was convinced the Communists were using."

Buckley also began to make regular trips to England and Germany. In London he came to know Dr. William Sargant. They traveled to Porton Down and other centers where British scientists were doing secret experiments in brainwashing.

On one journey to Porton Down Buckley and Sargant stayed the night at an old coaching inn close to the research establishment. Over dinner Sargant told Buckley the purpose of their visit was to collect the results of the latest tests in which terminal cancer patients at St. Thomas' Hospital in London had been injected with two rare viruses: the deadly Langat virus and the even more lethal Kyasanur Forest Disease virus. These patients had no idea they were being used as medical guinea pigs. The viruses were being considered as possible biological weapons. The tests had ended with the death of all the patients. In addition to their cancers, they had contracted encephalitis. Dr. Sargant was to collect the paperwork on the autopsies carried out at Porton Down; Buckley was to take the material back to Dr. Gottlieb.

They arrived at the establishment in the midst of a minor crisis. The facility had nearly run out of animals upon which to conduct experiments; monkeys, guinea pigs and rats and mice were all in short supply. But elsewhere in England, the search to find the answer to mind control continued.

At a secret facility near Maresfield in Sussex, Buckley was intrigued to see a windowless building contained a mock-up of what a Chinese interrogation center might look like. Soldiers were kept virtually naked in filthy cells and subjected to a variety of abuses: hosed down with cold water, deprived of sleep and beaten. He was assured the men were all volunteers.

From England Buckley flew to Germany, landing in the American zone. On his way to a CIA safe house, he was shown a secret dump in the Black Forest. Buried deep underground were enough canisters of biological and chemical weapons to counterattack any Soviet assault for a year. The dump epitomized what Buckley later described in his pocket diary as "Gottlieb's patriotic necklace around the Soviets." He had seen similar dumps on the island of Okinawa in the Pacific. Between them, these two dumps contained sufficient biological weapons to kill every man, woman and child in the Soviet Union.

Part of Buckley's work on his visit to Germany was to assess the suitability of targets to be experimented upon. "I checked their records and questioned them. Those who showed Nazi or Communist sympathies I passed on to our doctors. I was also on the lookout for our own people we could use." Sometimes he did not have to look far for a target. At a dance at an USAF base outside Frankfurt, he met a nurse: "A stunning looker who said she was ready to do anything to fight the Russians. I arranged for her to see some of our psychologists. They gave her a battery of tests and concluded she was ready to sleep for her country. There was a Russian agent in Nuremberg we wanted to recruit. The nurse agreed to go to bed with him. In three months he was in our camp, having defected." But sexual entrapment was something that soon lost its appeal for Buckley. Not only was it "tacky, but sexual blackmail isn't a good way to turn an agent. It shows an inherent weakness in his psyche," he later said to the author.

Early in February 1958, Buckley travelled once again to the Institute in Montreal. This time he brought a suitcase containing several newsreels, which CIA technicians had assembled. The clips showed U.S. prisoners in North Korea making their confessions. Dubbed onto the sound track was a commentary by Dr. Wolff, analyzing how the North Koreans had managed to brainwash their captives. Arriving at the Institute, Buckley was shown into Dr. Cameron's waiting room, having been informed the psychiatrist was making his rounds.

Once more Buckley was struck by "a sense of something strange about the place." That feeling came dramatically into focus when a young woman in a dressing gown went screaming past the waiting room, pursued by two nurses. The woman had reached the front door to the Institute before she was overpowered and dragged back into the hospital. By then Dr. Cameron had appeared. He ordered the patient to be taken to a side room. There she was given an injection; electrodes were attached to her temples and she received electroshock. Unconscious, as quiescent as a baby, she was wheeled away on a trolley. Realizing Buckley had witnessed the episode, Dr. Cameron led him into his office and explained that "depatterning" consisted of extensive periods of "sleep therapy" followed by electroshocks. "The biggest problem we have," Dr. Cameron confided, is "making sure our patients don't wake up unexpectedly and try and make a run for it." The young woman had been in the early stages of "depatterning." She was beginning to lose her memory, explained Dr. Cameron, but she "still knew where she was and why she was here. In the next stage she would show anxiety when asked where she was, and why she was here. The third, and final stage, would come when her anxiety would be gone." Dr. Cameron added the patient would only have a "sensation of the moment, and will only talk about and remember that moment. The past will have gone. She will be living in the immediate present."

In the Institute's projection room, Dr. Cameron and Buckley watched the newsreel footage of U.S. prisoners of war in North Korea. Dr. Wolff's voice explained that each man was initially held in solitary confinement, usually in complete darkness. The only contact with the outside world was through his guards when they fed him, usually once a day. Each meal was accompanied by acts of humiliation. The guards made a prisoner eat his food standing up and then urinate lying down. When he was allowed to sleep, a prisoner was awakened whenever he made the slightest movement.

"Slowly but steadily," Dr. Wolff's voice intoned, "the prisoner finds the stress so unbearable that he breaks down. He weeps. He mutters aloud. He prays for God to save him. Then curses God for failing to do so."

Dr. Cameron continued to write notes while Dr. Wolff explained what followed this initial stage.

"The prisoner is taken for interrogation. He is not confronted with any specific crimes. Instead he is told he knows what they are. If he wishes to share them with the interrogator, he can. But the prisoner doesn't know what to share. He doesn't know what his specific crime is. Slowly but surely, he is driven ever deeper into his own mental mire."

After weeks of this, the prisoner was ready for what Dr. Wolff said his captors called "re-education." To achieve that meant the prisoner must confess.

"To make a confession, the prisoner must be properly prepared. That requires he studies Marx and Mao, attends lectures and engages in self-criticism. As he developed these new skills, the prisoner has the pressure eased on him. His interrogators show their esteem. They reward him with extra food, a hot drink, another blanket."

And so, concluded Dr. Wolff, each prisoner had been led to stand before a camera and denounce all he had once cherished. Buckley was to recall that Dr. Cameron sat for a long moment in silence.

"We need to replicate what was done to those prisoners," he said at last. "We must not only replicate it, but do better, much better."

Without another word, Dr. Cameron walked out of his office.

Madeleine lay in the narrow, rubber-sheeted bed, watching the first gleam of daybreak bring into focus the furniture and her dressing gown hanging from the hook behind the door on South

Two. Her case file showed she had lost count of how many times the machine had been wheeled to her bedside, each time to shock her into unconsciousness. The file noted that when she awoke, she would complain that her head throbbed with pain and her mind "felt like a blurred, pounding emptiness." Yet, while her memory had been affected, the treatment had not as yet banished the Wise Men or the creature on the floor by the door, which she called the Sloth.

She told Dr. Cameron the Sloth was now part of her life, like telling Eddie she still loved him when she didn't, like saying to Dr. Cameron she wanted to live when she didn't, like promising the Wise Men she would take them away from South Two if only they would first drive out the Sloth. Madeleine confided to a nurse that the room had been the creature's and that Dr. Cameron had assigned it to her as one of "his punishments." He had recently restricted her privileges, after she had been caught trying to steal a knife from the dining room. She was no longer allowed outside her room. The Sloth appeared every night after the nurse watched her swallow her bedtime medication and switched off the light. The creature was about the size of the beach ball her father used to throw behind their house. As she watched, too horrified to scream, her mouth dry from the drugs, the Sloth unraveled and slithered over the carpet to settle itself on the floor by the door, blocking any escape, cutting off any help. In the darkness it gave off a pale glow — and Madeleine imagined it smelled of the sour earth of the cemetery where her father was buried. Her nightmare was plainly revealed in her growing case file.

Over the past three years Madeleine had been hospitalized five times; forty-four weeks in all, almost a year of her life spent on South Two. In that time, scores of syringes had been emptied into her arms; she had swallowed thousands of pills, and enough electricity had passed through her brain to power dozens of light bulbs.

Each time Madeline had been readmitted to the Institute, a doctor ran through a check list. Had she heard voices? Did she sometimes think people were plotting against her? She had refused to answer. A nurse would unpack her case, the one Eddie called her "going-away-coming-home-bag." When he visited, he sat on the bed, and she clung to him oblivious to everything. Dr. Cameron finally told him it was best if he stayed away and not upset himself. Madeleine had been grateful for that. That was also the moment she had been most conscious of the dreadful pain on Eddie's face. She had wanted to comfort him but could not. Gradually her feelings for him had receded so that most of the time she felt nothing but a deadness, broken only by another sudden overwhelming desire to try to kill herself so she could be with her father. Realizing she had no way of doing so, she would once more feel totally incapable of any emotional response.

In the corridor, Madeleine heard the sound of the trolley bringing the machine. She felt the familiar panic nibbling at her mind. Her nightdress and bedclothes were damp from perspiration, as was her hair. Once more she knew she had neither the energy nor the courage to get out of bed and open the door and escape before the machine arrived. A nurse wheeled in the trolley with its black box, a tube of lubricating jelly and two wooden spatulas covered with lint to form a mouth gag. The nurse spoke cheerfully, trying to turn Madeleine's attention away from the machine's dials, knobs and switches. She unplugged the lamp above the bed and connected the cable from the machine to the power supply. She watched the dials flicker when she adjusted some of the controls.

Madeleine begged the nurse to give her an injection to help her relax. She was told she must wait for the doctor. He explained that Dr. Cameron had said a sedative was not necessary in her case. The doctor fiddled with settings and adjusted the automatic timer. He rubbed some of the jelly on her temples. He told her to blow her nose and breathe deeply and to keep her mouth open. He next placed the gag between her teeth, checking it was in contact with the lower jaw to prevent her tongue from protruding. He asked her to close her mouth as tightly as she could, adding if she wished she could also shut her eyes. She felt something colder than the jelly on her skin, hard and pressing against the sides of her head. They were electrodes saturated with saline which the doctor held in position. The nurse checked a dial and announced " On." As she always did at this point, Madeleine began to struggle. She could not help herself. The doctor held the electrodes more firmly against the skin, ordered her to relax and not be afraid and that she would feel nothing. Over his shoulder he called to the nurse, "Ready here. Go!" The nurse touched a button.

In the split second between the doctor saying "Go!" and the nurse pressing the button, Madeline perhaps only imagined the great searing flash of pain that passed through her brain. In actual time, it lasted only for a second. In electrical measurement it was 150 volts. The electricity made her body twitch uncontrollably, and she began to dribble spittle. After a four-second delay, the machine's automatic timing device repeated the electroshock. It did so four more times — six separate shocks in all. The doctor removed the electrodes and the nurse pulled out the plug and reconnected the lamp. She then wiped off the jelly and removed the gag. Finally, she placed a linen square over Madeleine's lips to absorb the saliva. The doctor checked her pulse and then preceded the nurse out of the room. The procedure had taken five minutes.

On Buckley's next visit to Montreal, Dr. Cameron invited him for a quick lunch in his office before the agent returned to Washington. His host used the meal to question Buckley about other research going on in the United States. In turn Buckley tried to learn more about the methods used at the Institute. He asked Dr. Cameron if patients had given consent to being treated in this way. Dr. Cameron bridled, saying he would do nothing to harm his patients, but what he was doing was at the cutting edge of medicine.

He had then astonished Buckley by asking if it would be possible for the CIA to provide him with a number of foreign nationals so that he could study them. "Ideally they should be Communists. Maybe they had left Europe for America. But that didn't matter. They would still have the psychology of Communism in their minds," Buckley later recalled Dr. Cameron saying.

Buckley had agreed to convey the request to Dr. Gottlieb. He just hoped he wouldn't be given the task of finding the suitable candidates. That evening, on the flight back to Washington, Buckley wrote up his report on his visit. It contained the revelation that Dr. Cameron hoped "one day soon he would have created a brainwashing machine."

In the Institute's corridor, Dr. Morrow checked the list of patients scheduled for early morning electroshock treatment. Jeannine Huard was next. Dr. Morrow opened her file to make sure there was a signed consent form for treatment. The doctor would spend another morning working in the white-tiled treatment room known as "the shock shop." She would act as Dr. Cameron's "button pusher" at the electroshock machine. All junior doctors took it in turn to be the "button pusher."

Morrow had come to question whether shock treatment was of benefit in all cases. But among the many things she had learned during her time at the Allan Memorial Institute was never to challenge the methods of Dr. Cameron. He often ordered her to set the timer to give six jolting shocks to a patient, each one twenty times more powerful than she had ever seen used elsewhere. The caring and sensitive Dr. Morrow had often been upset to see the only immediate effect of repeatedly sending a current of very low amperage through a patient's brain was to create confusion and loss of memory.

She was glad to be on Dr. Cleghorn's service. In everything he said or did, the tall gentle-voiced psychiatrist exemplified the rational being brought to bear on the irrational. She had assisted him as he spent long hours in his laboratory working on such complex mysteries as the effect of electroshock on the adrenal cortex or investigating the chemicals excreted by the pituitary gland and hypothalamus. Because of his reputation as a researcher, some of the most prestigious names in medicine had come to work with him. Among them were the vivacious biochemist Marian Birmingham, and Paula Ward and Edward Schonbaum, painstakingly making progress toward their eventual triumph of isolating a new steroid. There were half a dozen scientists in Dr. Cleghorn's laboratory seeking answers to all kinds of affective disorders.

Dr. Morrow enjoyed being associated with such distinguished figures. That made it all the more distressing to learn that Dr. Cameron had introduced a rogue scientist into Dr. Cleghorn's team, a fast-talking persuasive clinician who would damage the reputation Dr. Cleghorn's leadership in applied research had given the Institute. The newcomer conducted an investigation into whether the color of a patient's eyes could help to identify the presence of schizophrenia. Cleghorn condemned the project as "something left over from the unfinished work of Dr. Joseph Mengele at Auschwitz," who had conducted similar investigations with Jewish women and children. Dr. Cleghorn's anger deepened when he discovered that Dr. Cameron had allowed the clinician to seek funds from "a thoroughly disreputable financier suspected of having links with the Mafia," he later stated in an affidavit he showed the author. The matter finally came to a head when Dr. Cameron approved publication of a paper by the clinician in a Canadian medical journal that listed Dr. Cleghorn as co-author of the study. Cleghorn insisted the journal should remove his name from what he castigated as "the worst piece of research I have ever seen in all my life." Dr. Cameron, who was on the editorial board of the journal, shrugged off the protests. The paper was published. The clinician, in the face of Dr. Cleghorn's unabated anger, left the Institute. Dr. Cleghorn made no secret that Dr. Cameron had "a serious personality flaw in not being able to spot a phony."

Dr. Morrow had tried to ignore the tensions between the two doctors who could most directly affect her future medical career — even though it was "a bit like walking on egg shells." Now, with Jeannine Huard strapped down on a trolley waiting for ECT, Dr. Cameron strode into the treatment room without a word of greeting. He plunged the needle into the patient's arm, watching the clear liquid flowing into a vein and told her to count backwards from ten. When she reached five, her jaw slackened and she breathed noisily. He placed the gag between her teeth, pressing his hand under her chin to force her jaw closed. He told Dr. Morrow to "hit the button." When the patient had received six jolting shots of electricity, Dr. Cameron marched from the room without saying a word, "his anger a palpable thing. I wondered what I had done wrong," Dr. Morrow was to recall.

Cameron's anger had nothing to do with her. He had just learned that William Buckley had filed a report to CIA Director Dulles describing his own sense of unease over what he had seen on his recent visits to the Institute. Dr. Cameron demanded Buckley be removed from any further involvement with MK-ULTRA. Normally, given a request from such a senior figure in the program, Dulles would have either fired Buckley or posted him to some remote CIA outpost. Instead he sent for Buckley and explained just how important Ewen Cameron had been in the past. In its own way, it was also a sign of the value Dulles placed on Buckley.

Dulles' own ties with Dr. Cameron extended back to the war years, to the days when the spymaster and the clinician had formed a common alliance to destroy Nazism. Dulles had been one of the founder members of the Office of Strategic Services, OSS, which was created in 1942. He had set about the business of sabotage, espionage and covert action with unabated enthusiasm, conducting these operations from a small office in Geneva, Switzerland. From there he carried out "the execution of all forms of moral subversion, including false rumors and support for fifth column activities inside Nazi Germany." He was credited with starting the rumor that Hitler only had one testicle and that Goering was a pedophile. At the end of the war, Dulles had helped set up Operation Paperclip, which successfully brought Nazi scientists to America to work for the United States government.

During this time Dr. Cameron met regularly with Dulles in the offices of the American Psychiatric Association in Washington. An immediate rapport developed between them; both found they had a suspicion of the English and a hatred of the Germans, only equalled by their antipathy for the Russians. Secret reports Dr. Cameron had sent Dulles carried such titles as "How to create mass hysteria in the German civilian population." After the war, the psychiatrist had written a document proposing that each German "over the age of twelve should receive a sufficient course of electroshock treatment to remove from their minds any remaining vestige of Nazism." The paper finally ended up in the CIA archives.

Dulles had arranged to send Dr. Cameron to Nuremberg to assess the mental state of Rudolf Hess prior to his trial. In

May 1941, the Deputy Fuhrer had flown to Scotland with the avowed aim of ending the war. Hess had been brought to Nuremberg to stand trial with other Nazi leaders, having been pronounced sane by a British psychiatrist. The Americans and the Russians were co-prosecutors in the war crimes trial and insisted on their own psychiatric evaluation. On a late autumn day in 1945, Dr. Cameron arrived in Nuremberg a city which had been the nursery of Nazism. Over dinner in the cavernous dining room of the refurbished Grand Hotel, Dulles told Dr. Cameron an astounding story. He said he had reason to believe that the man Dr. Cameron was to examine was not Rudolf Hess but an impostor. The real Deputy-Fuhrer had been secretly executed on Churchill's orders. Dulles explained how Dr. Cameron could confirm the point by a simple physical examination of the man's torso. If he was the genuine Hess, there should be scar tissue over his left lung, a legacy from the day the young Hess had been wounded in World War I. Dr. Cameron had agreed to try to physically examine the prisoner.

The next day, Cameron was taken to the prison where the Nazi leaders were held. A British military policeman brought a handcuffed figure to an interview room and formally introduced him as "Hess, Rudolf, prisoner awaiting trial." The deep sockets of Hess' blue eyes gave his pallid face the appearance of a skull. He wore an old tweed jacket and baggy trousers. He had on neither collar nor tie nor a belt around his waist — precautions against an attempted suicide. His feet were encased in the Luftwaffe flying boots in which he had flown to Scotland. Prisoner and escort remained handcuffed to each other while Dr. Cameron questioned Hess for several hours, but when he had asked the policeman to remove the handcuffs so that Hess could be physically examined, the escort refused, explaining he had no authority to do so. Dr. Cameron did not press the matter, but later reported to Dulles what had happened. If the spymaster was disappointed, he kept it from the psychiatrist. No one would ever know whether Dulles' story about Hess was any more than what he called one of "my little tests."

In the days they spent together at Nuremberg, Cameron and Dulles discovered they had a similar long view of history, believing that with Nazism defeated a new and in many ways even greater threat had emerged. Russia, Dulles was convinced, was ready to spread its pernicious influence as widely as possible. When they went their separate ways — Dr. Cameron having pronounced Hess "clinically not insane" — both agreed they must do everything possible to protect the world from Communism.

Now, Buckley sat in the director's office and listened to Dulles explain that Dr. Cameron was vital to the battle for mind control. Buckley would recall how Dulles had sat there, tapping tobacco into his pipe and drawing the flame of a match into the bowl so that the smoke wreathed his head.

"I didn't need convincing of the threat Communism posed to the United States, but Dulles had this way of making it sound even more dangerous. It was like having a master class in global strategy. At one point he surprised me totally by saying that during World War II the OSS had conducted its own drug program. Military hospitals had reported that some anaesthetics had made patients speak while under their influence. This had led to a number of attempts to use cannabis as a truth drug. The point Dulles made was that now cannabis was widely regarded as respectable, and that in time the pioneer work of Dr. Cameron would be similarly looked upon," Buckley told the author.

Abruptly the meeting switched direction. The director raised the case of Frank Olson. He began by saying the biochemist had been "one of the brightest on Dr. Gottlieb's staff." In Buckley's earlier readings into biological weapons, Olson's name had surfaced time and again. Now, as he sat listening to the director, he asked a question. Why had Dulles telephoned Olson's wife shortly after her husband plunged to his death? Buckley would remember how Dulles had looked at him. "Yes, there was that risk. There is always a risk in something like that. I liked Frank Olson. He was a good scientist. But in the end things got out of control," the director said.

In which way? Buckley had asked.

"In all sorts of ways. Dr. Gottlieb should have taken care of that. At least I hope so. But just go and check the files to make doubly sure," Dulles said.

And so William Buckley found himself assigned to make sure one of the great cover-ups in the history of an agency steeped in hiding the truth remained intact.

CHAPTER EIGHT

On Dulles' order, Buckley was taken off all duties and reassigned to a room down the corridor from the director's suite. "Dr. Gottlieb had looked at me curiously, but asked no questions," Buckley recalled to the author. When he entered his new office, he found the Olson files waiting. There were four, each several inches thick and each section carrying its own tab. Red ones were marked "Secret," green ones bore the warning "Sensitive: Handle With Care" and blue ones were marked "Eyes Only Director."

In one of those blue-tab sections Buckley learned that shortly after 2:00 A.M. on Saturday, November 23, 1953, Dulles had been awakened at home by the night duty officer at Langley. The officer said that Dr. Frank Rudolph Olson appeared to have committed suicide by jumping from a thirteenth floor bedroom window in the Statler Hotel in Manhattan, New York. In his first note on the case, Dulles had written: "I had met Olson on several occasions. He was the last person I expected to commit suicide. This was the makings of a serious problem."

Dulles' first response was to order the duty officer to summon Dr. Gottlieb to a meeting in his office. Next, he called the Police Commissioner in New York and told him there had to be a news blackout concerning Olson's death. If that turned out to be impossible, then the scientist's links with the CIA were to be kept absolutely secret. Dulles' third call was to Olson's wife, Alice, who told Dulles she had been very worried about her husband and that he had not seemed himself in the past few days. In a memo-to-file on the conversation, Dulles reported that he told her it appeared Frank had been "overcome by a sudden, inexplicable bout of depression that had driven him to end his life."

Years later Buckley would recall to the author: "Dulles was clearly a worried man. Keeping the lid on was his first concern. Calling Alice Olson was one way of doing that. He had to remove any suspicion from her mind. Dulles could be very sympathetic when needed. I had seen him when one of the staff lost a relative. Then he would, as my father used to say, 'cry to the edge of the grave'. In something like this Dulles was the right man to call Olson's widow."

The files showed Alice Olson knew "next to nothing" about what Frank did except that he worked at Fort Detrick. At home he was a model father, always ready to spend what little time he had with the children. Eric, the eldest, was born in 1944, then Lisa in 1946 and Nils in 1948. Frank came from Swedish farming stock. He had met Alice when they were both students at the University of Wisconsin and they had married in 1940 after Frank graduated with a Ph.D. in biochemistry. Alice liked to think theirs was a good marriage, solid rather than passionate. And though Frank worked long hours, at least he managed to come home most days, not like husbands stationed in post-war Europe, awaiting a Soviet invasion. Dulles explained that the police would not be troubling her, but, on the remote chance that the newspapers called, she was to direct them to a telephone number he gave her. It was for a safe house that Dr. Gottlieb had set up in New York as a cut-out for any press inquiries MK-ULTRA might spark.

A red-tab section of a file showed that in New York, the police commissioner put two rookie detectives in charge of the case. He ordered their precinct captain to brief them that they should proceed on the assumption that Olson had held a low grade post with the Defense Department and that he suffered from "chronic ulcers." The condition had probably driven him to commit suicide. The detectives did not speculate as to why Olson had traveled all the way from Washington to New York to kill himself, or how he had managed to gain sufficient speed to race across a bedroom and hurl himself through a thick plate-glass window. After taking a statement from the hotel's night manager, Armand Pastore, who had found Olson's body, the detectives did not seek any of the other witnesses who had been outside the hotel at the time. They were told by their captain there was no point in interviewing Alice Olson about her husband's previous mental state. Having spent a few hours on the case, the detectives filed a report that this was just another suicide in a city where jumping from skyscraper to sidewalk was all too commonplace. The first steps had been taken, orchestrated by Dulles, to cover up the fact that Frank Olson had become expendable because he posed a direct threat to the brainwashing program — and much else the CIA had been involved in.

Now, fourteen years after that cover-up had been put in place, Buckley sat at his desk reading the files to establish it still remained watertight. The personnel file on Olson told him little; it was a familiar story of a boy from a humble background. Olson's father, Johan, had run an ice business, cutting it from the lake in winter and selling it to shops and housewives in the hot summers of northern Wisconsin. There was a note that Frank had helped out in the summers.

As with everything he did, Buckley focused his considerable analytical skills not only checking on how the cover-up had been put in place, but the reason why Frank Olson had to die. The files were a paper trail on how the CIA had assembled the most sinister biological and chemical program ever engaged in by an agency of an American government. For years the boyish-faced Frank Olson had been deeply involved in that work, more so than his family would even begin to suspect, more so than Dulles himself probably knew, more so even than his colleagues in the CIA knew. Only Sidney Gottlieb and the most senior of scientists at Fort Detrick had the full details of Olson's work.

Frank Rudolph Olson was born in the small town of Hurley in Wisconsin on July 17, 1910. His school years were uneventful, distinguished only by his high grades in science. He was imbued with a strong patriotic streak and had been among those who had lined the streets of Hurley to welcome home its soldiers who had fought in the Great War in Europe. There is little doubt that to young Frank, they epitomized all that was good about America.

Olson reached adulthood during the Depression. It was an era marked by widespread disillusionment, the hateful racist broadcasts of Father Coughlin, the birth of swing music and *Gone with the Wind*. It was also a time when Isolationism was at its peak. Events in Europe barely intruded into Olson's daily life. In those grim years of Depression, Frank guarded his personal integrity; he refused to exchange idealism for despair. He was ready to confront inequality and any form of gross exploitation. He subscribed to the belief that the secret of the good life was to have the right loyalties and to balance them with the right scale of values. He was a patriot to the core.

War, when it came, was a shock to Frank. But Europe was still a long way away. Even the fall of France in 1940 did not bring it much closer. The war only exploded in Olson's life, as it did for millions of other Americans, on December 7, 1941, when the Japanese all but destroyed the United States Navy at Pearl Harbor. Frank Olson did not have to be told his patriotic duty. He joined the army. His skills as a chemist immediately singled him out. He was sent to Camp Detrick in 1943 (only later would it be called Fort Detrick, an indication of its increased importance).

Buckley continued to pore over the files trying to gain an insight into what had led to Olson's death.

For Olson, Camp Detrick was a place of uncomfortable billets, but the food was good, and Washington was only an hour's drive away on a weekend pass. Security at the camp resembled that surrounding the Manhattan Project, which was developing the atomic bomb at Los Alamos. The other link between the two sites was the regular visitors from Los Alamos to Camp Detrick. They came to discuss the creation of bombs and shells capable of carrying chemical warheads. There were also scientists from Porton Down who made the long and dangerous wartime flight from England to Washington.

The United States had been secretly supplying Britain with mustard gas since 1940. It was manufactured in U.S. factories and then sent in foreign-registered ships to England. Secretly providing weapons was President Roosevelt's way of helping Britain without appearing to break America's neutrality. Pearl Harbor put an end to that subterfuge.

Frank Olson arrived at Camp Detrick as it was becoming the fountainhead of a nationwide expansion into chemical warfare. Near Denver, Colorado, the Rocky Mountain Arsenal, spread over 20,000 acres and employing 3,000 people, worked around the clock to produce toxic chemicals. A quarter of a million acres had been taken over by the government to create the Dugway Proving Ground in the Great Salt Lake Desert in Utah. In the files, Buckley found that one of Olson's first trips was to go to Dugway with scientists from Porton Down to observe how replicas of German and Japanese buildings survived a variety of chemical attacks. They studied the effect of mustard gas sprayed from the air, and, as a result of Olson's report, the U.S. army ordered over 100,000 spray guns. In those first wartime years at Camp Detrick, Olson helped to devise chemical agents for grenades, bombs and shells.

Like other staff at Camp Detrick, Olson knew that President Roosevelt hated the idea of chemical warfare. To him it violated "every Christian ethic I have ever heard of and all of the known laws of war." To overcome the President's qualms, the Army publicity machine let it be known that Churchill had no aversion to chemical warfare and arranged for photographs to be published of the victims of mustard gas bombs dropped by the Japanese on a Chinese city that had caused the death of over 1,000 people in 1941. The carefully coordinated campaign, backed by public opinion polls, showed that almost 50% of those questioned favored using gas against the Japanese. Roosevelt was forced to warn Japan and Germany that the use of chemical warfare against Americans would be met with a similar response on a massive scale.

At Camp Detrick, Frank Olson, having proven himself at chemical warfare, was now engaged in an altogether more deadly area – biological weapons. Once again Britain's Prime Minister, Winston Churchill, had been the instigator. On the eve of D-Day, June 6, 1944, he had sent a secret memo to his War Cabinet to "examine the possibilities of biological warfare and of the form which enemy reprisals might take." There had been reports from underground sources in Germany that the Nazi biological warfare program was well advanced, working out of the Military Medical Academy at Posen. Experiments had been carried out on concentration camp prisoners, including women and children, at Dachau and Buchenwald. These experiments had included using typhus-infected lice and inhaling anthrax spores.

This had been enough for Churchill to order that Porton Down manufacture a supply of anthrax bombs. These were to supplement those Detrick was also making for use against the Japanese. Again, the fear of what the Japanese possessed overcame any scruples in the White House about attacking Japan with biological weapons.

The Japanese biological program far exceeded anything America had developed. Almost 6,000 Japanese scientists were employed in eighteen separate institutes. Hundreds of Allied prisoners were exposed to the full range of diseases in the Japanese biological arsenal. Some were force-fed with rice tainted by botulism; others were injected with brucellosis. Many more were forced to breathe in anthrax spores, or injected with tetanus, smallpox and bubonic plague. Often victims were dissected while still alive to gauge what effect the toxins had on their organs.

After the war at Fort Detrick and at Porton Down, the knowledge of what the Japanese had done proved to be a stimulant for further research into biological warfare. Now it was the Soviet Union that was perceived to be the threat.

Reading the files, there was little doubt in Buckley's mind this was the moment Olson's fate had taken a critical turn.

Olson did not appear to have any qualms about his work. What the Japanese and Germans had done was wrong. It had been right for him to make his contribution to destroying them. He would do the same to defeat the Soviets. To him this fully justified his continuing research at Fort Detrick. The Soviet Union was a threat to the United States — to all Frank Olson believed in. He had no hesitation about answering Dr. Gottlieb's beguiling siren call to create tools to fight them.

The files showed that some of Olson's early research had a verged on the bizarre. He developed a substance that he hoped would alter a person's sexual identity. The potion was tried out on prisoners in a Kentucky jail. There was no discernible effect. Another device was based on the theory nothing would embarrass an enemy more than the smell of his own excrement. Olson hoped to create a compound which perfectly reproduced the smell of diarrhea. The revolting liquid would then be packed into toothpaste tubes. These were to be distributed behind the

Iron Curtain in the hope Soviet troops would use them. The idea was not taken up. Soon Frank Olson had found himself working on finding an answer to mind control.

Olson first did what he had always done: he investigated what had been previously attempted and tried to find out why it had failed. To discover answers, he had to leave his high-security laboratory and travel into a world he had only vaguely heard about. According to what Buckley found in the CIA files, Dr. Gottlieb had assigned Olson a "guide," George Hunter White.

Built like a wrestler, with biceps bigger than most men's thighs, White had worked for the OSS during World War II under Dulles. In 1943, he had been sent to Calcutta to kill a Chinese spy who had turned out to be working for the Japanese. White killed him on a crowded street with one fist blow of such sufficient force that it made a hole in the man's skull. Later he boasted he had used the same technique on secret missions toward the end of World War II to kill suspected Nazis. During a spell as an instructor at an OSS training camp in Maryland, he taught trainee agents how to administer the blow. It had to be delivered to the side of the head with the knuckles acting as a pile driver to weaken the bone. White claimed that no skull could withstand a well-aimed blow.

At the end of the war, White had joined the Federal Narcotics Bureau as a field agent. His work tracking drug shipments took him back into Europe and down to South America. It was his proud claim that he often injected suspects with massive doses of cocaine or heroin to make them talk. Others he killed with his fist. Like many members of the OSS, White had remained in contact with his wartime colleagues in subversive warfare. At one reunion, he met Stanley Lovell, the former chief of scientific research in the OSS, whose philosophy was summed up in the slogan "once at war, to reason is treason." White told Lovell he was looking for a job with "a little more action."

Lovell wasted no time in calling Dr. Gottlieb to tell him that if he wanted someone ready do to anything to help America beat the Communists, then White was that man.

Dr. Gottlieb recruited White to set up safe houses — in San Francisco, New York, New Orleans and Miami — where people could be lured so that White could slip them drugs. Some of the houses were brothels. White recruited prostitutes, either by coercion or through cash payments from the slush fund Dr. Gottlieb had authorized him to draw on. The women were taught how to spike drinks with LSD. White would spend hours watching through two-way mirrors placed in the women's bedrooms. With him was a CIA psychologist who interviewed the prostitutes about what their clients had said.

Buckley continued to follow the paper trail. After Frank Olson returned to his lab, he began to experiment with a variety of "cocktails" that he hoped "might provide the answer to mind control." These were couriered to CIA safe houses in Europe. Olson focused on the possibility that a species of mushroom, *amanita phalloides*, could be effective in controling minds. The fungi grew in the jungles of Central America, where it was known as "God's flesh." Dr. Gottlieb had dispatched a team to harvest the mushrooms. They returned with sacks full of the fungi. Olson spent fruitless months trying to create a behavioral altering substance out of the mushrooms.

One of the blue-tab sections in a file recounted that Dulles had received information from a Soviet defector who claimed that a special hospital was operating in North Korea where Soviet and Czech doctors were conducting human experiments on American POWs. The experiments were designed to test the effects of chemical and biological agents as well as to discover the limits of the physiological and psychological endurance of the captives. The hospital was also a test bed for various mind-control drugs. Attached to it was a crematorium where bodies were burnt after they were experimented on. Some of the surviving prisoners had been secretly taken to the Soviet Union. At a facility in the Ukraine, they were subjected to further experiments before being killed. "Discovering more about these experiments must be top priority for the Agency," Dulles had written.

It was not until forty years later that the truth about these reports would finally emerge. On September 17, 1996 a smartly dressed, middle-aged man rose in Room 2118 of the Rayburn Building in Washington at the stroke of noon. For a moment he surveyed the men facing him behind a raised desk on a dais. They were members of the House of Representatives National Security Sub-Committee on Military Personnel. They had convened for some of the most remarkable testimony any of them had heard about lethal experiments on American prisoners of war captured in Korea.

The man testifying before them was Jan Sejna. He was the former First Secretary of the Czechoslovakia Communist Party and onetime Chief of Staff of that country's Ministry of Defense. He had held those high offices for thirteen years until, sensing he was about to be arrested for "political crimes" against the State, he had fled to the West. In two days he was in the United States, granted citizenship and given a post in the intelligence community. His testimony took only thirty-five minutes to deliver, in strongly accented English. Along with Dr. Gottlieb's Assassination Manual, it remains as one of the most shocking documents of the Cold War. It is published here for the first time:

"I was in the process of responding to Soviet directions in 1956 when I first became aware of the use of American and South Korean POWs by Soviet and Czech doctors. I certainly would not pretend to know what happened to all the missing POWs, but I do know what happened to many of them. In

brief, hundreds were used in Korea and in Vietnam as human guinea pigs. At the beginning of the Korean War, we received directions from Moscow to build a military hospital in North Korea. The advertised purpose of the hospital was to treat military casualties. But this was only a cover, a deception. The Top Secret purpose of the hospital was to experiment on American and South Korean POWs. The POWs were used as bodies for training military doctors in field medicine — for example treating serious wounds and conducting amputations.

The POWs were used to test the effects of chemical and biological warfare agents and to test the effects of atomic radiation.

The Soviets also used the American GIs to test the physiological and psychological endurance of American soldiers. They were also used to test various mind control drugs. Czechoslovakia also built a crematorium in North Korea to dispose of the bodies after the experiments were concluded.

The Americans and South Koreans were not the only humans used as guinea pigs. Thousands of prisoners within the Soviet Union and Czechoslovakia too, were also used. The Americans and South Koreans were very important to the Soviet plans because they believed it was essential to understand the manner in which different drugs and chemical and biological warfare agents and radiation affected different races and people who had been brought up differently; for example on better diets. The Soviets also wanted to know whether there were differences in the abilities of soldiers from different countries to stand up to the stress of nuclear war and keep on fighting.

The Soviets were deadly serious in their preparation for nuclear war and in their development of various drugs and chemicals that were to be used, and this included detailed tests on the people from the various countries that were their enemies. Because America was the main enemy, American POWs were the most highly valued experimental subjects.

At the end of the Korean War, there were about 100 POWs who were still considered useful for further experiments. I believe all others had been killed in the process of the experiments because I do not recall ever reading any report that indicated that any of the POW patients at the hospital left the hospital alive — except the 100 that were still alive at the end of the war. These 100 were flown in four groups first to Czechoslovakia where they were given physical exams and then on to the Soviet Union.

I learned all this from the Czech doctors who ran the hospital, and from the Czech military intelligence officer in charge of the Czech operations in Korea, and from Soviet advisers, and from official documentation that I reviewed in the process of responding to a Soviet request for Czechoslovakia to send medical doctors to the Soviet Union to participate in various experiments being run on the POWs who had been transferred to the Soviet Union. I also reviewed reports on the results of autopsies of the POWs and received briefings on various aspects of the experiments.

While what I have just said describes what happened in Korea, I want to point out that the same things happened in Vietnam and Laos during the Vietnam War. The only difference is the operation in Vietnam was better planned and more American POWs were used both in Vietnam and Laos and in the Soviet Union. On several occasions my office was responsible for organizing the shipments of POWs and their housing in Prague before they were shipped to the Soviet Union. I personally was present when American POWs were unloaded from planes, put on buses whose windows had been painted black, and then driven to Prague where they were placed in various military intelligence barracks and other secure buildings until they were shipped to the Soviet Union. Between 1961 and 1968 when I left Czechoslovakia, I would estimate at least 200 American

POWs were shipped to the Soviet Union through Czechoslovakia. I believe there were others who were shipped to the Soviet Union through North Korea and East Germany, although I have no first-hand knowledge of those transfers. I know that many were given to the Chinese for experiments during the Korean War, and Czech intelligence reported that the North Vietnamese also provided American POWs to the Chinese.

I want to emphasize this operation was conducted at the highest level of secrecy. Information on this operation was labelled State Secret, which was higher than Top Secret, and no one who did not have a real need to know was aware of the operation. My estimate is that fewer than 15 people in all of Czechoslovakia were aware of the transfer of American POWs to the Soviet Union. I will never forget the written directions on the original Soviet order that started the operation in 1951. It said that the operation was to be conducted in such a way that "no one would ever know about it."

Sejna was followed to the witness stand by a silver-haired man, dressed in a dark business suit that did not hide his lifetime in military service. He was U.S. Army Colonel (ret.) Philip Corso. During the Korean War he was Head of Intelligence in the Far East Command, first under General Douglas MacArthur, then General Matthew Ridgeway and finally General Mark Clark. Corso's sworn testimony was delivered in a calm, authoritative voice. Like Sejna, he was listened to in stunned silence. Again his extraordinary testimony is published here for the first time:

"The brainwashing and atrocities against American prisoners were conscious acts of Soviet policy. Not only was it used on our prisoners, but on their people and others under their control. The basis for their action was the Pavlovian theory of conditioned reflexes. I had information on medical experiments (Nazi style) on our prisoners. The most devilish and cunning

was the techniques of mind altering (Pavlov). It was just as deadly as brain surgery and many U.S. POWs died under such treatment. Many POWs willed themselves to death.

My findings revealed that the Soviets taught their allies, the Chinese Communists and North Koreans, a detailed scientific process aimed at molding prisoners of war into forms in which they could be exploited. Returned prisoners who underwent the experience reported the experts assigned to mold them were highly trained, efficient and well educated. They were specialists in applying a deadly psychological treatment which often ended in physical torment. The Soviet approach was a deliberate act of their overall policy which actively rejects, subverts and destroys decent standards of conduct and the whole structure of human values.

Upon my return to the United States I was assigned to the Operations Coordinating Board (OCB) of the White House, National Security Council and handled virtually all projects to U.S. prisoners of war. Here I found out that U.S. policy forbade that we win in Korea. The policy amounted to an actual paralysis and diversion of activity to force the return of our prisoners in enemy hands, including those in the Soviet Union.

Years later I discussed this situation with Attorney General Robert Kennedy in his office and he agreed with me. This "no win" policy is contained in policy directives NSC-68, NSC68/2 and NSC-135/3. The basis for this policy was in directives ORE-750, NIE 2, 2/1, 2/2, 10 and 11. We called this the "FIG LEAF POLICY." In 1953, 500 sick and wounded American prisoners were within ten miles of the prisoner exchange point in Panmunjom but were never exchanged. Subsequent information indicated that they died afterwards. During my tour of duty in the Far East Command, I received numerous reports that American POWs had been sent to the Soviet Union. These reports were from many sources: Chinese and North Korean

A STUDY OF ASSASSINATION

DEFINITION

Assassination is a term thought to be derived from "Hashish," a drug similar to marijuana, said to have been used by Hasan-Dan-Sabah to induce motivation in his followers, who were assigned to carry out political and other murders, usually at the cost of their lives.

It is here used to describe the planned killing of a person who is not under the legal jurisdiction of the killer, who is not physically in the hands of the killer, who has been selected by a resistance organization for death, and whose death provides positive advantages to that organization.

EMPLOYMENT

Assassination is an extreme measure not normally used in clandestine operations. It should be assumed that it will never be ordered or authorized by any U.S. Headquarters, though the latter may in rare instances agree to its execution by members of an associated foreign service. This reticence is partly due to the necessity of committing communications to paper. No assassination instructions should ever be written or recorded. Consequently, the decision to employ this technique must nearly always be reached in the field, at the area where the act will take place. Decision and instructions should be confined to an absolute minimum of persons. Ideally, only one person will be involved. No report may be made, but usually the act will be properly covered by normal news services, whose output is available to all concerned.

CIA Assassination Manual composed by Dr. Sidney Gottlieb

JUSTIFICATION

Murder is not morally justifiable. Self-defense may be argued if the victim has knowledge which may destroy the resistance organization if divulged. Assassination of persons responsible for atrocities or reprisals may be regarded as just punishment. Killing a political leader whose burgeoning career is a clear and present danger to the cause of freedom may be held necessary.

But assassination can seldom be employed with a clear conscience. Persons who are morally squeamish should not attempt it.

CLASSIFICATIONS

The techniques employed will vary according to whether the subject is unaware of his danger, aware but unguarded, or guarded. They will also be affected by whether or not the assassin is to be killed with the subject. Hereafter, assassinations in which the subject is unaware will be termed "simple"; those where the subject is aware but unguarded will be termed "chase"; those where the victim is guarded will be termed "guarded."

If the assassin is to die with the subject, the act will be called "lost." If the assassin is to escape, the adjective will be "safe." It should be noted that no compromises should exist here. The assassin must not fall into enemy hands.

A further type division is caused by the need to conceal the fact that the subject was actually the victim of assassination, rather than an accident or natural causes. If such concealment is desirable the operation will be called "secret"; if concealment is immaterial, the act will be called open"; while if the assassination requires publicity to be effective it will be termed "terroristic."

Following these definitions, the assassination of Julius Caesar was safe, simple, and terroristic, while that of Huey Long was lost, guarded and open. Obviously, successful secret assassinations are not recorded as assassination at all. [Illeg] of Thailand and Augustus Caesar may have been the victims of safe, guarded and secret assassination. Chase assassinations usually involve clandestine agents or members of criminal organizations.

THE ASSASSIN

In safe assassinations, the assassin needs the usual qualities of a clandestine agent. He should be determined, courageous, intelligent, resourceful, and physically active. If special equipment is to be used, such as firearms or drugs, it is clear that he must have outstanding skill with such equipment.

Except in terroristic assassinations, it is desirable that the assassin be transient in the area. He should have an absolute minimum of contact with the rest of the organization and his instructions should be given orally by one person only. His safe evacuation after the act is absolutely essential, but here again contact should be as limited as possible. It is preferable that the person issuing instructions also conduct any withdrawal or covering action which may be necessary.

In lost assassination, the assassin must be a fanatic of some sort. Politics, religion, and revenge are about the only feasible motives. Since a fanatic is unstable psychologically, he must be handled with extreme care. He must not know the identities of the other members of the organization, for although it is intended that he die in the act, something may go wrong. While the Assassin of Trotsky has never revealed any significant information, it was unsound to depend on this when the act was planned.

PLANNING

When the decision to assassinate has been reached, the tactics of the operation must be planned, based upon an estimate of the situation similar to that used in military operations. The preliminary estimate will reveal gaps in information and possibly indicate a need for special equipment which must be procured or constructed. When all necessary data has been collected, an effective tactical plan can be prepared. All planning must be mental; no papers should ever contain evidence of the operation.

In resistance situations, assassination may be used as a counter-reprisal. Since this requires advertising to be effective, the resistance organization must be in a position to warn high officials publicly that their lives will be the price of reprisal action against innocent people. Such a threat is of no value unless it can be carried out, so it may be necessary to plan the assassination of various responsible officers of the oppressive regime and hold such plans in readiness to be used only if provoked by excessive brutality. Such plans must be modified frequently to meet changes in the tactical situation.

TECHNIQUES

The essential point of assassination is the death of the subject. A human being may be killed in many ways but sureness is often overlooked by those who may be emotionally unstrung by the seriousness of this act they intend to commit. The specific technique employed will depend upon a large number of variables, but should be constant in one point: Death must be absolutely certain. The attempt on Hitler's life failed because the conspiracy did not give this matter proper attention.

Techniques may be considered as follows:

1. Manual.

It is possible to kill a man with the bare hands, but very few are skillful enough to do it well. Even a highly trained Judo expert will hesitate to risk killing by hand unless he has absolutely no alternative. However, the simplest local tools are often much the most efficient means of assassination. A hammer, axe, wrench, screw driver, fire poker, kitchen knife, lamp stand, or anything hard, heavy and handy will suffice. A length of rope or wire or a belt will do if the assassin is strong and agile. All such improvised weapons have the important advantage of availability and apparent innocence. The obviously lethal machine gun failed to kill Trotsky where an item of sporting goods succeeded.

In all safe cases where the assassin may be subject to search, either before or after the act, specialized weapons should not be used. Even in the lost case, the assassin may accidentally be searched before the act and should not carry an incriminating device if any sort of lethal weapon can be improvised at or near the site. If the assassin normally carries weapons because of the nature of his job, it may still be desirable to improvise and implement at the scene to avoid disclosure of his identity.

2. Accidents.

For secret assassination, either simple or chase, the contrived accident is the most effective technique. When successfully executed, it causes little excitement and is only casually investigated.

The most efficient accident, in simple assassination, is a fall of 75 feet or more onto a hard surface. Elevator shafts, stair wells, unscreened windows and bridges will serve. Bridge falls into water are not reliable. In simple cases a private meeting with the subject may be arranged at a properly-cased location. The act may be executed by sudden, vigorous [excised] of the ankles, tipping the subject over the edge. If the assassin immediately sets up an outcry, playing the "horrified witness", no alibi or surreptitious withdrawal is necessary. In chase cases it will usually be necessary to stun or drug the subject before dropping him. Care is required to insure that no wound or condition not attributable to the fall is discernible after death.

Falls into the sea or swiftly flowing rivers may suffice if the subject cannot swim. It will be more reliable if the assassin can arrange to attempt rescue, as he can thus be sure of the subject's death and at the same time establish a workable alibi.

If the subject's personal habits make it feasible, alcohol may be used [2 words excised] to prepare him for a contrived accident of any kind.

Falls before trains or subway cars are usually effective, but require exact timing and can seldom be free from unexpected observation.

Automobile accidents are a less satisfactory means of assassination. If the subject is deliberately run down, very exact timing is necessary and investigation is likely to be thorough. If the subject's car is tampered with, reliability is very low. The subject may be stunned or drugged and then placed in the car, but this is only reliable when the car can be run off a high cliff or into deep water without observation.

Arson can cause accidental death if the subject is drugged and left in a burning building. Reliability is not satisfactory unless the building is isolated and highly combustible.

3.	Drugs.
In all types of assassination except terroristic, drugs can be very effective. If the assassin is trained as a doctor or nurse and the subject is under medical care, this is an easy and rare method. An overdose of morphine administered as a sedative will cause death without disturbance and is difficult to detect. The size of the dose will depend upon whether the subject has been using narcotics regularly. If not, two grains will suffice.

If the subject drinks heavily, morphine or a similar narcotic can be injected at the passing out stage, and the cause of death will often be held to be acute alcoholism.

Specific poisons, such as arsenic or strychine, are effective but their possession or procurement is incriminating, and accurate dosage is problematical. Poison was used unsuccessfully in the assassination of Rasputin and Kolohan, though the latter case is more accurately described as a murder.

4.	Edge Weapons
Any locally obtained edge device may be successfully employed. A certain minimum of anatomical knowledge is needed for reliability.

Puncture wounds of the body cavity may not be reliable unless the heart is reached. The heart is protected by the rib cage and is not always easy to locate.

Abdominal wounds were once nearly always mortal, but modern medical treatment has made this no longer true.

Absolute reliability is obtained by severing the spinal cord in the cervical region. This can be done with the point of a knife or a light blow of an axe or hatchet.

Another reliable method is the severing of both jugular and carotid blood vessels on both sides of the windpipe.

If the subject has been rendered unconscious by other wounds or drugs, either of the above methods can be used to insure death.

5.	Blunt Weapons
As with edge weapons, blunt weapons require some anatomical knowledge for effective use. Their main advantage is their universal availability. A hammer may be picked up almost anywhere in the world. Baseball and [illeg] bats are very widely distributed. Even a rock or a heavy stick will do, and nothing resembling a weapon need be procured, carried or subsequently disposed of.

Blows should be directed to the temple, the area just below and behind the ear, and the lower, rear portion of the skull. Of course, if the blow is very heavy, any portion of the upper skull will do. The lower frontal portion of the head, from the eyes to the throat, can withstand enormous blows without fatal consequences.

6.	Firearms
Firearms are often used in assassination, often very ineffectively. The assassin usually has insufficient technical knowledge of the limitations of weapons, and expects more range, accuracy and killing power than can be provided with reliability. Since certainty of death is the major requirement, firearms should be used which can provide destructive power at least 100% in excess of that thought to be necessary, and ranges should be half that considered practical for the weapon.

Firearms have other drawbacks. Their possession is often incriminating. They may be difficult to obtain. They require a degree of experience from the user. They are [illeg]. Their [illeg] is consistently over-rated.

However, there are many cases in which firearms are probably more efficient than any other means. These cases usually involve distance between the assassin and the subject, or comparative physical weakness of the assassin, as with a woman.

(a) The precision rifle. In guarded assassination, a good hunting or target rifle should always be considered as a possibility. Absolute reliability can nearly always be achieved at a distance of one hundred yards. In ideal circumstances, the range may be extended to 250 yards. The rifle should be a well made bolt or falling block action type, handling a powerful long-range cartridge. The .300 F.A.B. Magnum is probably the best cartridge readily available. Other excellent calibers are .375 M.[illeg]. Magnum, .270 Winchester, .30 - 106 p.s., 8 x 60 MM Magnum, 9.3 x 62 kk and others of this type. These are preferable to ordinary military calibers, since ammunition available for them is usually of the expanding bullet type, whereas most ammunition for military rifles is full jacketed and hence not sufficiently lethal. Military ammunition should not be altered by filing or drilling bullets, as this will adversely affect accuracy.

The rifle may be of the "bull gun" variety, with extra heavy barrel and set triggers, but in any case should be capable of maximum precision. Ideally, the weapon should be able to group in one inch at one hundred yards, but 21/2" groups are adequate. The sight should be telescopic, not only for accuracy, but because such a sight is much better in dim light or near darkness. As long as the bare outline of the target is discernable, a telescope sight will work, even if the rifle and shooter are in total darkness.

An expanding, hunting bullet of such calibers as described above will produce extravagant laceration and shock at short or mid-range. If a man is struck just once in the body cavity, his death is almost entirely certain.

Public figures or guarded officials may be killed with great reliability and some safety if a firing point can be established prior to an official occasion. The propaganda value of this system may be very high.

(b)   The machine gun.

Machine guns may be used in most cases where the precision rifle is applicable. Usually, this will require the subversion of a unit of an official guard at a ceremony, though a skillful and determined team might conceivably dispose of a loyal gun crow without commotion and take over the gun at the critical time.

The area fire capacity of the machine gun should not be used to search out a concealed subject. This was tried with predictable lack of success on Trotsky. The automatic feature of the machine gun should rather be used to increase reliability by placing a 5 second burst on the subject. Even with full jacket ammunition, this will be absolute lethal is the burst pattern is no larger than a man. This can be accomplished at about 150 yards. In ideal circumstances, a properly padded and targeted machine gun can do it at 850 yards. The major difficulty is placing the first burst exactly on the target, as most machine gunners are trained to spot their fire on target by observation of strike. This will not do in assassination as the subject will not wait.

(c)   The Submachine Gun.

This weapon, known as the "machine-pistol" by the Russians and Germans and "machine-carbine" by the British, is occasionally useful in assassination. Unlike the rifle and machine gun, this is a short range weapon and since it fires pistol ammunition, much less powerful. To be reliable, it should deliver at least 5 rounds into the subject's chest, though the .45 caliber U.S. weapons have a much larger margin of killing efficiency than the 9 mm European arms.

The assassination range of the sub-machine gun is point blank. While accurate single rounds can be delivered by sub-machine gunners at 50 yards or more, this is not certain enough for assassination. Under ordinary circumstances, the 5MG should be used as a fully automatic weapon. In the hands of a capable gunner, a high cyclic rate is a distinct advantage, as speed of execution is most desirable, particularly in the case of multiple subjects.

The sub-machine gun is especially adapted to indoor work when more than one subject is to be assassinated. An effective technique has been devised for the use of a pair of sub-machine gunners, by which a room containing as many as a dozen subjects can be "purifico" in about twenty seconds with little or no risk to the gunners. It is illustrated below.

While the U.S. sub-machine guns fire the most lethal cartridges, the higher cyclic rate of some foreign weapons enable the gunner to cover a target quicker with acceptable pattern density. The Bergmann Model 1934 is particularly good in this way. The Danish Madman? SMG has a moderately good cyclic rate and is admirably compact and concealable. The Russian SHG's have a good cyclic rate, but are handicapped by a small, light protective which requires more kits for equivalent killing effect.

    (d)   The Shotgun.

A large bore shotgun is a most effective killing instrument as long as the range is kept under ten yards. It should normally be used only on single targets as it cannot sustain fire successfully. The barrel may be "sawed" off for convenience, but this is not a significant factor in its killing performance. Its optimum range is just out of reach of the subject. 00 buckshot is considered the best shot size for a twelve gage gun, but anything from single balls to bird shot will do if the range is right. The assassin should aim for the solar plexus as the shot pattern is small at close range and can easily [illeg] the head.

    (e)   The Pistol.

While the handgun is quite inefficient as a weapon of assassination, it is often used, partly because it is readily available and can be concealed on the person, and partly because its limitations are not widely appreciated. While many well known assassinations have been carried out with pistols (Lincoln, Harding, Ghandi), such attempts fail as often as they succeed, (Truman, Roosevelt, Churchill).

If a pistol is used, it should be as powerful as possible and fired from just beyond reach. The pistol and the shotgun are used in similar tactical situations, except that the shotgun is much more lethal and the pistol is much more easily concealed.

In the hands of an expert, a powerful pistol is quite deadly, but such experts are rare and not usually available for assassination missions.

.45 Colt, .44 Special, .455 Kly, .45 A.S.[illeg] (U.S. Service) and .357 Magnum are all efficient calibers. Less powerful rounds can suffice but are less reliable. Sub-power cartridges such as the .32s and .25s should be avoided.

In all cases, the subject should be hit solidly at least three times for complete reliability.

    (f)   Silent Firearms

The sound of the explosion of the proponent in a firearm can be effectively silenced by appropriate attachments. However, the sound of the projective passing through the air cannot, since this sound is generated outside the weapon. In cases where the velocity of the bullet greatly exceeds that of sound, the noise so generated is much louder than that of the explosion. Since all powerful rifles have muzzle velocities of over 2000 feet per second, they cannot be silenced.

Pistol bullets, on the other hand, usually travel slower than sound and the sound of their flight is negligible. Therefore, pistols, submachine guns and any sort of improvised carbine or rifle which will take a low velocity cartridge can be silenced. The user should not forget that the sound of the operation of a repeating action is considerable, and that the sound of bullet strike, particularly in bone is quite loud.

Silent firearms are only occasionally useful to the assassin, though they have been widely publicized in this connection. Because permissible velocity is low, effective precision range is held to about 100 yards with rifle or carbine type weapons, while with pistols, silent or otherwise, are most efficient just beyond arms length. The silent feature attempts to provide a degree of safety to the assassin, but mere possession of a silent firearm is likely to create enough hazard to counter the advantage of its silence. The silent pistol combines the disadvantages of any pistol with the added one of its obviously clandestine purpose.

A telescopically sighted, closed-action carbine shooting a low velocity bullet of great weight, and built for accuracy, could be very useful to an assassin in certain situations. At the time of writing, no such weapon is known to exist.

7.   Explosives.

Bombs and demolition charges of various sorts have been used frequently in assassination. Such devices, in terroristic and open assassination, can provide safety and overcome guard barriers, but it is curious that bombs have often been the implement of lost assassinations.

The major factor which affects reliability is the use of explosives for assassination. the charge must be very large and the detonation must be controlled exactly as to time by the assassin who can observe the subject. A small or moderate explosive charge is highly unreliable as a cause of death, and time delay or booby-trap devices are extremely prone to kill the wrong man. In addition to the moral aspects of indiscriminate killing, the death of casual bystanders can often produce public reactions unfavorable to the cause for which the assassination is carried out.

Bombs or grenades should never be thrown at a subject. While this will always cause a commotion and may even result in the subject's death, it is sloppy, unreliable, and bad propaganda. The charge must be too small and the assassin is never sure of:

(1)reaching his attack position, (2) placing the charge close enough to the target and (3) firing the charge at the right time.

Placing the charge surreptitiously in advance permits a charge of proper size to be employed, but requires accurate prediction of the subject's movements.

Ten pounds of high explosive should normally be regarded as a minimum, and this is explosive of fragmentation material. The latter can consist of any hard, [illeg] material as long as the fragments are large enough. Metal or rock fragments should be walnut-size rather than pen-size. If solid plates are used, to be ruptured by the explosion, cast iron, 1" thick, gives excellent fragmentation. Military or commercial high explosives are practical for use in assassination. Homemade or improvised explosives should be avoided. While possibly powerful, they tend to be dangerous and unreliable. Anti-personnel explosive missiles are excellent, provided the assassin has sufficient technical knowledge to fuse them properly. 81 or 82 mm mortar shells, or the 120 mm mortar shell, are particularly good. Anti-personnel shells for 85, 88, 90, 100 and 105 mm guns and howitzers are both large enough to be completely reliable and small enough to be carried by one man.

The charge should be so placed that the subject is not ever six feet from it at the moment of detonation.

A large, shaped charge with the [illeg] filled with iron fragments (such as 1" nuts and bolts) will fire a highly lethal shotgun-type [illeg] to 50 yards. This reaction has not been thoroughly tested, however, and an exact replica of the proposed device should be fired in advance to determine exact range, pattern-size, and penetration of fragments. Fragments should penetrate at least 1" of seasoned pine or equivalent for minimum reliability. Any firing device may be used which permits exact control by the assassin. An ordinary commercial or military explorer is efficient, as long as it is rigged for instantaneous action with no time fuse in the system. The wise [illeg] electric target can serve as the triggering device and provide exact timing from as far away as the assassin can reliably hit the target. This will avid the disadvantages olitary or commercial high explosives are practical for use in assassination. Homemade or improvised explosives should be avoided. While possibly powerful, they tend to be dangerous and unreliable. Anti-personnel explosive missiles are excellent, provided the assassin has sufficient technical knowledge to fuse them properly. 81 or 82 mm mortar shells, or the 120 mm mortar shell, are particularly good. Anti-personnel shells for 85, 88, 90, 100 and 105 mm guns and howitzers are both large enough to be completely reliable and small enough to be carried by one man.

The charge should be so placed that the subject is not ever six feet from it at the moment of detonation.

A large, shaped charge with the [illeg] filled with iron fragments (such as 1" nuts and bolts) will fire a highly lethal shotgun-type [illeg] to 50 yards. This reaction has not been thoroughly tested, however, and an exact replica of the proposed device should be fired in advance to determine exact range, pattern-size, and penetration of fragments. Fragments should penetrate at least 1" of seasoned pine or equivalent for minimum reliability.

Any firing device may be used which permits exact control by the assassin. An ordinary commercial or military explorer is efficient, as long as it is rigged for instantaneous action with no time fuse in the system.

The wise [illeg] electric target can serve as the triggering device and provide exact timing from as far away as the assassin can reliably hit the target. This will avid the disadvantages of stringing wire between the proposed positions of the assassin and the subject, and also permit the assassin to fire the charge from a variety of possible positions.

The radio switch can be [illeg] to fire [illeg], though its reliability is somewhat lower and its procurement may not be easy.

EXAMPLES

([illeg] may be presented brief outlines, with critical evaluations of the following assassinations and attempts:

Marat	Hedrich
Lincoln	Hitler
Harding	Roosevelt
Grand Duke Sergei	Truman
Pirhivie	Mussolini
Archduke Francis Ferdinand	Benes
Rasputin	Aung Sang
Madero	[illeg]
Kirov	Abdullah
Huey Long	Ghandi
Alexander of Yugoslvia	
Trotsky	

Flash

Secret

THE WHITE HOUSE

WASHINGTON

July 11, 1975

Cheney

MEMORANDUM FOR: DON RUMSFELD

FROM: DICK CHENEY   *R. Cheney*

SUBJECT: The Olson Matter / CIA Suicide

Attached is a proposed brief statement for the President to use at
his Press Conference. It would be best for him to use it in response
to a question, although if he wished, he can use it as an opening
statement.

There is also attached a four page memo prepared by the Civil
Division, the Department of Justice, based upon information
obtained from the CIA regarding the events surrounding
Mr. Olson's death.

Rod Hills has questions concerning the last paragraph of the
Justice Department memo which expresses the Justice Depart-
ment opinion that court action against the U.S. would be barred.
He will pursue the matter with the Attorney General.

At this point, we do not have enough information to be certain
we know all of the details of this incident. Furthermore, there
are serious legal questions that will have to be resolved concerning the Government's responsibility, the possibility of
additional compensation, and the possibility that it might be
necessary to disclose highly classified national security
information in connection with any court suit, or legislative
hearings on a private bill intended to provide additional
compensation to the family.

Documents pertaining to cover-up of circumstances surrounding the death
of Frank Olson. Declassified photocopy from Gerald R. Ford Library.

Therefore, Marsh, Hills and Cheney strongly recommend that the President limit his remarks to an expression of regret over this tragic event and a willingness to meet personally with Mrs. Olson and her children to offer an apology on behalf of the Government. Any discussion that goes beyond those issues raises questions which we are not yet in a position to answer.

In response to any questions which go beyond the above, we would recommend that the President indicate that the entire matter, both with regard to the adequacy of compensation and circumstances surrounding Mr. Olson's death, are under review by the Justice Department.

Attachments

cc: Jerry Jones

THE WHITE HOUSE

WASHINGTON

August 4, 1975

MEMORANDUM FOR: DICK CHENEY

FROM: RODERICK HILLS

SUBJECT: Attorneys for the Olson Family

The attorneys for the Olson family are pushing very hard for
information and are claiming a lack of cooperation with the
CIA and DOD. I cannot be certain, of course, but it appears
to me that they have been increasingly belligerent. Rex Lee,
Assistant Attorney General, Civil Division, believes that
there is no way to settle the case and wishes to take a tough
stance. I remain somewhat reluctant at having the Attorney
General refuse the Olsons' claim on what will be proved to be
a technicality and what may eventually seem to be an attempt
to "cover up." Accordingly, I believe that sometime in the
next week or two we should attempt to contact the attorneys
with the help of the Attorney General or perhaps through an
intermediary (Mitch Rogovin, Special Counsel to the CIA has
a partner at Arnold and Porter who is quite close to the Olson
children) to see if a settlement might not be arranged.

Copies of their letters are attached.

cc: Donald Rumsfeld
    Philip Buchen

*Memo, Hills to Cheney, 8/4/75, folder
"Frank Olson Gen CIJ" Box 20, Edward C.
Schmults Files.*

Photocopy from Gerald R. Ford Library.

THE WHITE HOUSE

WASHINGTON

September 30, 1975

MEMORANDUM FOR THE PRESIDENT

THROUGH: RICHARD CHENEY

FROM: RODERICK HILLS

SUBJECT: Olson Family Compensation Claim

The pending law suit by the Olson family against the United
States Government by reason of the death of Dr. Olson
threatens to be a reality this week if no new effort to settle
the case is made. The Attorney General has made a final
offer of $500,000 which has been rejected by the Olson
family.

The Olson family has countered with a request for $3
million but has indicated a willingness to settle for less.

Essentially, the Attorney General concludes that the claim
of the Olson family is worth $1 million, but must be dis-
counted by $500,000 by reason of the possibility that the
government will ultimately succeed in the case on the
grounds that exclusive remedy for the Olson family comes
from the benefits provided by the Federal Employees
Compensation Act. In short, the Justice Department
argues that there is a substantial possibility that a court
will find that Dr. Olson died in the course of his employment

I frankly disagree with this analysis and believe that there
is a real probability that an appellate court would decide
that as a matter of law when one dies under the circumstances such as those causing Dr. Olson's death, he
cannot be said to have died "in the course of his employment." In any event, the Department of Justice will not

*memo, Hills to GRF, 9/30/75, folder
"Frank Olson Gen. (1)" Box 20
Edward C. Schmults Files.*

Photocopy from Gerald R. Ford Library.

offer a larger sum in settlement. However, the Justice
Department would support a private bill which would waive
the FECA defense for a total of $1 million and would not
object if a private bill provided "compensation for the
extraordinary deceit" employed in the case of Dr. Olson.
For this element of damages they would provide $250,000.

Adding all the elements of the Justice Department together,
they would then support a private bill for $1,250,000 and
they would also forego an offset of the approximately
$150,000 that the Olson family has received to date in
compensatory benefits.

The Justice Department analysis is attached at Tab A.

RECOMMENDATION

I recommend that you authorize Special Counsel to the CIA
Mitchell Rogovin to attempt a settlement with the Olson
family at a sum not to exceed $1,250,000 plus a waiver of
an offset of the monies received to date by the Olson family.

In the event a settlement can be reached within these guidelines, the CIA and the Olson family can jointly petition the
Department of Labor to re-consider its 22 year old decision
that Dr. Olson did die in the course of his employment.
Should the Labor Department so rule, the Justice Department is on record as supporting a settlement of $1 million
without an offset.

The CIA could agree in a settlement with the Olson family
that any excess amount would be made the subject of a
private bill and supported by the Administration.
Alternatively, if the Labor Department does waive the
FECA decision, we could ask the Justice Department to
re-consider its settlement limitation. In the event that
the Labor Department should reaffirm the 22 year old
decision that Dr. Olson did die in the course of his
employment, we would agree that the private bill would
be in the amount of $750,000.

Mitchell Rogovin should be authorized to attempt
a settlement of the Olson family claim for a sum
not to exceed $1,250,000 without an offset.

The Rockefeller Report states on p. 226:

> "In the late 1940's, the CIA began to study
> the properties of certain behavior-influencing
> drugs (such as LSD) and how such drugs might
> be put to intelligence use. This interest was
> prompted by reports that the Soviet Union was
> experimenting with such drugs and by speculation
> that the confessions introduced during trials
> in the Soviet Union and other Soviet Bloc
> countries during the late 1940's might have
> been elicited by the use of drugs or hypnosis.
> Great concern over Soviet and North Korean
> techniques in 'brainwashing" continued to be
> manifested into the early 1950's. "

Dr. Frank A. Olson, a bio-chemist, was a civilian

employee of the Army working at Fort Detrick in a

cooperative effort with the CIA. On November 19, 1953,

at one of the periodic meetings of Ft. Detrick and CIA

personnel, a dosage of LSD was placed by CIA personnel

in drinks consumed by Dr. Olson and others, all of whom

were members of the group. Prior to receiving the LSD,

Dr. Olson had participated in discussions where the

testing of such substances on unsuspecting subjects was

agreed to in principle. However, neither Dr. Olson,

nor any of the others was made aware that they had been

given LSD until about 20 minutes after the fact.

Justice Department Report. Declassified photocopy
from Gerald R. Ford Library

During the next several days Dr. Olson developed side
effects, as a result of which he was taken to New York
City on November 24, 1953, to be treated by a doctor
who was a consultant to the agency on drug-related matters,
Dr. Harold A. Abramson. On November 24, 25 and 26,
he met with Dr. Abramson.

After seeing him on the 27th, Dr. Abramson believed
that hospitalization would be in Dr. Olson's best interest.
Arrangements were made for a hospital room near Dr.
Olson's home (in the Washington area), but his room
could not be prepared until the following day. Consequently, Dr. Lashbrook, of CIA, and Dr. Olson stayed
at the Hotel Statler in New York on the night of November 27.

Dr. Lashbrook reported that during cocktails and dinner
Dr. Olson appeared cheerful and spoke freely of his
forthcoming hospitalization. Lashbrook and Olson
retired at about 11:00 PM. They occupied separate twin
beds in the same room on the tenth floor. At approximately
2:30 Saturday morning, Lashbrook was awakened by a
loud noise; he reported that Olson had crashed through

the closed window blind and closed window and had

fallen to his death.

The CIA General Counsel rendered an opinion that
the death resulted from "circumstances arising out of
an experiment undertaken in the course of his official
duties for the U. S. Government.

The Bureau of Employee's Compensation adopted this
view, thus awarding survivor benefits to the widow and
children. To date $143,582.22 have been paid to the
widow and three children. These tax-free benefits
continue to be paid in the current total amount of
$792.00 per month. The payments to the children
terminate when they reach majority (as two already
have), but the widow's benefits continue until death or
re-marriage, and are periodically adjusted for cost
of living increases.

The CIA has never made any contact with the family.
Prior to the publication of the Rockefeller Report, no
government representative has ever disclosed the full
details concerning Dr. Olson's death.

Upon a preliminary review of the facts, it is the
opinion of Justice Department lawyers that any tort
action against the United States arising out of the above-

nty of Frederick)
) ss
te of Maryland)
)

AFFIDAVIT

Mrs. Alice W. Olson, being duly sworn, deposes and
ys:

1. I am the widow of Dr. Frank Olson who died when he
mped from a window of a hotel in New York City on November 28,
53 as the result of negligent and reckless conduct of the
ntral Intelligence Agency.

2. The circumstances surrounding this tragedy which
ded Frank's life, shattered mine and deprived our children of
eir father, are as follows: In 1953 my husband was a distin-
ished biochemist working as a civilian employee of the United
ates Army at Camp Detrick, Maryland. My husband and three of
s colleagues were given LSD, without warning, by CIA officials
dney Gottlieb, Chief of CIA's TSS Chemical Division and his
puty, Robert Lashbrook, as part of the CIA experimental brain-
shing program designated as MKULTRA and operating under the
irection of Richard Helms, Chief of Staff of CIA's Clandestine
rvices. Gottlieb and Lashbrook fed the LSD to my husband and
he others in their after-dinner liqueur without telling them
hat there was LSD in the cointreau glass, nor that they were the
ubject of CIA experiments.

DOCUMENT THIRTEEN

Sworn affidavit of Mrs. Alice Olson about the death
of her husband at the hands of the CIA.

3. When Frank came home on the Saturday following the CIA experiment, he was uncharacteristically moody and depressed. He was in great distress and in obvious need of help. But, instead of being taken to a psychiatrist in Washington or Maryland, Gottlieb and Lashbrook took him to an allergist in New York City, Dr. Harold Abramson, who was working with the CIA on its LSD experiments. Frank had two sessions with Abramson. After the first session he returned to this area, but when he got as far as Bethesda, he told me on the telephone that he was afraid to return home because he might do something wrong in front of the children. So he and Lashbrook returned to New York for a second session with Abramson. That night he jumped from a window of a tenth story hotel room in New York in which he was staying with Lashbrook. There is evidence from the hotel telephone operator that Frank's death may not have been a suicide, but I do not have sufficient proof to make that charge against the CIA in addition to their negligence and recklessness. When I spoke to Abramson years later, he could remember nothing whatever about my husband except that Frank "was a very sick man who needed help" and that he, Abramson, had destroyed all his records on the case. I still find it strange that Abramson destroyed records of a case of such significance.

4. My husband was a remarkably stable man. He had never had any psychiatric problems before he was fed the LSD [...]

2

CENTRAL INTELLIGENCE AGENCY
WASHINGTON 25, D. C.

OFFICE OF THE DIRECTOR

Allen Dulles
To: Gottlieb

FEB 10 1954

93

PERSONAL

Dr. Sidney Gottlieb
Chief, Chemical Division
Technical Services Staff

Dear Dr. Gottlieb:

I have personally reviewed the files from your office concerning the use of a drug on an unwitting group of individuals. In recommending the unwitting application of the drug to your superior, you apparently did not give sufficient emphasis to the necessity for medical collaboration and for proper consideration of the rights of the individual to whom it was being administered. This is to inform you that it is my opinion that you exercised poor judgment in this case.

Sincerely,

Allen W. Dulles
Director

Letter from CIA Director Allen Dulles to Sidney Gottlieb.

DRAFT/JJM
26 February 1957

EX IMPDLT; CL MEMORANDUM FOR: THE RECORD

SUBJECT: MKULTRA Subproject 68

1. Subproject 68 is being initiated as a means to support a research program, the effects upon human behavior of the repetition of verbal signals. The program will be under the direction of Dr. (D. Ewen Cameron, Chairman of the Department of Psychiatry at McGill University, Montreal, Canada.) The program will be for a period of two years, starting 18 March 1957.

2. The scope of the project will encompass studies upon the effects of predetermined signals upon (a) physiological functions, (b) patterns of behavior. The immediate objectives of the program will entail a study of methods to (a) improve the technique of heteropsychic driving, (b) to investigate the range of physiological functions which can be changed by these procedures. More specifically, these studies will include:

(1) A search for chemical agents which will breakdown the ongoing patterns of behavior:

    more rapidly
    more transitorily
    with less damage to the perceptive and cognitive capacities of the individual than the present physiological agents.

(2) An attempt to develop better methods of inactivating the patient during the period of driving (exposure to repetition), and at the same time maintain him at a higher level of activity, by physiological and chemical agents, than by the present physical effects. Among the chemical agents which we propose to explore with respect to their capacity to produce inactivation are the following (used either singly or in combination):

    Artane
    Anectine
    Bulbocapnine
    Curare
    LSD-25.

Extracts from CIA document outlining goals and procedures for Dr. Cameron's participation in the MK-ULTRA program.

D. Our studies now turned to attempts to establish lasting changes in the patient's behavior, using verbal signals of a predetermined nature and of our own devising. After considerable experimentation, we have developed a procedure which in the most successful case has produced behavioral changes lasting up to two months. The procedure requires:

    i. The breaking down of ongoing patterns of the patient's behavior by means of particularly intensive electroshocks (depatterning).

A-13.

TOP SECRET -4-

    ii. The intensive repetition (16 hours a day for 6 or 7 days) of the prearranged verbal signal.

    iii. During this period of intensive repetition the patient is kept in partial sensory isolation.

    iv. Repression of the driving period is carried out by putting the patient, after the conclusion of the period, into continuous sleep for 7-10 days.

3. Specific Proposals

    We now propose to carry on further studies upon the effects of predetermined signals upon: (a) physiological functions; (b) patterns of behavior. To further this, we have two major, immediate objectives:

    i. To improve the technique of heteropsychic driving (the repetition of predetermined verbal signals of our own devising).

    ii. To investigate the range of physiological functions which can be changed by these procedures.

First Objective: Among the studies which we propose to carry out in pursuit of our first objective are:-

    (a) Can we find chemical agents which will serve to break down the ongoing patterns of behavior:
> more rapidly
> more transitorily
> with less damage to the perceptive and cognitive capacities of the individual than the present physiological agents.

(c) Can we develop better methods of inactivating
the patient during the period of driving (exposure to
repetition), and at the same time maintain him at a
higher level of activity, by physiological and chemical
agents, than by the present physical effects. Among
the chemical agents which we propose to explore
with respect to their capacity to produce inactivation
are the following (used either singly or in
combination):-

        Artane
        Anectine
        Bulbocapnine
        Curare

We propose to use LSD 25 and other similar agents
as a means of breaking down the ongoing patterns
of behavior.

Procedure to be followed:

The initial procedure which we propose to employ
is that already outlined under section D. From the
context, however, it will be clear that we hope to be
able to modify and improve the procedure as we proceed.

The patients selected are almost entirely those
suffering from extremely long-term and intractable
psychoneurotic conditions. In the case of results of
physiological driving, the validity of the findings
can be assessed by statistical analysis. Repeated
estimations of the particular physiological function
are made prior to driving and at various periods
subsequent to driving (exposure to repetition).
In the case of the studies upon the effects upon
behavior of exposure to repetition of verbal signals,

the patients are studied exhaustively in psycho-
therapeutic interviews and by psychological test
procedures prior to exposure to repetition, and
by the same means at various intervals subsequent
to exposure. In addition, follow-up studies are
carried on through our Social Service section
subsequent to the discharge of the patient.

In the case of physiological studies, results
can be based on relatively small groups of from four
to six cases in each category, where the results are
as consistent as those which we obtained with muscle
potentials. In regard to shifts in behavioral pattern,
considerably larger numbers are required—up to twenty
patients.

The other aspects of our procedures have
already been indicated under the heading of "Specific
Proposals."

1 December 1953

MEMORANDUM FOR: Inspector General

SUBJECT: Use of LSD

1. Pursuant to your request, Dr. William Gibbons, Chief, TSS, was contacted on the evening of 30 November 1953 concerning points hereinafter noted.

2. Dr. Gibbons has impounded all LSD material in CIA Head-quarters in a safe adjacent to his desk. No one else has the combination to this safe; the material was so impounded on 29 November 1953.

3. Dr. Gibbons stated that he is stopping any LSD tests which may have been instituted or contemplated under CIA auspices. A cable will be sent to the field on 1 December 1953 to this effect.

4. Only two (2) field stations, Manila and Atsugi, have LSD material. There is none in Germany although Mr. William Harvey recently expressed interest in the subject. A cable to the field on 1 December 1953 will instruct the field as to non-use and request data as to how much is on hand and who has custody and access.

5. CIA has furnished a limited quantity of LSD to Mr. George White, Chief of New York District, Narcotics Division, Treasury Department. Dr. Gibbons does not now know the exact amount in Mr. White's possession. White is fully cleared according to Dr. Gibbons.

6. In summary, LSD material over which CIA has or had distributive responsibility is located in four places: (a) Dr. Gibbons' safe, (b) Manila, (c) Atsugi, and (d) that in possession of George White. Exact amounts in each location are not yet available.

7. There are several "grants in aid" units and individuals in the United States doing research with LSD. None of these received

Details regarding CIA's use of LSD.

material from CIA; some know of the CIA interest and furnish reports to CIA. Only volunteers are used. While some of the work is done with knowledge of CIA interest, it does not appear to be done under the auspices of CIA.

8. Dr. Gibbons said there is very little or no correspondence, either internal or external on the subject, but that he would collect such as existed for the Inspector General.

9. Dr. Gibbons was also asked to collect and have carried to the Inspector General all reports on the use and effects of LSD. He thought by this definition he would have a drawer full of papers.

10. Dr. Gibbons was asked to prepare a list of known clinical grants in aid units and individuals in this country engaged in LSD research. It appears that Dr. Abramson has experimented with this drug.

11. Dr. Gibbons was not clear as to the mechanics of CIA acquisition of LSD but said he would get the answers. The material is not under Federal U.S. Governmental control to the best of his knowledge. It is an experimental drug, and as such, is not allowed to be sold in this country. Most LSD obtained by CIA comes from the Eli Lilly Company with head offices in Indianapolis, Indiana. Dr. Gibbons thought some might have been obtained from other parties but he was not certain. The Eli Lilly Company apparently makes a gift of it to CIA. Dr. Gibbons was not certain whether the company brought it here, to a cut-out arrangement, or whether it is picked up in Indianapolis. The manner of receipting for the material is not clear.

12. Answers to the questions asked by the Inspector General which are not given by the above are being obtained by Dr. Gibbons and will be furnished as soon as he is able to get them to this Staff.

Chief, Inspection and Review

Distribution:
  Orig. & 1: addressee
        1: I&R Subject file

DRAFT/eip
17 August 1960

MEMORANDUM FOR: THE RECORD

SUBJECT : Supplement - MKULTRA, Subproject 68

1. Subproject Number 68 is being continued as a means to sustain a research program, the effects upon human behavior of the repetition of verbal signals. The program is under the direction of Dr. D. Ewen Cameron, Chairman of the Department of Psychology, McGill University, Montreal, Canada.

2. The scope of the program will encompass the same studies outlined in the previous draft dated 27 March 1959 which is attached.

3. It is anticipated that long term support for this study will be provided by other organizations (one such organization is the U.S. Air Force) where negotiation assisted by the Society for the Investigation of Human Ecology, Inc) has been underway for approximately 6 months), therefore, this project is being continued for a three month period only. In view of this short continuation, McGill will be authorized delay of the final reporting on expenditures and a terminal technical report.

4. This project will be funded through the Society for the Investigation of Human Ecology, Inc) The cost of the program for a period of three months will be $4,775.00. Charges should be made against Allotment 1525-1009-1902.

5. In lieu of higher overhead rates, title to any permanent equipment purchased by funds granted the University shall remain with the University.

Evidence of CIA link to Dr. Cameron. It is interesting to note that in 1988 the documents were deemed so sensitive that the names of the "Research Director and "Chief TSD/Research Branch" are blacked out.

TOP SECRET

19 August 1960

MEMORANDUM FOR: CHIEF, FINANCE DIVISION

VIA   : TSD/Budget Officer

SUBJECT   : MKULTRA, Subproject 68, Invoice #4
                 Allotment 1525-1009-1902

     1. Invoice No. 4 covering the above subproject is attached.
It is requested that payment be made as follows:

            Cashier's check in the amount of $4,775.00, drawn
            on a (local bank) payable to the (Society for the
            Investigation of Human Ecology, Incorporated.)

     2. The check should be forwarded to Chief, TSD/Research
Branch, through TSD/Budget Officer, no later than Monday, 29 August
1960.

     3. This is a final invoice. However, since it is antici-
pated that additional funds will be obligated for this project, the
files should not be closed.

Chief
TSD/Research Branch

Attached:
    Invoice & Certifications

Distribution:
    Orig & 2 - Addressee

PAID
2-00.3633
AUG 20 1960

I CERTIFY THAT FUNDS ARE AVAILABLE
OBLIGATION OF FUNDS . ___123___
CHARGE TO ALLOTMENT NO. _1122-1009-1912_
_____
AUTHORIZING OFFICER

TOP SECRET

26 February 1957

MEMORANDUM FOR: THE COMPTROLLER

ATTENTION: Finance Division

SUBJECT: MKULTRA, Subproject 68

Under the authority granted in the Memorandum dated 13 April 1953 from the DCI to the DD/A, and the extension of this authority in subsequent memoranda, Subproject 68 has been approved, and $33,180.00 of the over-all Project MKULTRA funds have been obligated to cover the subproject's expenses and should be charged to Allotment 7-2502-10-001.

SIDNEY GOTTLIEB
Chief
TSS/Chemical Division

APPROVED FOR OBLIGATION
OF FUNDS:

(Original signed by)
(Willis A. Gibbons)
Research Director

Date:
27 FEB 1957

Distribution:
Orig & 2 - Addressee
    1 - TSS/OC
    1 - TSS/FASB
    1 - TSS/SRB
    2 - TSS/CD

TSS/CD (26 Feb 57)

Confirmation of payments for MK-Ultra.

16 April 1958

MEMORANDUM FOR: CHIEF, FINANCE DIVISION

VIA   : TSS/Budget Officer

SUBJECT   : MKULTRA, Subproject 68, Invoice #2,
                 Allotment 7-2502-10-001

       1. Invoice #2 covering the above subproject is attached.
It is requested that payment be made as follows:

       Cashier's check in the amount of $19,100.00, drawn on
(a Philadelphia bank) payable to (the Society for the
Investigation of Human Ecology, Incorporated.)

       2. The check should be forwarded to Chief, TSS/Chemical
Division, through TSS/Budget Officer, no later than 30 April 1958.

       3. This is a final invoice. A total of $38,130.00 was
obligated under this subproject during FY 57. However, since it
is anticipated that additional funds will be obligated for this project,
the files should not be closed.

                                Chief
                     TSS/Chemical Division

I CERTIFY THAT FUNDS ARE AVAILABLE
OBLIGATION   1727
CHARGE TO   7-2502-10-001

ALLOTTING OFFICER

Attachments
     Invoice & Certifications

Distribution:
     Orig & 2 - Addressee
         1 - TSS/FASB

Dr. Ewen Cameron (Photo Canapress Photo Service)

William Buckley

Buckley on video filmed by his captives shortly before his execution.
(Photo © Rex Features)

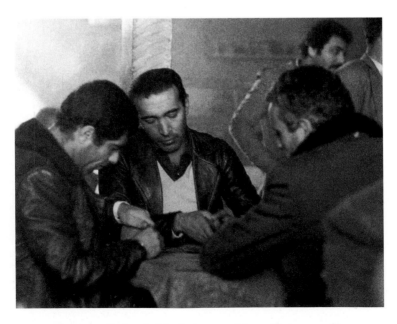

Doctor Aziz al-Abub (center) in a Beirut café.

*POWs, agent reports, Nationalist Chinese reports, our guer-
rillas, NSA intercepts, defectors and from our own returning
POWs.*

*My intelligence centered around three train loads of 450
POWs each. Two of these trainloads were confirmed over and
over, the third was not as certain. Therefore, the final figure
was "confirmed 900 and 1,200 possibly." These were the figures that I discussed with President Eisenhower while I was a
member of his National Security Council.*

*The bulk of the sightings were at Manchu-il, on the border of
Manchuria and the USSR. Here the rail gauge changed and the
U.S. POWs had to be transferred across a platform to a waiting
train going into the Soviet Union. These POWs were to be ex-
ploited for intelligence purposes and subsequently eliminated.
The methods of exploitation were not only practiced on our
POWs but all others falling into Communist hands.*

*To the sceptics and debunkers I have only this to say: by
some flashback in time I wish you could be present with me
at the prisoner exchanges in Korea in 1953 and look into
the faces of those sick and wounded prisoners — Americans
and Allied soldiers — as they came across in the exchange. If
you had witnessed their sacrifices and what they had suffered
by Communist hands, you would not be a critic or sceptic
today."*

Though there were gaps in the terrifying paper trail Buckley followed in the Olson files as he checked to make sure the
cover-up remained secure, the files inevitably led him back to
biological warfare — and the role the United States had played
while those American prisoners in the Korean War were being
experimented upon. He sent for more files.

He began by reading copies of the CIA's voluminous reports on the Soviet Union's huge stockpile of both chemical
and biological weapons at the end of World War II. These

were stored in the Ukraine, in the Ural Mountains and in the Islamic republics. In the files Buckley came across a number of World War II German intelligence files that detailed the Soviet capability in biological warfare. During World War II research had been conducted in laboratories outside Moscow. After the war, the work was transferred to the Red Army Biological Institute situated on the banks of the River Volga. Later still it had been moved to the town of Ostashkov, northeast of Moscow, where the focus was on anthrax and cholera and plague.

One report in the files described how rats were to be infected with plague and then parachuted in cages which would break-up on impact, releasing the rodents to spread the disease widely.

China had also stockpiled huge amounts of biological weapons. They had begun their biological program after 1940 when a Japanese plane had scattered rice and wheat grains saturated in anthrax over the city of Chunsein, in Chekiang province. A year later another Chinese city, Changteh in Hunan province, had been similarly sprayed, this time with bubonic plague. Scores had died from the virus. In World War II, thousands of Chinese soldiers were killed by a variety of germs released from aircraft. But China had never retaliated. With the outbreak of the Korean War, the fear had grown in Washington that Beijing would now use biological weapons. Four diseases were chosen to form biological weapons to be used by the U.S. in North Korea: anthrax, brucellosis, tularemia and psittacosis. Frank Olson had worked with all four. Buckley concluded it was this experience which had led to Olson's accompanying Gottlieb to South Korea in 1952.

Buckley studied the report of the International Scientific Commission for the Investigation of the Facts concerning Bacterial Warfare in Korea and China. Published in 1952, the 700-page report concluded that "the peoples of Korea and China did actually serve as targets for bacteriological weapons." The report listed a range of weapons that had been used against North Korea: these included fountain pens filled with infected ink; anthrax-polluted feathers; fleas, lice and mosquitoes which were carriers of the plague and yellow fever. Buckley knew from his own experience that these were all methods that Dr. Gottlieb had promoted. But how far had Frank Olson gone in assisting him? Tantalizingly the files did not say. Was the fact that Olson knew the terrible truth sufficient reason for his death — and the cover-up that Dulles was so anxious to ensure remain in place?

Frank Olson was among those sent to England to explore biological warfare with Dr. William Sargant, who later recalled to the author that Olson was "the quintessential American abroad. Everything he saw fascinated him. The food, the way people dressed, spoke and behaved. He kept saying that it was all so different back home. He was the typical apple-pie-and-salute-the-flag man. Given what I knew he did, there was something endearing about him, almost an innocence."

Working his way through the files, Buckley discovered that Olson had made several trips to Britain. On May 9, 1950, he flew into Bovingdon Airfield, an RAF base used by CIA and MI6 officers coming and going to Europe. Bovingdon is close to Porton Down. On that visit Olson spent five days there before flying out of Hendon, near London. He was back again on June 2, for another spell at Porton Down. There were hints in the files that some of those meetings had touched on the bizarre. A researcher at Porton Down told Olson he was trying to obtain a crocodile to create a poison based upon an extract from the animal's gall bladder. The crocodile had to be alive for the extract to be effective. The researcher had thought of asking Harrods, the Knightsbridge store, if their boast — "we supply everything" — extended to importing a crocodile from Africa.

The idea had been rejected by his superior as a security risk. Another chemist had come up with a plan to impregnate building cement widely used in the Soviet Union with a substance that would cause it to crumble. During those visits to Britain, Olson also collected a variety of shellfish poisons to bring back to his lab at Fort Detrick.

In May 1953, Olson was back in Europe. The entry point showed he had arrived in Liverpool on May 3. Buckley concluded the likeliest explanation was that Olson had come by ship, possibly from Norway or Sweden. Had he simply gone to Scandinavia to visit relatives? Or could there have been some other reason? There were reports that Buckley had read which suggested Dr. Gottlieb had authorized experiments to be conducted on quislings — Norwegians who had supported the Nazis in World War II. The brief hints in the files carried the restriction they could only be fully accessed on the order of director Dulles. Buckley wondered if Olson had gone to Norway to check on those experiments. Olson's 1953 visit to England included a notation in his passport that he had permission to visit the British, French and American zones in West Germany, plus the right to go to Berlin.

Before Frank Olson left England on that trip to Europe, he had dinner with Dr. Sargant in London. The psychiatrist was to recall to the author:

"Given how phlegmatic he had been in previous meetings, he seemed a little excited and perhaps even apprehensive. He said for the first time he was going to see something of how his creations worked on "expendables." Until then it transpired he had never seen what he called 'terminal trials.' I was surprised at this, given he had been doing his kind of work for so long."

Dr. Sargant suggested they should meet after Olson returned from Germany and was on his way back to the United States. It was a meeting that would settle fate Olson'.

CHAPTER NINE

When Frank Olson returned to London, Dr. Sargant was immediately struck by the psychological changes he saw in the scientist. Sargant believed that Olson had, for the first time, "come face to face with his own reality. He made no secret that he had witnessed murder being committed on those "expendables" the CIA was using in their experiments in Germany. There was a strong element of soul searching and seeking reassurance that it would be right for him to report what he had seen to his own superiors. Olson was a classic example of a research lab scientist who had seen the end result of his work," Dr. Sargant later told the author.

The one certainty is that the "expendables" would have died horrific deaths. Had Olson witnessed that? If so, it would explain much of what was to follow, beginning with the anxiety he expressed to Sargant upon his return to England.

Olson flew back to America from Northolt, an RAF base just outside London. By then Dr. Sargant had performed what he considered his duty. He had recommended to his own superiors in Britain's Secret Intelligence Service that Olson no longer have access to ongoing research at the various secret establishments he had visited in Britain. In the psychiatrist's judgment, Olson was "someone who could go to the media and reveal what was going on. Olson would see this as his patriotic duty. He didn't understand that real patriotism required he must accept what he had seen," Dr. Sargant recalled to the author. He knew his report would be passed on to Olson's superiors at the CIA. "There was no question of not doing that. We and the Americans were joined at the hip in all such matters. There were common interests to protect," he explained.

Working away in his office, Buckley continued to piece together the events that had followed upon Olson's return to Washington. There was excitement over what Dr. Gottlieb believed could be a significant breakthrough in mind control. Another of the Agency's staff researchers, Morse Allan, had been working on fungi brought back from the jungles of Central America, including the piule plant. He had crushed seeds from the plant and tested them on people George Hunter White had lured into his safe houses. Morse reported the effects of the drug in a paper to Dr. Gottlieb: "After thirty minutes anxiety became quite definite and was expressed as fear that something evil was going to happen; fear of insanity or of death. At times, subjects had the feeling they could see the blood and bones in their own bodies. They reported many fantasies in which they seemed to be elsewhere, such as taking trips to the moon or living in gorgeous castles. Several reported they felt their minds were being controlled."

Dr. Gottlieb told Dulles that these results had been reported to Olson, since he was on the need-to-know list, but Olson had shown little interest. A few days later Olson showed up in Dr. Gottlieb's office and strongly challenged the ethics of what Morse Allan had done. The meeting ended in a heated exchange. Alarmed, Dr. Gottlieb discussed the matter with Richard Helms, the tall, smooth-talking head of the Agency's Directorate of Operations. Helms told Dr. Gottlieb about the report the CIA had received from Britain's Secret Intelligence Service, MI6. It was Dr. Sargant's evaluation that Frank Olson was "deeply disturbed over what he had seen in the CIA safe houses in Germany. He had displayed symptoms of not wanting to keep secret what he had witnessed."

On the Saturday morning after he telephoned Alice Olson with the news of her husband's death, Dulles convened a meeting to go over what steps had been taken to deal with Olson upon his return from London. Helms explained Olson had been placed under close surveillance. A memo described how Dr. Gottlieb had perceived a "sea-change" in him. "Olson was no longer cheerful, but had become withdrawn. He was a man with something on his mind." Dr. Gottlieb arranged for one of the CIA psychologists to see Olson in his lab. There was nothing unusual in such visits; he often sent psychologists to see how researchers were coping with the undoubted stress of their work. The psychologist reported he found nothing untoward in Olson's behavior. On that note, Dulles ended the meeting.

In the days leading upto Olson's death, Dr. Gottlieb had been focusing his search for mind control on one substance: LSD. The indications were that even a speck of the drug could produce dramatic results. Subjects lost their inhibitions, abandoned their pretensions and spoke their inner thoughts freely. Solid, sane men became temporarily crazy; women free with their bodies. A man whose drink had been spiked with LSD suddenly "saw rainbows coming out of the ground. Then monsters emerged from walls. He fell to the floor and said he would admit anything if this would stop," Dr. Gottlieb had observed.

A number of those tested showed marked symptoms of paranoia. After having the drug slipped to him in a CIA Washington safe house, one man had rushed out into the street, and tried to remove all his clothes. He had been overpowered by colleagues and held in a strait jacket until he recovered. Another man believed he was the only survivor of a nuclear holocaust and over the course of several hours recited his entire life, in the belief he was talking directly to God. These encouraging results led Dr. Gottlieb to believe he should use Frank Olson as his next guinea pig. It would be the ideal opportunity to test his reliability. Buckley had found the "smoking gun."

Early in November of that 1953, Olson was invited to attend a three-day seminar to review the latest stage of the MK-ULTRA program. On the eighteenth of the month, Olson drove out to Deep Creek Lodge, a stone-walled cabin deep in the woods of western Maryland. Close to a lake with the peaks of the Appalachian Mountains as a backdrop, the lodge was a secure safe house. Two other senior men from Fort Detrick, Dr. John Schwab and Lt. Colonel Vincent Ruwet, were already there when Olson arrived. Dr. Gottlieb — who would host the seminar — arrived with his deputy, Dr. Robert Lashbrook and Richard Helms. Frank Olson found the others gathered in the lodge's spacious living room, standing before a log fire in the walk-in fireplace. In all there were a dozen people invited to the seminar. George Hunter White was among those present, as well as other men trained in the art of assassination.

Dr. Gottlieb gave an introductory address, explaining the problems with mind control that had still to be faced, but he said he was confident they would be overcome. Over dinner, Dr. Gottlieb made a point of seating Olson next to him. During the meal the talk was mostly about Olson's impression of life in Britain. He believed the country was on its way back to recovery.

One of the Fort Detrick team, Benjamin Wilson, sensed that Dr. Gottlieb was making "a real effort to integrate Olson into the group." He asked him about Alice and his three kids. Frank began to reminisce about how he had met his wife when they were both students at the University of Wisconsin. Helms asked if Olson was still playing practical jokes and everyone laughed when Frank said he didn't have time nowadays, Helms would later recall to the author.

Dinner over, Dr. Gottlieb invited everyone to join him in a nightcap. White acted as barman, making a show of writing down each man's preference. Olson chose a Cointreau. Wilson was to recall that Olson swallowed it in one mouthful, then bade everyone goodnight and went to bed. During the next day the gathering divided up into groups which Gottlieb, Schwab and Ruwet addressed. These meetings were devoted to such matters as the efficacy of suicide pills made from shellfish toxin and the effect of brucellosis. Dr. Gottlieb then gathered them all together once more and gave a detailed analysis of the work Dr. Cameron was doing in Montreal.

Dinner followed the same seating plan as the previous night. Dr. Gottlieb led a lively discussion on an article in the *Washington Post* attacking the use of dogs for experimental purposes. The newspaper's robust defense of the canines had created high amusement around the table. After the meal, Dr. Gottlieb once more invited everyone to join him in a drink. Showing his bartending skills, White had everyone's drinks waiting on a tray. He handed Olson a glass of Cointreau. The drink had been spiked by White on Dr. Gottlieb's orders. It contained a substantial amount of LSD. The most graphic account of what followed came from Benjamin Wilson. His account was transcribed in the files Buckley was reading:

"After about twenty minutes, Olson asked us if we had noticed anything wrong. He kept saying he couldn't understand what was happening to him. He said someone was playing tricks on him. He kept saying 'You guys are a bunch of thespians'. He was really weird. He sat down, stood up, and said people were watching him."

Dr. Gottlieb tried to question Olson. Was his reference to "thespians" connected with friends he had made in the media? Had he spoken to his Congressman about his last trip to England? What had he told Dr. Sargant? Frank Olson kept saying,

"You are all a bunch of spies," and "I mustn't speak to you."
He drove home, still in the grip of the drug. Alice would remember how he sat on the davenport in their living room. "He said nothing. No greeting. No 'How are the kids?' No question on how my day had been. Just nothing. He sat there, just silent."

This was not the Frank she knew. For the first time Alice became "a little frightened. Something had happened to Frank, something he couldn't or wouldn't speak about." When she put the children to bed, she found Frank slumped on the davenport. Alice asked him, "Did you break security?"

"No."

"Did you falsify data?"

"No."

"Well, you've nothing to worry about," Alice said.

Olson abruptly stood up and said he needed a shower. This was also unusual. Normally he never took a shower at home because regulations required he did so at Fort Detrick before entering or leaving his lab. After showering, he came back down to the living room and sat once more on the davenport holding Alice's hand. "He was in a world of his own and I was damned scared," Alice remembered.

The next day, a Sunday, he remained in the grip of this torpor. Outside the weather was as depressing as his mood. Alice tried to lift his spirits by suggesting they could all go to the movies. Ironically, the film turned out to be *Luther*, about a man confronting an all-powerful institution. Olson came home and went to bed without saying a word. Next morning he left home. telling Alice he had an "important decision to take care of." Before she could question him, he was out of the house and on his way to Fort Detrick. Arriving there, he entered the office of his boss, Colonel Ruwet. Before Ruwet could speak, Olson was leaning over his desk and, close to shouting, said "You either fire me or I quit."

According to his own statement, Ruwet spent the morning trying to "get to the bottom of Olson's agitation. I kept saying there was no need for him to quit, and I had no reason to fire him. Frank kept saying, 'Are you sure?' After a while he calmed down and I suggested he should take off the rest of the day." Instead, Olson went to his lab and worked until it was time to go home. Alice was relieved to find he was in a lighter mood, joking and laughing and playing a board game with the children. Whatever had caused the crisis seemed to be over. Olson went to bed and slept deeply. But next morning he awoke unusually early and drove to Fort Detrick. Ruwet arrived at the office to find Olson pacing up and down "like a caged animal."

Olson started to say he was "all screwed up. . .that he should never have done what he had done…that he was not the right person for the job. It was an endless catalogue of his imagined failures," Ruwet later recalled. After failing to calm him, Ruwet decided that Olson needed "professional help." He called Dr. Gottlieb who spoke to Dr. Lashbrook. They decided to send Olson to a doctor named Harold Abramson who had a private practice in New York. Although Abramson had no formal training in psychiatry, he had a high security clearance with the CIA. He was an allergist and immunologist who was interested in what he called "problems of the mind." Dr. Gottlieb had chosen Abramson because he had been working with LSD for some months, conducting experiments on selected patients for the MK-ULTRA program.

Ruwet and Lashbrook drove Olson to New York. During the car journey the biochemist displayed severe mood swings; one moment he was joking with them, the next accusing them of plotting against him. "He kept saying we were out to get him," Ruwet would later say.

The three men checked into the Statler Hotel near Penn Station in New York. George Hunter White had made the reservations. That evening a man answering White's physical description was seen in the hotel lobby by a hotel guest. The witness spoke years later to Eric Olson about "the person." At ten thirty that night, Dr. Abramson took the elevator to Olson's room. Lashbrook and Ruwet were waiting. From his bag, Abramson produced a bottle of bourbon and a vial of Nembutal sedatives. He ordered Olson to take a swig from the bottle and two of the tablets. In a phone call to Dr. Gottlieb, Lashbrook admitted this was "kind of unusual to give to someone with depression."

Dr. Gottlieb suggested that in the morning Lashbrook and Ruwet should take Olson to see a New York magician named John Mulholland. Dr. Gottlieb had recently enlisted his services so that he could "apply the magician's skills to covert activities." He wanted Mulholland to teach agents how to slip drugs into drinks and "deliver various materials to unwitting subjects."

In the CIA files, Buckley discovered what happened when Olson and his two companions turned up at the magician's home. Mulholland began to perform, pulling a rabbit out of his hat and discovering a silver dollar behind Olson's ear. This triggered an outburst with Olson insisting the coin was poisoned. To prove it wasn't, the magician bit down on it. Olson demanded they leave at once because Mulholland was probably in the pay of the Russians. Lashbrook and Ruwet dropped the biochemist off at Abramson's office, having arranged to meet him back at the Statler. Olson spent an hour with the doctor who said he was showing "signs of good recovery" and should go home to his family the following day, Thanksgiving.

Olson returned to the hotel. Ruwet made reservations for them to catch a plane next morning. In the meantime, following Dr. Gottlieb's order to "keep on coming up with diversions," Lashbrook booked them all to see the Rodgers and Hammerstein hit, *Me and Juliet*. They had barely taken their seats before

Olson began to shout that "Outside there are people waiting to arrest me for what I have done." Bewildered theater-goers watched Ruwet hurry Olson from the auditorium. Lashbrook remained to watch the show, according to his statement in the CIA file. Back at the Statler, Ruwet decided it was prudent to occupy the spare bed in Olson's room. But he soon fell asleep and did not see Olson leave the hotel. It was reported that Olson had wandered around Manhattan tearing up his money and finally throwing away his wallet, which contained his Fort Detrick pass and ID. Having searched all night for him, Lashbrook returned to the hotel at 5.30 AM. At some point White joined the search, checking the safe houses to which he had previously taken Olson. Later when Olson returned to the hotel, White arranged for a limousine to drive the three men to La Guardia airport to catch their flight back to Washington. White also arranged for a CIA driver to meet the flight and take Olson home to Frederick. Arriving at Washington's National Airport, Ruwet thought it "sensible" to accompany Olson home.

As the CIA car made its way up Wisconsin Avenue, Olson ordered the driver to pull into a motel parking lot. He turned to Ruwet and began to weep, saying he was fearful that if he returned home, he would attack his wife and children. He could feel this inner compulsion to do so, Ruwet later claimed Olson had said. The documents in the CIA files, also described how Ruwet had become sufficiently alarmed at Olson's behavior to order the driver to take them to Lashbrook's home off Dupont Circle. Given the state Olson was in, Lashbrook telephoned Dr. Gottlieb. He ordered Lashbrook to accompany Olson back to New York to see Dr. Abramson. Meanwhile Ruwet was to drive out to Frederick to explain to Alice Olson what was happening. He decided to call Alice in the morning.

Lashbrook and Olson flew back to La Guardia and then took a cab to Abramson's home. He said he had never seen a case like this, that Olson was "in a psychotic state… filled with persecution mania." Lashbrook now took the initiative. He called a private mental hospital in Maryland and spoke to a young psychiatrist on the staff, Dr. Robert Gibson who agreed Olson could be admitted. But Lashbrook had less success with flights out of New York to Washington. None were available until the following morning. Lashbrook booked them in for another night on the 10th floor of the Statler.

Seven hours later, Frank Olson was dead.

When he had heard this recital of the facts in his office on the following Saturday morning, Dulles asked how it was that, sleeping in the next bed no more than a couple of feet away, Lashbrook had not heard Olson get up, go to the opposite end of the room, turn and run toward the window and plunge through the drawn blinds and the closed window to his death? Lashbrook had no explanation other than he was in the bathroom when Olson had gone through the window. Dulles looked at each man seated before him in his office and said nothing for a while. Then he had turned to Richard Helms, the senior man present, and said: "This mess needs sorting out. I want it done properly and I want it done quickly." The cover up had officially begun.

The first step was to make sure that Ruwet, Lashbrook and Dr. Gottlieb told the same story at the internal CIA enquiry that would follow. They agreed Olson's death would be presented as suicide. Abramson was told by Lashbrook to stay with the same story. Ruwet visited Alice Olson. He told her that it was a personal tragedy that he had not realized that Frank "my good friend, had overworked himself to the point where he had lost control of the values which had always guided him." It was just "a terrible, terrible tragedy," Ruwet repeated. Alice Olson, gracious even in grief, politely said she could not accept that Frank had killed himself; he had so much to live for. He adored his children, especially young Eric, who was so like him in looks and mannerisms. By the time Ruwet left the family, Dr. Gottlieb had contacted George Hunter White. The man who had served Olson his spiked drink and who had a reputation for killing with his fist was told to make sure he had left no trace of his presence in New York.

The suicide story satisfied the press. Alice Olson received no calls. The funeral was a large one and included a number of colleagues from Fort Detrick, led by Ruwet. Dr. Gottlieb and Lashbrook also came to the service and watched Olson's coffin go into its grave.

Two weeks later, Dr. Gottlieb telephoned Alice. He wanted to come to the house with Lashbrook. She still did not know who either of them was; Frank had never mentioned them. She asked who they worked for and Dr. Gottlieb said "We are with the government." Alice was so nervous in their presence that her hands were shaking, and she could scarcely hold her coffee cup. Alice Olson did not ask the questions other widows might have. What had Frank been doing in New York? Why had no one at work noticed his odd behavior? Why had she not been allowed to see his body in the coffin? Why had no one from the New York police department contacted her? How had they decided so quickly that it was suicide? There were no answers. Not yet.

Nor were the complete details of what had transpired to be found in the files Buckley was immersed in. If fell to Eric, Frank and Alices son, to unearth the full story. In Eric Olson was endowed with the ability to ask questions. From the day his father had died, Eric had taken on the role of head of the family, comforting his mother, his brother Nils and sister Lisa. Not only had his father been taken from him, but Eric had also been robbed of his own childhood. He grew up asking himself the kind of questions his mother "may have tortured herself with privately." He could see what the death of his father was doing to her, eventually driving her to alcoholism. She had begun to meet regularly with Vincent Ruwet. She considered Ruwet's companionship as "an act of kindness and support." Neither she nor Eric knew until much later that Ruwet had been instructed by Dulles "to keep track of the wife."

Eric embarked upon a career in psychology; during a class at Harvard he learned about the connection between alcoholism and repressed grief. He arranged for his mother to undergo therapy. Alice began to recover and played a key role in creating a halfway house for recovering alcoholics in Frederick.

Eric recounted that on entering analysis his first dream was "of me probing the upholstery of an old chair for a coat which had belonged to my father. The analyst said that the dream should be interpreted as 'my coming into my father's legacy.'"

On the afternoon of June 12, 1975, Eric sat, completely stunned, after reading the front page of the *Washington Post*. Prominently displayed was an account of his father's death, twenty-two years before. With the help of his family, Eric arranged a press conference in the backyard of the family home on July 9, 1975. Reporters came from all over America to hear Eric, Nils and Lisa demand full disclosure of all relevant information about their father's death. The story was carried on the three major networks and made front page news around the world.

On July 21, 1975, President Ford publicly apologized to the Olson family and said he was rushing a bill through Congress that would provide the family with $1.5 million compensation. Behind the scenes, Gottlieb and Lashbrook sought to avoid full disclosure by buying the Olsons' silence.

For the family the settlement was followed by yet another personal tragedy. In March 1978, Lisa, pregnant with her second child, died with her husband and their small son in a plane crash near Lake Placid. Thankfully, the tragedy did not drive Alice back to drink.

With the settlement paid — in the end it had been cut in half to $750,000 by the House of Representatives — Eric Olson embarked on his own investigation into his father's still mysterious death. He spent a night in the Statler, room 1018A, which his father occupied on the night he died. He was "overwhelmed" by the possibility that his father had been thrown to his death, but he kept such thoughts to himself.

On August 19, 1993, Alice Olson died from cancer. Eric felt he had a duty to discover the truth she had gone to her grave without knowing. He went to see an old family friend, Professor James Starrs, Professor of Law and Forensic Science at George Washington University. He wanted to know if it was possible to have Frank Olson's body exhumed and if Starrs would conduct a forensic examination of his death. Starrs agreed.

On June 2, 1994, Frank Olson's body was exhumed. The CIA issued a statement repeating that Frank Olson's death had been a "tragic event and we have no indication whatsoever to suspect that homicide was involved." Eric was there to watch his father's concrete burial vault hoisted from its hillside tomb at Frederick Memorial Park in Maryland. The emotion on his face was raw as he saw the dark wooden coffin removed from the asphalt sealed vault, then wrapped in black vinyl and loaded into a van.

When the time came to open the coffin, Starrs took Eric aside. Concerned Eric might become more upset, Starrs urged him to leave. From experience, the pathologist knew there was a good chance that a gruesome shrunken cadaver lay inside the coffin. When the coffin lid was removed, Starrs was "very surprised at what we found. Frank Olson's skin was brown and shrunken, but he was clearly recognizable and looked good after all this long time," he told the author. More important for the pathologist, there was an absence of cuts on Frank Olson's head or neck, "which I would have expected if he had shattered the window as he jumped. Most stunning was the large bruise above Olson's left eye near the temple which to me immediately suggested a blow to the head of great force," said Starrs.

Eric Olson continued his investigation noting every twist and fragment of evidence in his files. On July 26, 1994, he met Ike Feldman at the Marriott Hotel in Uniondale, Long Island. Feldman had supplied a number of the prostitutes used in MK-ULTRA's safe houses. He introduced himself as "a close associate of Sidney Gottlieb and George Hunter White." It was not the first time Eric Olson had heard White's name. Feldman sketched in some of White's background. Then he stunned Eric Olson by saying that Frank Olson had been murdered. He wouldn't say any more and shuffled out of the motel leaving Eric Olson with the impression Feldman felt he "had said too much already."

Filled with what he admitted later was "a mixture of horror and excitement," Eric Olson hurried back to Washington to brief his lawyer, Harry Huge, on what he had been told. The lawyer pointed out that under the terms of the settlement President Ford had announced, the Olson family had forfeited all rights to a civil suit unless they could prove fraud on the part of the government. Huge, a powerful and much respected figure in American law circles, said the way forward was to persuade New York District Attorney Robert Morganthau to open a criminal investigation "based upon suspicion of homicide" for which there was no statute of limitation.

On November 28, 1994, after almost six months of forensic examination, Professor Starrs concluded Frank Olson's death "was rankly and starkly suggestive of homicide." His conclusion was based on the fist-sized hole on the left side of the skull.

It was a blow which could have been caused by the type of blow that George Hunter White had often used. The hematoma on the skull had convinced Starrs that Frank Olson had been hit prior to exiting the window. The evidence of the blow was reinforced by the details in Dr. Gottlieb's Assassination Manual. Eric made note: "the most effective way to disguise a murder and make it look like an accident or suicide was first to hit the victim in the head, at precisely the place where Starrs had discovered the hole in my father's skull, and then to drop the subject from a high window. It bore the hallmark of a White killing."

By now Eric knew a great deal more about George Hunter White.

In 1950 the CIA sent White to Europe to help find suitable "expendables" among the sizeable number of SS and Gestapo officers held in a number of prisons. White headed a team of interrogators who, having selected suitable "expendables" would subject them to torture. Some of those selected were women. Ostensibly this rough treatment was to learn more about their wartime activities. Having tortured them to a point where no further information was forthcoming, White then handed over the "expendables" to the CIA operatives working in the MK-ULTRA program in Germany. Buckley told the author that he was sure some of those "expendables" were ones Frank Olson had witnessed being subjected to a variety of terminal experiments shortly before his death.

After a stint hunting magic mushrooms in South America, White returned to Europe. He became a member of a CIA-driven operation centered in a compound outside the German city of Frankfurt. The building was known as "Hotel Himmler." The experiments conducted there were part of the MK-ULTRA project known as "Artichoke." This program used human subjects who would be shot full of drugs, including biological agents, and then killed if they survived and could serve no further purpose.

Eric Olson discovered that for George Hunter White some of those doomed victims provided him with a means to practice his own skills as a trained killer. Crude and ruthless, devoid of the slightest scruple, he was far removed from the fine manners and veneer of respectability that Dr. Gottlieb cultivated. White was the man who delivered what Dr. Gottlieb required. Eric now felt certain that White was the man selected to murder Frank Olson and that he had used one of the methods detailed in the CIA Assassination Manual that Dr. Gottlieb had authored: a single blow to the head. According to Eric Olson's reconstruction, what happened was this: White entered Frank Olson's room in the early hours of that November morning. He had, almost certainly, gained access to Room 1018A by using a pass key. Either he had obtained it from a contact in the hotel — he boasted of having one in every Manhattan hotel — or the Statler had been chosen because it was easy for White to come and go undetected. Lashbrook — either by chance or design — had placed himself in the bathroom. White delivered his fatal blow and then hurled Olson out of the window. By the time the former night manager, Armand Pastore, had run out into the street, White had made good his escape, possibly by using the stairs. It was a route prostitutes often used when attending to hotel guests.

But legal proof was needed. Eric Olson persuaded the Manhattan district attorney, Robert Morgenthau, to re-open an investigation into Frank Olson's death. Morgenthau assigned an experienced prosecutor from his cold-case office, Steve Sorocco. The problems Sorocco faced began almost at once. Former CIA director William Colby, a key witness to what had happened to Olson, disappeared. His body was eventually found after what appeared to be a boating accident. Then Lashbrook fought off Sorocco's subpoena to testify, claiming frailty and "memory lapses."

It was only in July 2002 that the full extent of the cover-up about Frank Olson finally surfaced. Documents obtained by the author show that Vice-President Dick Cheney and Secretary of Defense Donald Rumsfeld had at one time been deeply involved in keeping the truth secret. Deposited in the Gerald Ford library, and written by Cheney and Rumsfeld, the memos fully justify Eric Olson's claim that both men had been "linked to the murder of my father."

Cheney and Rumsfeld had the task of covering up the details of Frank Olson's death. At the time, Rumsfeld was White House Chief of Staff to President Gerald Ford. Dick Cheney was a senior White House Assistant. The documents include one that states: "Dr. Olson's job was so sensitive that it is highly unlikely that we would submit relevant evidence." In another memo, Cheney acknowledges that "the Olson lawyers will seek to explore all the circumstances of Dr. Olson's employment, as well as those concerning his death. In any trial, it may become apparent that we are concealing evidence for national security reasons and any settlement or judgment reached thereafter could be perceived as money paid to cover up the activities of the CIA."

Both the offices of Rumsfeld and Cheney continued to decline in 2006 to comment on their role in the murder of Frank Olson. But Eric Olson said the documents involving Rumsfeld and Cheney "show they have questions to answer. The documents show the lengths to which the government was going to cover up the truth. For decades there was a cover up. And then, under the guise of revealing everything, there was a new cover up."

It was a verdict that William Buckley had long ago come to support.

Throughout his assignment to look into the events surrounding Olson's death Buckley had been taking copious notes.

When he finished reading the Olson files, he took a day to write his report to Dulles recommending that the files be sealed and marked to be opened only by the incumbent director. He took the files and his report to Dulles' suite and handed them over to the director. Dulles thanked him, lit his pipe and settled back to read the report. Putting it aside, Dulles thanked Buckley again and said he was being returned to duties in Dr. Gottlieb's department.

Years later, when the author had established a relationship with Buckley, the CIA officer showed him the original notepad which he had kept in the trunk of books and papers which accompanied him to all his postings. The notes helped Buckley to recall the events leading to the death of Frank Olson. He said: "I have no doubt White murdered Olson." By then White was dead.

On November 20, 1998, at the request of Steve Sorocco, the New York public prosecutor investigating the murder of Frank Olson, the author provided him with a statement that included both the information Buckley had provided and details of the author's interviews with Dr. William Sargant. The statement reads in part: "He [Sargant] could remember exact details with compelling clarity. For instance, we once had an esoteric conversation on how Patty Hearst, at whose trial Dr. Sargant had been an expert witness, would have survived some of the techniques the CIA had developed in mind manipulation. From time to time he referred to the 'murder of Frank Olson' and expressed the view that from all he had learned through his own intelligence contacts in London and Washington, there was a strong 'prima facie' case for murder. Dr. Sargant, while granting me permission to use his material, stipulated it could only be published after his death. He died in 1988." The statement gave a detailed account of Olson's murder, as provided by Dr. Sargant and William Buckley. Both saw the murder as "a classic operation."

In January 1999, Sorocco told the author that the statement was going to be valuable in arguing his case before the grand jury that Dr. Gottlieb should be charged with Frank Olson's murder.

The public prosecutor was still pursuing the case when Dr. Gottlieb died. Sorocco closed the file. He told the author: "There is no more I can do."

CHAPTER TEN

William Buckley appreciated the fine spring weather as he made his way up Mount Royal to the Institute. The trip was a welcome relief from the tensions within the CIA over the effect of "mechanical" intelligence-gathering on traditional methods. Buckley had been among those officers who believed "gadgets cannot divine man's intentions." But there was a powerful lobby at the Agency that held that satellites would gather far more important data than any human agent could obtain.

Buckley's brief on that April morning in 1957 was to make sure that MK-ULTRA Project 68 was not going to attract undue attention. Project 68 was designed to replicate what Dr. Cameron believed were the physical conditions under which U.S. prisoners made their confessions to their North Korean captors. He had created an interrogation center in the basement of the hospital. Buckley arrived at the Institute to find that the basement area, on Dr. Cameron's orders, was now off-limits to all staff except two of his assistants Leonard Rubenstein and Jan Zielinski. Dr. Cameron greeted his visitor with "cold politeness." Buckley assumed it was because Dulles had rejected the demand Buckley should be removed. Before coming to Montreal, Dr. Gottlieb told Buckley he had sent Dr. Cameron a letter stating that Buckley was to stay on board with MK-ULTRA.

Dr. Cameron's program called for patients to remain in the basement for weeks, even months. He now believed the North Koreans had selected only those prisoners who could be reduced to a state of infantile dependency, and consequently ready to accept their interrogators' views. Dr. Cameron intended to emulate the North Korean methods by stripping his patients of their selfhood and introducing into their minds what he wanted them to believe. That they were already mentally ill made the challenge greater. The Chinese had only had to deal with healthy fighting men. He would have the infinitely harder task of brainwashing those who were disturbed, often seriously so. By successfully manipulating their psychological mechanisms, he was certain he could solve the mystery of mind control.

Cameron had been encouraged by Dr. William Sargant, many of whose own observations had been applied by English police interrogators and employed by Britain's intelligence service. Dr. Cameron had carefully noted that one method Dr. Sargant approved was "having found a sore spot, to keep on touching it." He wrote it was also important to make a person fill in long questionnaires. "This is intended to fatigue him further rather than produce new information of value. When his memory begins to fail him, the difficulty in keeping to the same story makes him more anxious than ever."

Dr. Cameron said he planned to start his tests later in the day. In the meantime, he suggested Buckley should catch up on other research going on at the Institute.

Buckley spent the rest of the day visiting well-endowed research laboratories. In one he found Dr. Cleghorn measuring the corticoid output in the urine of a number of his patients. It was another way to evaluate stress. On previous visits, Buckley had established a sufficient rapport with Dr. Cameron's deputy to convince Dr. Cleghorn that he could be trusted. Now, as Buckley watched the doctor setting up an experiment, he was not altogether surprised to be told of new dissension between the psychoanalysts on staff and the psychiatrists who sought cures with drugs and electroshocks. The psychiatrists had little patience with their analytical colleagues whose methods depended almost totally on observation. While Dr. Cleghorn admitted psychoanalysis had the structure of a science, he believed it had little value in supporting drug-oriented treatments. The analysts doggedly clung to their belief that patients could be helped through being encouraged to reveal themselves to an attentive, patient and sympathetic physician. They spoke of "the danger of chemicals" and electroshock destroying that region of the mind where thoughts, feelings, impulses, wishes and instinctual drives exist, awaiting to "be properly motivated under analysis." The latest disagreement between both factions had been over "transference neurosis." The psychiatrists doubted if it really existed. The analysts said not only did it exist, but its comprehension was vital, adding that often the extent of physical treatment — especially electroshock — ruined any chance they had of a successful follow-up.

Buckley had already seen that Dr. Cameron encouraged dissension; he thought the squabbling made for "better doctors." And, like Allan Dulles, he had long known the advantages of ruling over a divided house. Bickering between the factions had increased with the opening of still more research units. Doctors eminent in their fields found themselves cramped together, fighting for space and for the merits of their theories. That had heightened speculation over what was going on in the basement. The consensus was that Dr. Cameron was setting up another of his "projects." He had sometimes said he would like nothing better than the chance to pursue all his theories free from the responsibility of administering what amounted to a sizeable corporation; ultimately hundreds of people answered to him.

Robert Cleghorn told Buckley that no one believed for a moment Ewen Cameron would ever willingly relinquish his unique position. At times, his deputy wondered what drove Dr. Cameron. It couldn't be money; he was wealthy enough. There was not a door closed to him in the medical world, and he was probably more powerful than many Canadian politicians. He could drum up money in a way few professional fund-raisers could match. So what was it? That question increasingly puzzled Dr. Cleghorn. And, he confided to Buckley, he did not like the way Dr. Cameron cajoled, maneuvered and — where need be — exploited his staff in a dazzling display of medical politics, supporting one group against another and then, just as quickly, switching sides. He was promoter and concert master of an orchestra that often played brilliantly, but rarely in complete harmony.

Doctors came and went. Mary Morrow had gone to another hospital in Montreal, and Dr. Cleghorn was hopeful she would find a niche for herself once she learned to handle her anxieties. If he had taught her nothing else, he was certain he had impressed her with the belief that psychiatry was no place for someone with a nervous disposition.

In other labs Buckley found researchers investigating, among much else, the extent to which emotional distress produced cardiac pain in some patients and whether this was caused by a diminished blood supply to the heart through vasoconstriction, or a sudden demand for oxygen because of an anxiety attack.

One team studied phobic reactions — intense emotional experiences that can be psychologically crippling. One clinician correlated the links between the obsessions some of the patients displayed and their uneven sleep patterns. Another tabulated the link between raised blood pressure and anxiety. He was trying to quantify pressure fluctuations when patients were asked about matters intended to agitate them: questions about their sex lives, families and relationships.

Dr. Charles Shagass continued to probe the quantity of barbiturate needed to induce sleep in various categories of mental illness. His research would eventually receive worldwide recognition as the sedative threshold test. Dr. Hassam Azima, rumored to be a blood relative of the Shah of Iran, was preparing psychological tests designed to tailor occupational therapy to individual psychiatric conditions. Tall and darkly handsome, the Iranian sometimes reminded Buckley of the skipper of an Arab dhow running before the wind, rather than a scientist whose capability was only limited by the amount of money that could be charmed out of the Society for the Investigation of Human Ecology.

Much of the research would take years to produce results; some of it would be abandoned. All of it ultimately depended on the whim of Dr. Cameron. He was the final arbiter of which projects needed his fund-raising skills. In Dr. Cleghorn's opinion this was not an ideal situation, because the Institute's chief doctor usually allowed himself little time to fully assess the merits of each proposed research project. Sometimes he made snap judgments, often on the move, going from ward to treatment room, pausing to listen briefly to a researcher waiting in a corridor. Once he had come to a decision, he could not be budged. Anyone who persisted was moved to the outer reaches of the empire Dr. Cameron had created. This empire, known as the McGill Psychiatric Training Network, embraced eight Montreal hospitals, had its own diploma course in psychiatry and gave its founder more power than any other doctor in the city. That too worried Robert Cleghorn.

Dr. Eve Lester, soon to become one of the youngest professors on the McGill faculty, worked with disturbed adolescent patients. Other researchers were measuring the body heat of schizophrenics, the effect of physical pain on depressives, the change of electrical brain waves during insulin treatment, the effect of small doses of adrenalin on certain of the higher mental functions. One scientist was preparing a study into nocturnal delirium. A therapist was studying the speech patterns of psychotics, while a behaviorist charted the changes in chronically tense people.

As usual, Buckley visited the Institute's well-stocked library to check on any new papers Dr. Cameron had deposited. There were boxes of such papers, each with catchy titles like *Remembering Not to Forget*, *Research and Society*, and *Psychiatry and the Citizen*. Buckley had found the theories readily understandable. There was none of the cant that marred so many of other papers he had read. In his writing as in everything else he did, there was a certainty about Dr. Cameron. His books were equally clear and persuasive. Dr. Cleghorn pointed out, however, that the chief doctor avoided crediting others who had often done crucial preliminary work, and he found this a revealing insight into Dr. Cameron's personality. More worrying to the deputy medical director was Dr. Cameron's obsession with "psychic driving." Cameron had created his own terminology to describe the treatments: "auto-psychic driving," "heteropsychic driving," "dynamic implant," "cue repetitions." To Dr. Cleghorn the language was nonsensical. Dr. Cameron had even promoted "psychic driving" through the columns of *Weekend Magazine*, a mass circulation tabloid normally preoccupied with the lives of movie stars and offering household hints. He had referred to the technique as "beneficial brainwashing." Accompanying the interview was a photograph of a young woman wearing headphones and the caption described her listening to her repeated "confession." Cameron was credited with inventing "a daring idea designed to help neurotic patients." He was quoted as saying: "Patients, like prisoners of the Communists, tended to resist and must be broken down."

Dr. Cleghorn was horrified by such statements. He told Buckley he had begun to feel equally concerned about his superior's use of multiple and massive electroshocks, for which Dr. Cameron had also created a special word, "depatterning." Dr. Cleghorn saw no long-term benefit in a treatment in which a patient was first put to sleep for three days and then, still comatose, given between thirty to sixty electroshocks over a short period and, in between, received doses of 1,000 milligrams of Largactil to combat anxiety.

It had disturbed Dr. Cleghorn's sense of medical propriety that, when he finally queried the total amnesia produced in patients by the treatment, the chief doctor had said the patients' families would have to "help them build a scaffold of normal events." For Dr. Cleghorn, "This word from the building trade was hardly appropriate and explained nothing — and scaffolds did fall with dire consequences." His sentiments had not improved the cooling relationship between the two most senior doctors in the hospital. All this Buckley filed away in his mind for the next report he would write when he returned to Washington.

Buckley's Washington office began to resemble a library, with books and journals overflowing from his desk onto the floor. The more he read, the more concerned he became about what Dr. Cameron was trying to accomplish in Montreal. But mindful of the psychiatrist's high standing with Dulles and Gottlieb, Buckley kept his thoughts to himself.

From the beginning the psychiatrist had presented himself to Buckley as a pioneer. But increasingly Buckley discovered that much of what Dr. Cameron was postulating had been adapted from the work of radical medical theorists. One was Frank Kellman, who had been the chief of psychiatric research at the New York State Psychiatric Institute and later professor of psychiatry at Columbia. Kellman had trained in Germany at the time Hitler came to power. During his studies in Berlin, Dr. Kellman had supported more radical sterilization measures than even the Nazis were to advocate. He wanted to sterilize "every possible member of any family tainted with schizophrenia and any person showing signs of eccentricity or minor anomalies that might suggest a latent gene for the disease."

Returning to the United States, Dr. Kellman had laid out a horrifying agenda in *Eugenical News* in 1938: "Even the most extreme eugenic measures at present accepted in this country would hardly dent the problem of eradicating the bad genes from our society. The only solution is to sterilize all the relatives of known carriers of such genes and prevent the marriages of all such patients. There must be legal power to sterilize tainted children and siblings of schizophrenics and to so prevent marriages involving schizoid eccentrics and borderline cases."

Dr. Cameron had enthused to Buckley that Dr. Kellman had been "a man before his time; someone to take seriously and admire for his courage and foresight." Increasingly Buckley wondered if that was how Dr. Cameron saw himself: as the natural successor to men like Dr. Kellman.

Dr. Cameron had given Buckley glimpses of a future world in which electroshock treatment would be used to, "for instance reprogram the mind of a woman and make her a more suitable housewife." He had spoken of his "search to successfully eradicate an identity or personality in order to reprogram it and called this 'memory loosening' and described how the infantile state produced by the electroshock made a patient amenable to drastic change." Dr. Cameron had said if the CIA would provide more funding, he could start a series of "clinical trials" to see if it was possible, through electroshock, to actually create new personalities that would "last for many years in a person."

Buckley had noted: "He called this 'psychosynthesis,' which he described as a therapeutic union, combining the psychodynamics of Freud with cybernetics and ECT for the transformation of a disordered personality into an ordered one."

Dr. Gottlieb turned down the request for funding this particular experiment. He told Buckley that he wanted Dr. Cameron to focus on brainwashing.

Returning to Washington, Buckley noted that Dr. Cameron was "increasingly, in my view, concerned about using fear as a means of creating suggestibility. For instance, I noticed on his desk was a copy of the book, *A Many Splendored Thing* by the writer Han Suyin. When I asked about the book, he insisted on reading me a passage. 'For Man will always strive to conquer the world, to establish the will of Man in the name of his God.' To the Communists each individual is a fortress to be taken by spiritual struggle alone. They are out to conquer souls and the bodies will follow."

Peggy Mielke, the head nurse on the Institute's South-Two Ward, a trim, vivacious twenty-four year old, sometimes wondered if her concerns over the Sleep Room — a dormitory of twenty beds kept in continuous semi-darkness and situated at one end of the wing — was no more than her inability to find an answer to a nagging question. Had she spent her years of training to end up working in this strange twilight world, supervising a treatment she had never read about in her textbooks or seen in any of the other psychiatric hospitals where she had nursed? Beyond the closed door of the dormitory, she could hear the sounds of the Institute going through its daily routine. The first of several thousand tablets were being dispensed and swallowed. The contents of ampules were being drawn up into syringes before being injected into veins and muscles; gel was being smeared on temples, electroshocks administered. It was a world Nurse Mielke understood. But in the Sleep Room each day was undistinguishable from the last. Some of the nurses called the place "the Zombie Tomb."

Nurse Mielke stood inside the dormitory door adjusting her eyes to the gloom and smell of chemicals and human odors. Some patients lay inert, listening to instructions endlessly repeated from speakers under their pillows. Sometimes they whimpered unintelligibly at the sound of their own recorded voices or Dr. Cameron's. Others shuffled around the dormitory wearing specially adapted football helmets. A few sat at the table in the center of the room being spoon-fed by nurses, oblivious of anything except the tapes being played through their helmets.

It was those helmets that had first given rise to Nurse Mielke's doubts. It was not merely that she thought it "very wrong" to see desperately ill people wearing them, or that they should have to listen through a drugged stupor for up to sixteen hours a day to looped tapes repeating the same words. What also concerned her was that Leonard Rubenstein and Jan Zielinski were allowed to come and go as they pleased, to replace tapes or fit a helmet on a patient.

When she had queried this arrangement, she was told the two men had "special permission" from Dr. Cameron — and were the only non-medical staff allowed in the Sleep Room. Nurse Mielke thought it a highly irregular arrangement. She had never before encountered a situation where patients were routinely handled by staff that had no formal medical or nursing training — let alone the special skills required to deal with the acutely disturbed. What especially upset her was that neither man appeared to fully understand that this was a ward for the seriously ill. Rubenstein could never resist joshing with the nurses or delivering his latest joke and braying at his own wit. Nurse Mielke thought at times he "was off the wall." Zielinski rarely spoke but peered at patients and often shook his head; she thought he resembled a barn owl.

She felt both were playing roles and that in their white coats they not only looked like doctors but imagined they were. When she spoke to Rubenstein, his language was peppered with medical terms, and he constantly spoke about his "ongoing research" in his "behavioral laboratory." Many of the doctors referred to it as "the workshop." It was housed in one of the converted stables at the back of the mansion. Rubenstein and Zielinski stored their tape editing machines and football helmets against walls which still bore the imprint of horse shoes.

At first Nurse Mielke had put down Rubenstein's attitude as egotism — in her time at the Institute she had encountered several highly-developed egos — and was mildly amused that he sounded so self-important, behaving at times as if he were "not only the chief's right hand, but also his closest confidant." But she had seen that Rubenstein was not above telling a nurse or even a doctor not to touch a pillow speaker or remove a helmet without him being present, insisting that was how "he and the chief" wanted the matter to be handled. She had considered raising this with Dr. Cameron on that day when Madeleine Lacroix somehow escaped from her room after her morning electroshock and ran out of the Institute in her nightdress, barefooted down the drive and out onto the street, dodging in and out of the traffic, causing cars to swerve.

Nurse Mielke had spotted Madeline from a window in South-Two and, after raising the alarm, ran in pursuit, sprinting so fast that her cap flew off. She caught up with Madeleine as she narrowly escaped falling under a van, grabbed her and led the exhausted and distressed woman back into the Institute. Dr. Cameron had appeared with Rubenstein. Madeleine had wept uncontrollably before crumpling up in a ball on the floor, her fists beating the ground. Dr. Cameron had looked down at her and said firmly, "Lassie, stop that. You will not get better like this." Rubenstein lifted Madeleine to her feet. The psychiatrist placed an arm around Madeleine's shoulders and said, "Lassie, I want to help you." The men led her to the Sleep Room. Madeleine was kept in a chemically-controlled sleep for thirty-six days and awakened only to eat. In between her meals she received multiple electroshocks.

*   *   *

Buckley returned once again to Montreal. He carried with him a reel of film shot by a CIA cameraman. Rubenstein set up the projector and settled down to watch the film with Dr. Cameron. The film showed hundreds of American soldiers at an undisclosed training ground undergoing a series of battle-field exercises: firing machine-guns, running assault courses, performing bayonet charges. Then each soldier was lined up and given a pill by a doctor. They were then told to repeat their exercises. But this time they behaved very differently, staggering about the training ground, laughing uncontrollably one moment, then reduced to tears the next. Dr. Cameron sat trans-fixed.

"Wonderful," he said. "One pill and their will to fight has been removed." Without another word of explanation had walked from the room, followed by Rubenstein.

Buckley wondered "what in the name of God had this to do with what Dr. Cameron was supposed to be doing, finding the answer to mind control." Late in the afternoon Dr. Cameron sent for Buckley and invited him to meet the first of two patients he had selected to kick-start Project 68. She was Velma Orlikov, the wife of a pharmacist and a long-serving member of the Canadian Parliament, David Orlikov. Four months before, when she had arrived at the Institute, Velma had told Dr. Cameron he was her "last port of call. Everybody else has tried and failed."

At their first interview Dr. Cameron stared at Velma for a long moment and then said, "Lassie, tell me your story." She did so, sometimes looking into his face, searching for hope, other times burying her own face in her hands and weeping uncontrollably. All she saw across the desk was an expression-less mask. The tape machine on his desk recorded every word: She was forty years old; David was a pharmacist and Lesley her daughter was eight years old; her marriage had once been happy, which was why she was all that more bewildered over her loss of sexual desire after her daughter was born. At first she thought it was no more than a passing phase and David had been patient. But months went by and she still refused to make love. Her loss of libido increased and was accompanied by a growing feeling of fatigue and mood swings. That feeling sometimes lasted for weeks, accompanied by splitting headaches and sleeplessness. David gave her Largactil, doing so without consulting a doctor. She took it for a year, even though it made her skin feel as if it were on fire. She persevered because she wanted to be a good wife. Finally, when Velma told her family doctor about the side effect, he took her off the drug. When the headaches returned, she turned to a tried and trusted remedy David sold over the counter to his lady customers — "Frosts' 2-2-2's" — tablets made from acetylsalicylic acid and codeine, sold to relieve premenstrual tensions. It was no help, and she entered the Mayo Clinic in Winnipeg. A psychologist told her that her symptoms were caused by frigidity. Velma spent almost four years in therapy during which she became so desperate that she actually begged the doctor for electroshock treatment. She hoped it would short-circuit her time in analysis.

Dr. Cameron stared at her across the desk. Finally he said, "Tell me it all, lassie. Everything."

She told him everything, how she talked over the idea of electroshock with David and how her husband suggested she should discuss the matter with her therapist who had finally agreed. She had no idea what the treatment entailed, and the doctor had not explained. Velma recalled her feeling of helplessness and fear as she was wheeled into the shock room at the Mayo Clinic and how, when she regained consciousness, there followed even more blinding headaches, accompanied by foggy confusion and memory gaps. She had begun to think she was incurable. Somehow she plucked up enough courage to make love with David and became pregnant. Her Winnipeg therapist strongly urged she should have a therapeutic abortion and the pregnancy was terminated; at the same time her fallopian tubes were ligated. The doctor also recommended she go to Montreal and consult Dr. Cameron. He was her last hope.

Cameron questioned her about her childhood and parents. Not really understanding why he was interested in such matters, she nevertheless answered him truthfully. Her father was "a very charming but irresponsible Irishman who carried on affairs of which my mother knew." He had deserted the family when she was seventeen. Her mother was very possessive.

When Dr. Cameron finished with his questions, Velma was taken back to her room thinking she had never felt lonelier. She pulled the sheets over her head to hide the misery which welled from a continuously renewing source deep within her. She cried and slept, slept and cried. Finally a young man arrived carrying a tape recorder similarly to the one Dr. Cameron had on his desk. He placed it on the bedside locker and plugged it in, smiling all the time. He had a strange accent. He explained, "I'm Rubenstein. I'm English." Seeing his white coat she assumed he was a doctor.

Dr. Cameron arrived carrying a kidney bowl holding a syringe. He said he was going to give her an injection. When she had asked what it was for, he replied, "just trust me, lassie," and slipped the needle into a vein in her arm. He patted her on the shoulder, turned on the recorder and walked out of the room telling her to say or write whatever came into her mind. Rubenstein handed her a tablet of paper and pencil and settled in the armchair, urging her to take no notice of him.

She looked at the paper. She had no idea what to write. She stared at Rubenstein. He smiled back. She looked around the room. It somehow seemed different. Then she realized the sink had moved. It was on the ceiling, upside down, the taps reaching

towards her, coming ever closer. She turned to the paper thinking she had to record this. But her hands were trembling so
badly she couldn't grip the pencil. She shook her head to clear
it, thinking it was not possible for sinks to move. She looked
again at Rubenstein. He sat unperturbed in the chair, smiling.
The taps were coming closer. There was no doubt about it.
Suddenly from faucets came fiery jets and she felt "a terrifying
panic. I had absolutely no control over me. And I felt that all
my bones were melting." She was locked in a room that was
shrinking; the walls and ceilings were coming closer and would
eventually crush her. The whirling in her mind grew. Her body
ached from a huge black bubble of fear. "I was a squirrel in a
cage. I couldn't get out. I tried to climb the walls. And I felt if
I was to lie down, I'd never get up." The turmoil in her mind
continued for hours until, exhausted, she fell asleep. When she
awoke, Rubenstein and the tape recorder were gone.

Velma telephoned David. The connection to Winnipeg was
poor but through the static her husband was reassuring. However dreadful it had been, there must be a good reason for the
treatment. He told her over and again: "Sometimes you have to
feel worse before you feel better."

Dr. Cameron questioned her further. What did her mother
symbolize to her? Her younger sister? She struggled to give
meaningful answers. He examined her feelings when her sister
was born. Had she felt rejected and overshadowed by her arrival? Was that when her shyness started? Was that the reason
for her inability to make love? Was this her way of punishing
her husband?

When the questioning finished, he walked Velma back to her
room accompanied by Rubenstein carrying a tape recorder. Dr.
Cameron once more switched on the machine. Her own voice
came through the speaker. She hardly recognized the words
through the tears. One minute she spoke about the death of

a young cousin for whom, when she saw him in the coffin, she had only felt resentment, "because they all paid great attention to him." Next she spoke of her mother driving her to achieve still better results at school. Then she rambled on about her father being charming and fun and how much she missed him and how her mother always seemed burdened by being breadwinner and housekeeper. She remembered she had said all those things during an earlier interview with Dr. Cameron. Velma pleaded with Dr. Cameron to switch off the tape. Instead he had given her another injection. When it took effect, she was once again gripped with the fear that the walls had turned into a cage and she was a squirrel.

A few days later, Dr. Cameron questioned her again. When her father had left home, how had she felt? Sad? Guilty? Had she drawn closer to her mother? Did her mother always regard her as a child even when she was an adolescent? Even when she had married David? Then she was taken back to her room and given another injection. Once more she began to hallucinate.

She finally learned what was in the syringe when she saw her name on a card in the nurse's office: "Mrs. Orlikov, lysergic acid diethylamide-25." She did not know what it meant — and no one would tell her. She called David. He was equally mystified. There was nothing about LSD in the literature the drug house salesman left with him on their calls.

Finally she came to a decision. No matter what Dr. Cameron said, she would refuse any more injections. Her mind made up, she waited resolutely in her bed. When Rubenstein arrived with the tape recorder, she ordered him to take it away. He looked at her in surprise. Dr. Cameron came and Rubenstein explained what had happened. Dr. Cameron spoke to Mrs. Orlikov.

"Lassie, don't you want to get better?"

She heard a tiny, distant voice saying what she had said many times before: Just as the hallucinations filled her with fear, so she could not cope with listening to her voice remembering things she thought she had long forgotten. Cameron told her to stand up.

"Come on, lassie, we'll walk down the hall." Outside in the corridor he put an arm around her shoulder and said: "Come on, lassie, you're going to take the injection for me. You know you are."

She looked at him, feeling the strength in his arm. The warmth of his body was calming. She looked at him. What if she didn't do as Dr. Cameron asked? Would the rest of her life be filled with that awful void and pain which filled her abdomen and made her fail David as a wife?

Dr. Cameron spoke again: "Lassie, you must have the injection."

She nodded.

Velma would be the first patient to be used in Project 68.

In their converted stable, Leonard Rubenstein and Jan Zielinkski spun through the spools of tape containing Madeleine Lacroix's innermost secrets – searching for the segment Dr. Cameron wanted turned into a loop. Surrounded by tape recorders, editing machines and shelves stacked with pillow speakers and football helmets, microphones and cables and boxes of new tapes, Zielinski felt the place was "more like a radio shack than a science lab." But, he also had to admit, the pay was good and the work always fascinating; he could think of no other job, outside of actually being a psychiatrist, or perhaps a priest, which allowed him to have such access and insights into human frailties. He often reminded himself, that although he was a Polish émigré with limited English and no medical training, he had ended up as one of the assistants to the most powerful psychiatrist in North America, if not the Western world.

Wandering through the rooms of the sick, Zielinski often looked at patients and tried to match what was said on tape with their appearance. Much of what Zielinski saw he did not understand. Why were patients kept asleep for so long? Some of those in the Sleep Room had been there for two months. Why were patients so frightened of the Shock Room? He'd seen grown men and women struggling desperately with nurses trying to hold them on the trolley as it was pushed into the room. Why was there so much tension between the doctors? And why did many of them make it clear they disliked Rubenstein and himself? That had hurt Zielinski. After all, he was only trying to help the patients.

Since Zielinski had begun working at the Institute, the back-stabbing had increased. He heard physicians and nurses ridiculing the idea of making patients listen to their own voices. Rubenstein told him the others did not understand the wealth of important psychological data that could be spotted by repeated replaying of the tapes: the shifts in cadence, the tiny mental blocks, the change in speed and emphasis, the hesitations and silences. Rubenstein called it "a whole universe of non-verbal communication carried on below the perceptual level."

Descriptions like that made Zielinski believe that Rubenstein was serious when he said that Dr. Cameron and he would one day become the world's authorities on "continuous radio telemetry of human activity." Rubenstein had envisioned the time would come when "there would be no secrets of the mind that we cannot probe electrically." All Cameron had to do was to ensure a continuous supply of patients and the wise-cracking Cockney would create the electronic equipment which "would enter the deepest corners of their minds."

Rubenstein, for all his banter and horseplay, remained a puzzling figure for Zielinski. The Englishman discouraged questions about his background. Despite his lack of formal medical training, he was one of the very few staff who could approach Dr. Cameron at any time. The psychiatrist never showed him the impatience he frequently displayed to others. The pair often spent hours alone together in the doctor's office, usually late in the evening. Rubenstein never said what they discussed. Sometimes the psychiatrist would come to the stable and talk to Rubenstein about such matters as the possible effect of "anti-gravity on posture" and the role that "electrical friction" had on the brain. Almost always the conversation returned to "psychic driving" — and the use of continuous repetition. Zielinski had been struck by one of Dr. Cameron's descriptions of his treatment: "It's like looking through a hole in the curtain of the mind at the world of things as a patient believes them to be, and to see another quite different world of how things could be — if the patient cared to see them differently."

Now, on this April evening, Rubenstein found on Madeleine's tapes the words Dr. Cameron wanted turned into a continuous loop.

"...I used to stay out late just to get him going. I wanted to arouse my father. I wanted him to love me so I could love him the way my mother never had. I wanted him..."

Madeleine would be the second human guinea pig for Project 68.

In the end, Dr. Cameron decided it would be "inappropriate" for Buckley to witness the start of Project 68. The CIA officer returned to Washington, to learn that he would shortly be posted to Bonn to act as deputy head of station. It would be a chance to put behind him the strange goings-on at the Institute. It was only later that he discovered that Dr. Gottlieb had arranged the posting. The head of MK-ULTRA did not like what the agent was discovering during his visits to Montreal.

CHAPTER ELEVEN

Buckley made one more visit to Montreal. He was invited to attend a staff meeting in the Institute's lecture theater. He saw that although Dr. Cameron had not yet spoken a word, the atmosphere crackled with tension. The psychiatrist sat, arms folded, shirt cuffs visible in all their starched whiteness, one ankle crossed over the other, socks held in place by garters, each shoelace identically tied with a reefer knot. His blue eyes were fixed on some point over the heads of his staff. He was forbidding, and intimidating, his expression ominous.

Over the course of six months Dr. Cameron's senior resident, Dr. Roper, had frequently encountered this intimidating stare and silence, usually when a patient asked questions or a doctor did not answer quickly enough. Years later he would recall Dr. Cameron's "ability, without saying a word, to instill fear." The English-born psychiatrist had not encountered anyone who could do so in quite the same way. Dr. Cameron's demeanor conveyed his anger more clearly than any words.

Dr. Roper spent longer hours at the Institute than any other staff doctor. Dr. Cameron often gave electroshocks late in the evening and afterward went from bed to bed in the Sleep Room, bending over a drugged patient to listen for a moment to the words coming from the pillow speaker or a football helmet. Dr. Roper remembered how Dr. Cameron would invariably murmur, "Take it all in. All of it. It's your only way to get better. You want to get better because I am telling you."

After giving further orders about medication to the nurses or duty doctor, Cameron would stride unsmilingly through the corridors, his brooding presence everywhere. Those were the times when Dr. Roper wondered about the compulsive forces that consumed Dr. Cameron, forces that had no doubt played their part in creating the cold, silent anger that enveloped him in the lecture room.

One of the first things to strike Roper on joining the staff was that, while doctors complained to each other about the chief psychiatrist, they were careful to make sure he was out of earshot. He had heard stories about Dr. Cameron's "little revenges:" refusing to support an application for funds from a researcher; moving a senior scientist to smaller quarters; banishing a doctor who failed to carry out a treatment exactly as specified to one of the city's workhouse-like asylums or to some remote township in the prairies. Dr. Roper had been told that the golden rule for survival was "you put up or shut up." When he had first heard some of the doctors muttering at the tag end of Dr. Cameron's daily round that "there but for God goes God," he thought they exaggerated. But he had come to see life in the Institute was "probably similar to entering a closed religious order." There was the same demand for total obedience and the same authoritarian figurehead. There was indeed something invincible about Dr. Cameron — "as if he really saw God as an equal. It really was very intimidating," Dr. Roper later recalled.

"He would appear unexpectedly in a treatment room, at a sick bed, or behind a researcher working in a laboratory, and after moments turn on his heels. He seemed to be always checking up, making sure that no one was doing anything he didn't know about. But he didn't reciprocate. No one knew what went on behind the doors of his office," Dr. Roper recalled to the author.

Now in the lecture theatre, Peter Roper sensed the restlessness increasing around him. Dr. Roper looked at Dr. Cameron. He was still staring impassively ahead. Dr. Cleghorn noisily cleared his throat and some of the other doctors fidgeted.

Chapter Eleven

Abruptly Dr. Cameron spoke. It had come to his attention there had been gossip over what was happening to patients undergoing treatment in the basement. He had been surprised to learn that some of his more senior colleagues were at the forefront of such talk. He paused and searched each face in turn, then continued, the Scottish burr still more pronounced. What he found especially distressing was not one of them had asked for an explanation. Once more he fixed them with a steely gaze. No one spoke. The burr gave the words a saw-like quality. Cameron paused, gathering himself together, the way Peter Roper had seen him move toward the climax of a fund-raising speech. Dr. Cameron reminded them he was primarily interested in mental motivations and discovering the laws which governed them. What he was intent on achieving in the basement was essentially no different from what the Chinese had done to American prisoners in the Korean War — except with one significant difference. The Chinese techniques were designed to harm. His methods were meant to be only beneficial. Did they understand — *beneficial*? Therefore he wanted an end — "here and now" — to the rumors. What was happening in the basement was "positive treatment." Dr. Roper would never forget "how the words fell upon us like a whiplash. Crack-crack. Positive treatment. We had better all understand that."

Dr. Cameron looked unblinkingly at his staff. Then he repeated: "Now. Here and now." He rose to his feet and walked from the silent room.

A month before, Dr. Gottlieb had visited the Institute. The MK-ULTRA chief was understandably a concerned man. The Eisenhower siesta years in the White House, as they were now being called, were coming to an end. Waiting in the wings was a vigorous young man, John F. Kennedy, twenty-six years younger than the seventy-year-old sitting president. In his campaign speeches Kennedy had shown himself to be a Cold War warrior, ready to confront Communism. But how far would he go in terms of combating its brainwashing techniques? Dulles had said that nobody would know until Kennedy was in the Oval Office.

Dr. Gottlieb traveled to Montreal, the last stop in a tour of all the research centers he was funding. What he had seen so far had reassured him that Kennedy, when elected, would have no reason to pull the plug on MK-ULTRA.

Before leaving Washington, Dr. Gottlieb had prepared a paper on the current state of America's biological-chemical warfare program, arguing that a further $4 million was required to bring it up to "an acceptable level." He had recommended the money should be used to expand existing facilities, including the new testing center in Utah. That site would be used to test an enhanced version of tularemia. He also recommended some of the money should be used to run tests on the possibility of seeding clouds with anthrax. Dr. Gottlieb had been pleased to learn that Kennedy had told Dulles the money would become available if he were elected.

Dr. Cameron conducted Dr. Gottlieb on a tour of the Institute, including the basement. No one paid Gottlieb any undue attention as he club-footed his way through the corridors and treatment and patients' rooms. Every day brought a number of visiting doctors.

After his tour, Dr. Gottlieb suggested it would be a good idea to defuse any lingering curiosity over the purpose of the basement facilities by telling the medical staff it was no more than an extension of "normal methods." As a result, Dr. Cameron summoned the staff to the lecture theatre to reinforce that the basement was being used for "positive treatment."

Back in Washington Dr. Gottlieb read the reports he had brought back from the Institute. Dr. Cameron was concentrating on "psychic driving." A report described his findings with twenty patients who had each been "driven" over a period of two months.

"In an attempt to explore the ramifications, a variety of possible applications were introduced. Among the variations in driving techniques which have been explored are the use of concealed ceiling microphones, and how to present the driving in a multiplicity of ways, such as the playing of a supportive mother role or of that of a youthful peer in terms of intonation and in terms of choice of words," Dr. Cameron had written.

Dr. Gottlieb knew the KGB used microphones concealed in ceiling light fittings. The disembodied voice of a Soviet interrogator suddenly boomed out from nowhere. More interesting for Dr. Gottlieb was that the length of time a patient was "driven" had been increased to as long as twenty hours a day. With only a four-hour break from the voices from the concealed microphones or through the pillow speakers or football helmets, Dr. Cameron was close to the optimum daily level of "driving." The report concluded that "twenty-four hour driving could be harmful."

Attached to the report were notes of a woman's case, identified only as "M." She suffered from what Dr. Cameron described as "marked feelings of inadequacy and ambivalence towards her husband, much of which derives from an earlier relationship with her mother." The notes described what had happened when "M" was forced to listen repeatedly to her own account of being beaten by her mother. The notes described her admission concerning her father. "M" had broken down and confessed her sexual longings for him. "M" was Madeleine Lacroix.

Dr. Cameron's success at breaking through into her secret world came at a time of mixed fortunes for the Agency.

The U-2 flights had been a spectacular success and the intelligence data they provided allowed Dulles to puff contentedly on his pipe as he studied vividly clear photographs taken from 45,000 feet above the earth not only of Russian installations but also installations in China, Manchuria and Tibet. The CIA's station chief in Taiwan, Ray Cline, had agents in place in Peking and Shanghai. But a carefully prepared Agency plan to overthrow the regime of the pro-Communist President Sukarno of Indonesia — an operation which Dulles had budgeted at $10 million — had failed. Alan Pope, one of the agents who took part in the operation, had been captured.

Dr. Gottlieb was convinced Pope had somehow been brainwashed: How else to explain Pope's abject admissions that he worked for the CIA? Dulles had persuaded his brother, Secretary of State John Foster Dulles, to authorize 37,000 tons of rice and $1 million worth of arms to be sent to Indonesia as a gesture of contrition. Attached to the gift was a polite request from the Secretary for Pope's safe and immediate return. Sukarno had accepted the offerings, but Pope still languished in a Jakarta jail. He would remain there until 1962.

A personal blow to Dr. Gottlieb had been the decision of Cornell University to sever its ties with the Agency. Dr. Harold Wolff, however, remained closely connected with MK-ULTRA. As president of the Society for the Investigation of Human Ecology, he had used his connections to fill the board with some of the most prestigious names in North American medicine. They included the energetic Carl Rogers, professor of psychology and psychiatry at the University of Wisconsin; the urbane John Whitehorn, chairman of the department of psychiatry at the Johns Hopkins University; Dr. Joseph Hinsey, president of the New York Hospital – Cornell Medical Center. Dr. Charles Hinkle, who had worked on the first study of brain-washing techniques, was the Society's vice-president. Soon to serve on the board would be Leonard Carmichael, head of the Smithsonian Institute; George Kelly, professor of psychiatry at Ohio State University and professor Barnaby Keeney, president of Brown University.

Chapter Eleven

Dr. Cameron continued to visit Washington regularly in his official capacity as president of the American Psychiatric Association. Velma Orlikov sat in his office listening to him making travel arrangements – and it struck her as "curious" that her doctor had so much business in the American capital. But she never dared broach the subject. To do so would have meant another period of Dr. Cameron ignoring her; several times he had walked past her in the corridor and refused to see her in his office because she asked him why she had to spend hours writing reactions to what she heard herself say on the tapes. "I had to write papers every morning, every afternoon and every evening. Over and over and over again. And over and over and over again. Until I just wanted to tear them up," she would later testify in court. Sometimes he would ignore her for days, leaving her "feeling in bits." He remained oblivious to her tearful pleas: "Please speak to me, doctor. Help me."

When Dr. Cameron decided to resume seeing her, he would always begin by saying, "Lassie. You must do exactly what I say." She had tried, but the hours and hours of writing increasingly distressed her, and when she failed she would be banished from his presence. She was upset from coping with all the memories he had stirred up. He wanted her to accept things she could not: that she felt sexual urges for her mother and that perhaps she didn't love David. "It seemed to me," she had thought through her tears, "he wanted my mind to be in a mess."

Dr. Cameron suddenly decided she should become a day patient — ordering her to take a room in Montreal and report daily to the hospital. "I had to go each day to this little room that had a bed, a chair with a recorder and me and create my tapes. And then I got my sleeping pills for the night and I went home. Every weekday I had to do my tape or I was not given my sleeping pills," she later said.

Dr. Cameron featured Velma's responses in his reports to Dr. Gottlieb. Patients who refused to perform tasks he gave them were restricted to their wards. His "operant condition approach" to Velma contained the underlying assumption she could be "motivated" to provide her tapes. Dr. Cameron had discussed his approach with Dr. Sargant. They continued to meet at medical conferences and spoke about what Dr. Cameron always referred to as the "project."

Dr. Sargant later confirmed to the author that the conversation sometimes turned to the use of biochemical weapons. Dr. Sargant had told Cameron about the use of terminal cancer patients at his own hospital in London. Dr. Cameron had wondered about the risks involved — "families finding out or someone going to the press with the news. I told him that we had everything pretty well under control in that area," Sargant recalled.

Dr. Roper detected, behind the self-accusations, the deep hopelessness of Jeannine Huard. Yet he knew that he could never allow her to believe he shared her sense of defeat.

"Jeannine, do you know where you are?"

She sobbed but no tears came, only a broken whimper. Finally she nodded.

"Do you know what day it is?"

After an interval, she nodded again.

"Do you know what time it is?"

Another nod. Then she asked a question.

"Why can't I be strong?"

He told her she would be and that he was there to help. She tried to speak. But no sound came from her lips; her mouth shaped noiseless words. Jeannine closed her eyes. Dr. Roper rose from the bedside chair. There was no more to be done for the moment. Like so many others, Jeannine kept on returning to the Institute, overcome once more by the pressures of her life. Dr. Roper wondered whether she was another of those who would spend the remainder of their lives in mental institutions. Yet he firmly believed she could be helped by another course of multiple electroshocks. She would receive them twice a day, each session comprising five separate measured bursts of electricity, administered either through the temples, bilaterally, or at the back and front of one side of her head, unilaterally. Ten shocks a day. Fifty a week. Two hundred a month. Dr. Roper would later admit to the author "it seemed a great number. But I had become used to giving such a high number of treatments under Dr. Cameron's direction."

His lack of knowledge of its effects had not dampened Dr. Roper's enthusiasm for a treatment he resolutely believed was "relatively safe and has the great advantage of treating an episode of depression very quickly, sometimes in a matter of days and usually within a month. A hundred shots of electricity is a small price to pay for getting rid of that dreadful feeling that the end of the world is nigh." That the treatment required a patient to be often periodically "topped up with electricity" — as with Jeannine — was "one of the crosses she had to try and bear," Dr. Roper said. Another was the confusion and amnesia that accompanied the electroshocks. Dr. Roper thought these might even be beneficial. "After all, the idea was also to remove the memories which caused her depression."

He knew it was no use explaining to Jeannine that the electroshock treatment was a relatively simple procedure, or that the muscle relaxant drug and the anesthetic he always insisted must be given before the treatment virtually eliminated any risk of bone fractures or other orthopedic injury caused by the procedure. He knew that patients still scared each other with stories of being threatened with the treatment "if they did not behave," of being strapped down and given the treatment without sedation, of waiting in the corridor outside the Shock Room listening to the screams from inside. But he was not about to "lead a protest movement to Dr. Cameron. That would see me banished to the outer regions of the Network."

Peter Roper also wondered whether his own wife Agnes could benefit from a course of electroshock. Over the past year her depression had become more noticeable. There was hardly a day when she would not make claims like "the Catholic Church is trying to brainwash our children." He realized he could not help her himself because he was too emotionally involved. Yet when he suggested she see another psychiatrist, Agnes angrily refused, accusing him of "trying to get rid of her." He did not discuss the matter further with her but hoped to raise it with Dr. Cameron. Yet there never seemed to be a good time. Besides, the chief psychiatrist had made it clear that, just as he kept his own private life outside the Institute, he expected the staff to do the same.

Dr. Roper stood for a moment looking at Jeannine curled up in her bed. She seemed so vulnerable and pathetic. But at least, unlike Agnes, she had once more showed her willingness and desire to get better by coming into the hospital.

Nurse Mielke moved from bed to bed in the Institute's Sleep Room. She was asking herself similar questions to those Dr. Roper had asked Jeannine, as she wrote her evaluations on each patient's chart. Her observations ranged from "unable to say her own name," "unable to write down his name" and "does not know time of day or date," to "infantile response" and "only babbles." Every day she or one of her nurses recorded that information. Dr. Cameron had said it was important to measure how far each patient had regressed under electroshock. The sight and sounds of heavily drugged men and women gibbering and mumbling had become "highly unpalatable" to Nurse Mielke. Yet only that morning Dr. Cameron had taken her aside. "Girlie. This treatment is helping. Never you forget that. When you take away everything that is bad, you have room to put back the good." He had turned on his heel and marched out of the darkened room, leaving a list of patients who were to receive further electroshocks.

One of the patients was Rosemary Bonner, the blonde twenty-year-old that Dr. Cameron generally referred to as "the catatonic at the end of the row." Rosemary had been his patient for seven months after he had diagnosed her as suffering from insomnia and depression. Prior to being sent to the Sleep Room, she had received insulin and LSD. Increasingly Rosemary had displayed symptoms of withdrawal. Sometimes she stood for hours on end on tiptoes, staring out of her bedroom window. In bed she would lay rigid, elbows to her side, fingers stiffly extended in the air. On other occasions when she awakened from a drugged sleep, she somehow found the energy to overcome her chemical stupor and used her bed as an exercise machine, repeatedly tumbling over it and doing headstands on the mattress. Then she would abruptly return to the window rubbing one thumb endlessly, or scratching one side of her nose for hours. It was after Dr. Cameron had surprised her pulling out her hair that he began the most intense course of electroshock treatment Nurse Mielke had ever seen.

Over a three-month period Rosemary had received one hundred and ninety-five separate treatments, each of five separate shocks. In all, they amounted to nine hundred and seventy-five electrical charges. Rosemary had continued to visibly regress. She could do nothing for herself and was incontinent, without speech, without any physical or mental coordination. She was as helpless as a newborn baby, whimpering pitifully when aroused from her drugged sleep, but otherwise incapable of any other response. She had become "the nearest person to one of the living dead," Nurse Mielke had ever seen. Yet, whenever he stopped at Rosemary's bed, Dr. Cameron would invariably say to the nurse that "a little bit more treatment and we could have a breakthrough here. But she needs to regress a little more. It's her only hope." Nurse Mielke wanted to maintain her faith in Dr. Cameron, but she could not shake off the feeling that Rosemary's condition "really did raise the question of whether the end justified the means."

But, despite her concerns, Nurse Mielke was not prepared to go much beyond that. She wanted so much to believe that "something tremendous" was happening in the Institute; that she was taking part in breaking new ground; rather than feeling apprehensive, she should be excited and totally committed to seeing it through. Dr. Cameron had once said, in a rare confidence, that "the landscape of the old days would be forever banished." He had loomed over Nurse Mielke sounding more like a prophet than a clinician with his vision of a new world. "Girlie, we are at a moment of history. You. Me. The patients. Everyone. We are all in this. Never you forget that."

When he said this, she had wanted to ask him so many questions. Would that do away with the need for such massive doses of Thorazine and the darkened Sleep Room with its slumbering figures and their pillow speakers and football helmets? Would that put a stop to Rubenstein and Zielinski coming and going as they pleased? Above all, would that mean no more electroshocks? But Cameron had already turned and walked away. Watching him go, she thought that if he believed, so should she. After all, she was still only a nurse, and Dr. Cameron was the most powerful and intimidating doctor she had ever worked for. He must know what he was doing.

And yet, there was Rosemary. Could it be right — shocking her until she had literally none of her senses left? The harder Nurse Mielke tried to push it aside, the more persistent the questions became. "Increasingly I asked myself how could this be right," she told the author.

*   *   *

"Doctor…"

Jeannine Huard could not continue. The word hung between them, a mocking specter of the reassurance she so much wanted to have.

"What are you afraid of, lassie?"

Behind Dr. Cameron was the nurse standing beside the trolley with the black box. Jeannine tried again.

"I'm… not afraid. It's just… the treatment."

Dr. Cameron looked at her. "I've told you before, lassie. There's nothing to be afraid of. Now, give me your arm."

She watched him searching for a vein, trying to keep her eyes off the box with its dials already flickering and the tiny lights glowing yellow.

Dr. Cameron lifted a syringe from a tray on the trolley. "Lassie, you have got to stop resisting me. You really have."

He drove in the needle, steadily depressing the plunger, telling her to start counting backwards from ten.

Jeannine had consented to further electroshocks because she didn't want to end up like one of the patients in the horror film she had seen shortly before coming back into hospital. They had all been abandoned by their doctor and locked in padded cells. She was certain Dr. Cameron would never do that to her. Yet, she also knew he did not understand her fears and why she trembled and felt worse after her treatment. Yet, in spite of the way he spoke to her, she believed Dr. Cameron wanted her to get well too. It was just that he could not realize what it was like for her to be locked up, drugged and shocked.

She felt the cold jelly being smeared on her temples, and Dr. Cameron's voice coming from a distance delivering his standard litany.

"This will help you, lassie. You won't feel anything. Ready, nurse? Voltage set? Go!"

In one split second she, too, had become another of what Nurse Mielke called "the living dead."

In February 1961 Buckley was posted to the CIA station in West Germany. The travel order had been signed by Dr Gottlieb. In a memo to Buckley, the scientist said he would remain attached to MK-ULTRA and his task was to develop "useful sources." Buckley's work included making frequent visits to safe houses the CIA had set up in West Berlin and staffed with prostitutes. His task was to analyze the reports the hookers provided about their clients. Most of the information gleaned in post-sexual "share-a-cigarette" time was of little value.

Buckley remembered Berlin as "a time when I learned a great deal more than I needed to know about sexual behavior. I used to get requests from Dr Gottlieb to see if some of the information could be adapted for operational purposes. Dr Gottlieb saw it as something worth pursuing. He said the Russians 'were using sex in a big way as a clandestine weapon, so we should try and do the same' ", Buckley recalled.

One of Buckley's informers was a German academic, Professor Adolf-Henning Frucht, who worked for the Institute of Industrial Physiology in East Berlin. His specialty was developing new methods to detect poisons in the atmosphere. Occasionally he traveled to the Western sector of the divided city. Buckley had met with him, once again assuming his cover as a science writer. Frucht had told him his latest invention was based on the idea that fireflies were affected by the presence of gas in the air; the principle was similar to the one in which miners took caged birds with them underground to warn of the presence of gas at the coalface.

After several convivial meetings in the city's Ku'Dam bars and clubs, Buckley recruited Frucht to become a spy for the CIA. "To be honest, he did not need much persuading. He was convinced that the Soviet Union was going to launch a new world war and that Germany would be in the front line," Buckley remembered.

Frucht soon proved to be highly useful. He managed to smuggle out of East Germany details of the Warsaw Pact's work in biological and chemical weapons. One weapon was a nerve agent that could remain potent at well below its freezing point. When Buckley sent the details to Dr Gottlieb, they caused excitement and consternation. CIA analysts concluded that the nerve agent was designed to attack America's early warning bases in Alaska.

In the coming weeks, Frucht, at huge personal risk, sent a wealth of data about chemical and biological agents that were being developed within the Soviet Union to a number of dead letterboxes in West Germany that Buckley had set up specially for the purpose. The center for this work was in Czechoslovakia, at the Prague Institute for Military Hygiene and the Institute for Biological Research in the village of Techonin. Frucht even managed to identify the very room in the Prague Institute where the most dangerous germs were kept. Room 625 housed such deadly germs as Nile fever, rabies and yellow fever, plus containers holding the spores of milled anthrax.

Suddenly this supply of priceless information stopped. It took Buckley weeks to establish what had happened. Frucht had been arrested by the German Stasi, its fearsome secret police. "There was always going to be that possibility," was all Buckley would later say. "It goes with the job."

Soon he would have work more to his liking; training a motley Cuban force to wrest control of their country from Fidel Castro. The operation would become known as the Bay of Pigs.

From the day he arrived to help train La Brigada, the 1500-strong Cuban force that would spearhead the invasion of Cuba, Buckley sensed the operation was doomed. He had attended several briefings given by Allen Dulles, and it was clear that the Director "had no love and affection for the operation. At best he was half-sold on the idea but had to go along with it because of pressure from the Kennedy Administration. One of the many problems was lack of security. Every night the Cubans would go into town and tell their friends what was going on. We knew that Castro had spies all over the place who reported every detail back to Havana," Buckley later recalled to the author.

Matters were not helped when a courier from Washington lost a briefcase filled with CIA documents that listed every agent and contact in Cuba. "That was the moment when we should have pulled the plug on the operation. But the pressure was on to make it work. Despite all that, the actual plan could have succeeded. The key to the success of the operation was for La Brigada to establish a beachhead in Cuba. That would trigger an uprising against Castro. But for that to work there was a need for adequate air cover. The CIA was going to provide that. But Kennedy said it was too risky because it could have some very unpleasant political repercussions for him. We were told to keep everything low profile. Absolutely zero profile if possible. From then on I knew it was going to be a disaster," Buckley remembered.

Among the warnings Buckley had given the Cubans was that, if captured, they could expect to be harshly interrogated by the Soviet KGB officers known to be on the island. "I threw in some of the stuff which was going on in the MK-ULTRA program. That really shook them up. But to their credit no one wanted to quit. They were full of the gung-ho bullshit which other CIA guys were filling them with."

Buckley would remember watching La Brigada setting out from their supposedly secret base in Guatemala – they had been moved there to try and tighten up security – and feeling "sick in my gut that it has all been a waste of time."

So it proved to be. Buckley was "too far down the totem pole for my head to roll. But it was the end for Dulles. Kennedy sent for him and said he must go. He would be given a few months' grace. But go he must. For those of us who had served him, it was a bitter blow. In many ways Dulles had been the Agency for us."

But the departure of Dulles did nothing to halt MK-ULTRA.

By then, the CIA had settled into its new headquarters in Langley and Buckley had begun driving out of Washington to take the turnoff on the George Washington Parkway, his destination marked by an overhead sign that stated simply: "CIA." It had struck him as "bloody weird" that a secret agency should advertise itself on the highway.

Every morning he parked his car in the area reserved for the Directorate of Operations — the clandestine side of the agency — and walked along a footpath that led into the main building. The layout of the main lobby reminded him of a bank; the watchful uniformed guards, the brisk coming and going. But no bank had a bald eagle carved into the marble of its floor. Seen in profile, the bird was the symbol of the CIA — along with the sixteen-point compass star on a shield which supported the eagle. All were encased in a circle. On its rim were carved the words, "Central Intelligence Agency," and "United States of America." Set into a wall was a verse from the Gospel of St.John: "And ye shall know the truth and the truth shall make you free." The first time he saw the plaque, Buckley had smiled ironically.

After showing his ID, he had a choice of five elevators. The sixth was reserved for the Director. Buckley's elevator would whisk him up past the first two floors — housing the library, medical facility, the travel office, the typing secretariat and the cafeterias. His office was on the third floor. The approach to it was along a corridor painted off-white and devoid of wall hangings. His office was small, carpeted with the same covering as every other office. At twelve-thirty sharp he left his office, locking the door behind him and joined all the others making their way to the cafeteria on the first floor for lunch. On his first day at Langley he had been briefed that, as a field agent, he must sit in an area away from the curious eyes of other staff or any visitors who were in the cafeteria. The Director and his senior staff ate on the seventh floor, close to their offices. Their food, Buckley had been assured, was the same as that in the cafeteria. "There was a standing joke that this was to reduce the chance of anybody managing to poison the supergrades," Buckley was to remember.

When he flew back from Montreal into Washington's National Airport, Buckley was reminded that pilots used the CIA building as a landmark. And most weekends KGB agents from the Russian Embassy in the city drove out past Langley to take a peek at the square, block-like headquarters not unlike some of the buildings Buckley had seen in post-war Berlin. But he had little time for such musings. There was, Buckley would recall, "one hell of a pressure to make sure that Cameron came up with answers. And pretty damn quick."

Back on what he called "the Montreal trail," Buckley found that the Institute had become its "own pressure cooker with Cameron controlling the valve." In March 1961, the psychiatrist had taken Buckley to the basement and opened the locked door to the isolation chamber.

Madeleine Lacroix's body odor was strong as she lay curled up in a corner of the sound-proofed chamber wearing only a hospital gown and a pair of panties. On her head was a football helmet secured in place by straps under her chin so that even if she had the strength to do so, she could not remove it. The helmet was painted the same lifeless black as the chamber. When the door was closed, there was no way Madeleine could have distinguished between the black rubber-foam floor and the similarly clad walls and ceiling.

Chapter Eleven

Elsewhere in the world on this morning, American astronaut Alan Shepherd had spent fifteen minutes in space, Freedom Riders had swept through Dixie, and President Kennedy had confronted Khrushchev in Vienna. None of this had penetrated Madeleine's isolated world, one in which there was no sense of time, of day or night, of anything but the stygian darkness that enveloped her. Her only escape was to be taken twice a day to the lavatory.

This was her thirtieth day in the Isolator, totally cut off from the world. At first, in spite of her drugged state, she had struggled to be let out, banging her helmeted head against the door. Dr. Cameron had increased her intake of sodium amytal, and she had quieted down. After two weeks he began to reduce her level of drugging so that she would become further aware of her surroundings and know she was cut off from all outside stimuli apart from the tape played continuously through the speakers in the helmet. The voice was Dr. Cameron's, repeating a new message Rubenstein had spliced together from comments the psychiatrist had made during earlier interviews with Madeleine.

"Your father is dead. You must forget thinking of him sexually. Eddie has gone. He is no longer a part of your life. You will accept that he has divorced you. You do not feel alone because you are strong. You will say to yourself that today is the start of your new life. You will say that and believe that."

Before being placed in the isolator, Madeleine had, all told, received nearly one thousand separate electroshocks. The treatments had been spaced out over a year. She had also undergone over one hundred hours of "psychic driving."

Buckley watched as Madeleine was brought to the Voice Analysis Room in the basement. The small, sound-proofed booth was in the charge of Zielinski and dominated by a spectrum analyzer. Dr. Cameron told Buckley it was designed to assess one of the most distinctive traits of schizophrenia — the abnormalities of speech that frequently accompanied the illness. It would differentiate between the euphoric language of the manic patient, the slow delivery of the melancholic, the babbling and stammering of the catatonic, the hesitant, singsong speech of the epileptic.

Zielinski's task was to operate the analyzer while Dr. Cameron put a series of questions to Madeleine. There were questions about where she was born, the names of her parents, what school she had attended, the date of her marriage, where it was consummated, the name of Eddie's best man, the name of her bridesmaids, the date of her father's death, the name of the cemetery where he was buried, the name of the radio station where she had last worked, the names of the shops where she bought groceries and clothes and their locations. Finally, the questions concentrated on her immediate environment. Did she know where she was, what year it was, what was the month, the day of the week, the time of day?

Many of her responses were no more than little grunt-like sounds. After each answer, Dr. Cameron paused so that there was a gap on the tape recording her responses to the questions. Later Zielinski would insert in each space the time and date, and cut up the tape into snippets and join them to previous tapes, forming loops that contained Madeleine's answers to each separate question since she had been in the Isolator. The loops were then fed through the spectrum analyzer and her responses compared at various given times. When asked about the date of her father's death, Madeleine had hesitated. Later, she had given it. Dr. Cameron told Buckley he did not yet know whether this was connected with Madeleine's biological body clock. As usual he had found a scientific way to describe what was done to Madeleine — "Psychological Stress Evaluation," PSE. It was neither a new nor uncommon technique, at least in police and intelligence circles. There, the use of a lie detector or voice analyzer was routine to help establish the degree of tension in the voice of a suspect. Dr. Cameron used the analyzer to try to detect when Madeleine told him the truth.

Over the past year, a hundred other patients had each answered a series of similar questions. Zielinski had observed that Dr. Cameron favored docile and compliant patients, those who made every effort to answer him quickly. He looked less favorably upon persons whose voices, in spite of their drugging, showed themselves to be still intractable. They were the ones who refused to answer, or said things like "You tell me," or "I've told you that before" or "I am not going to answer any more questions." Sometimes those patients did not return to the Voice Analysis Room, and the next time Zielinski saw them was in one of the beds of the Sleep Room listening to tapes that included injunctions from Dr. Cameron such as "You will listen to all I say," and "You will be cooperative."

Madeleine's latest session in the Voice Analysis Room had once more produced slobbering and choking sessions. Dr. Cameron noted on her chart she had regressed "that much more than on the previous day."

He took Madeleine to the Grid Room and Buckley watched Rubenstein tape a potentiometer on her upper thigh and lower trunk. The technician then strapped to her arm a miniature transmitter, smaller than the size of a packet of cigarettes. He had recently developed the unit so that he could dispense with wires leading to what he called his Body Movement Transducer. The transmitter picked up signals in the potentiometer and relayed it to the transducer.

In the Grid Room, Dr. Cameron said, marks on graph paper identified the complexities of patients' personality and illness. The way they moved, sat, inclined their head, intertwined their hands, mumbled and muttered, drooled and dribbled or stared vacantly became carefully plotted dots and lines. He reminded Madeleine she was free to move as she pleased in front of the lines on the wall. Together with Buckley, the psychiatrist and technician left the room and Rubenstein began to film Madeleine's movements, the concealed microphone in the ceiling picking up her animal-like whimpers.

Dr. Cameron noted what he identified as "the typical waveform activities" of Madeleine's movements. From time to time he issued commands to her through the speaker, ordering her to stand up, to move in one direction and then another, and perform simple movements such as clasping her hands and raising first one and then the other arm. Her case notes showed that in the beginning she had appeared puzzled as to where the voice came from. She no longer showed any interest. She had regressed too far to be concerned with such matters.

Watching the spiky graph emerging from the transducer Cameron dictated into a recorder: "Repeatedly walks over the same course. Movements slow and disorganized. Sits in chair and rises again. The overall shift in baseline indicates the body produces a lower center of gravity. Her whole action is retarded."

CHAPTER TWELVE

Following the departure of Allen Welsh Dulles, a new director, John Alex McCone, was appointed by President John F. Kennedy. Gottlieb persuaded McCone to authorize further substantial payments to be channeled through the Society for the Investigation of Human Ecology — the CIA front organization in New York — for Dr. Cameron and other researchers at the Institute and elsewhere. The money would be spent on such lines of investigation as hypnotism, the analysis of the extrasensory perception of African witch doctors and voodoo's potential for brainwashing. It was an unrestrained, scattershot approach in which researchers were granted total freedom from the academic restrictions and red tape their work would normally attract.

Dr. Donald Hebb, the head of the psychology department at McGill had received $30,000 from the Society for the Investigation of Human Ecology to continue his pioneer work in sensory deprivation. He had already received grants from the Rockefeller Foundation and the Canadian Department of Defense. The money had been used to convert a room in his laboratory into an "isolation box" into which volunteers, who had been fully briefed as to the purpose of the test, were placed. They were encased in high-altitude flying suits and wore goggles and ear muffs. The air in the box was filtered and from time to time the subjects were exposed to a constant beeping. Each volunteer was told he could be released as soon as he pressed a panic button. No one, whether he wished to or not, had been allowed to remain in the box for extended periods. Dr. Gottlieb had tried to persuade Dr. Hebb to keep volunteers for longer periods in isolation and to give them drugs. The psychologist flatly refused to entertain the proposals. Subsequently he had been "horrified" to discover the CIA was the source of part of his funding and discontinued his research.

No such qualms affected an Agency staff researcher, Morse Allen. He had persuaded Dr. Maitland Baldwin at the National Institute of Health to perform "terminal-type" experiments. Dr. Baldwin had come to Allen's attention after keeping an Army volunteer in isolation for forty hours. The soldier had broken down and, in Dr. Baldwin's account, "he began to cry and sob in the most heartbreaking way."

Dr. Baldwin agreed to cooperate with the Agency on certain conditions. The CIA would provide the volunteers and accepted that, after a week in isolation, there would be almost certainly irreparable brain damage. Dr. Gottlieb chaired a number of meetings to see how best to fund Dr. Baldwin. It was decided the Society for the Investigation of Human Ecology was not a suitable conduit because of the potential "terminal" nature of the research. A dead "expendable" on American soil could lead to awkward questions and expose the Society's cover. But before a satisfactory way of funding was agreed, McCone ordered the project to be abandoned as "altogether too risky to perform within the borders of the United States." Once more Dr. Gottlieb's attention focused upon Dr. Cameron.

Cameron's reports had become a vindication of what Dr. Gottlieb had always maintained: the human mind was far more resistant than people realized. That made it all that more baffling as to how "the enemy" — Dr. Gottlieb had come to lump together both the Russians and the Chinese — were so successful. There had to be a point where the strongest of wills could be broken. Clearly it depended on knowing just how far to take a subject. The enemy had discovered the secret, so why couldn't Dr. Cameron?

Dr. Gottlieb noted the psychiatrist's preliminary interviews with patients were now conducted so that they had to go over their past life in even more minute detail. Dr. Cameron had explained he was looking specifically for "a sore spot, something that was what he called 'tremblingly alive' in a patient's mind. As a result, a patient often became more and more nervous and confused and inevitably his or her memory fell apart," he had written to Dr. Gottlieb.

Dr. Cameron made a patient write down all he or she could remember. When answers did not precisely match what he had been told previously, Dr. Cameron focused on the discrepancies. It was classic police interrogation methodology. But Dr. Cameron had explained that "this method leads to a controlled disorganization in the patient's mind. The patient then becomes vulnerable to suggestions and he becomes easier to handle."

"In my view much of what Cameron said has been achieved by the Chinese in terms of brainwashing is based upon tested techniques passed on to them by the Soviet Union," Dr. Gottlieb wrote in a memo to Director McCone on May 21, 1961, but he had ended the memo saying he was convinced Dr. Cameron was going to achieve the breakthrough which would allow the United States to match the Chinese discoveries. Once more Buckley was dispatched to the Institute to report on progress.

Throughout the summer of 1961, Dr. Morrow continued to believe what Dr. Cameron had promised, that when she was well again he would consider taking her back on his staff so that she could complete her fellowship in psychiatry. He had insisted he must treat her medically before that could happen.

Looking back, she felt she should have spotted the signs of her illness. There had been that first nervous quiver in the stomach, the first skipped meal, the first gulped Dexedrine to keep going just a little longer, the first Phenobarbital capsule to snatch a few hours sleep, the first outburst of tears and then the creeping exhaustion. The symptoms had fed off each other, creating the crisis that had finally taken over her life.

She had admitted herself to Montreal's Royal Victoria, one of the hospital's within Dr. Cameron's "Network." Shortly afterwards he had shown up. She was genuinely flattered that he had regularly come to her room and sat on the chair in the corner, a tall, still figure in a conservative suit. Sometimes the afternoon sun caught his face, making it even harder to see his eyes. Somehow he always managed to avoid her catching his gaze. He always seemed so composed and in control, whereas she sat on the bed, her hands fidgeting on her lap, not certain what to say. After a while he would rise to his feet in one elegant movement and looked down at her. She had often wondered if she should smile and say something like she wasn't feeling that bad, after all. But his manner left no room for flippancy. Each time after he left, she tried to control her racing thoughts and calm her thumping heart. She would tritry to put out of her mind her previous impression of him as being cold, humorless and indifferent. She had convinced herself he would treat her with compassion and care. She wanted to believe so much in the "doctorness of Dr. Cameron. He must have had medical judgment and insight I did not possess and would know what had made me so frightened and desperate. I had to trust him. I kept saying to myself it was my only way back, my only hope of going forward," she recalled to the author.

Dr. Morrow wanted to discuss all that with him, to speak to him about her symptoms. All she wanted from him was an assurance when she did recover, she could return to medicine and help others. She endlessly told herself it was only a matter of finding the correct treatment, perhaps in her case no more than the right combination of drugs. She was a doctor and knew she had a reactive depression complicated by an amphetamine psychosis. When she said it like that, what had happened to her did not sound either so shameful or terrifying. Before she had been hospitalized, her life had become an endless round of falling asleep exhausted and waking slowly to another day of greyness during which her body had been wracked in pain, and she had wept, which did nothing to relieve the agony and the blackness imprisoned inside her.

When Morrow left Dr. Cleghorn's team to work in another hospital, the demands of her work left her little time to study for her higher qualifications in neurology. Weeks before her final examinations, she was admitted as a patient to the Royal Victoria for surgery. As soon as she was discharged, she plunged back into work. She developed otis media in both ears, a painful condition. Determined to obtain the coveted Royal College certification, she drove herself even harder and passed her written paper. But at the oral test, with her ears still troubling her, she had been presented with a patient suffering from bruit — blockage or obstruction in an artery that causes a rushing sound — a difficult ailment to diagnose at the best of times. With her impaired hearing, she failed to recognize the symptoms through her stethoscope and was failed. Tears of helplessness welled up behind her eyes.

Without the higher qualification, her career prospects had dramatically altered. Her stipend at an epilepsy clinic was given to a colleague. She felt an outsider. She took more pep pills during the day and sleeping tablets at night in order to cope. One day, to her embarrassment, she suddenly burst out in tears during ward rounds. She knew the Dexedrine was responsible, just as she knew she could only "hold my head up" by continuing to take the amphetamines. Colleagues had expressed sympathy but no one offered to help. The uncontrollable crying bouts persisted, as did her need for the pharmacological props that barely kept her going. She struggled on, missing meals, swallowing pills, sensing that colleagues now exchanged glances which made her "want to disappear in a puff of smoke — forever." Filled with continuous despair, she wondered why she should go on pretending she had any worthwhile future. Increasingly she felt unable to cope with her inner pain. At times it seemed to envelop everything around her. Day and night she took her tablets. She hated the demeaning ritual. But it was the only way she could cope. She had no one to talk to, to explain the tensions which filled her, the drug-dependant loneliness and the feeling that her very mind was atrophying. There was really nothing to live for.

No sooner had the thought taken root than she had nurtured it. Death would be infinitely preferable to this existence. She had the pills. Why not take them — all of them at once? The question raced around her mind. Why not? She should just take them. A part of her, what she knew to be the small voice of reason, urged her to cling to life, that her pain and her sense of being beaten could not last forever.

Dr. Morrow found no answer to her questioning. Why not? While she had never been able to imagine what death would be like, she knew it could not possibly be more terrifying than the way she felt. Finally, she chose the day which would be her last on earth. She went through it all in a daze, seeing patients, encouraging them to believe in the future. That night she went back to her apartment and swallowed the sleeping pills — not bothering to count them, just taking what she thought would be sufficient — and lay down on the bed. It was done. There would be no more tearful outbursts, no more anguish and shame over her future. Soon there would be nothing. She fell asleep. The next day, she had opened her eyes. There was a roaring noise in her ears, and her vision was blurred. Her first conscious reaction was to say aloud, "I am alive." But the words would not pass her dry lips. She would not remember how long she lay there or what else she had thought, or if she thought at all. But gradually her mind cleared and she began to concentrate. *She was alive.* Her suicide bid had failed, just as she had failed in so many other ways. Then, through her pounding headache and parched mouth, she told herself that whatever had been her intention, she still had no solution to the torment which returned as soon as she was capable of thinking clearly. Days dragged on into sleepless nights, she felt almost nothing except a deepening numbness in her body, was only dimly aware of the storm still raging somewhere below the surface of her mind.

Morrow's last formal ties to her medical practice were severed when she was asked to leave the Neurological Institute. After weeks of being close to the breadline, she took a position as a nurse in a convalescent home. The $200 a month salary paid her rent, but there was little left over for food. She grew more undernourished, and she continued to swallow Dexedrine. The combination of drugs and not eating or sleeping continued to take its toll.

She finally told herself the only way out of her present crisis was to confront it head-on. It was not all over! She would fight her way back! The way to do so was obvious. Dr. Cameron.

Morrow telephoned Cameron asking for a job. He listened politely, but said she must first agree to be medically examined. Finally, she admitted herself to the Royal Victoria.

In the four weeks she had been in the Royal Victoria hospital, apart from a thorough physical check, Morrow received little treatment except bed rest. On his last visit, Dr. Cameron said he wanted to transfer her to the Institute. She wanted to explain that she would feel "humiliated and embarrassed" to be a patient at a place where she had once worked. What would old colleagues say and think to see her lying in bed? And how could she ever work again in a hospital where she had once been treated? Was that even allowed? And what would be done to her? There were lots of questions she badly wanted to ask, but she could not bring herself to ask any of them. Dr. Cameron sat staring at her impassively and said again, "I want to help you." Too depressed to speak, she nodded. He left without saying another word. A few days later she entered the Institute as a patient.

In Langley, Buckley had been given yet another bizarre assignment. Dr. Gottlieb sent him to New York to ask a hypnotist who had recently been put under contract to the CIA to teach him the technique of hypnotism. Over a week, Buckley proved to be an adept pupil. By the end of his visit he had hypnotized the magician's wife into believing she wanted to have sex. Buckley brought her out of her hypnotic trance as she began to undress.

Back at Langley Dr. Gottlieb had devised his own test. He told Buckley to approach two secretaries who worked in the Clandestine Operations section and hypnotize them. Within moments both women were under Buckley's spell. Watched by Dr. Gottlieb, Buckley asked the women to steal files he had marked TOP SECRET. They did so, leaving the files in a corridor where anybody could see the documents. Next, he told one of the women to go to her companion's locker and steal its contents. This she did. Under Dr. Gottlieb's watchful eye, Buckley snapped his fingers to bring the women out of their trance. Neither remembered what they had done.

The next day, Buckley was asked to hypnotize two more secretaries, once more putting them into deep trances. He told one of them that her friend was a Russian spy, and she must kill her with the revolver Dr. Gottlieb had placed on a table. Without hesitation the woman pulled the trigger and "shot" her companion. Buckley was ordered to bring them out of their trances. Again, neither woman recalled what had happened. The secretary who had pulled the trigger recoiled when Buckley showed her the gun. She told him she had a horror of all firearms.

Dr. Gottlieb was delighted. He believed he had made another "significant breakthrough," he told Buckley, in the use of hypnosis in mind control. He added that Buckley was going to be sent to Vietnam to select Vietcong "expendables" to be tested. But first he would accompany Dr. William Sargant on a visit to the Allan Memorial Institute.

Buckley welcomed the chance to leave Langley. In the aftermath of the Bay of Pigs disaster, the Kennedy Administration's obsession with removing Castro had been rekindled into what Buckley later called "a bonfire of ideas." Stoking the fire was Dr. Gottlieb. Urged on by Operations Director, Richard Helms, who in turn was being personally spurred on by Attorney General Robert Kennedy, the President's younger brother, Dr. Gottlieb had created a whole range of toxins and devices to kill the Cuban leader. The project was code-named Operation Mongoose; Buckley had not been involved. "But I had seen and heard enough to know that the pressure to come up with a way of terminating Castro was producing some nutty ideas. The heat was coming from Robert Kennedy. Nothing was too crazy for him to dismiss out of hand. A proposal that really sums it all up was the one that was based on Cuba having a largely Roman Catholic population. The idea was to spread the word that God had chosen the island for the Second Coming — but Jesus would only appear on the island if the people got rid of the Anti Christ, Fidel Castro. To give the idea a semblance of normality, the Navy would be asked to provide a submarine. It would arrive off Havana one night, surface and launch a succession of star shells that would burst over Havana. At the same time a radio station run by Cuban exiles and funded by the Agency would broadcast to Cuba that the glorified fireworks display was the sign for people to expect the Second Coming was imminent and dump Castro.

The whole idea was shelved when the Navy said no way would it go along with the idea," Buckley told the author.

When Buckley left Langley to meet Dr. Sargant, Dr. Gottlieb was busy concocting new schemes to murder Fidel Castro. Driving him on was a report from a Cuban defector that KGB specialists in biological warfare had arrived in Havana and had set up a research institute in a heavily guarded area outside the city. True or not — and no corroborative evidence would ever surface — it was sufficient for Dr. Gottlieb to believe it was imperative to murder Castro before he launched a biological attack on Florida. CIA meteorologists were asked to prepare detailed weather forecasts when the wind would be most favorable to launch a wind-borne attack of the plague or anthrax. Agency chemists were asked to look again at the possibility of seeding clouds with anthrax. Could the Russians do that? Could Cuba be the launch pad for the very kind of weapons that America itself had created? The conclusion of his analysts that this was highly unlikely did nothing to deter Dr. Gottlieb in his hunt for a way to assassinate Fidel.

Resembling an invincible phalanx, the morning medical round proceeded through the Institute with Dr. Cameron at its head and, matching him stride for stride, the equally commanding Dr. Sargant. Doctors and nurses strove to keep pace with the two senior psychiatrists. With them marched Buckley.

He had accompanied Dr. Sargant from the time he had stepped off the plane from London to New York two days before. The psychiatrist had proven to be an engaging companion and insisted Buckley should dine with him at the Plaza. Over dinner and one of the Oak Room's finest clarets, the conversation turned to intelligence matters, and Buckley had raised the case of Frank Olson. Dr. Sargant had described Olson's death as a "bad business" and revealed his own role in the affair, beginning with his report on his last meeting with Olson. Buckley was later to remember he had a feeling that Dr. Sargant regretted having played any part in the murder of the biochemist.

Before collecting Dr. Sargant in New York, Buckley had learned he was to be transferred to the CIA station in Saigon. The prospect of seeing "real action" at last had pleased him. Knowing he would be away from the United States for some time, Buckley suggested to Dr. Sargant they should travel by train to Montreal. It would be Buckley's last chance to take with him memories of how beautiful New England was. The journey furthered Buckley's impression of how cultured and intellectual the psychiatrist was, able to express his views intelligently on the intricacies of international affairs. Dr. Sargant saw Vietnam as "a hiding to nothing" for the United States, adding from his own experience a people could never be bombed into submission. The Blitz of London had proved that.

Now, two days later, Buckley walked beside Dr. Roper, another quintessential Englishman, listening to his murmured opinion that the relationship between Dr. Cameron and Dr. Sargant was proof that the attraction of opposites worked. Dr. Cameron was his usual taciturn self. "Give the lassie an extra fifty milligrams of sodium amytal;" "The manic depressive in bed three needs more Thorazine;" and "Write him up for another course of ECT." As the round wheeled in and out of wards, Dr. Cameron remarked how great the changes were since Dr. Sargant's first visit to the Institute in the mid-fifties. Then only about a third of depressives and schizophrenics — still by far the commonest types of mental illness — recovered sufficiently to be sent back into the world. Dr. Sargant said he was getting similar results in London.

Walking past stretcher patients waiting outside the Shock Room, Dr. Sargant enthused, "Nowadays we may only need to prescribe four or five electrical shock treatments and the patient is himself again without any need for elaborate case history or social investigation and all the jaw-jaw of the Freudians." It was the first time Buckley had seen Dr. Cameron smile that morning.

Dr. Roper told Buckley he felt a real sense of pride that he was part of an ongoing revolution though it had become increasingly difficult to push back the frontiers. The psychoanalysts on staff continued to resist physical treatments. Within the Institute opposition had become united after Rosemary Bonner, a patient of Dr. Cameron's had died after receiving her one thousand, three hundredth shock. Dr. Cleghorn raised "the implications of the case" with Dr. Cameron. He reluctantly agreed to a committee being set up to decide in future which patients were most suitable for "depatterning." Its members were drawn equally from among staff psychiatrists and psychotherapists. However, Dr. Cameron insisted that in a deadlocked situation he would have the final decision.

It was not only clinical problems that continued to sow dissension. There was growing friction among French-speaking doctors about the way Dr. Cameron ridiculed their language and culture. Many analysts complained he had little or no understanding of the ethnic background of many patients, an important consideration when it came to treatment. There was a marked difference between the ideas and attitudes of a Montrealer and a patient from the Canadian Rockies. The debate had swirled around the doctor's common room until Dr. Cameron finally said he would authorize funds for a research project into the matter. Buckley knew it would be another project funded by the CIA.

Buckley saw that Dr. Cameron asked patients familiar questions. "Are you sleeping better, lassie?" "Eating well?" "Listening to the tapes?" Most responses of patients who were conscious were monosyllabic. If a patient tried to elaborate, Dr. Cameron cut them off with an imperious, "We'll talk about that later," or "Lassie, I've already told you that is unimportant."

Leaving another ward, Dr. Sargant observed that in his own hospital he had found traumatic events must be "relived by a patient in the present tense. It's not a bit of good if a patient just describes what has happened to him or her in a dull recital of events. We always try and get them to go right back into the situation which has caused their mental problems. We make them live through the crisis once more, only this time they have all their feelings and rememberings noted down." Buckley saw Dr. Cameron was visibly pleased.

On their journey back to New York, Dr. Sargant told Buckley that his visit to the Institute had greatly disturbed him. He could find no scientific rationale for much of what he had seen. He was prepared to accept that it was difficult to be certain what part of a particular treatment, such as electroshock or drugs or their use in combination, helped patients to recovery, but he was quite sure of one thing: "What was being done to Cameron's patients was wrong, wrong, wrong."

In the privacy of their rail compartment, Dr. Sargant continued to forcefully express himself: "I was frankly horrified. And I suspect I didn't see everything. For instance I never went into the Sleep Room or down to the basement. In helping out Washington, Cameron seems to have forgotten his prime concern must always be for the welfare of his patients. I want no part of this. It has a bad taste to it," Dr. Sargant was to later recall to the author.

Buckley suggested that the psychiatrist should convey his views to Dr. Gottlieb. Dr. Sargant had said he would "think about that." In the end he did not do so. Years later he would defend his decision: "It was not my business to tell Gottlieb what he should do."

But on that train ride back to New York, William Buckley decided the prospect of a spell in Vietnam was infinitely more appealing than being ordered to make another visit to Montreal.

Mary Morrow was becoming increasingly upset. She had been a patient in the Institute for a week, and Dr. Cameron had still not come to see her. No one seemed able to tell her where he was — or what was going on with her case. All that had happened was that a junior doctor had taken her history and she had been visited by a resident whom she had once worked alongside. Yet she felt that if she discharged herself, she would almost certainly forfeit any chance of returning to medical practice. Cameron would pass the word through the "Network" that she was unfit to practice. Later that morning she heard his voice in the corridor. She began to relax. Everything was going to be fine. But, by the end of the day she wondered why he had not come to her room.

The next morning she once more heard a rush of approaching footsteps: the morning round. She braced herself to face old colleagues as well as young interns. It would be embarrassing knowing they all probably realized she was a doctor, but she would try and put on a brave face. She recognized Dr. Cameron's voice but could not make out his words. She had been waiting for this moment and the opportunity to begin her journey back to health under his guiding hand.

The footfalls came closer. Dr. Cameron was still speaking, but his voice had dropped. She remembered from her own days on his round that sometimes before entering a patient's room he lowered his tone when giving instructions about treatment. But in her case he hadn't even spoken to her about any treatment. The footsteps in the corridor slowed. She could visualize the junior doctors and nurses grouping themselves around Dr. Cameron. She composed herself, anxious he should see no signs of her concerns. She even tried to smile. At last Dr. Cameron was outside the door and she was ready to admit to him how helpless she was and how much she needed his help. The time-stopping agony of waiting for him to come was almost over. In a few moments he would be striding into her room and the fearful hopelessness, the feeling of being separated from the rest of the world would cease.

She heard Dr. Cameron outside her door announce: "We'll give this lassie shock treatments." The rush of footsteps moved on.

Mary Morrow screamed. "Why? Why?"

CHAPTER THIRTEEN

In the summer of 1963, Dr. Gottlieb was among a number of experts in bio-chemical warfare called to Washington to advise the Arms Control Agency on how best to negotiate a treaty with Moscow intended to outlaw all nuclear tests. Buckley accompanied Dr Gottlieb and the Harvard biologist, Dr. Matthew Mendelson, who had recently found the answer to how DNA copies itself. At the meeting, Mendelson proposed he should look into what he called "biological issues." Dr. Gottlieb then invited Mendelson to Fort Detrick where he was shown its arsenal of chemical and biological weapons and told they were "infinitely cheaper to manufacture than a nuclear bomb," Buckley recalled. Mendelson went to see McGeorge Bundy, President Kennedy's national security adviser. Bundy told the biologist there was no cause for alarm over what he had been shown. While the germ weapons would remain an integral part of America's defenses, their presence would, in Bundy's words, "be kept out of the war plans." Given his own close interest in military matters, it is unlikely President Kennedy was unaware of what was stored at Fort Detrick.

In the mid-1960s, the American air force started to bomb North Vietnam, focusing on the Ho Chi Minh Trail. Dr. Gottlieb was asked by the Pentagon's commanders if biological weapons would stop the southward flow of weapons for the Vietcong in its war against the South. A number of possibilities were discussed. They included the U.S. dropping canisters filled with smallpox. The virus had a track record of killing most of its victims, leaving those who survived scarred and blinded. The Center for Disease Control estimated it had claimed more lives down the centuries than any other infectious disease. The CIA kept a small supply of the virus at Fort Detrick that, according to Buckley, "was a weapon for special operations." Its presence was not listed on the official arsenal of weapons stored at Fort Detrick. Desperate though they were to close the Ho Chi Minh Trail, the Air Force chiefs decided against using the virus after Pentagon analysts pointed out that dropping smallpox would most likely lead to North Vietnam retaliating with its own germ agents, which China and the Soviet Union had supplied. But the ever persuasive Dr Gottlieb had another idea: if not smallpox, then his scientists would like to ground test another biological agent against the Vietcong. It was Venezuelan equine encephalitis ; not only was it highly contagious, but also debilitating, producing nausea and all the symptoms associated with severe influenza. The weapon was intended to make an enemy unable to fight once the disease had been inhaled. The one drawback was that it would also infect American and South Vietnamese troops. After several trials, the planned widespread distribution of the agent was halted.

However, by the time Buckley arrived in Vietnam in 1964, another Fort Detrick program called "Black Magic" was in operation. CS gas was being sprayed over wide areas of jungle where the Vietcong were thought to be hiding; usually there were villages in the area and their inhabitants were also subjected to the highly unpleasant effects of the noxious chemical. Originally developed by Porton Down for British troops to use in Malaysia, the gas had been considerably improved for Vietnam. Temporarily blinded and suffering with severe skin burns, the Vietcong were forced out of their tunnels — to be killed with fragmentation bombs after the U.S. helicopters had sprayed the area. Gas-masked American troops were then sent in to kill any Vietcong survivors.

Buckley knew that while CS gas did not kill, back in the United States a crash program was underway to manufacture a range of lethal nerve gases, ready to be used on a scale never before seen in any war. At least twenty universities, many already involved in the MK-ULTRA program, were now working on biological or chemical weapons. All over the country huge stocks of chemical and biological weapons were ready to be shipped to Vietnam. The Rocky Mountain Arsenal in Colorado held tens of thousands of cluster bombs filled with mustard gas, phosgene and nerve agents. At the old mining town of Toole near Salt Lake City, a depot held millions of pounds of similar weapons in silver drums that stretched over half a mile into the desert. It was estimated they alone contained sufficient poison to wipe out any major city in the United States.

But in Vietnam, pride of place in the American bio-warfare arsenal rested on a chemical designed to strip the jungle of its dense foliage and, of course, injure anyone exposed to it. It was called Agent Orange, after the color of the drums in which it arrived in South Vietnam. To create the agent, Fort Detrick scientists had tested a staggering 26,000 varieties of chemicals before getting the mix they desired. C123 transport planes, slow and low flying, set about systematically defoliating the countryside.

A combination of two chemicals — one code-named 245T and the other dioxin — made Agent Orange probably the most horrific weapon used in Vietnam. It caused trees to explode, plants to wither in moments; in its wake entire jungles were left stunted and bare. The Vietnamese called the destroyed land "the ground of the dead." But for American commanders the result was gratifying: the Vietcong, caught in the rainstorms of defoliant, found themselves developing the first signs of cancer. This was caused by the dioxin in Agent Orange. A few ounces in the water supply would have been sufficient to poison the entire population of New York.

In all, 250 pounds of dioxin were dropped on Vietnam. Indications that the mass spraying was doing more than destroying vegetation came after the first year. Doctors at Saigon Children's Hospital reported a significant upsurge in the number of babies born with spina bifida and cleft palates. Worse followed. Hospitals throughout South Vietnam reported an increase in still births. Autopsies revealed dioxin in the dead infants' blood. But the spraying went on. And now it was not only the civilian population who were exposed to Agent Orange. The deadly weedkiller was mistakenly dropped on no fewer than forty U.S. bases. Servicemen reported in sick with severe skin eruptions; eventually some of them also developed skin and other kinds of cancer.

For Buckley, hardened as he was by fighting in Korea and what he had witnessed in Europe with the "expendables", "what was happening was a Grade A horror story."

In Montreal another horror story was coming to its climax.

Madeleine Lacroix had been transferred by Dr. Cameron from the Institute to a Montreal neurosurgical unit to undergo a prefrontal lobotomy. The night before, a nurse shaved her hair with shears and lathered her scalp with a shaving brush before using a barber's cut-throat razor to leave her head shiny and bald.

The day of her operation, April 13, 1963, marked the tenth anniversary of MK-ULTRA. Its initial budget of $300,000 had been multiplied many times. Although only Dr. Gottlieb knew the exact figure — for he was the sole paymaster for the secret fund he controlled — the amount ran into millions of dollars. Hundreds of doctors and scientists from different disciplines had been enlisted. But Dr. Cameron remained the program's flag-bearer. He imparted the academic tone that Dr. Gottlieb asserted gave MK-ULTRA "its respectability."

Gottlieb and Cameron's relationship was now one of mutual respect. Dr. Gottlieb knew he did not have to push Dr. Cameron to create new experiments; Cameron in turn issued a steady succession of requests for further funding, and he was always available to take Dr. Gottlieb's calls asking for progress reports. In their latest telephone call he explained the decision he had taken in Madeleine's case.

After forty days in the Isolator followed by a further period in the Sleep Room, Madeline's chronic schizophrenia was now going to be treated by a surgical procedure Dr. Cameron still called "the new psychiatry." Most psychiatrists had concluded that lobotomy operations did not alleviate illness. Many patients became more confused, alternating between inertia and stubbornness. Others developed symptoms such as over-eating, child-like emotional crushes on nurses and doctors, rolling on the floor and alternately weeping and laughing. Lobotomized patients generally lived out their lives in asylums.

Dr. Cameron had become an advocate of the procedure through his contact with Walter Jackson Freeman. A goateed, flamboyant surgeon, Jackson was Professor of Neurology at George Washington University. He often carried with him a human brain in a pickling jar and used a sharp-pointed wooden stiletto — which doubled as his toothpick — to expose nerve pathways. Freeman had long been the acknowledged expert in North America on lobotomy. He had promised his first patient, a woman with a fine head of hair, he would preserve her curls. At the last moment he had shaved her head. But, as he told Dr. Cameron, "afterwards she no longer cared." Since then Freeman had performed over 4,000 further lobotomies to destroy the brains of those suffering from apprehension, anxiety, depression, compulsions, obsessions, as well as drug addicts, sexual deviants and, of course, schizophrenics. He was convinced

the frontal lobe was responsible for a patient's refusal to cooperate in what he termed "an acceptable way."

Dr. Cameron had decided Madeleine fit those criteria. In her
drugged condition she had made sounds in the Isolator that the
voice analyzer in the Radio Telemetry Laboratory had identified as "...father...," "...want baby...," "...father...." Transferred back to the Sleep Room, she had somehow found the
strength to use her helmet to butt a nurse. Such behavior fell
within Freeman's guidelines for those who could benefit from
psychosurgery. "It is better for the patient to have a simplified
intellect. Society can accommodate itself to the most humble
laborer. But it justifiably distrusts the mad thinker," he had
written.

Madeleine was to be operated upon by a Canadian neurosurgeon. She was wheeled into the operating room and transferred
from the trolley to the table. Naked except for a surgical gown,
Madeleine stared, fully conscious, into the powerful overhead
light. The radical lobotomy would be performed under a local anesthetic so that the surgeon could immediately judge her
level of disorientation, indicating how successful his severing of
her frontal lobes was. Until he saw the required signs, he would
continue to destroy portions of Madeleine's brain.

Dr. Cameron arrived in the OR and began to scrub alongside the surgeon and his assistant. The psychiatrist frequently
attended the lobotomy of one of his patients. The three men
emerged from the alcove and stood behind Madeleine's head.
The surgeon fitted an eye-shield over Madeleine's brow to protect her eyes while he swabbed her scalp with antiseptic. The
skin gleamed under the powerful light. The surgeon called for
a scalpel and drew a scratch mark around the area to be in-
cised. The resident handed the surgeon a syringe filled with a
local anesthetic. He injected around the circle, and the skin
bubbled under the effect of the drug. The surgeon was handed

a second syringe of anesthetic and injected this in the same area. It would act as a hemostat, reducing bleeding when the cutting started.

"Do you feel anything, lassie?" Dr. Cameron asked.

Madeleine mumbled. Blood marked the knife's progress. The resident used a curved forceps to hold back the skin flap. The only sound was the discarded instrument being dropped into a bucket. The surgeon continued to use a retractor to peel another portion of scalp from the bone.

"All right, lassie?"

The surgeon dipped his gloved hands in an antiseptic solution. He found it easier to work with damp gloves; they gave more sensitivity to his fingers. The resident sluiced the operative area with an antiseptic solution. A nurse handed the surgeon the surgical brace with its bit already in place. He drilled for a few moments and a fine spray of bone shavings flew into the air. The surgeon asked for a dural hook, an instrument very similar to the one dentists use to locate tooth cavities, and probed the hole. If he detected a crack he knew he had gone through the skull. Madeleine had a rather thick skull. There was no crack. The drilling continued. After he finally retracted the brace, the resident collected the skull shavings and placed them in a small galipot. The dust would be used to fill up the burr hole at the end of the operation. The surgeon used a syringe to wash the cavity clean. He asked for a tenotome. The nurse handed him the small scalpel with its finely honed blade. He snipped a corner of the dura mater, the tough membranous covering of the brain. Then, using a dural scissors, he began to cut away the skin, fraction by fraction. Madeleine's brain was exposed, milky pinkish in color.

"Do you feel anything, lassie?"

Madeleine made a grunt sound.

"Lassie, count to ten."

A series of grunts came from Madeleine. The surgeon inserted a spatula into the burr hole. He worked to a definite routine; down a few millimeters, then a pause to move the instrument a few millimeters laterally. Each move destroyed more of Madeleine's brain.

"Lassie, can you sing your favorite song?"

There were more grunts from Madeleine. The surgeon continued to destroy her brain.

"Do you feel sleepy, lassie?"

She gave Dr. Cameron a grunt. The surgeon withdrew the tube and asked for a cannula, a heavy-gauge hypodermic needle. He inserted it into the hole and, using steady pressure, drove it down to the spheroidal, the bony ridge at the base of her skull. He withdrew the cannula and once more inserted the spatula and forced its handle upwards so that the blade could be drawn along the base of her skull and a cut made as far to the side as possible in her brain. The spatula was pulled out and the burr hole rinsed of the oozing fluid. In all, four cuts were made, two to each side of the hole.

Dr. Cameron continued to ask Madeleine questions. They were part of what he termed "the disorientation yardstick" – his means of knowing how much brain destruction was being achieved. The surgeon continued his work, poking and cutting.

"Lassie, speak to me."

A further grunt. The surgeon continued, crushing forever Madeleine's prime areas of emotional responses. Finally, she made no more sounds, closed her eyes and fell into a stupor. Dr. Cameron bent over Madeleine. Removing the eye-shield, he lifted one and then another of her eyelids. She stared vacantly back at him.

"Lassie, it's all over, no more pain."

He left the operating theater to return to the Institute for his morning ward round. Later that day Madeleine was transferred to St.Jean de Dieu Hospital to enter the custodial care of the religious sisters who maintained a number of zombies like her.

On the other side of the world in Saigon, William Buckley once more thrust aside his doubts about American involvement in a war he believed could not be won. From his small office in a house on Pasteur Street, the CIA's headquarters in the Cholon suburb of the city, he bent to his task of making it as hard as possible for the North Vietnamese to win. He had established a reputation for being able to ease his way through the brutal freak show the war had become. From the day he saw a Buddhist monk pour gasoline over his head and immolate on a crowded Saigon street while other monks formed a protective circle around him, he had concluded: "This is going to be a different kind of war for me, for America, for the whole world."

Yet, Vietnam suited his mentality, just as Korea had. Very quickly, he had turned a motley group of Vietnamese hill tribesmen into one of the best clandestine fighting groups operating in the country. Using Gottlieb's Assassination Manual, he trained the tribesmen to kill in a variety of ways. In his broken-in combat boots, rumpled fatigues and cap, Buckley led from the front; no challenge was too great to meet. He had taught them neither to show nor expect mercy. A confidential report to Richard Helms, soon to be head of Clandestine Operations in Langley, from Elliot Richardson, the CIA chief of station in Saigon, described Buckley as that "rarity out here, a man who can analyze a situation and then kill without compunction."

Buckley would remember it as "a real charge. The first time I went down a tunnel, I thought 'Hey, this is what I really want to do. Go after the enemy and take him on hand-to-hand'. I also needed to show my men how to do it." He took few prisoners for a "God-damned simple reason. The interrogation centers were overcrowded. The whole business of bringing in a Vietcong and interrogating him was a lengthy one. There was also a drive on for building up the body count. It came all the way down from the top. So it was just simpler to eliminate a person in the field rather than having to deal with all the paperwork that goes with a good interrogation. I encouraged my people to never forget the body count. The head of a Vietcong, or his ear, or an ID card, was sufficient to earn a reward of anything up to ten thousand piasters. Maybe some of the wrong guys did get killed. But an awful lot of the bad guys were also taken out."

But Buckley had also seen that brutality alone did not work. The more the South Vietnamese pushed their Vietcong prisoners out of American-built aircraft, the more the Vietcong spitted babies in village compounds to terrorize villagers into hiding and feeding them, and acting as informers.

Operating with the free hand given all CIA agents in Vietnam, Buckley began to use the hypnotism he had learned in New York to deadly purpose. Captured Vietcong were hypnotized and, under his spell, they were told they would be provided with hand grenades and other weapons. They should then return to their outfits. The signal for them to attack their colleagues would be when they were welcomed back. How successful the experiment was would never be known. But Buckley made use of a number of the "dirty tricks" he had learned from contact with Dr. Gottlieb. In the villages he strongly suspected the Vietcong controlled, he planted foods that had been poisoned with anthrax or one of the other lethal substances that were sent from Langley for his use.

Unlike the distaste he had felt over what was happening at the Institute in Montreal, Buckley had no hesitation in using such methods in Vietnam. For him it was "all out war." This philosophy contributed to his legendary stature. Around the building on Pasteur Street he became known as "Top Spy." Some colleagues even went so far as to say he was the reincarnation of Lawrence of Arabia. Buckley would later admit he had the single-minded purpose of destroying the enemy by all possible means. He knew the Vietcong had targeted him for assassination. He knew they tried to stalk him, ready at the first opportunity to eliminate him. But that did not change his lifestyle. He bedded women with an ease other men envied; he could hold his liquor as well as any soldier. He also had a barely concealed contempt for many of his superiors. In turn they came to resent him. But to those who really mattered — the Vietnamese agents he ran — he was a genuine hero.

It was the happiest time of his life. The rotting jungles of Vietnam had finally wiped away the memory of the pungent aroma of chemicals that always lurked in the corridors of the Institute in Montreal.

Mary Morrow had screamed for hours that she had not consented to electroshock treatment. When she no longer had the strength to shout, she repeatedly sobbed. Every morning she heard Dr. Cameron striding past her room. She thought he was "cruel, savage, inhumane," not to visit her. Waiting was as bad as not knowing what to do. She increasingly felt weak and exhausted and finally didn't have the energy to get out of bed. She was left with a sense of "nothingness." The numbing apathy was as agonizing as any pain. Fear seemed to squeeze her heart. Outside in the corridor, she heard nurses occasionally laughing as they passed. When they brought meals she told them over and again that she didn't belong here, that she wanted to go back to the Royal Victoria and that she was not going to allow herself to be electroshocked. They said nothing. One morning Dr. Cameron appeared with a junior doctor. He carried a tray covered with a surgical towel. She knew what was underneath and repeated she had not given her consent for electroshock. Dr. Cameron didn't answer, only stood, towering above her.

She couldn't stop the rush of words: "I don't want it. It's wrong for me. I don't want to be zapped like that. I don't want electroshock. You can't force me. You can't make a patient have treatment she doesn't want. I'm a doctor. I know what I'm talking about. Do you understand? I know what I'm talking about," she recalled to the author.

"Lassie, listen to me." Dr. Cameron spoke precisely. "We're going to put you to sleep. And we're going to give you shock treatment when you're asleep."

"No!"

Dr. Cameron removed the cover from the tray and picked up a syringe, already filled with clear liquid. He removed the sheath from the needle. She thought, "My God, he can't do this! He can't! He can't!" A great band seemed to be stretched around her chest, cutting off words.

"Give me your arm, lassie."

"No! Please, no!" Somehow she managed to speak.

"You've seen it help others. Don't you want it to help you?"

She shook her head. Once more she couldn't speak. It was terrifying. She knew what she must say but no sound came from her lips.

"Your arm, lassie."

She hated him. He had lied to her; it had all been a trick on his part to get her to voluntarily come into hospital. He stood over her with the needle poised.

"No shocks! Please!" She screamed, all control gone. "No shocks!"

He injected her. Through the door came a nurse wheeling the electroshock trolley.

"N-o... No..........!"

Darkness.

Robert Cleghorn was coming to feel that Dr. Cameron's methods were "lacking in validity." Observations like that run through the notebooks filled with his account of life at the Institute. They record his private thoughts about his superior. He later gave a copy of his notebooks to the author.

"Dr. Cameron's methods take little or no account of the fact that psychiatry, like other branches of medicine, is changing, often dramatically. Diagnosis is becoming more sophisticated. Schizophrenia is no longer simply called just that, but there is now "latent," "pseudoneurotic," "pseudo-pathopathic," "borderline" and "creeping" schizophrenia. Organic brain damage has been separated into "minimal brain damage" and "minimal brain dysfunction." At the same time the methods of treating an illness are more specific. Every few months a new antidepressant appears: a range of tranquilizers and the more powerful phenothiazines help to control the physiological function of almost every organ system in the body. The age of the blunderbuss approach when a patient was shot full of everything in the hope some of it would work is almost over," Dr. Cleghorn had written.

It was the time when there were also the first indications of public awareness of the dangers of over-medication, the first stories in the press about the first lawsuits brought by patients in the United States who claimed they had been maltreated, the first calls for government regulation. Dr. Cleghorn had reminded his own staff, never to prescribe drugs indiscriminately and never to do so without the most thorough physical examination. No drug was ever to be used on his patients simply for "institutional management."

Nevertheless, Dr. Cameron continued to preside over a divided institute, cleverly exploiting the division between the psychotherapists and the neurologically oriented psychiatrists. With a few words he could set researcher against researcher, physician against physician. More disturbing to the fastidious

Dr. Cleghorn, whose own scientific publications continued to place him at the forefront of medical research in North America, Dr. Cameron continued "to support bootleg research. He still had a blind spot for psychopaths. His acceptance of such characters in his entourage was deeply worrying."

Dr. Cleghorn had no inkling that the dark shadow of the drug culture which had swept across North America had been triggered by MK-ULTRA. LSD was being described in new ways. It was called "psychedelic" and "mind expanding." On university campuses, students and teachers were experimenting with the drug. "Taking a trip," or "turning on," became a status symbol. In discotheques, flashing colored lights suggested the impact of the LSD experience. Tripping, freaking out and blowing one's mind had become Dr. Gottlieb's gift to the nation. But now the first reports were surfacing of the downside of the drug: bad trips that led to psychotic episodes, even suicide.

The news confirmed Dr. Cleghorn's worst fears that LSD was a dangerous substance that should have no place in treatment at the Institute. Publicly he still displayed a sense of loyalty to Dr. Cameron. He studiously avoided voicing any open criticism about his treatments — and detested the personal gossip about his senior. Junior doctors had spread the story that Dr. Cameron was having an affair with a private patient he saw in his office twice a week late in the evening. The doctors claimed they heard giggling coming from the office. One of the nurses on South-Two insisted she had seen Dr. Cameron embracing the woman. Working late one evening, Dr. Cleghorn had passed Dr. Cameron in a corridor and had been astonished to see what looked like a lipstick smudge on his collar.

In his notebook, Dr. Cleghorn had reminded himself "people who could not even spell 'paranoia' thought they knew how best it should be treated." A short while earlier Dr. Cleghorn had discovered that his chief had manipulated evidence. In his latest paper on "psychic driving," Dr. Cameron claimed a total success in all patients treated. Yet Dr. Cleghorn knew that the treatment — one which he steadfastly refused to use on his patients — was anything but effective. Nearly half of the several hundred who had received "psychic driving" in the past five years and then been discharged, had to be re-admitted to the Institute within a year. Depatterning had also proven to be equally ineffective for curing schizophrenia. Yet Dr. Cameron boldly claimed a high success rate for the method by using a "mumbo-jumbo of statistics dressed up in fancy tabulations." Dr. Cleghorn had noted that "Madison Avenue language sits ill in what proposes to be a scientific explanation of serious psychic mechanisms."

Dr. Cleghorn had come to see that what was wrong with Dr. Cameron's approach was it lacked a properly organized system. "There were too many assumptions and inconsistencies. Dr. Cameron seemed primarily concerned with pacification, sedation and repression. He was too quick to label, to fall back on jargon," he wrote in his diary.

Dr. Morrow awoke with a blinding headache. "I was in a deep, dark pitch-black hole with no sense of appendages, like a worm. There was no sense of solidity, like I was not on ground and I was not on water. It was like being suspended in an eerie, black hole."

Next morning she received another series of multiple shocks. That night she dreamed she was being electrocuted. Two mornings later Dr. Cameron, accompanied by a nurse with the trolley, came again. They came three more times the following week. She wondered how much longer she could endure the searing pain in her head. She lay in bed, terrified her mind had begun to disintegrate under the amount of electricity passing through her head.

On the eleventh day, a Saturday, Dr. Cameron gave Mary Morrow, twelve consecutive electroshocks. No other patient had received so many in one session. He then went home for the weekend. Mary was unconscious for most of the day. That Saturday evening her sister, Margy, came to the Institute. She had traveled from New York after receiving a phone call from their mother. Mrs. Mathilda Morrow had suffered a recent stroke and because of that had been unable to visit the Institute from her home in Montreal. But her daily calls to her daughter's bedside thoroughly alarmed her. "Mary," she told Margy, "sounds more and more strange."

At the Institute Margy was refused permission to see her sister. Already emotionally wrought, Margy threatened to call the police and was reluctantly allowed to visit. The sight of Mary deeply upset Margy. She rushed from the hospital to their mother. In spite of her infirmity, Mrs. Morrow was a calm and resourceful woman. Having listened to Margy's report, she telephoned Dr. Cleghorn. He was sympathetic, but he said that because Mary Morrow was not his patient, there was no way he could intervene. He recommended Mrs. Morrow call Dr. Cameron. It was Saturday evening when she contacted Cameron at home in Lake Placid. He was politely distant and interrupted: "The best you can hope for is that your daughter will go into a home. She'll never again practice medicine." He hung up.

Mrs. Morrow called the Institute and told several nurses and doctors that under no circumstances was her daughter to receive any further treatment. The senior doctor on duty telephoned Dr. Cameron. He ordered that Mary Morrow be given 300 milligrams of Largactil. For the next two days she was maintained in a drugged stupor as the dosage of Largactil was stepped up to 600 milligrams. She developed an itchy rash.

Back at work after the weekend, Dr. Cameron did not visit Mary Morrow. His absence struck a new fear in her. He was probably preparing something else. The possibility gave her strength she thought she never possessed. The glimmer of anger took root and quickly grew, wild and raw and therapeutic. He had been like a "seducer" sitting in her room in the Royal Victoria and dangling the prospect of taking her back as a doctor, yet all the while "scheming to use me like a pink mouse in a laboratory experiment." Her anger grew, surfacing through the Largactil, nourished by the way he had treated her. She began to feel alive, truly, for the first time in a year — perhaps in years. She reminded herself she had been very ill and was not fully recovered. But she was not helpless. And he was not going to make her dependent on him. He had treated her as if she was a "no-hoper." Well, she wasn't — and she would show him. The anger continued to surge through her, powerful and invigorating. He had not once asked her how she felt as a person and never discussed her feelings as a human being. Yet he had gone ahead and blasted electricity through her brain. My God, how he had duped her! Looking back on her whole relationship with him, she realized he had not even bothered about her as a patient. She had just been someone else "on whom to try out his theories."

Her anger deepened. She had suffered greatly those past years and much of the pain she had borne stoically. The past weeks had been especially horrible. Deeply troubled and desperate, she had been treated inhumanely. Even now it was not finished. There was a choking feeling in her larynx — and she wondered if somehow the electroshock had damaged her vocal chords. Mary Morrow used her bedside telephone to call a doctor she trusted at the Royal Victoria. When she explained her symptoms, he promised to come at once.

Waiting, she continued to fuel her fury, knowing it was one way to keep her mind alert. She had always wanted to believe Dr. Cameron cared for his patients. "But he didn't. They were just symptoms to be injected, shocked and put to sleep. He never related to a patient, but remained behind his own line of demarcation: he was healthy, a patient was sick. He had actually made me feel guilty for daring to resist his methods. There was something about him that was mad and evil," she recalled to the author.

The doctor arrived. He arranged for Mary Morrow's immediate transfer to the Royal Victoria Hospital. As she left the Institute, she again thanked God that she had escaped whatever fate Dr. Cameron had planned for her. But what of others? That question filled her mind as the taxi drove her to the Royal Victoria. What about all the hundreds of patients who over the years had come into Cameron's hands? What had happened to them? She felt a sense of kinship with them. If what had happened to her was typical, and she increasingly believed it was, then he had also treated them as less than human. They needed to be helped — and the sooner she found a way back into medicine, the better she could offer to do so.

In Vietnam Buckley wrote in a postcard to a colleague at Langley: "Here it's a life like no other. Life is whatever day it is and wherever I am. I'm eating well and keeping fit. Hope you are all ok. Best, Bill." Buckley had no wife, children, house; not even a steady girlfriend. He wasn't close to his family any more.

"Vietnam suited me," he would say years later. "I knew that from the first time I went out into the jungle. It touched me, something in me. Out there, especially at night, the silence was like a time that didn't move, the darkness was like no other darkness. Silence and stillness. It's a great way to focus your mind. In the jungle you learn to breathe differently; breathe so that the enemy can't hear you. That kind of breathing brings a sort of peace to your mind; helps to dampen down the fears.

Sure you are scared. God Almighty, if you weren't, you would become too relaxed."

CHAPTER FOURTEEN

William Buckley would remember everything about the morning of October 4, 1963: the rain scudding across the military airfield outside Saigon; the tall, gaunt-faced figure of William Egan Colby standing ramrod stiff beside him; the carbine-toting MPs forming a cordon toward which the United States Air Force transport was taxiing. The tension was like a living thing, a dangerous mix of hoped-for success and the fear of failure.

The operation started at midnight. The plan was to literally wipe out the Vietcong leadership in one massive push through Saigon and its environs. No city, town or hamlet was to be left untouched by the assassination teams the two men had put together. Attached to each unit were veterans from Buckley's special Vietnam forces, men he had trained when he had first come to Saigon. They had passed on to their teams the knowledge he had given them. In turn the teams had been ordered to do one thing: kill. Kill the guerrillas. Kill those who succored them.

Since midnight several hundred units had set about doing this. Early reports indicated that they were close to running out of control, driven by a terrible bloodlust. Buckley feared there might be a backlash when news of what was happening reached the United States, as it surely would. Vietnam had become the most reported war in history. If Colby shared a similar concern, he did not show it as the transport's engines died to a murmur. Colby rarely showed any emotion. He was a graduate of Princeton and Columbia, and during World War II he served with the OSS in Europe for two years. It was there he had developed the philosophy of kill-or-be-killed. Among his circle of close friends from that time was George Hunter White.

Buckley regarded Colby as "having the warmth of a glacier." Nevertheless they had worked well together in helping to put the operation in place. Buckley had used his detailed knowledge of the Vietcong structure, identifying its ambush units, its secret police units, its medical units, and the eleven separate units in the air which made up the Vietcong in the Saigon area. Colby had ensured the operation had the full approval of President Kennedy. With that authority, Colby had forced the rival intelligence and police agencies in Saigon to pool their information so that dossiers and blacklists could be drawn up on those targeted for assassination. Colby wanted a minimum of 1,000 guerrillas killed every month and twice that number captured and held for interrogation.

In the run-up to the operation's launch, Buckley had detected that Saigon's already corrupt officials saw the operation as a new way to blackmail innocents and extort bribes from those who should be arrested. He could do nothing about that; corruption was an integral part of Vietnamese society. Waiting for the passengers to emerge down the rear ramp of the plane, Colby offered his first judgment: "This operation is going to do wonders for the body count." Nevertheless, Buckley knew there was an element of desperation in the White House's approval. Kennedy hoped this operation would force the North Vietnam regime in Hanoi to come to the negotiating table. Buckley figured that failure would leave Kennedy only two options, both of which could irrevocably damage his hopes of re-election. The first was to withdraw from South Vietnam and face severe political damage at home and diplomatic humiliation abroad. Or he could escalate the war by launching an all-out bombing offensive against Hanoi, which would mean committing more men and hardware into an already costly war.

In silence Colby and Buckley watched Dr. Sidney Gottlieb coming down the aircraft's ramp with a handful of men.

Buckley knew who these people were; the MOST SECRET cable he had received from Dr. Gottlieb described the men simply as "medical personnel of various disciplines." Dr. Gottlieb was in Vietnam to use the war as a test bed for MK-ULTRA. He knew there would be no shortage of "expendables" for his latest experiments. He had ordered Buckley to make sure everything was in place by the time he arrived.

Buckley had chosen Bien Hoa Prison situated on the outskirts of Saigon. In the past hours its already crowded cells had been crammed with those arrested in the new operation. On his way to the airport, Buckley had stopped by the prison to ensure that Dr. Gottlieb's instructions had been fulfilled. A building in the compound had been set aside. In one room were half a dozen operating tables that had been requested from a U.S. military hospital in Saigon. Attached to the room was an anesthesia induction area. Close by was a pen where the first batch of prisoners were already held. Some showed signs of having been severely beaten. Beyond the makeshift operating room was another room, windowless and empty.

Buckley and Colby hurried forward to welcome Dr. Gottlieb and the members of his team whom Gottlieb introduced only by first names. They carried medical bags which Buckley guessed were filled with surgical tools. He had heard that surgeons liked to work with their own equipment. That night, after a short rest, Dr. Gottlieb asked Buckley to take them to Bien Hoa. He explained: "My people want to get started as soon as possible."

At night the prison seemed even more sinister. Harsh lights cast shadows over the compound. There was constant shouting and screaming from the cell blocks. Dr. Gottlieb and his team set to work. Prison guards brought a man to the induction room. One of the team anaesthetized the prisoner. The guards carried him into the makeshift operating room. Meantime, another prisoner was being anaesthetized. Dr. Gottlieb asked Buckley to join him in the OR. They watched one of the surgeons perform the same technique that had been used to open Madeleine's skull. Once the brain was exposed, one of the neurologists implanted electrodes in different parts of the brain. While another surgeon closed-up the opening, a second prisoner was on another table, undergoing similar surgery. Soon all the tables were occupied. Buckley would remember the scene: "Gottlieb was going from table to table, commenting and nodding approvingly. There were no proper OR lights for the surgeons to see. They had to make do with overhead strip lights. There was no attempt at sterilization. The surgeons wore gowns and masks, but that was really only to protect their clothes from the blood. That was everywhere. The OR smelled like an abattoir. Once a prisoner's head wound was closed, the guards carried him away."

Each man was taken to the empty room adjoining the OR. There he was placed on the floor and allowed to recover. By midnight the floor was littered with prisoners in various stages of recovery. Dr. Gottlieb moved among them, placing a bayonet beside each man. Then he went to an adjoining room and began to manipulate switches on a black box to transmit signals to the electrode implants. To a baffled Buckley, Dr. Gottlieb explained he wanted the electrodes to stimulate anger in the men, to the point where they would use their bayonets to attack one another. He said if he could achieve that, he would have created assassins to order.

"He was almost dancing a jig in his excitement. He said the black box could be developed to have a range of up to a mile. At that distance it would be possible to infiltrate an assassin into the area of an unsuspecting target and signal him to kill. Gottlieb's excitement did not last long. The prisoners just sat there fingering their head wounds and showing no signs of violence. The scientist ordered the guards to remove them. The guinea pigs were later shot and their bodies burned," Buckley would remember.

All told, twenty-four prisoners were subjected to this treatment. Not one displayed any signs of violence despite Dr. Gottlieb's repeated tweaking of the black box dials. All were executed. Over the next two days a further sixty prisoners suffered the same fate. On the third day, Dr. Gottlieb and his hardworking team flew back to the United States. Watching them go, Buckley decided to report the whole matter to Colby. Colby told him to "forget you ever saw anything."

In the Institute in Montreal, Jan Zielinski had increasingly come to dread the Sleep Room. He found the "groaning and moaning" too upsetting. What he had seen had started troubling his sleep: a woman sobbing at what she was forced to listen to, a man reduced to drooling after weeks of chemically controlled nightmares. Worst of all, he hated those times when a patient begged him not to fit another tape into a football helmet or pillow speaker. He knew he was not alone in feeling horrified at what was happening. Some of the Institute's doctors had expressed shock that Dr. Cameron now gave patients curare to paralyze them so there was no way they could physically stop the tapes. When Zielinski tried to discuss matters with Rubenstein, he was reminded how much they both owed Dr. Cameron, but Zielinski felt the Institute was no longer the place he first came to work in. Then it had been a close-knit community. Now new faces regularly appeared; every square foot of the mansion was being utilized.

In the watchtower of what, a century earlier, had been a shipowner's mansion, researchers worked in renovated broom closets, a shoe black's cubbyhole and a maid's bedroom. The dialects of Africa, Asia and the Middle East ran through the wards and corridors. Zielinski had noticed some of the Iranian staff did not even know how to read the settings on the electro-shock machines.

Nevertheless, that was no defense for what the physician everyone called "Ataturk" had done to the patient called Sammy. Sammy had been admitted to North-Two and soon regaled everyone on the wing with his outlandish stories of life in the outback. He said he had wrestled with a grizzly bear and survived a bison charge. He insisted he had been a fighter pilot in Korea, a submariner in the Atlantic, a Marine on duty in the frozen North. At various other times he also claimed to have been a gold miner, a fairground boxing-booth champion and a big-game hunter. There was nothing Sammy had not done — at least in his mind. He was an engaging fantasist. A small, vigorous man, clear-eyed and fair-haired, he was charming and outgoing and always managed somehow to suggest the situation he now found himself in was slightly embarrassing. His pleasant well-modulated baritone voice intrigued Zielinski, and Sammy had confided that not only was he born in Wales, but he was a druid. His case file gave his birthplace as Nova Scotia.

There was no mistaking where Dr. Ataturk came from: dark-skinned, muscular and swarthy, he looked like what he was, a man from one of the mountain villages of eastern Turkey. He had graduated from medical school in Ankara and had been sent by his government on a student visa to Montreal. The Institute was increasingly staffed by such doctors. They came for a year and were given wide clinical responsibilities. Dr. Ataturk had been assigned to Sammy's case. There had been immediate conflict. Sammy had claimed he was descended from the Caliph of Baghdad and objected to being treated by a peasant. Dr. Ataturk had demanded his patient apologize. Sammy said he would have the doctor banished from the Institute for "insulting his Royal personage." The physician prescribed 1000 milligrams of Largactil a day for Sammy and sent him to the Sleep Room.

To the analysts on the staff, Sammy appeared an excellent case for psychotherapy. Instead, over a two-week period, Ataturk gave Sammy one hundred and twenty separate electroshocks. On the fifteenth day Sammy died of a heart attack. The distress felt by many of the staff turned to whispered anger when they realized Dr. Cameron did not intend to reprimand Ataturk. Instead the medical director left on another of his trips, this time to Japan. Each time he went abroad, his return was marked shortly after by the arrival of yet more foreign doctors. None were as absolutely detested as Ataturk. After Sammy's death he was tagged "Dr. Death."

Dr. Cleghorn had been treating Agnes Roper as a patient for a few weeks. She had come into therapy on the strict condition her husband not know. Dr. Cleghorn had reluctantly agreed, though he knew it would only be a short time before Peter Roper discovered the truth. Cleghorn liked both of them. Agnes Roper still showed glimpses of what she had once been, a witty and vivacious woman. Her husband was one of the most dedicated psychiatrists on the staff. He willingly took on cases that were labeled as "no-hopers" and "FRs" — final referrals. Dr. Cleghorn's concern was that the senior resident drove himself too hard and, having begun to treat Agnes' fears and frustrations, he understood why her husband did so. With her manic-depressive illness she had turned their home into a battleground. Dr. Cleghorn realized Agnes' symptoms were well advanced, and he could not be certain any treatment would do more than partially help. As he made his morning rounds, he knew he could not put off much longer discussing Agnes Roper with her husband.

Dr. Cleghorn's rounds were altogether more leisurely than Dr. Cameron's. Dr. Cleghorn spent considerable time discussing each patient's progress. He invited junior doctors to ask additional questions and used the answers to help him judge the overall clinical picture. The rounds included visiting Dr. Cameron's patients when he was away from the hospital. Their case notes indicated many were treated very differently from the way he would have handled their cases himself. This had not struck Dr. Cleghorn more forcibly than it did when he came to the bedside of a teenager, Simone, a friend of his daughter's. Simone was a tall, vibrant girl and on her visits to his home, Dr. Cleghorn had briefly wondered at her mood changes; she could switch from being voluble to withdrawn in the space of an evening. But he had not given it much thought. In his judgment she was a long way from needing professional help.

Now, in her hospital bed, she resembled what he imagined a zombie would look like, one of the "living dead" of Haiti that a researcher was studying in the Institute's Transcultural Behavior Laboratory. Simone had the same vacant stare and deathly pallor the researcher had shown Dr. Cleghorn in photos of zombies he had brought back from the island. In the two weeks since admission, Simone had received fifty separate electroshocks. Dr. Cameron had diagnosed her as schizophrenic. Dr. Cleghorn ordered the treatment stopped. More than that he felt he could not do.

Back from Vietnam, Dr. Gottlieb mulled over the way Saigon's prostitutes had seemed able to manipulate U.S. servicemen. He wondered how many of them were in the pay of the Vietcong. From that Gottlieb developed another operation to investigate the role of sexual entrapment in covert operations. Once more he chose San Francisco as the city where it could be carried out; in his mind it resembled the licentiousness of Saigon in many ways.

Richard Helms, a man Dr. Gottlieb openly revered, was now Deputy Director of the CIA. He was a dyed-in-the-wool Agency man, having earned his stripes with the OSS. Throughout his steady climb to his seventh floor office, Helms had encouraged Dr. Gottlieb to develop MK-ULTRA to its maximum potential. Although he appeared bureaucratic to outsiders, to those in his inner circle Helms was the can-do-leader Dr. Gottlieb had yearned for since the departure of Allen Dulles. Helms thought Dr. Gottlieb's proposal to use sex as a weapon was "one heck of a hoot."

Over a quarter of a million dollars was set aside for what became known as "Operation Climax." An apartment was rented in San Francisco's Nob Hill area. Whores were recruited from the city's Tenderloin district. They would be paid between $200 and $500 a week, depending on the hours worked. They were questioned by CIA psychologists. Why had they come into the business? How did they feel about selling their bodies? What did they normally talk about to their clients? The psychologists had compared their observations and pondered if it was possible to actually train prostitutes to become intelligence officers. The spirit of Mata Hari permeated the apartment.

To launch the operation the agents decided to hold a cocktail party and spray the unsuspecting guests with LSD, sending them on a collective trip. The prospect was warmly endorsed by Dr. Gottlieb. He ordered his technicians to fill aerosols with LSD. They were variously labeled as insect repellents, deodorants and perfumes. In the meantime, CIA agents spent a week visiting the bars in downtown San Francisco issuing invitations to a party to launch a new club. The chosen day was a Bay Area broiler — sultry and humid. The whores looked their best. Trays of canapés had been provided. Beer and wine was on ice. The windows were closed so that the sprayed LSD would not escape. Guests who did not know each other or their hosts arrived and, as with all such parties, there were a number of gate-crashers. The apartment was soon overflowing. The psychologists decided to wait until everyone was at "second drink level" before beginning the spraying. But while the guests happily swallowed CIA booze and pawed CIA-paid-for tarts, they also began to open the windows. In vain the Agency men rushed around closing them. Soon every window in the apartment was wide open to let in the first evening breeze. The psychologists began to spray, going from room to room explaining that they "wanted to freshen-up the place," or "kill off the roaches." No matter how diligently they worked, the LSD drifted out of the windows.

Another MK-ULTRA project had failed.

After Operation Climax came to an inglorious end, Helms told Dr. Gottlieb that in his meetings with the Canadian Department of Defense and the country's Royal Canadian Mounted Police secret intelligence branch, it had become clear that both were becoming more sensitive about their collaboration with the CIA. At the last meeting Helms had attended in Ottawa, there had been questions about what was going on at the Institute. Helms had reassured them that Dr. Cameron's research was still at an early stage and would, naturally, be shared with Canada.

After the San Francisco debacle, Helms suggested to Dr. Gottlieb that it "may be a good idea to pull in the reins as far as the Institute went." Dr. Gottlieb argued that Dr. Cameron was still the most powerful figure in North American psychiatry, if not in the entire Western world and that in every way he remained the ideal cover for MK-ULTRA's quest for mind control. Helms repeated his caution that Dr. Gottlieb keep a close eye on matters.

In early November 1963, Dr. Gottlieb summoned three staff psychologists, Walter Pasternak, John Gittinger and Dr. Wolff to his office to discuss how best to monitor what was happening at the Institute. Dr. Gottlieb suggested the ideal way to do so would be to involve Dr. Cameron in Gittinger's latest program. Called the Personality Assessment System, PAS, it was intended to predict future behavior. Dr. Gottlieb saw it as yet another key to mind control.

Over $1 million had been spent developing PAS, which had involved testing no fewer than 29,000 unsuspecting subjects across the United States. When patients consulted their own physicians, they found themselves answering Dr. Gittinger's questionnaires. He fed their responses into a computer. PAS broke down personalities into two broad categories: Regulated, R-type; Flexible, F-type. Dr. Gittinger claimed that by placing a personality into one category or the other, a number of important judgments could be made. It was possible to predict whether a person would remain faithful, become a drunk or a sexual deviant, whether he or she had a tight control on imagination, a thorough grasp of detail, a high boredom tolerance — or had an unstable or over-indulgent type of personality. PAS allowed for cultural variables and could be applied equally successfully to a North American or a Russian or Chinese. For the Agency it would be an invaluable tool for case officers to use when handling agents or interrogating suspected spies. The one drawback was that PAS required accurate measurements using an entire battery of Weschler intelligence tests, themselves among the more complex of psychological assessment scales.

Dr. Gittinger now had a splendid new office in Washington from where he ran Psychological Assessment Associates. It had opened offices in Tokyo and Hong Kong to test potential employees for commercial firms, which was one way for the CIA to recoup MK-ULTRA's huge investment in PAS. Dr. Gittinger wanted to test PAS on schizophrenics. By using a checklist of forty "personality pattern trends" he hoped to be able to focus on the psychological differences between a healthy and chroni-

cally sick personality and to uncover at an early stage schizoid
symptoms in a supposedly normal person. But first he needed
a readily available supply of schizophrenics that Dr. Cameron's
Institute could provide.

Dr. Wolff was present because he had recently conducted a
review of Dr. Cameron's work with Dr. Pasternak. Some of his
research, in their view, was bizarre. Dr. Gottlieb reminded them
that Einstein had been considered crazy. With growing passion,
he said that Dr. Cameron continued to publish in some of the
world's leading journals, papers that suggested he could at last be
on the verge of the long-awaited breakthrough on mind control.
In the *American Journal of Psychiatry* his "Repetition of Verbal
Signals: Behavioral and Psychological Changes," claimed that
"attitudes and interpersonal relationships and self-concepts"
had been dramatically changed under "psychic driving." Another paper, "Images of Tomorrow," envisioned a future where the
"restructuring of personality" would be routinely achieved with
"suggestion and extra-sensory perception." It had been published in Britain's *Journal of Psychiatry*. Dr. Gottlieb wanted one
question answered: did all this published evidence indicate Dr.
Cameron had, in the past three years, made significant progress
that was of potential benefit to the Agency? It was agreed that
Dr. Wolff and the two psychologists would travel to Montreal
to evaluate Dr. Cameron's work and see if there were a number
of suitable schizophrenics for Dr. Gittinger's purposes.

Walking up the drive to the Institute, Velma Orlikov again
thought it was "a spooky place." Even the sunshine of an autumn day did not remove that feeling. Driving from Ottawa —
the family had moved from Winnipeg so that David could better tend to his duties as a Member of Parliament — Velma had
struggled with a feeling that as far as her therapy went, she was
"standing still or losing ground." For the past three years she

had come at regular intervals, a week at a time, to the Institute. Each day as an outpatient she sat in a room with a tape-recorder and a notebook listening and writing. Rubenstein regularly came and replaced a spool or took away her full notebook. He often made some remark that set her teeth on edge. Dr. Cameron still gave her injections of LSD and her mind would fill with gothic images of cages and creatures, coffins and bodies. When she came out of the nightmares, her symptoms remained: the depression and the feeling that life was not worth living. Yet there were also times when she believed herself "cured" and her distress was all that greater when the depression returned.

Dr. Cameron's tape recording — a copy of which the author later heard — provides confirmation of her feelings as she sat in the chair before his desk.

"Well, lassie?"

He always began with the same question.

"I... I don't want to... come anymore."

He asked her to repeat what she had said.

"I-I-I don't want to come. It isn't working."

"Yes?" The question hung.

"I don't feel... any better." The last two words came in a rush.

"Why don't you want to be helped?"

Silence. She was once more frightened.

"Well, tell me why you don't want to be helped."

There was nothing understanding or compassionate in his tone.

"I can't help you if you don't tell me what is bothering you, lassie."

"David..."

"Not your husband, lassie. It's not what bothers him. But you. That's what I want to know."

Another silence on the tape.

"Lassie, what is this about?" His voice was sharp and probing.

Another silence. He rose to his feet.

"Lassie, go to your room and write it all down. It's the only way I can help you. Write it all down. What your husband said. Everything that comes into your head. What you feel like when you make love. What you think about your husband. Everything."

"I want to go home. I want to try and get better myself. I'm upsetting everybody. Please try and understand. Please."

"Lassie! Stop this!"

"Thank you for seeing me."

Her voice on the tape is low and dispirited.

"Lassie, you'd better think about coming back in. Never mind what your husband says. It's what I say that matters here."

She ran down the corridor to her room. Behind its closed door she burst into tears. Though there was no tape to record her words, she would remember them well: "Will it never end?"

CHAPTER FIFTEEN

After Dr. Gottlieb had decided to send Dr. Wolff and his two associates to Montreal to reassess the value of Dr. Cameron's work, he sent a "MOST SECRET" message to the telex machine in Buckley's office in Saigon, saying that three more "medical specialists" would be arriving to conduct further "research." Buckley was to ensure there were sufficient numbers of "subjects" available for testing. Afterwards, Buckley was to return with the specialists to Langley. When the message arrived, Buckley was out of Saigon on a field trip up on the Ho Chi Minh Trail. Named after North Vietnam's legendary leader, the trail was the supply route along which men and supplies from the North reinforced the Vietcong guerrillas. Buckley had placed his own "assets" along the trail, men the Vietcong called *my-nguy*, American puppets. If caught, they were tortured and executed. Buckley had lost scores of *my-nguy* over the past year. The purpose of this trip was to find replacements for them. He would make the usual offer — in return for working for him he would arrange for them to go to America with their families when the war ended.

Buckley returned to Saigon to find Dr. Gottlieb's message. He set about making preparations. There may have been a time when he would have questioned what he was being asked to do. "But long ago I had learned that if I did not do it, somebody else would. And whoever did, it would probably make no difference to the outcome of the war in the end. America had supremacy in its fighter-bombers, napalm and rockets. But the guerrillas knew how to take advantage of the terrain. However hard the *Stars and Stripes* newspaper tried to promote America's eventual victory, the truth was that every night our transports left with our dead in our body bags for home. MK-ULTRA had become a big, bad, black game which men like Gottlieb and Cameron and others like them played because they wanted to believe. Not actually believed, but wanted to," Buckley later recalled.

Nevertheless, on that tropical energy-sapping day in November, he went to Bien Hoa Prison and arranged for some fifty of Vietcong prisoners to be placed in the same holding pen Dr. Gottlieb's surgeons had previously used for their human guinea pigs. The next day, two staff doctors, a pathologist and a psychiatrist from Pacific State Hospital in California arrived. Each had brought with him a portable ECG machine. That afternoon the first dozen prisoners were strapped down on tables. Each man was given six electroshocks. In the next two hours all fifty were similarly shocked. After six hours they were brought back and given a further twenty separate shocks. Twelve hours later the process was repeated. In between, the psychiatrist questioned the prisoners. He was trying to establish if the shocks would produce an admission from each prisoner that he had come to recognize that Communism was "bad." All the captives said was they feared further treatments. The doctors raised the settings on the ECG machines. Within two days the first prisoner was dead. Ten more soon succumbed. Autopsies carried out by the pathologist showed the men died from heart failure. That night Buckley flew with the team back to Los Angeles. Hardly anyone spoke on the long flight. "It was more than a sense of having failed. It was the feeling they should not have started in the first place," Buckley decided.

Upon landing, he found a message from Dr. Gottlieb ordering him to take the next flight to Mexico City. Waiting at the airport was the hypnotist who had taught him in New York. He handed Buckley a sealed envelope. It contained Dr. Gottlieb's instructions for Operation Mindbender. This centered on turning a Mexican CIA informer, who was now suspected of working for the KGB, into an assassin. It would involve the hypnotist putting the man into a trance and Buckley then taking him to the restaurant where the local KGB station chief was known to dine. The agent was to shoot the Russian. In the expected confusion, Buckley was then to shoot the Mexican. To hypnotize the agent, a suite had been booked in the city's Sheraton Hotel. For two days Buckley and the hypnotist waited for the Mexican to turn up. He never did. It was only later that Buckley learned the KGB resident, suspecting something was afoot, had arranged to have the man flown to Cuba. His fate there remained unknown. Operation Mindbender took almost $4,000 more out of the MK-ULTRA budget.

During his stay in Mexico, Buckley met with the CIA's station chief in the city. The man told him that the only excitement in his work had been the discovery that a former radar operator in the U.S. Marine Corps, having defected to the Soviet Union in 1959, had shown up in the city in the company of a KGB officer. They had made several trips to the Soviet and Cuban embassies as well as mixing with various groups of Cuban exiles in the city. The station chief said he had filed a report on the matter but there had been no follow-up from Langley. The man was Lee Harvey Oswald.

Arriving in Langley, Buckley was told by Dr. Gottlieb that he was to travel with the assessment team to Montreal. The team took the morning flight from Washington to Montreal, arriving there in the early afternoon of November 22, 1963. The newspapers on the flight were filled with accounts of President Kennedy's progress in Texas and how he appeared to be healing the factionalism between State Governor John Connolly and Senator Ralph Yarborough, which at one time had threatened to destroy the Texas' Democratic Party. By the time the team reached the Institute, the cab radio announced that the

Kennedy entourage had landed at Love Field, Dallas, and the presidential motorcade was heading into the city.

Dr. Cameron greeted his visitors and led them on a tour of the wards. At each bed, Dr. Wolff flicked through a case file before questioning those patients who were conscious. Others lay there, eyes open, staring fixedly, too regressed to communicate. The physicians did not bother to disguise their disquiet. Dr. Wolff repeatedly asked Dr. Cameron: "Are these typical of your successes?" He was told they were good examples of "positive treatment" either from "depatterning" or "psychic driving." Buckley heard Dr. Wolff murmur to his colleagues he had a feeling, "We are living in two worlds. Cameron's and the real one."

They had reached South-Two when a nurse ran from a day room shouting, "He's been shot! Someone's shot the President!" Dr. Cameron stared at her: "Lassie, control yourself. What nonsense are you saying?" Buckley, followed by Dr. Wolff, ran to the day room. On the television screen, an announcer had interrupted the afternoon soap opera with news from Dallas that President Kennedy had been shot. For long minutes they all stood before the television listening to the updates coming over the screen from Dallas. What made it even more surreal for Buckley was the giggling that came from one of the patients slumped in a wheelchair. Dr. Cameron ordered a nurse to take the man outside. Finally came the news that Kennedy was dead. Buckley's first response was to ask himself, how could this have happened? Where was the warning? Then he remembered the MOST SECRET report he had received before leaving Saigon. It was a CIA appraisal of the threat level to the President, based upon the growing opposition to the Vietnam War. Could this be the start of a second Civil War in America?

Beside him Dr. Wolff was whispering to his colleagues. Buckley caught some of the words, "enough... let's get out... back to Washington... seen enough..." Dr. Cameron was speaking: "There is much more to see. You can't leave like this! I have important projects to show you. New ones to discuss." Buckley remembered later that the protest in Dr. Cameron's voice had been "unreal. Here we had our President assassinated and he was talking about his projects. Wolff was right. The man was out of touch."

Thirty minutes later, with his visitors heading to the airport, Dr. Cameron sat alone behind his desk. Before he left, Dr. Wolff had said he would not be recommending that the Society for Investigation of Human Ecology support any new grant applications for the Institute.

On the way to the airport, Dr. Wolff told Buckley: "This madness has to stop. What I have seen today makes it clear that Cameron is a liability. His links with us have to be severed."

When Buckley returned to Langley, he found the Agency gripped in a collective paranoia. The belief in an elaborate plot to murder the President had taken root early on when an Associated Press wire message announced that a Secret Service agent and a Dallas policeman had been shot and killed in the vicinity of the assassination. The message had been quickly corrected. But it took many hours before the CIA was ready to let go of the idea that the Russians had struck. That belief was reinforced when Buckley mentioned what the station chief in Mexico had told him about Lee Harvey Oswald, the man who had been seized for carrying out the killing. "In moments," he was to remember, "the whole of the Operations area was in uproar. Men were sent to Mexico, to Florida, to infiltrate the Cuban community. To anywhere where Oswald had been, may have been, could have been — and sometimes where he manifestly had not been."

Buckley found himself back at his analyst's desk trying to figure out the genesis of a plot. On a TV set, he watched the unfolding drama: Lyndon Johnson taking the presidential oath of office on board Air Force One; the bloodstained and grief-stricken Jacqueline Kennedy beside him, the body of her husband in the aircraft hold. Buckley watched the plane land at Andrews Air Force Base a little over two hours later, then the separation of the old and the new: Johnson taking the short helicopter ride to the White House, the Kennedy entourage following the coffin to Bethesda Naval Hospital for an autopsy that continued through the night. Just before dawn the casket, covered with the American flag, was carried into the White House and placed on a catafalque in the East Room. Buckley could barely suppress his tears as Mrs. Kennedy knelt at the side of the coffin and hid her face in the flag's field of stars.

For Buckley, like the rest of America and the whole western world, the next three days passed in a blur. He ate at his desk, catnapped on a couch, didn't bother to wash or shave as he tried to make sense of what had happened. On the fourth day he was ordered to get some proper rest. Instead he sat before the TV in his apartment and watched the funeral. Like the assassination, it was televised around the world. The next day, he was back at Langley "trying to pick up the pieces again." Richard Helms took him aside and said the assassination had been the work "of a lone nut. We are now certain of that."

The day after the President's funeral, Buckley was back in Montreal with a sealed envelope from Dr. Gottlieb. Buckley handed over the envelope to Dr. Cameron explaining he was to read it in his presence. Dr. Cameron did as instructed.

"Have you fully understood the contents, Dr. Cameron?" Buckley asked. The psychiatrist nodded. It was the only indication he had heard the question. Buckley reached across the desk and retrieved the letter and its envelope. He replaced the letter in the envelope and resealed it with a piece of Scotch tape. "It was written on Cameron's face. Finished" Buckley was on the next flight back to Washington.

Dr. Cameron's secretary, Dorothy Trainor, would recall that, almost overnight, he became aged and withdrawn. On November 26 he dictated to her a memo to all research staff that they were to wind up their projects. He told Dr. Roper, "They are out to get me." He did not amplify who "they" were. To the medical staff he sent a separate memo stating that "for the time being" treatments he had implemented could continue. For the next seven months Dr. Cameron made repeated visits to pharmaceutical companies he hoped would be sources of funding for his work. He showed medical director's published papers and tried to excite them with his own convictions. Each time he was turned away empty-handed. Within a year the seemingly unlimited funds that had once flowed into the Institute's finance department had slowed to a trickle. The Institute kept going on little more than fees from private patients and already-in-place grants from McGill University. Dorothy Trainor remembered that Dr. Cameron became "increasingly more withdrawn and showed signs of real depression." His future looked bleaker by the day. He made several attempts to call Dr. Gottlieb and Dr. Wolff. Their assistants promised the calls would be returned. They never were.

The winter passed into the spring of 1964 and then summer itself. Even the sunshine and blue skies could do nothing to lift the gloom that had settled over the Institute. Staff had been let go, research labs closed down, new patients were few and far between. Invitations for Dr. Cameron to address medical conferences in Canada and elsewhere had all but stopped. He had given up calling Dr. Gottlieb and Dr. Wolff after the operator informed him the direct line numbers he had for both men had been disconnected.

In Langley, Dr. Gottlieb continued his immersion in the biological warfare program. At Edgewood Arsenal, CIA-sponsored scientists had been working with mescaline as a potential weapon. Their experiments included using a tennis coach, Harold Bleur, who was undergoing psychiatric treatment at the New York State Psychiatric Institute. Unknown to most of the staff, that Institute had become enrolled in the CIA's mind control program. Mescaline, code-named EA-1298, had been sent to the Institute for "human evaluation." Bleur was given an injection. Within minutes he fell into a coma from which he never emerged.

Dr. Gottlieb now wanted the scientists at the Edgewood Arsenal to develop a biological weapon based upon the glycolate drug. In a memo, he wrote that there was an "urgency to the research as the Soviets are known to be actively engaged in the glycolate area." Twenty volunteers — five of them serving prison sentences and fifteen servicemen — were injected with a glycolate-based drug and developed seriously incapacitating symptoms that lasted for two months. They were not told the purpose of the trial, the nature of the drug, or whether it would leave any long-term effects. The trial was deemed to have been "satisfactory."

Meanwhile, Buckley was busy in New York checking that the Society for the Investigation of Human Ecology had removed any links from its files between Dr. Cameron and overseas research institutes in Finland, Holland, Switzerland, Burma and Israel. Subsequently all files about those connections were incinerated. But these locations were, Buckley later recalled, all involved in experiments using the surreptitious delivery of drugs.

With Dr. Cameron gone, Dr. Gottlieb could still call upon a formidable academic arsenal to do his bidding. Forty-four universities and colleges in the United States remained in the mind control program, along with fifteen research institutes, twelve hospitals and three penal institutions; the latter provided guinea pig prisoners. Over the years these ran into many thousands. How many died and how many were permanently damaged from being experimented on has yet to be established.

At noon on July 24, 1964, Peter Roper did something he had never done before. He stormed into Dr. Cameron's office without knocking, brushing aside the shocked Dorothy Trainor who was about to enter to take dictation. He closed the door in her face. Dr. Roper's anger was motivated by what he had heard in a Montreal court earlier that morning, the testimony given by his wife in their divorce case. His compassion for Agnes had turned to disbelief and finally anger when, towards the end of her testimony, she revealed that, as well as consulting Robert Cleghorn, she had also been Dr. Cameron's patient. A dumbfounded Roper listened as Agnes recounted how Dr. Cameron had said her husband possessed "this character fault which showed in his work and, as far as he was concerned, my husband would get no further in his profession because he had been pushy and aggressive." Standing before his desk, Dr. Roper confronted Dr. Cameron: had he said any of that?

The chief psychiatrist said nothing. The senior resident felt suddenly sorry for the gaunt-faced man sitting behind the vast expanse of desk with the tape recorder that symbolized his treatment methods. "He's finished," Dr. Roper thought to himself, "the man is a spent force." Dr. Roper's own anger evaporated. What did it matter now what Dr. Cameron had said to his wife? His life with Agnes was over, ended that morning by the judge's decree. Dr. Cameron broke his silence: "It's the French. They ruined everything. Your lassie. Everything." His voice was little more than a hoarse whisper. He slumped back in his chair, staring at some point over Roper's head.

On July 26, 1964, Ewen Cameron summoned the entire medical and nursing staff to the Institute's lecture theatre. When they were assembled, he addressed them: "As of this moment, I am resigning." For a moment he surveyed the stunned faces: "I don't want a party." Within an hour, he had driven away from the Institute. By nightfall Robert Cleghorn was appointed to replace Ewen Cameron. His first instruction to the staff was, "Okay. No party. But no wake either. We've all got plenty to do." Dr. Cleghorn later confided in his notebook: "The resignation is unfathomable. It was too big, too sudden, too overwhelming."

Within twenty-four hours Dr. Cleghorn ordered a halt to all "depatterning" and "psychic driving." The Radio Telemetry Laboratory was closed and the Isolator Chamber dismantled. The basement was stripped of everything that had made it resemble an interrogation center. Leonard Rubenstein was among the first of the staff Dr. Cleghorn dismissed. The technician returned to London — as mysterious a figure as when he had arrived. Zielinski left soon afterwards. Among the doctors who were sacked was Ataturk.

Before he left, Dr. Cameron had loaded several boxes of files into his car. They contained all his paperwork relating to MK-ULTRA, the proof that what he had done to his patients had been in the name of the CIA and, ultimately, the government of the United States. Watching him drive away, filled with her own sadness, Dorothy Trainor felt "the magic was gone." So was the sorcery.

Ewen Cameron's resignation caused consternation in Langley. Buckley was to recall "Cameron had to be, in Agency terms, urgently secured." Buckley was sent to Lake Placid to do so. He arrived in the early evening of July 27. Buckley was astonished at the changes in the psychiatrist. He appeared to have shrunk physically. Instead of the well-cut suit he had always worn, he was dressed in baggy trousers and a cardigan. After fixing drinks, the two sat facing each other in armchairs in Dr. Cameron's den. On the floor were the files Cameron had brought from the Institute. Buckley explained he had come for them and any other relevant papers. Dr. Cameron nodded. Buckley asked why he had resigned.

Dr. Cameron broke the silence: "What has that to do with the Agency?" His irritation was clear. Rattling the ice in his glass, he added, "I'm not interested in the problems of your people." Abruptly he rose to his feet and stared at Buckley. There was the hint of the imperious Dr. Cameron that Buckley remembered. The agent gathered up the files and took them to his car. Dr. Cameron closed the front door even before Buckley drove away.

On August 4, 1964, Buckley sent Dr. Gottlieb a memo stating that after reviewing the files, he had found nothing of "any significant importance." He ended by saying he was certain that Dr. Cameron would never reveal his connections to the Agency. Dr. Gottlieb did not acknowledge the memo, but later that day he told Richard Helms a potentially difficult situation had been contained. There was no need to give up the search for the answer to mind control.

CHAPTER SIXTEEN

Exactly one month after Buckley retrieved all the material from Dr. Cameron, Dr. f gave the project a new acronym: MK-SEARCH. With a new president in the White House and Richard Helms riding shotgun for the project, things were, "very much business as usual," Buckley remembered Gottlieb saying.

Dr. Gottlieb was concerned that the KGB's Technical Operations Directorate, whose purpose was identical to the division Dr. Gottlieb controlled at the CIA, was ahead of American research in poisons and gases. His fears were grounded in a case involving a White Russian, Georgi Sergeivich Okolovich, who had run a vocal anti-Soviet propaganda campaign from Frankfurt. Germany. A KGB assassin, Nicholai Khoklov, was assigned to murder him. Instead, as he later admitted, arriving in Frankfurt, Khoklov was seduced by the lifestyle in the West. He sought out Okolovich to confess why he was there. Okolovich fled to South America while Khoklov went to the U.S. Air Force base at Rhein-Main and asked for political asylum.

Within an hour Khoklov was in a CIA safe house, one that Buckley knew from his own work in Germany. Once he had satisfied his interrogators of who he was, Khoklov took them to the Black Forest. Using a map he had been given in Moscow, he led the CIA men to a tree trunk. It had been daubed with a spot of white paint. Buried beneath the tree roots was a small package. It contained a gold cigarette case. Khoklov revealed how it had been adapted by KGB armorers to become a gun that fired dum-dum bullets designed to look like cigarettes. Buckley was among those in Langley who recommended Khoklov should be used as a propaganda weapon. He became a regular speaker at meetings throughout West Germany, describing the Soviet Union's vast arsenal of bio-chemical weapons. One evening in Frankfurt, while delivering yet another lecture, he suddenly collapsed. The KGB had managed to poison his food with minute radioactive particles. No one ever discovered how.

Two years later the KGB launched a similar attack against another Soviet dissident, Stefan Bandera, in Munich. He had returned home for lunch at his apartment in a city suburb when a KGB agent, Bogdan Stashinsky, used a tube-shaped gun to fire a quantity of prussic acid into Bandera's face. Bandera swallowed a quantity of the acid, which caused his blood vessels to contract, creating what appeared to be a heart attack. Two years later Stashinsky defected to the West bringing with him the latest details of the KGB's biological weapons. Buckley spent several days reviewing his interrogation report. He was then posted back to Vietnam.

Before leaving, Buckley had lunch with Helms in the executive dining room on Langley's seventh floor. Helms explained that Buckley's task in Saigon would not be an easy one. Opposition to the war was hardening and both the U.S. Air Force and Defense Intelligence Agency were trying to regain control of the situation. The battle over technology versus human intelligence-gathering methods was heating up. In his first meeting with President Johnson, Helms was told that Johnson wanted the CIA to keep him informed. Buckley's job was to ensure that the analysis from Saigon "was rock-solid and would make the President look good so that he could say that's how it really is."

Meanwhile, Dr. Gottlieb was busy setting up MK-SEARCH. He had authorized $30,000 to be set aside for new safe houses in Chicago and Los Angeles. Another $150,000 had been given to a Baltimore laboratory to research micro-organisms that could "induce anything from kinky sex to simulating death by carbon-dioxide." Dr. Gottlieb hoped the research would eventually provide additions to his Assassination Manual. He had ordered Dr. Cameron's Isolator Room to be rebuilt at a laboratory of the National Institute of Health. Lobotomized apes were kept for months in total isolation. Rubenstein's radio telemetry techniques were adapted so that "radio frequency energy" was beamed into the brains of the already crazed animals. Several were then decapitated and their heads transplanted onto the bodies of other headless simians — to see whether the "energy" from the radio frequency could somehow bring back the animals to life. In a moment of unusual humor, Dr. Gottlieb called it Operation Resurrection.

A new conduit for drug funding was created. The Amazon Natural Drug Company had a registered office in Iquitos, Peru. It was run by J.C. King who had headed the CIA's Western Hemisphere Division until the Bay of Pigs fiasco. He had left with Dulles. Dr. Gottlieb discreetly brought King back into the Agency and provided him with a budget of nearly $1 million. King used some of the money to buy a houseboat, stocked it with bourbon and sailed the backwaters of the Amazon with a small team of Agency botanists who gathered leaves, roots and barks. Back at the laboratories in Langley, these were pulverized into powder and fed to still more apes to see if they were driven mad or killed each other. Many were, and did.

For Dr. Gottlieb, Helms was the perfect patron. He made decisions quickly and never hesitated to take risks or cut corners. Helms remained convinced that one day Dr. Gottlieb would discover the answer to mind control and allowed him to continue, unfettered and untroubled, devising new and better ways to disorient and discredit, to maim and kill. The key to Pandora's Box was once more firmly in his immaculately manicured hands. MK-SEARCH expanded rapidly. Abandoned projects were reactivated, old ideas revived. Among them was the use of hypnotism. After the fiasco in Mexico City, the idea had been written off. Dr. Gottlieb gave that project a new code-name, Operation Spellbinder and assigned an initial $50,000 to try once more to create an assassin who would strike upon receiving a key word planted in his mind under hypnosis. A member of the American Society of Clinical and Experimental Hypnosis was recruited for the purpose. The hypnotist was dubbed "Fingers" by Dr. Gottlieb from the theatrical way he used his hands to put a patient into a trance. Dr. Gottlieb chose him because his file said Fingers had no qualms about "terminal" experiments.

The hypnotist's intended victim was, once again, Fidel Castro. Dr. Gottlieb's drive to murder the Cuban leader remained strong. Fingers and two Agency psychologists traveled to Miami and began to move through the city's large Cuban community posing as potential employers to the largely jobless immigrants. Likely candidates for Fingers hypnosis were invited to a motel room. The hypnotist sat the first unsuspecting Cuban before him and sent the man into a trance. Then he spoke to him about the need to kill Castro, and that doing so was not a crime but the only way to liberate Cuba. The man nodded. Encouraged, Fingers set about planting the key word. When the man heard it, instructed the hypnotist, and he was in the presence of Castro, he must immediately kill him. The word was "cigar." To prove how effective he had been, Fingers ordered the man to imagine he was at Castro's side. Watched by the Agency psychologists, Fingers uttered the word. Nothing happened. He tried again. Nothing. Finally, perplexed, Fingers brought the man out of the trance and once more said "cigar." The man looked at him blankly and said he didn't smoke. The next man refused to awake on command and the alarmed Agency men hurriedly drove him back to the Cuban quarter and dumped him on a street corner, still asleep. A third became violent under hypnosis when Castro's name was mentioned and started to smash-up the motel room. He was quickly brought out of his trance. The defeated Agency team returned to Langley.

By late 1966, the dozen MK-SEARCH projects had cost almost $1 million without any real results. Euphoria turned sour. There were bitter recriminations. Men spent days writing reports to justify failure. There were a growing number of resignations within the Agency's scientific division. Many found work in the drug companies the CIA had originally approached for help. Researchers who had worked on pain-inducing projects used their talents to create pain-killing drugs. Others who had been solely concerned with "terminal" work were now using their skills to discover new cures for arthritis, lumbago and heart disease.

Fearing the brain drain would cause the Agency to fall behind the Soviets and Chinese in the black arts of scientific intelligence, Helms called in an old friend, William Casey. In the years since the lawyer had been introduced to Clover Dulles at her party as an investment expert, Casey had created a formidable reputation and fortune for himself through his astute financial dealings. Casey traveled to Washington. Helms met him for lunch in a suite at the Jefferson Hotel. Over poached salmon and Chablis — Casey's favorite meal — Helms outlined the problem. The government's pay structure did not allow the CIA to compete with the salaries offered by the drug companies. What could be done? Casey had a practical solution. The Agency should create a foundation to help its staff with long-term, low-investment loans for house purchases, college education and such matters. He would not only be happy to structure such funding, but would like to make a personal contribution of $50,000. Almost twenty years after working with the OSS, Casey became more actively associated with its successor. When he heard the news, Buckley predicted that it was only a matter of time before the big, shambling man would be a permanent fixture at Langley.

One evening in September 1967, the telephone rang in Ewen Cameron's home at Lake Placid. It was Allen Dulles calling from Mississippi. He had been brought out of retirement by President Johnson, first to be a member of the Warren Commission, which had investigated the assassination of President Kennedy, and now to act as a one-man presidential mission to investigate racism in the Deep South. For the old spymaster, who had once ruled over the murky world of intelligence and where plots involving the murder of heads of state had been commonplace, enquiring into the deaths of Civil Rights workers was a long step down. Hobbling through the enervating heat of a Southern summer, his left leg throbbing with gout, a residue of the childhood operation on his club foot, Dulles was also troubled by a failing memory. He had to write everything down on a little pad he carried in his pocket. The problem was, he sighed on the phone to Dr. Cameron, he couldn't always read what he'd written. "Lord, Ewen," he added, "what shall I do? I seem to remember you were pretty good in the memory field." It was an old friend seeking, perhaps, no more than advice. William Buckley, who had been recalled by Helms from Vietnam to accompany Dulles on his trip, would remember how the former director put down the telephone in the hotel and repeated, in a slightly puzzled voice, what Dr. Cameron had said: "Find yourself a good doctor, Allen."

Buckley had returned to the United States after a year in Vietnam during which he had helped put together an operation that, more than any other, marked the turning point in America's involvement in the war. It was called Phoenix, and once more Buckley had found himself working closely with William Colby. The plan called for the mass murder or capture of all the Vietcong leaders in South Vietnam. Phoenix would rely on the techniques the Vietcong had made their own: assassination, kidnapping and intimidation.

Buckley later recalled that Colby told him: "It's push comes to shove time. If Phoenix works, we will be able to start the de-Americanization of the war. The old problems of Vietnamese corruption and nepotism will not be our concern. And that way we will calm public opinion back home. Success with Phoenix will also mean we will slash the present cost of the war by two-thirds." But hardly had Phoenix begun, when it came under fierce public attack, not only in the United States, but in Europe. U.S. Army publicists pointed out with success that South Vietnamese forces were responsible for the excesses; they were using Phoenix to settle their own personal scores. The evidence clearly showed, however, that the CIA had played a key role in preparing and helping to carry out the operation.

Buckley noted in a memo to Helms: "There is now an uncontrolled bloodletting among the MACV (the South Vietnamese) that we have instilled by measuring everything by the body count. I have daily reports of MACV killing people who owed them money, or where there was some kind of personal disagreement. Phoenix has become a wild program, run on vendettas. This is one of the things we have to live with. Nobody wants to condone wildcat killings and settling personal scores. Obviously that's immoral, and I want us to have no part in that. But our people can't be everywhere. That's the truth."

In the end, Buckley felt he had become one of the scapegoats for Phoenix, though Helms tried to soften the blow by saying that Buckley's talents for analyzing the direction the war was taking were needed back at Langley. Buckley found himself desk bound again until he was assigned to accompany Dulles on his fact-finding investigation across America.

Their trip was through an ever-more divided nation. There were those who cheered news footage from Vietnam showing peasant villages being put to the torch and exulted when the Pentagon announced that the weekly bomb tonnage being dropped on North Vietnam already exceeded that of all the explosives dropped on Germany in World War II. Cheers from the war's opponents came when the Secret Service confirmed that since President Johnson's arrival in the Oval Office, over 500 persons had been arrested for threatening his life.

In the meantime, violence had increased within the United States. No longer confined to the black metropolitan ghettos like Watts and Harlem, it had swept across America creating the kind of desolation that matched the images from Vietnam. Activist John Lewis had appeared on the evening news to say: "The government is contradictory in telling oppressed black people not to be violent in the streets while it carries out the terrible slaughter in Vietnam and finances it with money it should be spending to get things right at home."

On his return to Langley Buckley once again found himself at the cutting edge of a CIA operation. He was to join Team Nosenko as one of its interrogators.

Russian KGB colonel Yuri Nosenko had defected to the United States in February 1964. He had provided the Agency with shattering information on how the KGB had bugged the American Embassy in Moscow. A CIA team had flown to the Soviet capital and reported back that Nosenko's revelations were only too true. The team also confirmed the efficiency of the KGB ability to target a victim with a biological weapon. A security officer, Horst Schwirkmann, at the West German embassy in Moscow had been on a sightseeing trip to a monastery outside the city when, surrounded by scores of other tourists, he had suddenly felt a burning sensation in his lower back. In moments he was paralyzed. His companions, two German diplomats, arranged for him to be rushed to the only experts they knew who could help: doctors at the United States embassy. By the time they reached the embassy compound, Schwirkmann was close to death. The doctors established he had been injected with nitrogen mustard gas that the Soviets had developed in World War II. But it was too late to save the security man. Flown back to Germany, Schwirkmann died shortly afterwards. Nosenko confirmed that the gas had been effectively used to silence a number of dissenters in various parts of Europe. He also gave the Agency the identities of over twenty Soviet sleeper agents in the West. Their names were passed on to MI5 in Britain and French intelligence, as well as the FBI. Once more Nosenko proved to be a totally credible source.

The Agency interrogators then questioned Nosenko about Lee Harvey Oswald. Nosenko was stunningly forthcoming. He said he had inspected the file the KGB had on Oswald – and discovered that it stated there was no Soviet involvement with the death of Kennedy. The Soviet file claimed Oswald had been a hit-man for a consortium of right-wing American millionaires who wanted the increasingly liberal President murdered. This assertion sparked questions among the interrogation team and Helms. Had Nosenko been allowed to deliberately sacrifice Soviet intelligence sleeper agents? Was he a modern-day human version of the Trojan horse, sent to wreak havoc within the United States intelligence community and government? Had Soviet psychiatrists spent years preparing Nosenko to pose as a defector? Was he the joker in the classical espionage game? Was he real or fake?

Team Nosenko included psychiatrists and psychologists as well as interrogators. Before commencing their work, Buckley had taken them through the Cameron files he had recovered from Lake Placid. Dr. Gottlieb had selected a number of drugs to use to try to establish if Nosenko was telling the full truth. He was taken to an Agency safe house in the Maryland countryside — coincidentally near the lodge where Frank Olson had been given LSD. Nosenko's new quarters contained a room with walls lined with heavy padded material designed to absorb electrical emissions. There was also a tape recorder and a machine sophisticated enough to measure minute involuntary responses: body temperature, the electrical conductivity of the skin and pulse rate. It could also calibrate and analyze variations in the pitch and delivery of words. Buckley recognized the machine as the latest refinement of the equipment he had seen Jan Zielinski use to monitor patients in the Institute basement.

Nosenko was strapped across the chest with an elastic belt to measure his respiratory functions. His wrists and forehead were daubed with a cold, conductive gel. Electrodes were attached to his head. The paper began to unravel under the swinging pens. One of the Agency psychiatrists told Nosenko to breathe deeply. The pens careened quickly over the paper. The variations were noted. They were a bench-mark for Buckley to begin his interrogation, the first member of the team to do so. Buckley had prepared himself carefully. Long ago he had concluded that finding the truth was no simple matter: There was "a truth you separate from what most people accept as truth, and search for a truth that can only be sensed. That is what a trained interrogator does." Questioning Nosenko he kept his voice at an even level. His questions, while touching on the most personal matters, the deepest issues in Nosenko's life, were asked in the same tone. Nosenko's responses came out as smoothly and automatically as his heartbeat.

After a week of watching the pens trace smooth curves on the polygraph paper, Buckley began to feel that Nosenko was telling the truth: "But the consensus was that it was still too early to say. He would have been trained to resist. To offer facts, but not to bend to them. We all knew that the relation between a defector and his interrogators is always difficult. We watched for any signs, the merest twitch, the gentlest of breaths, anything that would warn us of danger. The art of good interrogation is to move slowly and painstakingly. We had to allow Nosenko to establish himself with us. We wanted him to understand we knew his wish to be accepted. We needed him to trust us but we didn't want to trust him until we were sure," was how Buckley later saw it.

One night Buckley escorted Nosenko into a specially prepared room. It was a replica of Dr. Cameron's Isolator, a free-standing cell-like structure in the basement of the safe house. After twelve hours Nosenko was brought out of isolation and again polygraphed. The same questions were put, just as Dr. Cameron had repeated the questions to his patients. At exactly the same point as before in his interrogation, Nosenko was asked to breathe deeply. The graph measurement was compared with the earlier one to see if solitary confinement had affected him. It had not. The Agency team decided that if Nosenko was lying, he was doing so superbly.

For a further month the questions alternated with periods of ever-lengthening isolation. The techniques Dr. Gottlieb had once posited as those used by the Communists to obtain their "confessions" were being used to try and break the defector. The unfolding strip of sensitized polygraph paper was evaluated. Every night, one of the team summarized the spiked chart and reported personally to Helms. Sometimes Helms would tell Buckley he was convinced Nosenko was telling the truth about the Oswald file. Other times he still wondered if Nosenko was a plant. After three months, Helms gave an order to increase the psychological pressure on the Russian.

Nosenko was moved to a new cell. A powerful light bulb burned continuously, and Buckley helped to stand guard over him around the clock, removing his last vestige of privacy. Nosenko was allowed nothing to read; even the writing on his toothpaste tube was obliterated. When he tried to occupy his mind by making a chess set from threads he pulled from his sweater, he was dressed in a nylon track suit. For Buckley, "This was the only way. Nosenko was one hard nut. He'd already admitted he had been taught by the best of the Soviets how to resist interrogation. They'd put him through what we were doing to him, of that I had no doubt. This was not the time to hold back. If we failed with Nosenko, then we may have let in probably the best agent the Soviets had ever sent to penetrate us."

The greater the pressure, the more insistent Nosenko became that he had only told the truth. After 500 days Nosenko was placed in a specially built vault, eight feet square and made of steel. It cost $2,500 to manufacture. On his seven-hundredth day in captivity, Nosenko finally broke down, weeping and pleading to be believed. The electrodes strapped to his skin confirmed he was not lying. But Helms refused to accept the evidence. The interrogations continued. A fresh group of psychiatrists were assigned to the case. Buckley remained the only member of the original team. He sat passively as Nosenko wept, his breath coming in short gasps as he repeated time and again the same words: "I am telling the truth." Buckley no longer had any doubts. "Nosenko had long passed the stage where he wanted to please. He was a man who had been through every stage of pain. I just knew he was telling the truth," Buckley recalled.

But Dr. Gottlieb's psychiatrists proposed even harsher methods. Nosenko was starved, in the belief that, physically weakened, he would finally lose his mental strength to resist. He did not. Guards used steel bars to beat for hours at a time on the vault. Earphones were strapped to Nosenko's head and a cacophony of sounds played for up to twenty-three hours at a time — Dr. Cameron's optimum level for "psychic driving." Nosenko still insisted he was telling the truth. He was given

LSD. The drug plunged him from manic elation to the depths of depression.

Nosenko continued to be tortured by the Agency's physicians and interrogators. Reluctantly they came to regard him with awe. If he was lying, he was simply the best liar they had encountered. For Buckley, the interrogation had reached the stage where he "hated the idea of putting him through it over and over. If there had been the faintest hint he was a liar at any one point I would have driven on and on and on. But there was no hint. In the end, I asked to be relieved from the interrogation panel." Buckley felt the psychiatrists had long overstepped every ethical boundary. Dr. Gottlieb urged Helms to continue; here was a rare opportunity to probe the wider issue of brainwashing.

Helms had listened for hours to the tapes of Nosenko's interrogations. Over the years the Russian's voice had lost its strong, vibrant quality and became reedy and less human. But was it the voice of truth — if no longer completely lucid reason — or of deceit? On September 21, 1967, the director called another case conference. He listened to argument and counterargument. Finally Helms ordered that Nosenko should be set free and he went home for dinner, drowning the last vestige of doubt in his brandy.

Out in his converted slave cabin, Dr. Gottlieb sipped a glass of warmed goat's milk. For almost fourteen years he had spearheaded the search for answers to mind control. Finally the hunt had come full circle in that safe house where Nosenko had been held. Everything the Communists were reported to have done had been tried out on Nosenko — without success. After weeks of rehabilitation, Nosenko was given a new identity and settled into the American witness protection program. As of 2006, his whereabouts and whether he was alive, or when he may have died, remained secret.

*　　　　　*　　　　　*

On September 9, 1968, the telephone rang in Dr. Sargant's office in Harley Street. The caller said that Dr. Cameron had died from a heart attack while climbing a mountain near his home. The caller, the editor of the *British Medical Journal*, asked Dr. Sargant to write an obituary. On September 23, 1968, the Journal carried his tribute:

"Cameron had great organizing abilities, but he remained a clinician till the end. He always insisted on treating a number of his patients himself personally rather than sitting too much in his professorial chair, which also carried so many administrative and teaching responsibilities. By this means he always remained aware of the individual patient's problems and was also able to discuss treatment matters from personal experience. He did not always tolerate fools gladly but supported with all his energies those he felt were doing all they could to improve the treatment of the mentally ill. He refused to follow the craze for psychoanalysis which swept American medical schools after the Second World War. Cameron died as he would have wished, in full and active harness still planning his future research programs. Ewen Cameron by his work and example, helped not only many psychiatrists to become much better doctors but directly and indirectly helped hundreds and hundreds of patients, both personally and through those he had inspired and taught."

Years later Dr. Sargant would comment to the author, "I have a policy of not speaking or writing ill of the dead."

On her fiftieth birthday, September 13, 1967, five days after Dr. Cameron died, Mary Morrow formally launched a legal action against his estate and the Allan Memorial Institute. She claimed $100,000 damages for unethical treatment. Preparation for the proceedings had consumed her for the past six years. One lawyer after another had listened with mounting disbelief as she described her seventeen days in the Institute. At times she had had to remind herself that she had indeed not imagined it. Part of the problem, she realized, was that when she had first consulted a lawyer, there had been considerable gaps in her memory as a result of the electroshocks. The more she had driven herself to remember everything Dr. Cameron had done to her, the greater the determination to find legal redress. It was not only the prospect of financial damages which spurred her, but the knowledge she had been cruelly experimented upon. She wondered how many others he had treated like her. She decided she wanted justice not only for herself, but for all those who had suffered at his hands.

She spoke to more lawyers. One after another shook his head and asked the same question. Where was her proof? Still she refused to give up, even when her mother and sister looked defeated. Their attitude helped trigger another depression. She felt herself struggling against fatigue and nightmares and prescribed anti-depressants for herself. Finally she found a lawyer prepared to take her case. But he had said that her only hope of winning was to find expert medical witnesses who would testify she had been the victim of gross malpractice. But she was unable to find Canadian psychiatrists willing to stand up in court and denounce what Dr. Cameron had done. She felt "the power of the McGill Network Cameron had created still spread far and wide. It was a brick wall Cameron had erected and nobody was ready to dismantle it," she recalled to the author.

She sat in one Canadian doctor's office after another, patiently explaining what happened, remembering a little more on each occasion of what Dr. Cameron had done to her. She no longer had to close her eyes to recollect how he had stood there, needle in hand, ignoring her protests and injecting her and then electroshocking her. She told her story quietly and matter-of-factly, the way her lawyer said she should. But still no doctor in Canada was prepared to pit his or her reputation against Dr. Cameron's. Dr. Morrow refused to give up. Finally, through the Law Medicine Institute at Harvard, she found three American psychiatrists prepared to tell a court that the recognized treatment in a case like hers was totally different from what Dr. Cameron had carried out.

When Velma Orlikov learned about Dr. Cameron's death, she fitted it all into what she was continuing to discover from her own suffering. Her mentor was a psychiatrist, Dr. Gordon Lambard. He helped her unlock some of the mystery of her own pain and see that ultimately the suffering which had driven her to seek help was not unique. Dr. Lambard made no secret of his own anger over the way Dr. Cameron had mishandled her.

Peter Roper had also learned to become philosophical. Dismissed by Dr. Cleghorn, he had fought a spirited and long-running battle for reinstatement. Finally he and Dr. Cleghorn attended a meeting of the staff relations committee of the Senate of McGill University. Dr. Roper submitted extensive documentation to show he had been unfairly sacked. The whole issue, he argued, revolved around personal conflict between himself and Dr. Cleghorn, who told the committee that "either Dr. Roper or I had to go." The committee decided Dr. Roper's dismissal would not be revoked.

In 1969, Dr. Roper opened a private practice close to the Institute and from time to time sent patients there, knowing that it no longer endorsed any of Dr. Cameron's methods.

CHAPTER SEVENTEEN

Buckley would refer to the day Candace Hammond came into his life as his Indian summer. He had been returning from a trip to the CIA training school at Fayetteville where he had undergone his induction into the Agency. With time on his hands he decided to explore the Carolinas. Driving through the hamlet of Farmer, he had spotted an antique shop. Over the door were the words "Candace Hammond. Prop."

The name intrigued him; Candace suggested a character from *Gone With The Wind*. He went in. Candace, he would always remember, was wearing a simple print dress, no make-up and her skin was burnished by the sun. He asked her how she came by her name. She said her dad had chosen it. By the time she finished taking him on a tour of the shop, talking knowledge-ably about the artifacts from the Civil War, he knew she was "someone special." The other women who had peopled his life left him feeling "empty and dissatisfied," Buckley later said. "Part of the problem was of my own making. Being out in the field isn't conducive to a lasting relationship. It's like being a soldier in the war, only worse. A soldier gets to know the risks of being killed. In this job you never know. And what makes it worse is that when you are killed, often nobody knows what happened to you."

He didn't share these thoughts with Candace at this first meeting. For the moment he was just happy to be in her company and enjoy the way she moved and the soft cadence of her voice. But Buckley knew he had found the relationship he yearned for: a woman who loved him, but would not impose on his other love, his work.

In December 1968, Buckley received an invitation to the Dulles Christmas party. Clover herself had called, saying that Allen and she were looking forward to seeing him again. She met him at the door and Buckley was struck at Clover's appearance. Although close to her seventieth birthday, she was dressed like a woman half her age. Yet, despite Clover's vivaciousness, Buckley sensed a tension among many of the other guests. Clover told him that Allen was in bed with a cold but had insisted there was no reason to cancel the party. Nevertheless, several guests kept glancing up towards his bedroom. Though almost six years had passed since President Kennedy had sacked Dulles, his reputation still drew the cream of the capital's intelligence community. There were, Buckley guessed, probably more than fifty active spies and counter-intelligence men sipping drinks and making polite conversation. A Dulles party, he thought, was still the place to be seen. Over by the fireplace a group was singing carols. Finally Jeanie Houston, the wife of the CIA's current in-house legal counsel, asked Clover whether there was too much noise for Allen. "No. He's fine," she replied, moving to the door to greet still more guests.

Jeanie Houston turned to her husband, "I think you should go upstairs and see how Allen is." Houston nodded. Helms, now Director of Central Intelligence, pleading he had to attend several more parties including one at the White House, made his farewells. Buckley thought the Director looked grim. The Washington rumor mill said that President-elect Richard Nixon wanted better results from the Agency's operations in Vietnam. It reminded Buckley that Washington could be the loneliest town in the world for those whose careers stood or fell during a changeover in the Oval Office.

Buckley recognized several senior officers and scientists from Fort Detrick. Their talk was of an embarrassing failure at the Dugway Proving Ground in Utah. An F4 Phantom jet fighter, adapted for aerial dispersion of a new nerve agent code-named VX, had mistakenly dumped some twenty pounds of the chemical in the wrong place. Caught by the wind, the nerve gas had drifted well away from the test site, settling in the aptly named Skull Valley. Grazing on the valley floor were some 6,000 prize sheep. They were dead in hours. The media had descended in force on the valley to witness crews from Dugway burying the carcasses in hurriedly dug deep trenches. The resultant publicity had caused an international uproar.

There was talk that President-elect Nixon intended to end the chemical/biological weapons program. In one of his election campaign speeches he had said: "Mankind already has too many of the seeds of its own destruction to have biological weapons included. I therefore propose that the United States should renounce the use." It would turn out to be a significant moment. In two years time Russia would give up its opposition to a germ warfare convention outlawing all biological and chemical weapons. Another eighty countries would eventually support the ban. Soon the mass-produced germs would be turned into fertilizer to spread over farmland.

But Buckley sensed that for the men from Fort Detrick at Clover Dulles' party, this was no more than a temporary glitch; simply too much money and resources had been invested in the program to surrender it all now.

Houston returned to the living room and went to Jim Hunt. Hunt was one of Dulles' oldest friends, as well as a long-serving officer with the Agency. Houston whispered urgently. The two men returned upstairs. Several guests looked pointedly at Clover. Smiling fixedly, followed by Jeanie Houston, she accompanied them. The carol singers were still going as Buckley went out into the hall. Raised voices came from Dulles' bedroom.

"God Almighty, Allen's sick, Clover," Houston sounded exasperated.

"It's just a cold, Larry. Really it is."

"Nonsense! He's sick as a dog. Maybe dying," Hunt's concerned rumble carried clearly.

Buckley heard Clover's pleading reply. "Don't be so dramatic. He saw the doctor only this morning. He's only got the flu. Stop worrying me like this. He's been getting these spells after his last stroke."

"Jesus, Clover! This is not just 'a spell'! Can't you see how ill he is?" Hunt was almost shouting.

From the living room, the carol singing was at full bellow. Hunt appeared at the top of the stairs. Pointing at Buckley, he shouted: "Shut those goddamn people up. And call an ambulance. Tell them it's urgent." Using a phone on the hall table, Buckley dialed the emergency service. Then he went into the living room and told the guests to quiet down.

As the guests started to head for the street, Clover stood in the hallway endlessly repeating, "Thank you for coming. Allen will be sorry to have missed you." Jeanie Houston led her back upstairs. The last guests were driving away when an ambulance arrived. Two male attendants ran up the stairs with a stretcher. Buckley followed them. They found their way into the bedroom blocked by a now suddenly resolute Clover. "No stretcher," she repeated firmly. "Absolutely no stretcher!" Buckley remembered Clover had once explained that the Dulles family detested stretchers. They represented a degree of helplessness that was unthinkable for a Dulles.

Motioning the attendants to stand back, Buckley went into the bedroom. Dulles had somehow found the strength to push back the bedclothes and sit up. He tried to stand, failed, and made a second attempt, once more falling back, gripping the bedstead with one hand to support himself. Between them, Houston and Buckley helped Dulles to his feet and half-carried him down the stairs. In the hallway, the ambulance men took over. Draping Dulles' arms around their shoulders, they hurried him to the ambulance. Clover followed, once more helpless and uncertain.

"You'd better go with him," Hunt said brusquely.

Jeanie Houston came running out of the house with a hat and coat for Clover. She was too late. The ambulance, siren wailing, was already down the street. Five weeks later, on January 29, 1969, Allen Welsh Dulles died.

Buckley was unable to attend the funeral. He was on another assignment for the indefatigable Sydney Gottlieb, accompanying a team of scientists from Fort Detrick to Okinawa, the Japanese island in the Pacific where the United States had a huge military base. The base contained a sealed-off area where chemical weapons were stored in containers. One container holding the VX nerve agent had developed a leak; twenty-three U.S. servicemen had been affected by exposure. A short while before, over one hundred Japanese children playing on a beach near the base had collapsed. Many had taken weeks to recover. The political fallout had led to the Pentagon agreeing to the Japanese government's enraged demand that all chemical weapons be removed from their soil. Buckley's task was to see that this happened.

Returning to Langley after this mission, Buckley found himself cast in the now familiar role of analyzing media coverage. The State Department, Department of Defense and the Pentagon had combined to show the world it was making good on President Nixon's promise to have America's chemical/biological arsenal destroyed. Containers of tularemia, anthrax, Q fever and Venezuelan equine encephalitis were mixed with carbolic acid and then heated to 1000 degrees in specially-made furnaces. The equipment that had been used to manufacture the germs was melted down. Once secret places like Pine Bluff and the Rocky Mountain Arsenal threw open their doors for visitors. But Buckley also knew that the other great preoccupation of Sidney Gottlieb life — mind control — remained a project of which Richard Nixon approved.

When Dr. Gottlieb took over the CIA's new Office of Research and Development, ORD, it quickly became his flagship for even more bizarre and potentially far-reaching experiments in mind control. The most innovative and daring Agency doctors had been transferred there, and a number of young consultants from civilian medical research laboratories had been recruited. The ORD team also included chemists, biologists and general physicians from the Army Chemical Corps. Dr. Gottlieb had persuaded Helms to authorize $150,000 as an initial grant to ORD's first project. It was called Operation Often. Dr. Gottlieb reminded colleagues that "often" they were close to goals before pulling back, and "often" they forgot the only scientific way forward was to learn from the past. That would not happen in Operation Often.

This operation was based on Dr. Cameron's earlier research into the supernatural. Operation Often was going to go further, exploring the world of black magic. In Dr. Gottlieb's mission statement the intention was to "harness the forces of darkness and challenge the concept that the inner reaches of the mind are beyond reach. The project will aim to create a new kind of psycho-civilized human being." Dr. Gottlieb's own version of Frankenstein's monster.

Operation Often members began by visiting palmistry parlors, the booths of fairground fortune-tellers and — in the larger cities — the well-appointed offices of the psychics who served the rich and powerful. The agents invariably introduced themselves as researchers from the Scientific Engineering Institute, a cover name Dr. Gottlieb had chosen. A number of clairvoyants were persuaded to become consultants to a vaguely defined educational research program. It was run from a Washington CIA safe house. Within its walls, it became a common sight to see long-bearded men or gypsy-garbed women talking earnestly to preppy, grey-suited CIA behaviorists about how to identify and interpret life-lines and interpret the different bumps on a person's head. An astrologer from San Francisco who specialized in delineating character through the color of a subject's eyes was recruited before being unmasked as a fraud. Undaunted, the search continued for ways to use the paranormal in spying and counter-intelligence.

In October 1970, the possibility of stationing psychics at strategic points around the Soviet Bloc was considered. The idea was to use their powers to "tune in" to places like East Berlin, Warsaw and Moscow, and see what "vibrations" were picked up. The proposal was abandoned when someone realized it would take years for the psychics to become fluent in Russian.

Buckley was ordered to escort a medium to the United Nations Building in New York and ask her to wander through its public areas. He was equipped with a small camera. Whenever the medium felt herself in the presence of an "evil type of personality" she should inform him. In the weeks that particular experiment ran, Buckley was not asked to take one photo. It was, he remembered, "Looney Toon time."

Considerable efforts were made to get the palm prints of that old CIA bogey man, Fidel Castro. These were studied by palmists who were not told to whom the prints belonged. They decided Castro was "a born leader," "possibly a future Pope," or "a male with strong homosexual leanings." The latter tidbit was passed along to the CIA's Political Psychological Division and incorporated into the Cuban's psychological profile.

By May 1971, Operation Often had three full-time professional astrologers on its payroll. Each received $350 a week plus expenses — to cover what they claimed would be their loss of regular earnings. Their task was to predict the future. They sat for hours in sound-proof booths in the safe house and read a wide selection of newspapers and magazines. They focused on items which "psychically alerted" them. They taped what came into their minds about how some particular event or happening would develop.

One astrologer forecast that President Richard Nixon would win a second term but would experience severe political damage during it, a prediction that would later prove true. Another foresaw that the Vietnam War would end in disaster for the United States — Buckley had thought that was not a difficult piece of forecasting for a conflict that was now costing $25 billion a year, with American dead approaching 40,000. Nearer to home, the astrologers all saw an increase in serious crime, while internationally, the hijacking of airplanes would become the single greatest threat to travellers. Asked by the behaviorists to produce a psychological profile of a typical skyjacker, the palmists settled for a "young, dispossessed, Cuban type of personality." The psychics were asked for suggestions to combat the hijackers. Among the more memorable ones were that airline stewardesses should be trained to seduce hijackers; passengers should be made to travel in their underwear with cloaks provided by the airlines to preserve their modesty. Before each flight, the pilot should play through the aircraft public address system the Cuban national anthem and arrest anyone who stood up. The only suggestion the Agency passed on to the airline industry was that every pilot should carry approach maps for Havana Airport.

By early 1972, Operation Often had taken on two more palm readers — both Chinese-Americans — to probe still further how palmistry could be adapted to intelligence work. The program's behaviorists already knew that different cultures produced varying personalities. The palm readers were asked to see how much of this they could detect. They set to work. Posing as educational psychologists, they visited a number of ethnic communities, traveling north to Alaska to study Eskimos and south to New Mexico to look at the palms of Indians. They never submitted their findings; their inquiries had been written off in favor of researching the Devil.

Operation Often was soon deep into demonology. In April 1972, an approach was made to the monsignor in charge of exorcisms for the Catholic archdiocese of New York. He flatly refused to cooperate. Undismayed, the Agency behaviorists approached Sybil Leek, a Houston sorceress who cast spells with the help of a pet jackdaw called Hotfoot Jackson. With the bird perched on her shoulders, Mrs. Leek gave the "two very nice gentlemen" from Washington a fast course on the current state of black magic in the United States: four hundred covens operated by five thousand initiated witches and warlocks. These people were the foot soldiers of a prediction industry which supported 10,000 full-time fortune-tellers and 200,000 part-timers, as well as a growing publishing business in tarot cards and factories producing a widening range of anti-Christian tokens. Satan was not only alive but thriving in the country. To corner him for the Agency, Dr. Gottlieb decided the Devil must be made respectable. Working through conduits, he financed a course in sorcery at the University of South Carolina. Two hundred and fifty students enrolled for lessons devoted to fertility and initiation rites and raising the dead.

Buckley, still a devout Catholic, found himself surrounded by "a mysterious and magical vortex in an agency that was supposed to deal in facts and predictions based upon them, that corner of the CIA which Gottlieb had set aside for his work with the Devil was an inner black hole from which came the constant cries 'There is no God!,' 'The cosmic deity is all!' Talk of Ouija boards and white witches, chaos magic made the whole place sound like Halloween forever. These people were intelligent; they understood for instance classical philosophy, but their sense of what was real was a chasm away from mine. I would start to get papers they had written to evaluate. They had titles like 'Cripple and Confuse Your Enemy with Satan,' 'How a pendulum can become a secret weapon in locating Soviet submarines.' What astonished me was the vast majority of Satanists were former Roman Catholics. Many said they had tried the Church and that it had nothing to offer," recalled Buckley.

The more bizarre an idea was, the more Dr. Gottlieb enthused about its possibilities. One was "chaos magic" in which "psychonauts" offered to travel for the CIA into what they called "the void." One occultist told Buckley that somewhere in the void was the most powerful magic of all, able to destroy any enemy. Dr. Gottlieb had agreed to finance this particular "psychonaut" on his journey into the unknown. The man said the trip would be the equivalent of the Argonauts' search for the Golden Fleece in Greek mythology. Armed with the $500 he had requested, the "psychonaut" retreated to his launch pad in San Francisco. He was never heard from again.

Soon afterwards Dr. Gottlieb moved on to investigations in another area.

He decided to resurrect research in the use of brain implants. He ordered a program to evaluate the results achieved by Jose Delgado, a Yale psychologist. Delgado had faced a charging bull fitted with electrodes in its brain. With no other protection against a couple of tons of lethal hooves, horns and muscle than the small black box in his hands, Delgado had deliberately goaded the bull by activating the implant which provoked the animal to become further enraged. With the bull almost upon him, the psychologist pressed another button. The animal promptly stopped in its tracks, the result of a signal transmitted to that part of the bull's brain which calmed it. Delgado had freely admitted his method of remote mind control was still crude and not always predictable. But Dr. Gottlieb was certain the day would come when not only animals, but humans, would respond to electrically transmitted commands.

Robert G. Heath, a neurosurgeon at Tulane University, had brought the prospect of human mind control closer through his experiments with electrical stimulation of the brain, ESB, to arouse his patients sexually. He had actually implanted 125 electrodes in the brain and body of a single patient — for which he claimed a world record — and spent hours stimulating the man's pleasure centers. Heath concluded that ESB could control memory, impulses, feelings and evoke hallucinations. It could manipulate the human will — at will.

Late in June 1972, Dr. Gottlieb jigged back and forth on the carpet of Helm's office insisting that at long, long last here was the answer to mind control: ESB was the key to creating not only a "psycho-civilized" person, but an entire "psycho-civilized" society. It would be a world where every human thought, emotion, sensation and desire could be controlled by electrical stimulation of the brain. The possibilities, Dr. Gottlieb insisted, were far beyond Heath's neurological masturbation of the pleasure centers. A human brain could finally be programmed to attack and kill on command. The scientist to prove that, Dr. Gottlieb had determined, was Dr. Stephen Aldrich.

A former medical director of the Agency's Office of Scientific Intelligence, Dr. Aldrich had long been regarded by Dr. Gottlieb as a genuine innovator. He began to spend his time experimenting with ESB. Using the latest computer technology, Aldrich developed Rubenstein's earlier work on radiotelemetry. Dr. Aldrich believed he could bring to fruition the unfulfilled dream the English technician had shared with Dr. Cameron — a world of electrically monitored people. In the safe house where Yuri Nosenko had been brutalized, Dr. Aldrich supervised much more sophisticated research. His equipment included the Schwitzgebel Machine. Developed by Ralph K. Schwitzgebel in the Laboratory of Community Psychiatry at Harvard Medical School, it resembled a small version of the cumbersome transducer Rubenstein had built in the Montreal basement. The Schwitzgebel Machine consisted of a "Behavior Transmitter-Reinforcer," BT-R, fitted to a body belt which received and transmitted signals to a radio module. In the official description of the machine, the module was "linked to a modified missile-tracking device which graphs the wearer's location and displays it on a screen." It was claimed that the Schwitzgebel Machine was able to record all physical and neurological signs from a subject up to a distance of a quarter of a mile. If so, it was an impressive improvement over the distance between the Grid Room and the cubby-hole where Dr. Cameron had monitored his patients in the Institute's basement.

On September 20, 1972, news reached Langley that Mary Morrow was actively pursuing her legal action against the Institute and Ewen Cameron's estate. Previous reports on her case had simply been filed away. But this time, Helms ordered Buckley to run a check on every patient known to have been used in Dr. Cameron's research. "He wanted to know if there was any way – any way at all – that what had been done to them could be traced back to the Agency," Buckley later recalled. Six weeks later he reported to Helms there was no way the CIA could be implicated – except through the material still in its own archives. On December 10, 1972, Helms ordered Operation Often cancelled. In a terse memo marked "Read. Destroy," the CIA director offered Dr. Gottlieb no explanation.

In January of 1973, Sydney Gottlieb resigned from the CIA. No effort was made by Helms to persuade him to stay. Before his departure, and acting on Helms' order, Dr. Gottlieb had shredded records of MK-ULTRA and MK-SEARCH. Later, when President Nixon replaced Helms as director, his successor, James Rodney Schlesinger, asked if there was anything in "the CIA's recent history which could cause problems?" Helms had replied, "Nope. Not a thing."

Several floors below where the two men sat in the executive dining room there were one hundred and thirty boxes in the archives containing incriminating material that Dr. Gottlieb inexplicably had failed to destroy. Buckley was to call it "the smoking gun that eventually destroyed Gottlieb and nearly the Agency." The archive was a Pandora's Box of unfinished experiments, of those about to be launched, of some that were only still at the blueprint stage. In those boxes was the proof of Ewen Cameron's wrongdoing; of links between the CIA and the Mafia articulated in one memorable phrase Dr. Gottlieb had written to Dulles: "Such a link is inevitable considering you have gentlemen wishing to be killers and killers wishing to be gentlemen."

In one box was the master copy of Sidney Gottlieb's Assassination Manual and paperwork which showed his long-lasting and clear obsession with finding a means to murder Fidel Castro. In another box was a file on Project 143 in which Dr. Gottlieb had agreed to pay Dr. Edward Bennet at the University of Houston, Texas, $20,000 a year to develop a bacteria that could sabotage petroleum products. Bennet, the file showed, had managed to produce a substance that could eat into the metal of a car engine. One file neatly listed payment for the safe houses that George Hunter White , now dead, had opened. Right up to his demise, the killer of Frank Olson had sent his expenses to the CIA for entertaining "undercover agents," his euphemism for prostitutes. Another file detailed payments made by Dr. Gottlieb to keep Frank Olson's old lab at Fort Detrick fully functional; that cost $100,000 a year. There were bills for the supply of three kilos of a deadly carbonate poison. There were bills for so many things. There were reports on biological and chemical programs in Germany, in conjunction with Porton Down. From all over the world there were bills, requests, orders, payments. Had Sidney Gottlieb deliberately left them all undestroyed? If so, why? Had it been an oversight? But for the moment they lay there, deep in the bowels of the Central Intelligence Agency, a silent paper bomb, Buckley's smoking gun.

James Schlesinger was forty-eight years old when he took over the CIA; he was deeply steeped in the politics of Washington. His few friends called him "Mr. Can Do," the man who was ready to step into anyone's shoes. An economist by profession, he had worked for the Rand Corporation and later the Bureau of the Budget. Before coming to Langley, he had been Chairman of the Atomic Energy Commission.

From his first day the director made it clear he had come to clean house. In no time almost seven percent of the CIA's total staff were either fired or forced to resign. Many of those driven out came from the Agency's clandestine side. Buckley waited daily for the memo that would terminate his employment. It never came. He was surprised, given that the new Director had made it clear human intelligence gathering was on the way out. The new emphasis was on spies in the sky and computers that could tabulate faster than any human. Buckley kept a low profile, stayed well clear of the seventh floor and, whenever possible, visited Candace in Farmer. In the meantime, in his Brooks Brothers suits and shirts with button-down collars, Buckley did little more than tidy up paperwork. He was glad of the chance to slow down. Vietnam had badly frayed his nerves, as had the Nosenko episode.

Meeting Candace had made Buckley realize there was more to life than Langley. There were even times when he had seriously considered resigning. He had received offers, routed through ex-colleagues, to head up security in a medium-sized bank or corporation. But he knew that was not for him, that he would soon become bored. He had been in the CIA too long to leave voluntarily. Now that he sensed he would not be pushed, he only had to wait until someone on the seventh floor once again recognized his value.

On Schlesinger's third day in office, John D. Ehrlichmann, Assistant to President Nixon for Domestic Affairs, had presented the director with a thick file on the latest purported Soviet infiltrations in the United States. Moscow was accused of being behind a grave-diggers' strike in New York, a walk-out by air traffic controllers and an attempt to undermine the morals of young Americans by getting teachers to introduce realistic sex education programs. And, who else could be behind the campaign for abortion on demand? Or the thousand bomb threats New York received every week? Who else stood to benefit from the call to revolution by Angela Davis, a daughter of the black middle-class, and the Soledad Brothers? Who else but Moscow?

The file also contained claims that Russian doctors had tortured captured Americans in North Vietnam and that the Patrice Lumumba Friendship University in Moscow had begun an even more intensive training of Third World physicians in the art of medical torture. There were allegations the KGB had created "torture centers" in Bulgaria and East Germany where victims endured a wide range of medical abuse.

Alarmed by these accusations, Schlesinger ordered urgent checks to be made concerning the agency's own operations, only to be told that, while reports of CIA's wrongdoing were almost certainly true, they were hardly new. Station chiefs had written about them on several previous occasions.

Nevertheless, Schlesinger circulated a memo to all employees that the director's office should be immediately informed of any evidence that in the past the CIA had been involved in "any illegal activity." Within days his desk was covered with piles of paperwork that included various MK-ULTRA operations. Schlesinger was stunned by the sheer scope of the Agency's previous black operations. Nothing had been too great or small, too risky or vile, to try. Blackmail, sexual harassment and violence of all kinds — often ending in murder — had been commonplace. It was genuinely horrific. Since the days of Dulles, bribery also had been a commonplace Agency practice.

William Colby admired Schlesinger. His view was expressed in his book *Honorable Men*, and later repeated to the author: "James Schlesinger came on strong. He not only conducted a comprehensive review of the CIA, but also of the entire intelligence community. He was shocked about what the KGB had done, and that had reinforced in him his already present belief of what was *right* and what was *wrong*. He abhorred all he knew about the KGB, but he arrived at Langley, running, his shirt tails flying. He had that bulldog determination that went with an abrasive temperament and his hell-and-high-water determination to have the slate wiped clean in the CIA. He didn't expect the KGB to change, but he sure was going to bring change to the CIA."

Every morning when he took the turnoff on the George Washington Parkway — identified with an overhead sign "CIA" — Buckley wondered if one of Schlesinger's brief memos would be waiting for him, asking him to explain what had happened at the Institute. But the memo never came. In all the digging into the past that the DCI had ordered, nothing was asked about what had happened in Montreal.

Buckley knew there was no way that what had become known around the seventh floor as "the family jewels" — the ever-mounting evidence covering years of illegal and unethical behavior by Agency employees — could remain hidden. Shredding was no longer a guarantee the lid could be closed. Who knew what else was squirreled away? What other incriminating paperwork was buried in some university campus office or stashed in a filing cabinet in one of the drug houses the Agency had used? Others might be tempted to reveal evidence of previous government misdoings. As it was, details of Agency operations were finding their way into the newspapers, leaked by some of the scientists who had resigned or been sacked from the CIA. The whole job had become a nightmare for Schlesinger.

On July 2, 1973, after only five months in the job, President Nixon appointed Schlesinger as Secretary of Defense — a post where he would have his hands full fighting with Secretary of State Henry Kissinger. He would no longer be asking awkward questions about the Agency's past. Among the many concerns he found himself faced with upon assuming his new post were the claims of powerful Pentagon lobbyists that the Soviet Union was back in the business of manufacturing biological and chemical weapons, and that NATO airfields in Europe could be prime targets for Russian missiles firing nerve gas agents. This fear had been reinforced by the start of the Six-Day War in Sinai on October 6, 1973.

A Red Alert message from Mossad, Israel's security service, to the CIA revealed that captured Egyptian tanks and support vehicles were all equipped with protective nerve gas suits and gas masks, along with a range of detection equipment that had been manufactured in the Soviet Union. The Pentagon immediately ordered almost $2 billion to be spent improving the chemical-biological warfare defenses of its troops in NATO and elsewhere. Porton Down had followed suit, working on developing new protective clothing against chemical and biological attacks. Other measures included the manufacturing of iodine-based tablets to be taken against nerve gas.

On both sides of the Atlantic, scientists were creating portable battlefield headquarters which were protected against chemical or biological weapons with a variety of alarms, detectors and decontamination units. NATO held war games which posited the Russians had launched a full-scale chemical/biological attack against Western Europe. At their conclusion, NATO Supreme Commander, General Alexander Haig (later President Ronald Reagan's Secretary of State) told the U.S. Chiefs of Staff: "Our ability to make war with chemicals is very weak. We need to urgently reassess the situation." He found ready support. Chemical and biological warfare was back on the agenda.

For Sidney Gottlieb it must have been a bitter-sweet moment: bitter because he was not there to once more take charge, sweet because it proved him right.

President Nixon hesitated for two months before appointing William Colby as Director of Central Intelligence. The move was welcomed in the increasingly dispirited Agency, by none more so than Buckley, who believed Colby was "one of our own." Colby was the perfect invisible man: grey suits, graying hair, glasses with translucent frames the color of pale white skin. He had a habit when he was asked a question he did not care to answer of tilting back his head so light reflected off the lenses of his glasses, turning his eyes into blank white discs. Seated at his desk, spectacles perched on the bridge of his nose, Colby liked nothing more than digesting vast quantities of information at top speed, the way he had done in Vietnam. Among the first people he sent for was Buckley.

"There was," he told Buckley, "no way of diverting the pack beginning to howl along the trail to Langley." But he was not going to make it easy for them. *Omerta*, the old code of silence, still meant a great deal to Colby. Nevertheless, his unpalatable task was to "take over where his predecessors had left off." He was going to look deep into the Agency's hidden history and discover "what illegal activities were hidden in the secret recesses of our clandestine past that might now explode at any time under our feet."

It was, for Buckley a time "when the moment of truth was approaching. What had happened in Montreal, in Vietnam, in a lot of places, was finally going to surface."

Meanwhile, the burgeoning Watergate scandal bought Colby time. On October 10, 1973, Vice-President Agnew resigned. Ten days later there was a further spate of resignations and firings from the Nixon Administration. Throughout the winter of that year, and into 1974, Watergate eroded the remaining credibility of the President and his men. Colby worked hard to distance the Agency from what, by July 27, 1974, had become inevitable. On that day the House Judiciary Committee passed the first article of impeachment against Nixon, accusing him of obstructing justice in his attempt to cover up Watergate. Two days later the second article of impeachment was passed by the House. On August 8, 1974, the President went on television, using a medium he had never fully mastered, to tell the nation he was resigning. The next day, Vice-President Gerald Ford became President. That night he sent for Colby and asked to be fully briefed on the problems ahead. Colby spelled them out, including what had happened in Montreal. President Ford shook his head. "My God," he repeated. "Oh, my God."

Buckley received a call from Colby the next morning. He simply said he thought it would "be a good idea if I would set down all I knew about the bad business in Montreal. Purely routine. Nothing to worry about. That was Colby's style," Buckley recalled. He also knew he would take his time about the report. What had happened in Montreal was not really his concern any more, any more than Nosenko was, or what had happened in

Vietnam. He had signed off on that business long ago. He had earned his immunity. Let others worry about theirs.

On a December morning in 1974, Colby and Buckley were among those who awoke to find that the *New York Times* carried a broad account of the Agency's illegal activities during the Johnson and Nixon Administrations. There was a hint that the rot went even further back. To curb the national outcry, President Ford appointed a commission, chaired by Vice President Nelson A. Rockefeller to investigate the allegations. Its eight members included the Governor of California, Ronald Reagan. The commission met at 716 Lafayette Park, a government-owned brick town house. The commission's brief included examining CIA biomedical research and suggesting ways to ensure that any proven malpractice could never happen again. Between his visits to Washington — he would attend only ten of the Commission's twenty-six hearings — Governor Reagan was using his considerable charm in an attempt to maneuver the California legislature into secretly financing a scheme which, when he had first heard of it, seemed to him as neat a solution as any ending to one of his old B-movies.

The Governor, like many wealthy middle-aged and middle-class Americans, was obsessed with the violence which permeated the nation. Serious crime had reached unprecedented levels. The answer, at least for California, Reagan believed, was the one proposed by one of the State's most eminent psychiatrists, Dr. Louis Jolyon West, Chairman of the Department of Psychiatry at the University of Los Angeles and Director of its Neuropsychiatric Institute. In the early 1960s, when he had been at the University of Oklahoma, Dr. West had run an LSD research program financed by the CIA. He suggested to an immediately enthusiastic Governor the creation of a financially well-endowed multi-disciplinary Center for the Study and Reduction of Violence. Within its confines, doctors would explore all types of violent behavior, what caused it, and how it could be detected, prevented and treated. Dr. West planned to site the Center on a converted missile site in the Santa Monica Mountains. The location had been chosen because it was "accessible but relatively remote, is securely fenced and includes various buildings where comparative studies could be carried out, in an isolated and convenient location, of experimental procedure for the alteration of undesirable behavior," West wrote in a memo to Governor Reagan.

The psychiatrist proposed the Center would deal with persons who displayed "antisocial and impulsive aggression." Its laboratories would be devoted to genetic, biochemical and neurophysiological studies of "violent individuals, including prisoners and hyperactive children." Other research would concentrate upon the "pharmacology of violence" and the best way to use "anti-violence inhibiting drugs." There would also be specialists in "combating life-threatening behavior during the menstrual cycle and in making comparative studies of the levels of violence among various ethnic groups." The Center would also develop tests which Dr. West hoped "might produce the answer to violence-predisposing brain disorders prior to the occurrence of a violent episode." He planned to achieve this through tiny electrodes implanted in the brains of persons suspected of "violent trends," which would be connected to small radio transmitters and monitors.

Methods used in MK-ULTRA and MK-SEARCH that Reagan was helping to investigate in Washington were being secretly promoted by him in California. He shared Dr. West's vision that one day the behavior of all persons with "violent tendencies" could be monitored by staff at central control stations. At the first indication of trouble, attendants would rush with "suitable psychotropic drugs" to overpower a person. The system would be expensive to operate, but Governor Reagan visualized the day when thousands of his fellow Californians would be permanently monitored in this way. As he liked to say to his friends, life sure beat the movies.

Despite his considerable powers of persuasion, Governor Reagan failed to convince the California Legislature to go ahead with Dr. West's proposal. However, when the Rockefeller Commission report was issued, the Governor was a dissenting voice to the damning conclusion that the CIA had conducted a highly unethical program to "study possible means for controlling human behavior by irresponsibly exploring the effects of electroshock, psychiatry, psychology, sociology and harassment techniques." Reagan, defending the Agency, claimed that "in any bureaucracy of about sixteen thousand people there are going to be individuals who make mistakes and do things they shouldn't do."

Later, over dinner with William Casey, Reagan had vowed that if he were ever elected to the presidency, he would make sure that the CIA would never have to fight with one hand tied behind its back. Instead he would give the CIA free rein to carry the war to the enemy — wherever it was and whoever it might be and by any means the Agency chose.

William Colby lasted as CIA director until January 30, 1976, grimly obeying the orders of Congressional committees to hand over Agency secrets. He had given the U.S. Department of Justice information, which had led to Richard Helms facing a perjury charge for not testifying "fully and completely" about CIA covert action in Chile while he was director. Helms had been fined $2,000 and drew a two-year suspended jail sentence. Colby became the leper of Langley, shunned and avoided for turning in Helms, who had lived by the old Dulles code: "We are the silent service and silence begins here." Years later, Colby stated that one of the "really low points of that time was my meeting with the family of Frank Olson to give them the CIA records and thus open up and overcome a twenty-year secret that had such an impact on their lives." Colby left a legacy of resentment, but the widely circulated accusation in Langley's corridors that Colby was a Soviet spy, a charge which finally found its veiled way into the *New York Times*, was patently absurd.

George Bush arrived as CIA director on January 31, 1976, and departed three hundred and fifty-six days later. Bush was followed by Stansfield Turner. A retired four-star admiral with a formidable intellect, Turner was a Rhodes Scholar and had been one of the Navy's brightest strategists. He saw his role as "steering the Agency away from the rocks that threatened to destroy it totally — a jagged coastline made out of compounded responsibilities stretching all the way from Korea, down through Vietnam to Watergate." What had happened in Montreal was especially shocking to Turner: "It was a horror story, a God-awful horror story that must never happen again," he later said.

Buckley's own report on the Institute had vanished into the CIA's labyrinthian filing system, as he suspected it would. Afterwards he thought "perhaps Colby had quietly had it shredded; there had been so much of that going on around that time." Turner ordered the code of *Omerta* to be urgently reactivated: Buckley recalled him saying at a senior staff meeting, "What has been done cannot be undone. But no longer must it be publicly spoken about."

Shortly afterward, Buckley was posted to Laos and then Africa while the purges Colby had instigated continued under Turner. Buckley did what he always did at such times: "Kept my head below the parapet, tried to ignore all the corrosive rumors and sent my condolences when a good man was gone." Returning to Langley, Buckley maintained his reputation as a methodical and careful analyst. His work attracted little comment from the seventh floor, which suited him. Like everyone else at Langley, Buckley had formed his own opinion of Stansfield Turner: "He had managed to get himself disliked from almost the first day when he had told us that the Agency was a 'disgrace'. His first job was to keep the Agency away from anything he could not control. He didn't want to hear anything about psychological assessment of a problem. The way to get results was to concentrate on using technology. Turner sacked two hundred of my colleagues. For some reason I was never able to figure out, I was spared. But that didn't make me like Turner any more. He avoided all personal relationships, and the seventh floor became his crow's nest, where staff from lower floors rarely came. He ran the Agency like it was his flagship. He had brought with him several naval staff officers whose sole role was to filter out anybody who wanted to see him," Buckley recalled.

Turner's first memo to the depleted Clandestine Division was to remind them that Executive Order 11905 remained strictly in force. Signed by President Ford in February 1976, it stated, "No employee of the United States Government shall engage in, or conspire to engage in, political assassination." Dr. Gottlieb's Assassination Manual had been recalled. Buckley, like a number of operatives, had made a copy of the document before returning it. He also knew it would be only a matter of time before Turner was himself sacked. Washington was awash with rumors of the low morale at the CIA.

On November 3, 1981, President elect Ronald Reagan offered the post of Director of Central Intelligence to William Casey, who had been his election campaign manager. Casey was approaching his sixty-eighth birthday, a shambling, mumbling man, but rarely a bumbling one. Behind his jowls and slack-mouthed smile was a finely-honed brain. Mentally quicker than men half his age, he could sense a weakness, exploit or close a gap, and destroy an opponent through a mush of words. Reagan had told Casey he was his first and only choice to run the CIA. He was one of the first appointments confirmed by Congress after the new Administration took office.

CHAPTER EIGHTEEN

One day in March of 1981, William Buckley sat beside William Casey, as the chauffeur for the new Director of Central Intelligence drove his limousine through the last of Langley's 219 acres of pleasant and partially wooded countryside along the banks of the Potomac River and headed toward Washington.

Buckley had accompanied Casey to several meetings on Capitol Hill and in the White House to discuss the worldwide threat of terrorism being fomented by Libya, Iran and Syria. In between congressional appearances, Casey had been holding meetings at Langley that began at dawn and ended in the small hours of the next day. People marveled at his stamina and grasp of detail. He had assured everyone their jobs were safe for the moment.

Casey read hundreds of Agency personnel files. He was particularly impressed by Buckley's. He questioned Buckley closely about his time in Korea and Vietnam, and his spells in Europe and Africa. Casey dismissed Buckley's work for MK-ULTRA and MK-SEARCH, saying "That kind of thing is dead and buried." Buckley would remember how Casey leaned back in his padded chair and studied him. Buckley was confident the Director would see nothing to concern him. Fifty-three years old, twenty-seven of them spent with the CIA, Buckley was still the same weight as he had been when he had charged the enemy on the Korean battlefield. Casey leaned forward and asked Buckley why he had stayed with the CIA. Buckley didn't hesitate. "I told him I had stayed in the hope that things would get better, get back to the days of Allen Dulles," Buckley told the author.

Casey smiled and said those days were back. He told Buckley he wanted him to be his "personal point man, the fireman who told him when the fire was about to start, not when it is out of control," recalled Buckley. The new Director said he sensed the Middle East was the site for the next conflagration. He wanted Buckley to focus his analytical skills on the area. Casey's request on how he wanted information presented had been clear-cut: "Be specific. Keep it short."

For the next month Buckley worked sixteen hour days pulling together the work of the Agency's specialists on the region. He dissected their reports and reassembled them, the technique he had used in Vietnam. Every morning when Casey arrived on the seventh floor, there was a briefing paper on his desk stamped "Sensitive Compartmented Information." The papers dealt with the roles of the Soviet Union and China in the region and tried to predict the trends that would dominate Middle East intelligence gathering in the next decade. Buckley saw that the biggest problem was going to be containing the region's many terrorist groups, and he predicted that they would zero in on the United States. He identified Iran's Islamic terrorism as the immediate major threat, and one which would be unlike terrorism sponsored by the USSR, Cuba and China. Islamic terrorism would be driven by deep-set religious beliefs and, in the end, would follow its own dynamic.

In one paper, Buckley urged the Agency to see that its agents in the region could read Arab newspapers (few had more than a smattering of the language). In another he argued for the need to conduct in-depth studies of the role of the mullahs and the imams and the importance of identifying the key ones. Buckley's papers — each no longer than one page — were a series of wake-up calls that fitted Casey's own philosophy perfectly.

On that March morning, as Buckley and Casey rode toward Washington, a copy of Buckley's latest briefing paper was in Casey's briefcase on the backseat of the car. It was an evaluation of the next stage of the holy war, jihad, in Lebanon. Casey said he found the document frightening reading. He hoped the Senate Intelligence Committee would feel the same. Copies had been hand-carried overnight to its members, to the Oval Office, and to Secretary of Defense Casper Weinberger. Buckley had become used to Casey's silence during the nine-mile drive into Washington.

Like Casey himself, the Lincoln Continental they were riding in was outwardly deceptive. The sleek, highly polished limousine looked like any other government car. But the driver was a CIA officer who had passed a demanding driving course. He was also practice-perfect in grabbing for the loaded shotgun kept in a door recess. The car's armor added some 2,000 pounds to the Lincoln's original weight. The windscreen and windows were blast-proof. The body was strengthened by titanium-ceramic armor tested to withstand a 155mm shell or a small mine detonating under the chassis. Built into the rear compartment were an oxygen mask and a fire-suppression system, a global positioning system, accurate to within one yard and a jam-resistant communications system that could instantly put Casey in touch with Langley, the Pentagon or the Oval Office. In the event that the limo's tires were shot out, the Lincoln would still be able to maintain a speed of sixty miles an hour on the rims of its wheels. Only one car offered comparable protection — the one used by the President of the United States. The Lincoln made Buckley feel as protected as it was possible to be, short of traveling in a tank. Nevertheless, the driver had been warned by the FBI that Iran could be planning "a spectacular" as a reminder that releasing the American hostages had ultimately changed nothing except to serve as a final humiliation for President Carter. The Iranians had waited a mere thirty minutes after Reagan had been sworn-in as President before allowing the hostages to leave.

Casey had told Buckley the story of the hostages' release. Known as the "October Surprise," it was an operation that

Casey had orchestrated over dinner one night with some of the future president's aides. Casey had raised the possibility of doing a deal with Iran and said there would "have to be something in it for the ayatollahs." He had proposed approaching a number of wealthy Republicans. In a week they had pledged $40 million. The money was to be laundered through a number of Swiss banks before ending up in Tehran. Earl Brian, a business associate of Reagan, agreed to handle the transfer because of his long-standing high-level contacts in Tehran. He arranged to fly to Paris on October 17, 1980, less than a month before the race for the White House was decided. His cover story was that he was going to sign a deal for one of his own companies. The next day, sixteen high-ranking Iranian government officials arrived. It took two days to hammer out the deal. Terms for the hostages' freedom were agreed upon.

Buckley asked himself why Casey had shared the story with him. Politically its implications could drive Reagan from the White House. Casey and all those involved would certainly face criminal prosecution. Was the story even true? Or had Casey told it as a litmus test to establish how far he could trust his new point man? Buckley couldn't decide. But he was not about to "start poking around," he later remembered thinking.

Buckley had himself been on the periphery of what happened after the hostages had been flown out of Tehran. He had accompanied a team of CIA doctors who helped examine the hostages when they landed at the U.S. Air Force base at Wiesbaden in Germany. The base was near a number of safe houses Buckley had visited during the MK-ULTRA experiments on "expendables." The physicians concluded that some of the hostages had been tortured psychologically and that this had required significant medical knowledge. The realization that the "sons of Gottlieb and Cameron were out there made me feel pretty sick," Buckley recalled.

Chapter Eighteen

On the drive to Capitol Hill, Casey had on the custom-made dark blue pinstripe lawyer's suit he wore for Senate committee meetings. Buckley waited in an anteroom while the Director went into the committee room. Two hours later, Casey emerged and told the driver to take them out to Fort George Meade. It was the first time Buckley had been to the sprawling National Security Agency headquarters.

The NSA Director, Bobby Inman, took them on a tour. He showed them banks of computers that analyzed information from satellites on the edge of space, and digital images of stunning clarity. Into sharp relief came bridges in Russia, rocket launching rigs and a close-up of a smoking chimney stack. Inman explained that NSA computers had analyzed the emissions and discovered they derived from cheap fuels. He showed them in real time a military truck in a street of a Russian city and faces of soldiers marching from a barracks. Buckley found Inman's enthusiasm infectious. The NSA chief was right when he said electronic spying had an increasing role to play in intelligence gathering. Yet Inman was careful not to suggest that this meant the end of human intelligence gathering. There was, he said, a place for both. Inman then revealed that NSA satellites had positively identified four prisons where Iranian doctors observed or actually took part in acts of torture. He produced a set of black-and-white prints. Each was marked with the time, date and location of the photo. One taken high above Evin showed a white-coated figure watching a man being whipped. The prints from Komiteh and Qasr were shots of other white-coated figures supervising more whippings and *falaqu*, the beating to pulp of a prisoner's feet. "Inman said he had more pictures. Doctors carrying out electroshocks or branding with red-hot knives. He asked if we would like to see them. Casey said it wasn't necessary," Buckley was to remember.

On the ride back to Langley, Casey told Buckley they were next going to make a series of short trips to CIA stations in the Middle East and North Africa.

Buckley later remembered it as a time "when we used to try and second guess what sauce they would use to cover the chicken. Some of the countries were strictly no booze places, so one of my jobs was to make sure that State used the diplomatic bag to bring in the whisky Bill Casey preferred. On those trips we came to know one another fairly well. I suspect some of the station chiefs were not altogether thrilled about that. But Bill made it clear that anything they wanted to say to him they could say in front of me."

The data Buckley collected on the region's leaders enabled the Agency to satisfy an early request from President Reagan. He wanted psychological profiles of these leaders to be made up as videos. Casey explained that the President and the First Lady enjoyed watching television. They would sit in their pajamas with their tray suppers and watch a favorite movie. Casey hoped the profiles would add to their knowledge.

Buckley was given the job of assembling the video on Ayatollah Khomeini. It began with the standard Agency warning that the material was "sensitive intelligence." The caption faded, then came the plaintive sound of music: a recitative and restricted range of notes: halves and quarter tones. The sound swelled: flutes and horns, tambourines and cymbals. The footage was a clip from a travel show from the days when Iran had been on the holiday itinerary of adventurous Americans. Mountains filled the screen. The sorrowful wailing faded. Iran, intoned the narrator — a voice-over actor from television commercials — had always been a hard land. The picture changed to newsreel footage of Ayatollah Khomeini receiving the adulation of the Tehran mob. The narrator identified him: "Ruhollah Mussavi Khomeini, the Glorious Upholder of the

Faith, the Sole Hope of the Downtrodden, His Holiness the Grand Ayatollah." For a further twenty minutes the video attempted to explain the personality of the Ayatollah: "Though he is a sayyad, a descendant of one of the twelve Imams the Shiites hold sacred, there is still in psychological terms, a definite conflict within him between ideals and purposes. He is old and dangerous and an example that religious fanaticism often springs from dissatisfaction with personal development in early life. He has cast himself in the role as God-instructor to his people. To maintain that myth, he will need to act in an increasingly dangerous manner toward the United States and Western world." The screen went momentarily blank. Then it was filled with that most endearing of Disney's creations — Mickey Mouse. With the gravity of a voice announcing a final significant revelation, the narrator said the Ayatollah's favorite relaxation was watching cartoons of the fabled rodent.

Buckley was hearing various reports of doctors engaging in state-sponsored medical torture in Syria, Lebanon, Egypt and Libya. Several of the physicians appeared to use methods similar to those developed by Ewen Cameron at the Montreal Institute: sensory deprivation, lengthy periods of isolation and electroshock. In Syria, he had been told there was a doctor who fitted helmets to the heads of his prisoners through which he played a tape endlessly demanding they admitted to being spies. Buckley wondered if any of these doctors had worked at the Institute. Casey told him to follow up the matter.

In the hope that Dr. Gottlieb may have kept a list of all those he had employed, Buckley drove out to see the now retired CIA scientist. He found Dr. Gottlieb milking his goats. The scientist declared that part of his life was over and virtually ordered Buckley off his land. His parting words: "Nothing worked for me, so why should it work for anyone else?"

Buckley flew to Montreal. The Institute itself was much as he remembered it, but he recognised none of the staff. He went to the administrator's office and, this time posing as an investigator for a law firm seeking a doctor who had come into a legacy, he asked to see the staff list for the past ten years. The administrator told him the document had been taken away by the Canadian security service. Knowing he had reached another dead end — to approach the CSS would be pointless after the debacle following Dr. Cameron's resignation — Buckley flew back to Washington.

During his travels Buckley found that the nervous exhaustion that had marked his last weeks in Vietnam had returned. He had trouble sleeping, and when he did, he awoke from nightmares. Many of these featured Dr. Cameron or the human experiments he had witnessed in Vietnam. Buckley became irritable on his weekends with Candace, showing little interest in her new passion for landscape gardening. She would remember how "Bill would sit there, glued to the television and switching from one newscast to another. When I asked him if there was anything that especially interested him, he would bark and say, 'Everything interests me.' There was something going on in his head that he was not going to share with me. Suddenly I felt left out." But before she could explore the matter with him, William Buckley was off again to the Middle East.

His assignment was to check the training of the bodyguards of Egypt's President Anwar Sadat. Buckley had met Sadat on a previous visit to Cairo with Casey, when the Director's offer to have the CIA train the bodyguards had been gratefully accepted by Sadat.

On Saturday, October 6, 1981, Buckley sat in the back of the presidential review stand in Cairo watching a military parade. Below him to his right was President Anwar Sadat, dressed in the uniform of Egypt's commander-in-chief. Buckley felt he could have been in West Point. The American equipped and trained Egyptian army look very different from the rabble he remembered seeing on television at the end of the Six-Day War with Israel. Yet, behind the impressive display of precision marching and the columns of armoured vehicles — the outward symbol that Sadat was the first Egyptian to have Washington's military support — Buckley also knew the Egyptian president found it increasingly hard to bear the isolation from his Arab neighbors.

Syria's President Hafez Assad had publicly said he would, given the opportunity, personally strangle Sadat for promising that Egypt would never again wage war against Israel. Despite King Hussein's years of being the CIA's most distinguished informer in the Middle East, Jordan's ruler had told Washington he would be unwilling to support Sadat should his enemies attack. A pariah beyond his borders, Sadat had also become hated by some of his own people, who had used the parade to publicly show their anger at his policies. Hundreds of thousands had obeyed the calls of their fundamentalist clerics to boycott the parade. Even some of the diplomatic corps had found excuses not to be present.

Over the preceding days, Buckley had had the opportunity to spend time with Sadat. He found him to be depressed and pessimistic about the peace pact's chances for success. The effects of Sadat's marijuana use were very clear; at times Sadat seemed spaced out. Those were the occasions when the president was most prone to say that it was Allah's will whether he lived or died — and that he felt God no longer favored him. Buckley had warned Sadat's bodyguards that they must never allow such fatalism to undermine their work. The parade was the first public chance for the guards to show off their skills. Suddenly, from behind the last tank, there was a break in the marching ranks. Instinctively Buckley rose to his feet, feeling for the gun in his shoulder holster. His shouted commands to the bodyguards were drowned in a burst of gunfire. The oncoming soldiers were raking the stand.

"Shoot! For Christ's sake, shoot!" Buckley screamed as he forced his way forward.

The bodyguards stared, dumb-founded at the approaching gunmen.

"Shoot!"

Buckley's orders went unheeded.

The gunmen were firing with deadly effect into the stand.

"Pick your targets! Chris'sake! Pick your targets!" Buckley once again screamed.

The gunmen poured shots into the stampeding spectators and President Sadat. Hemmed in, there was no way Buckley could return the fire. Sadat sat slumped in his seat. Only then did the bodyguards form a protective shield. They began to pick off the gunmen. From the parade, soldiers broke ranks to help. The assassins were trapped between two fields of fire, but Buckley knew it was too late. One look showed him the President was beyond help. Blood poured from his mouth, ears, nose and chest. Unable to help, Buckley headed for the U.S. embassy compound. He arrived to find the place in uproar. A line had been opened to the State Department, and a diplomat was yelling down the phone.

"He's still alive! The Egyptians are saying he's still alive!"

Buckley walked into the office shaking his head, mouthing the word: dead. The diplomat waved him away. Buckley shrugged and walked to the Agency's offices at the rear of the building. The Station Chief was on the phone to the new Deputy Director of Operations in Langley, John H Stein.

"The latest we have is that State is saying he's alive," said Stein.

"He's dead," yelled Buckley. "As dead as a dodo!"

"Buckley says he's dead!" the Station Chief said into the phone.

Buckley motioned for the phone. He explained to Stein what he had seen, speaking slowly, knowing that the DDO was writing it all down. That was Stein's style: no matter how great the crisis, keep a record, remain cool, ask only essential questions. When Buckley finished, Stein said that he should take the first plane to Washington.

Three weeks later, Buckley was confronted with the legacy of MK-ULTRA. Ottawa Station reported that Dr. Mary Morrow and Velma Orlikov would soon be joined by other plaintiffs in their case against the CIA.

Velma Orlikov had filed a lawsuit in Washington on December 11, 1980. She was asking for $1 million damages. Her attorney was Joseph Rauh, America's most renowned civil rights lawyer. Shortly afterward Mary Morrow had become a co-plaintiff. Casey asked the Agency's general-counsel, Stanley Sporkin, to defend the action — and legally delay its coming into court for as long as possible. But Rauh pushed his case along. He talked to Alice Olson about how her husband died; he tracked down Dr. Gottlieb; he spoke to a number of doctors who had worked at the Institute. He dug out all of Dr. Cameron's papers from the archives and had them evaluated by psychiatrist Robert Jay Lifton, who was conducting research into the behavior of Nazi doctors at Auschwitz and elsewhere. Additionally, Rauh spoke to relatives of patients at the Institute and to senior medical men who had known Dr. Cameron. Now Rauh wanted to question Helms. He wanted the key to Pandora's Box.

On Monday, November 9, 1981, Buckley was dispatched to Canada to try to get background on all the plaintiffs whose names Ottawa Station had provided. He was to concentrate upon their current medical state. Buckley realized it was "dogs-body time again."

In Montreal he read the *New York Times* report that a five-man Libyan hit squad had secretly entered the United States. Within forty-eight hours, the number reported had grown to ten — and there was additional information that the Libyans may have entered the U.S. by crossing the Canadian border. Buckley telephoned Langley and asked if he should momentarily drop his enquiries to try and pick up the trail of Qadaffi's men. He was told the matter was well in hand. On the next day Qadaffi scored a public relations coup by appearing live on American network television from Libya to deny he had sent any assassination squads to North America. President Reagan swiftly publicly branded the Colonel a liar: "We have the evidence and he knows it!"

Buckley called a friend in Langley. What was this evidence?

"It's White House evidence! Pure Hollywood!"

On January 4, 1982, Buckley turned in a report to Casey on the medical and mental conditions of Velma Orlikov, Mary Morrow and the other plaintiffs. They were all elderly now and in poor physical health. But they were united in a common determination to fight for justice. Years later Casey would admit: "This was the time I realized we were not going to win this one unless all sixteen plaintiffs died." Casey denied he was being insensitive, or motivated by any consideration other than to prevent the CIA suffering further humiliation as well as having to pay a substantial sum in damages. "The Montreal business was a hangover from the past. What had happened would not have done so on my watch."

Though the plaintiffs were indeed in poor physical shape and one of them died soon after being named as a co-plaintiff, the Canadian government not only expressed its outrage over what had happened at the Institute, but also promised to provide all possible support for its citizens in suing the United States Government. Every day public anger in Canada grew.

Nevertheless, Rauh had not reckoned with the legal machinations of William Casey — the CIA Director mounted a counter-offensive of stalling actions. These included resisting the release of documents on the grounds of "national security." Frustrated by Casey's tactics and himself in poor health, Rauh lashed out at the one ally he could have counted on, the Canadian government. He publicly accused it of inertia, and of being "in cahoots" with the CIA. Overnight the goodwill from Ottawa evaporated. In Washington, the State Department formally told the Canadian government that it rejected any legal responsibility for funding Dr. Cameron. Rauh found the case slipping from his grasp. He made a personal and impassioned appeal to Canada's Prime Minister, Brian Mulroney. It was a further serious tactical error on the part of a once astute lawyer. A furious Mulroney rejected every allegation Rauh made, including: "Is it Canadian fright of the Big Brother in the south, aggravated by the fear of the CIA, that holds back your government?" In Langley, Casey followed every move and predicted that the case would "die a natural death like the plaintiffs." There were by now only nine left, including the redoubtable Dr. Mary Morrow.

In January 1987, Joe Rauh retired on his seventy-sixth birthday. He had become as physically frail as his clients. His place was taken by a partner in Rauh's firm, Jim Turner. A tough and capable lawyer, Turner realized that the CIA could run out the clock until the last of his clients was dead. Turner came to the conclusion it was better to try to obtain the best possible settlement before that happened. He began a protracted round of discussions that concluded on October 5, 1988, when the Central Intelligence Agency, represented by the Department of Justice, settled $750,000 on the nine plaintiffs, to be divided between them on an equal basis. Each plaintiff signed an undertaking they would never discuss the case in public. The author of this book had agreed to testify if the case had gone to trial and to provide the plaintiffs with all the documentation in his possession.

Like every director, Casey found he had to grapple with the fear that the Soviet Union and China were once more stock-piling chemical and biological weapons. Buckley found these matters added to his daily docket. He made a trip to Laos, where CIA-backed tribesmen claimed they had been attacked with gases that had produced horrible skin blisters and often agonizing deaths. Buckley recovered a canister of the substance and brought it back to Fort Detrick. The tribesmen had described it as falling like "yellow rain." Analysis of the canister showed its contents did not fit any chemical known at Fort Detrick. Victims complained of burning — associated with mustard gas derivatives — and of choking — symptomatic of phosgene. But no weapon in the Fort Detrick inventory matched those symptoms or could account for the fatal internal bleeding the tribesmen had suffered. These symptoms had, however, been reported in other Soviet-supported wars in Cambodia and Yemen. The conclusion was that Russian scientists had created a deadly new weapon.

Buckley was sent back to the Thai/Cambodia border with a team of researchers from Fort Detrick. Pro-American tribesmen led them into the jungle to a spot where the vegetation was covered in a slimy white mould. Samples were taken and placed in a hermetically sealed container. Buckley flew with it back to Washington. There, scientists at Fort Detrick discovered the mould contained mytoxins known as tricothenes or T-2 toxins. They knew the Soviets had focused research on those toxins as a possible cause of the poor harvests that regularly affected vast areas of Russia. Russian scientists had turned the T-2 toxins into a lethal weapon.

Richard Nixon had halted American participation in chemical/biological warfare research. But in 1981 it resumed and America, in the utmost secrecy, began the search for new and altogether more terrifying weapons. The "patriotic germs" Sidney Gottlieb had once spoken of were once again alive and marching under the banner of the Stars and Stripes.

As this was going on, Casey told Buckley to prepare a list of countries where there was evidence of medical torture. Buckley found that in Ethiopia, physicians employed by the regime poured boiling oil and water on parts of prisoners' bodies and then tested various blood coagulants and serums to treat the massive blistering. The medications had been supplied by the Russians. Many of the victims died in agony. From the tiny Marxist state of Djibouti, he obtained proof that doctors injected coma-inducing drugs, gave prisoners electroshock and carried out amputations, immersed victims in vats of brine water for weeks at a time, pickling their skins until they rotted from the bone. In Somalia, physicians employed by the National Security Service at its headquarters in Mogadishu had created a "noise room." Prisoners were subjected for days to increasingly amplified sounds until they became permanently deaf. In Uganda, a dozen centers through the country had physicians who supervised or participated in castration, burning-off of breasts and genitalia, and surgical removal of tongues.

For the past thirty-five years the Agency had filed reports on many thousands of cases of medical torture in Russia. When required, these were fed to U.S. politicians to attack the Soviet system, using the names of the doctors and the hospitals where the abuses occurred. Soviet physicians routinely prescribed psychotropic disorienting and pain-inducing treatments for perfectly sane persons whose only "illness" was opposing the regime. Many of the drugs were given in massive quantities with a total disregard of contraindications. Those who received them frequently became permanently physically incapacitated or mentally deranged.

Inevitably, Buckley found his research could not be neatly compartmentalized. While medical torture was uniform within the Soviet Bloc, elsewhere it recognized no geographic boundaries. What doctors did in Libya was duplicated in adjoining Egypt. In the aftermath of Sadat's assassination, thousands of people had been taken to several notorious Cairo torture chambers: the Citadel, Tora Reception Prison and Al Marg Prison. In all those places doctors routinely supervised whippings, sensory deprivation and incarceration in underground vaults. Saudi Arabia, long deemed "friendly" by the Agency, was, in terms of medical torture, really no different from Syria. In both countries doctors used an instrument called the al-Abd as-Aswad, the Black Slave. It consisted of a metal chair with a hole in its seat. A victim was strapped, naked, to the chair and then through the hole came a heated metal skewer which entered the anus, slowly mincing its way into the intestines. A doctor was often on hand to ensure the skewer was withdrawn before killing a person — though death generally followed from massive internal hemorrhaging. In Turkey, another "friendly" nation, doctors supervised beatings, administered electroshocks and decided how long a victim should be hooded. At Bien Hoa Prison in Saigon where Dr. Gottlieb had sent Agency doctors to experiment upon Vietcong prisoners, Communist physicians now tortured those who refused to accept the new regime.

In the Philippines, physicians in the employ of the national security service — yet another organization the CIA had trained — authorized similar treatments for opponents of the Marcos regime. From Africa to Asia, to Latin America, to the Middle East, in over eighty countries, Buckley gathered evidence of medical torture. With the help of the specialists in the Political Psychological Division — whose contacts reached into every corner of the medical world — Buckley arranged for the material to be fed to human rights workers. Some of the evidence Buckley had gathered was included in Amnesty International's regular reports on torture.

As Buckley continued his investigation, he was reminded of a meeting he had in Tel Aviv in the office of Ari Ben-Menashe. The darkly handsome quick-witted Ben-Menashe held a key post in the Israeli intelligence community. He worked in the External Relations Department, ERD, one of the most powerful and secret organizations in a nation of secret organizations and ran the desk that handled ERD's relationship with friendly intelligence networks. Ben-Menashe had confirmed the reports of doctors conducting torture and he called special attention to an Iranian, Aziz al-Abub. The latest Mossad intelligence suggested al-Abub had undergone training in Moscow and was now in Beirut where he was torturing hostages captured by Hezbollah.

The physician had arrived in Beirut on Saturday, March 15, 1982. He had come directly from Moscow to Beirut equipped with a range of drugs. It turned out that Dr. al-Abub had devoted considerable time to the study of Sidney Gottlieb's methods. He had graduated from Tehran University in late 1978 swearing his physician's oath to the sound of a dying dynasty. In Iran, the Shah had only weeks of rule left. Entire cities were already closed citadels controlled by the clerics of the Ayatollah Khomeini. Despite his waning authority, the Shah continued to fill the prisons with the suffering innocent. Perhaps that had convinced the doctor, who had sworn to harm no one, to play a direct role in the overthrow of the regime. On entering medical school he joined the Revolutionary Guards. Within a year he had been elected their leader in the school.

In late 1979, with the Shah finally deposed and the Ayatollah Khomeini installed in Tehran, Dr. al-Abub was given a scholarship to Patrice Lumumba Friendship University in Moscow. In

March 1980 he took a flight from Tehran to Moscow. The next two years were spent in the university's post-graduate medical school. He had been selected for a course in brainwashing techniques.

The CIA Moscow station provided Buckley with details of the course. Dr. al-Abub had been taught that brainwashing depended on carefully calculated psychological pressure. This included the use of repetition, harassment and humiliation. Students took turns acting the roles of "interrogators" and "prisoners." Those cast as "prisoners" were made to memorize lengthy and increasingly complex Communist tracts. An inability to answer correctly was dealt with by petty harassment. A "prisoner" would be summoned from his meal and lectured by his tutors on the necessity of paying attention. When he returned to the table he would find his food gone. His sleep was disrupted in the small hours, and he was asked to repeat portions of text he had earlier failed to correctly deliver. He was subjected to humiliation, a technique aimed primarily at turning his fellow students against him. The tutors explained to a "prisoner's" fellow students they were also responsible for his mistakes; he became, at least momentarily, the object of dislike to the rest of the class and ostracized. Only when the instructors decided a student had been driven close to collapse was he reinstalled and another "prisoner" chosen to replace him.

Behaviorists analyzed the students' responses, showing them their increasing vulnerability and suggestibility. Students were then taught how to achieve these effects in others. At Patrice Lumumba, Dr. al-Abub also learned how to strip an individual of his selfhood by creating a state of dependency, and how to establish a sense of guilt. This could lead to the destruction of long-cherished ideals and a growing compulsion to confess. He was told that when a person had purged himself of his past, he could be encouraged to accept new substitute beliefs.

Although Dr. al-Abub's receding hairline and a slight stoop gave him the bearing of an older man, he was still a few weeks from his thirty-first birthday. Physically there was little about him to show he had once been the leader of the Pasadaran, the Revolutionary Guards, in the medical school at Tehran University.

Dr. al-Abub's training and temperament made him an ideal candidate for Hezbollah. By this time, Hezbollah comprised a number of radical fundamentalist groups unified into a political, social and military organization that closely resembled the ideology and militancy of the Iranian revolution. Hezbollah's immediate goals were to remove all Western influence from Lebanon and to destroy Israel. Its ultimate aim was to create a worldwide Islamic republic headed by Shiite clerics. Since its founding, Hezbollah had become the most dangerous terrorist organization in the Middle East. What distinguished Hezbollah from other terrorist groups was the thoroughness of its planning. Every operation it had carried out confirmed that. Sheikh Muhammad Husayn Fadlallah, who was head of the group's Leadership Council as well as the spiritual leader of the movement, had, from the very outset, insisted that their planning must equal that of Israel's operations. Every attack needed Fadlallah's prior approval. He had insisted that before Dr. al-Abub was recruited his background be carefully checked to establish that he felt intense hatred for any view contradicting Hezbollah ideology. Now the physician was an integral part of Hezbollah tactics in Lebanon. These included political kidnapping.

Kidnapping was not new to the city; it was a plague that the rich had long lived with. To be wealthy in Lebanon was to be a permanent target for the gangs who had long supported their drug habits, violence, and overall antagonism to society through kidnapping. They thrived on the slackness of the authorities, the poor quality of police training and the pervasive corruption that had seen local bodyguards bought off. For the really wealthy there was the possibility of hiring foreign bodyguards, men who had served in Lebanon either with the British or French armies. But they were expensive and their services were already in demand all over the world. Insurance — knowing that money would be paid in return for a kidnapped victim — was available from Lloyds of London. But the premiums were high, and Lebanon was regarded as a high-risk area and coverage would not generally exceed a person's assets. Three other companies, all American based, were ready to underwrite kidnap insurance but again the premiums were high and hedged with caveats. No company, however, was prepared to underwrite a person kidnapped for purely political reasons. Though no one would say so, it was assumed that in the event of such a kidnapping, the person's government would intervene using its own considerable Special Forces to recover a kidnapped person.

Hezbollah had succeeded in garnering considerable support in Lebanon. But no other single factor guaranteed their rapid ascent to power and influence more than the Israeli invasion of 1982. Beirut inhabitants recalled how, after months of Israeli planes dropping leaflets filled with threats — which enterprising local shopkeepers had collected and stapled together and sold as toilet paper — and a stream of warning broadcasts from Tel Aviv, which the city's radio stations had quickly learned to jam, the Israelis attacked. On Sunday morning, June 6, 1982, fifteen years to the day after Israel had launched a pre-emptive strike against Egypt to assure its victory in the Six-Day War, Israeli forces swept into Lebanon. The pretext was to exact a swift and terrible retaliation for the assassination of Israel's ambassador to Britain. A few days before he had been shot pointblank in the head by an Arab gunman outside a London hotel.

By nightfall on the Sunday, the sky over West Beirut was fiery with the glow of exploding Israeli shells and rockets. Tens of thousands of refugees fled from the city to escape the Israeli ground forces. It was no comfort to them that the ferocity of the attack had drawn worldwide condemnation. Peace, so fragile at the best of times during the years of Lebanon's civil strife — in which Lebanese Christians had fought Muslims and elements of the Shiite community had turned upon each other, often fighting for no more than control of a street in West Beirut — was shattered into bloody shards as hour after hour came the crump of exploding Israeli bombs.

No one would ever know how many died. Day and night, the grimy white ambulances with green crescents painted on their sides careened through the streets, first to the hospitals with the dying and then to the morgues with the dead.

The Palestine Liberation Organization was everywhere, distinguished by their red checkered *kaffiyehs* and their Russian small arms. They stood alongside the soldiers of the Palestine Liberation Front and the fighters of Islamic Amal. Until recently they had been bitter opponents.

Sheikh Fadlallah perceived all this new unity with profound satisfaction. Terrible though the carnage was, God, he would say later, had ordained it. It had a divine purpose to which he must give human voice. Now. Now was the time. That was how the recruiting began — the precursor which had led to Dr. al-Abub's own arrival in the city. Within weeks, Hezbollah had fired the imagination of the deprived and fuelled a dormant belief that only Islamic law and justice was pure: all else was evil and must be destroyed before it devoured Islam. Inside of a year there were thousands of followers, each spreading the word with missionary zeal throughout West Beirut, into the fertile Beka'a Valley and the hinterland, and out to the stark Shiite villages in the rural south of the country. The message was carried to the very border with Israel that the hour of Islamic retribution was at hand.

Despite the relentless siege by Israel's forces in Beirut, the will to resist grew. It became a matter of honor to sit, drinking tiny glasses of sweet tea, while Israeli rockets whistled overhead. A man's courage was measured by whether he flinched at the whine of Israeli aircraft. Children learned to control their hysterical screams when the alleys vibrated with the noise and the ground heaved and was torn asunder by explosives. That was when the organized chanting began. Hezbollah! Hate Israel! Hezbollah! Hate America! Hezbollah! Hate the West! Hezbollah! Hate the World beyond our World!

Filled with a sense of sacred mission, every Friday evening the Hezbollah clerics delivered the same uncompromising message. After the faithful spread their prayer rugs and prostrated themselves three times — on each occasion touching their foreheads to the ground and murmuring the name of Allah, The Great, they squatted on their haunches and listened to an ever-increasing list of targets the clerics read out. As well as Israel and the Great Satan — the label Fadlallah had given the United States — the list included Saudi Arabia for refusing to stop selling its oil and so cripple the West; the Pope for his support for Lebanese Christians; the governments of France and Germany; Western newspaper and media representatives in Beirut for biased reporting; all the cafes and shops in the Christian sector of the city that sold hamburgers, ketchup and foreign magazines. Sometimes it could take a cleric a full hour to remind his congregation of all the foreign products and where they were still on sale in the deeply divided city.

No fulmination was complete without a concluding reminder that ultimate victory meant not only banishing all those evils, but also required confronting and defeating forces poised beyond the narrow frontiers of Lebanon. The adversaries were always identified as being led by the United States and Israel. To that list would soon be added a new name, the U.S. Embassy's Protocol Officer. In the mosques, he was called Buck-lee.

CHAPTER NINETEEN

Shortly after his return from Southeast Asia, William Buckley was sent back to Beirut as the CIA station chief. Director Casey said that Buckley's accumulated years of tradecraft made him the ideal choice for the post. In Beirut, Buckley set about establishing a network of informers which extended into the upper echelons of the shaky Lebanese coalition government. Among them was Walid Jumblatt, the Druze leader, a warlord who survived by sleeping under a different roof every night in the Christian sector of the city. Jumblatt was the government's Minister of Tourism — a post that entailed constant visits to foreign embassies to encourage their staff to think of ways of attracting tourists to what had already become probably the most dangerous city on earth. In each of those embassies Jumblatt had his own man in place, gathering up tidbits of intelligence that the Druze leader conveyed to Buckley. Another informer was a PLO man who, at huge personal risk, met Buckley to brief him on Yasir Arafat's latest thinking. A third informer, a Syrian, supplied details of the latest groupings around President Assad in Damascus. At times the sheer volume of raw intelligence was overwhelming.

As well as keeping tabs on events in Lebanon, Buckley maintained a watch over Iran, using foreign businessmen who passed through Beirut on their way to and from Tehran. They briefed Buckley often in return for no more than a good meal. On a daily basis Buckley handled up to a hundred separate items. Each one had to be assessed and sent on to Langley. Sometimes he worked a twenty-hour stint for several days at a time before sleeping round the clock in his penthouse.

By this time Dr. Aziz al-Abub had solidified his position within the Hezbollah hierarchy and established a powerful name for himself in Beirut. His task was to keep the hostages kidnapped by the Hezbollah alive for ransom or political reasons. Most of them were wealthy Lebanese. But recently some new "patients" had come under Dr. al-Abub's "care." These were an American academic, Frank Regier; Christian Joubert, a French construction engineer; and Jeremy Levin, the CNN bureau chief in Beirut. But their capture had done nothing to achieve Hezbollah's aims. This failure was discussed at a meeting of the Leadership Council. Sheikh Fadlallah raised the question of what more could be done to embarrass the United States. Copies of the Lebanese government's list of foreign diplomats accredited to the country were produced, and attention was focused on the names of the remaining American diplomats in Beirut. Sheikh Fadlallah reminded everyone that those who worked for the Great Satan took their security most seriously. Whenever they left their compound, they traveled with heavily armed U.S. Marine escorts. The ambassadors said they had learned the Americans were determined to either capture or kill Dr. al-Abub, whom they believed was mistreating the hostages. Because of Dr. al-Abub's importance, Fadlallah offered him protection. The physician declined, insisting he knew how to protect himself.

A month after that meeting, Dr. al-Abub once more met with the Leadership Council. All around him was daily evidence that Beirut, once the pride of French colonization, was slipping into the Third World. Black-marketeering and inflation were rampant. The virtual collapse of living standards had produced a debilitating effect on a population forced to live check-by-jowl with the Hezbollah. The aura of violence and sense of defeat were everywhere. The Hezbollah fighters were accustomed to poverty. They were ready, even eager, to see the city, indeed the whole of Lebanon, lurch into an irreversible depression. From its depths they would spread their doctrine of extremism. Dr. al-Abub was there to help make that possible. That was why he could walk with such confidence and immunity through the most dangerous city in the world. Its streets were part battleground, part demolition site. Barricades blocked roads; cars were forced to negotiate between oil drums filled with rubble, the route between them marked with black streamers, the color of the Hezbollah. Guarding the barricades were groups of youths in *kaffiyehs* and remnants of khaki fatigues. Behind each barricade was a brazier, cooking pots, boxes of fruit and vegetables, bed-rolls. The youths lived and slept on the barricades and, if need be, would die defending the posts. For this they each received the equivalent of U.S. $3 a month, a vast salary amid the economic collapse of Lebanon.

Dr. al-Abub, it was widely believed in West Beirut, received many times that income, along with an apartment and a car. Such status symbols, together with his education and authoritarian manner, further marked him out in the community. He was looked upon with something approaching awe. Everybody knew he had the power of life or death over the hostages and would exercise it without a moment's hesitation. His doctor's bag contained drugs capable of reducing the strongest-minded captive's will to resist. His skill at using them was part of a campaign whose visible and harrowing apex were the video recordings of the hostages the Hezbollah had started to release to the media. The tapes were designed to force governments to accede to the demands of the hostage takers. So far the pressure had met with no success. But the warning that the Americans had identified Dr. al-Abub as a target for elimination had given the physician the status of a folk hero. And, in the depths of West Beirut, he knew he was safe.

On either side of the road were ruined buildings, dumps for burnt-out cars and trash. A pile of rubble was all that remained of the United States Embassy, destroyed by a car bomb that had left sixty-three dead. The surviving Americans had moved to a compound in the eastern sector of the city. Those had been heady days for the youthful bombers; they had clamored to be the next to die. Now the skills of Dr. al-Abub had largely supplanted their actions. While their methods spoke directly to the enemy, his approach was far more subtle, and the morality of his actions had not been challenged, unlike those of the suicide bombers. Before they had been allowed to launch their attacks, there had been intense debate as to whether they could be granted absolution from the inviolate Islamic prohibition against suicide.

Inside the mosques the arguments among the clerics had been heated. The conservatives insisted that religious law did not condone suicide attacks. More radical priests combed the Koran and maintained it supported the position that oppression requires that the oppressed discover new strength and weapons. That argument was countered by the claim that suicide bombing was itself so intrinsically dramatic as to actually obscure the real purpose of an attack. World attention focused on the bomber rather than the ideology behind the bombing. Hezbollah was accused of exploiting unbalanced youngsters who, like the Japanese kamikaze teenagers of World War II, went to their deaths either drugged or in a state of religious fervor. The proponents of suicide bombing claimed that while it was indeed perfectly correct that Dr. al-Abub and other physicians provided pep pills for the death drivers and that clerics preached to them before a mission about the glory of dying, the sheer number of young people lining up to be the next to die meant that it must be the will of God that motivated them.

Hezbollah's two newspapers, *As Sabi* and *Al Ahd*, both supported the suicide bombers, praising their sacrifice, making a virtue of the fact that no one outside the Shiite community understood such commitment. The newspapers editorialized that there was no difference between a young fighter who died with a gun in his hand or one who drove a truck of explosives into a target; both could be assured of a place in heaven because their sacrifices advanced the common cause. It had become a matter of honor for a family to provide a son, or sometimes even a daughter, for sacrifice; girls often had a better chance of reaching a target before suspicions were aroused and, indeed, they had shown themselves to be as fearless as their brothers. Those who were chosen were remembered each day after the *muezzin* wailed through the crackling loudspeakers, calling the faithful to prayer. Then, in the shadowy coolness of the mosques the suicide bombers were lauded and their memories kept alive. The souls of the children of the Hezbollah needed no more.

On Friday morning, March 16, 1984, William Buckley began his three hundred and forty-third day in Beirut. He was alone in his tenth floor apartment in the Al-Manara building in the western suburb of the city. Beyond the picture windows of his living room were views of the Chouf Mountains and the Mediterranean Sea. It was going to be one of those sublime days which compensated for what Lebanon had become for the few foreigners still living there: a dangerous and volatile hell hole. At that early hour the city could be seen at its best. Below Buckley, stretching into the distance, were more than a hundred spiraling minarets, the filigree on each iron-rimmed balcony already glinting in the sun. From those balconies loud-speakers would soon summon the faithful to morning prayers.

There were streets that ran long and straight, magnificent boulevards, reminders of the time of French dominance; the language remained but could be heard only in the Christian quarter. In the streets around Buckley's apartment block — curved, narrow and frequently winding back on themselves — Arabic was spoken. By seven o'clock, the peace would once more be broken by a roar of voices and traffic; the tidal wave of human and mechanical sounds reverberating against the buildings helped to provide Beirut's unique character.

Although his apartment was large — four bedrooms, dining room, living room, maid's room — Buckley insisted on keeping house himself; he hated the idea of anyone snooping through his personal belongings. Evidence of bachelor life was all around him: dishes scattered casually about the living area and the laundry bag overflowing. Buckley had awoken at his customary pre-dawn hour. It was his favorite time to "strategize and do my real thinking," he said when the author visited the apartment.

Despite hard work and some results, his attempts to cultivate informants and gain information about Lebanon's disparate political factions had met with mixed success; methods that had served him well in Vietnam had not always worked with his Arab contacts. Part of the reason, he believed, was that he still found it difficult to communicate in Arabic. But the trait of personal bravery that had marked his time in Vietnam had not deserted him. Within days of arriving in Beirut, a fire fight had broken out between two groups contesting claim to the area around Buckley's apartment block. He immediately went down into the street and demanded that both sides lay down their weapons. When they did so, he invited the militia leaders to join him for coffee in a nearby café. On another occasion, he and an embassy colleague came under artillery fire on their way to dinner. With shells exploding dangerously close, Buckley took his time parking and then led the way into the restaurant — to find the other diners cowering under tables. He calmly ordered a meal for himself and his companion and carried it from the kitchen. While such bravado impressed the Arabs, it also drew attention to him, as well as gaining him a reprimand from his ambassador for exposing himself to unnecessary danger.

No one at the embassy knew that Buckley's risk-taking was a deliberate tactic to gain entry into the Arab community and that it had begun to pay off. His reports to Langley contained hard intelligence about the plans of Hezbollah. He was also assembling valuable information about Sheikh Fadlallah and other Muslim clerics: their movements around the city, the number of their bodyguards, the cars they used. In gathering this data, Buckley also came to learn more about Dr. Aziz al-Abub.

Early on in his time in Beirut, Buckley had made contact with the senior Mossad *katsa*, a field agent, in the city. The relationship between the Israeli intelligence service and the CIA was close at the time. despite rumors that Mossad had prior knowledge of the embassy bombing in October 1983. The Mossad vehemently denied knowing about the attack, which killed 285 Marines. The relationship between CIA chief William Casey and Mossad chief Nahum Admoni was one of mutual respect, resulting in what Casey called "back door cooperation." He had also characterized Admoni to Buckley as "a Jew who'd want to win a pissing contest on a rainy night in Gdansk."

The Beirut *katsa* was close to Admoni — they had gone to the same school, Jerusalem's elitist Rejavia Gymnasium, and shared a passion for languages. Previously the *katsa* had also served in some of the cities where Buckley had operated undercover. It had eased the way for professional cooperation between them. A few days before this March morning, the two men had met in the George Washington café on the Beirut seafront. The *katsa* handed Buckley an envelope. Inside was a photograph of Dr. al-Abub. It showed a sallow-faced man with a receding hairline. Buckley studied the picture closely, so that he would be able to pick Dr. al-Abub out of a crowd. To be able to do so was crucial to the plan Buckley and the *katsa* were developing to rescue the foreign hostages. A team of Green Berets would be flown from the United States to Tel Aviv and sail with

Israeli Special Forces on gunboats that would drop them off the coast of Beirut. The craft would wait off-shore while the team hid in the sand dunes waiting for the "go" signal. That would come once other Mossad agents had infiltrated into the city to place bombs outside the homes of Sheikh Fadlallah and his key aides. The ensuing panic would be the signal for the force in the dunes to make its way into the city and join Buckley. He would lead them to Dr. al-Abub and force the physician to take them to the hostages. The gunboats would come inshore, providing covering fire while the force and the rescued hostages would be ferried out to the craft. Dr. al-Abub would be brought along to be put on trial in the United States.

Dangerous and daring though the plan was, Buckley believed its element of surprise would ensure success. He had carried out similar operations in Vietnam. The previous day, March 15, 1984, the plan had been green lighted in an "Eyes Only" coded signal to Buckley from William Casey.

It is almost certain that on that Friday morning of March 16, 1984, Bill Buckley followed his daily routine. He fetched his briefcase from the safe in his bedroom. Known as a "burn bag," at a twist of the key clockwise, the case would incinerate its contents by triggering flames from a ring of gas jets. Buckley placed a number of files marked "Top Secret," "Secret" or "Confidential" in the bag. Sandwiches for his lunch went on top. He deadlocked the apartment door behind him — the only other key was held by the Ambassador at the embassy — and walked across the hall to the elevator. It stopped at a floor below. A man entered. He was young, well dressed and carried a leather briefcase. A few floors further down the elevator paused again. This time a woman tenant whom Buckley knew joined them. He exchanged polite greetings with her. The man did not speak. At the ground floor the woman stepped out, wishing Buckley "have a nice day," no doubt proud of her grasp of American idiom. The two men rode down to the basement garage where Buckley kept his car. Normally his embassy driver would have been waiting, but this morning Buckley had decided to drive himself to his appointments. He had told no one at the embassy of this violation of security; it was an unbreakable rule that no American official travel alone in the city.

As he walked towards his car, the fierce blow from the man's briefcase to the back of his head, powerful enough to leave traces of blood and hair on the must have caught Buckley by surprise. The attacker dropped his bag — when it was later recovered, it was found to contain several rocks. From somewhere inside the garage a white Renault drove up. There were two men in the car, the driver and his companion in the rear. He may well have assisted Buckley's assailant get him and the burn bag into the back of the car. With Buckley half-sprawled on the floor and the other two men squatting on top, the Renault roared out of the garage, its rear door flapping open dangerously.

The woman who had exchanged pleasantries with the CIA station chief moments before was standing at a bus stop near the garage exit. She glimpsed what had happened and started to scream for help. If he heard her shrieks, they were almost certainly the last entreaties William Buckley would have heard being made on his behalf.

William Buckley was kidnapped shortly after eight o'clock in the morning, Beirut time. Several hours passed before the United States embassy learned he was missing. Another full hour passed before senior embassy officials concluded he had been abducted and that his kidnappers knew who he was, where he lived and his precise movements. That pointed either to Buckley having been grossly careless, or to his kidnappers having received inside information from a Lebanese employee inside the embassy.

While those possibilities were being investigated, a priority signal was sent to the State Department and the Central Intelligence Agency. It was still early morning in Washington. At the State Department, news of what had happened was passed to Chip Beck who had served with Buckley in Beirut. He was "too stunned to take it in. I was having a hard time emotionally," he said later. At Langley the signal was delivered to William Casey's office on the seventh floor. Until then the flow of messages onto his desk from the communications center had been routine. The news from Beirut shocked the CIA Director. Years later he would recall to the author how: "I just sat there and read the thing two, three times. For three decades, on three continents, Bill had served the CIA and this nation with unfailing loyalty and without question. He was one of the bravest men I ever met. He was can-do, go-anywhere. He was street savvy in a way few agents were. So how the hell had this happened?"

An ashen-faced Casey asked that question of anyone who could possibly provide the answer. Receiving none, he shouted in frustration, "Find him! I want him found. I don't care what it takes, I want him found!" So began an operation like no other the CIA had organized.

Claire George, the Agency's deputy director, was ordered to "turn the Middle East upside down." A special in-agency committee chaired by Casey was set up to monitor the search. The National Security Agency was ordered to provide high-resolution satellite photos of known terrorist hideouts in Beirut and the Beka'a Valley. The intelligence services of Israel, Germany, France and the United Kingdom were asked to help. Every CIA station in the Middle East was ordered to treat the hunt for Buckley as a top priority. A joint FBI/CIA team flew to Beirut. Shortly afterward they were joined by NSA technicians, each a specialist in ground communications. They were to use their equipment to probe deep beneath the rubble of West Beirut where satellites could not penetrate.

In Langley, psychiatrists, psychologists, behavioral scientists and analysts were mobilized to assess how Buckley would withstand being kidnapped and to determine the mindset of his captors. Dr. Jerrold Post was put in charge of the task. The fastidious, soberly dressed psychiatrist also held a senior teaching post at George Washington University. One of the first people consulted was Dr. Gottlieb. He expressed the view that Buckley would be able to withstand both psychological and physical torture for a considerable period.

Casey informed Secretary of State George Schultz and Secretary of Defense Casper Weinberger of the kidnapping. Schultz briefed President Reagan, then he briefed the foreign ministers of a number of European nations, informing them that one of the CIA's most important agents had been lifted. Those ministers ordered their own security services to redouble their efforts to trace both Buckley and Dr. al-Abub. Within twenty-four hours, the joint CIA/FBI team in Beirut had established that embassy security had not been compromised. Buckley's high profile behavior was almost certainly why his captors had gotten to him. In their first reports back to Langley, the team painted a picture of the missing agent as being idiosyncratic. Buckley was known to spend time cleaning mud from the inside of his car's mudguards with a toothbrush. His apartment had been thoroughly searched and its untidiness unfavorably remarked upon. His trunk of private papers had been taken to the embassy. It was later shipped to Langley, and its fate remains unknown to this day. His habit of bringing his own food to work had received adverse comment. The picture that emerged was of an agent who was eccentric and possibly past his prime. This judgment infuriated Casey. He said later, "Buckley may have had unusual traits, but he was not a has-been." But the feeling grew in Langley that Buckley was an "oddball," someone who had "goofed up."

Reconstructing what had happened, the CIA/FBI team concluded that the white Renault had roared through the Muslim quarter and was waved past several Hezbollah checkpoints before reaching a well-prepared safe house. Buckley would have been manhandled out of the car and into the house. Very likely Dr. al-Abub would have pulled a stethoscope from his black bag and listened to his breathing. He may then have injected Buckley with a fast-acting narcotic, rendering him unconscious in moments. It was a common way to treat hostages. The team was equally certain that one of the kidnappers would have unclipped the briefcase from Buckley's wrist and found the key in his pocket. They could only guess if he had been able to open the burn bag correctly.

A statement was taken from the woman eyewitness, more for form than for any real hope of a lead. The team was quickly satisfied that the Hezbollah had kidnapped Buckley, and that most likely he remained somewhere in the sprawl of West Beirut, between what remained of the heavily shelled port in the north and the Hotel Sands to the south, near the international airport. There were simply not enough Green Berets to go in to rescue Buckley from probably the most hostile area on earth.

At the State Department, Chip Beck sensed that within the CIA there was a "mood that Buckley knew too much and that he could blow away a lot of people if he was forced to talk. There was a feeling that if Casey couldn't rescue Buckley, no agent was safe," recalled Beck. Slowly but surely, with no hard leads emerging about Buckley's whereabouts, the search began to concentrate on Dr. al-Abub. Casey himself reiterated: "We are going to get that sonofabitch."

In London, in the headquarters of MI6, analysts worked up their psycho-profiles of the physician. In Paris the multi-disciplined physicians of French intelligence began to piece together Dr. al-Abub's background. Within the sprawl of buildings at Pullach near Wiesbaden, the BND, West Germany's foreign intelligence service, had like-minded doctors doing the same. Further east in Vienna, Austria's small, but highly efficient security service mobilized a team of specialists to work under the direction of a burly, hard-drinking lawyer, Otto Kormek, whose contacts in the Middle East were legendary. In Rome, in the drab headquarters of DIGOS, the Italian national antiterrorist squad, specialists tried to fit together their mosaic of Dr. al-Abub. They were helped by Dr. Franco Ferracuti, Professor of Criminological Medicine and Forensic Psychiatry at the University of Rome, another world-ranking expert on the behavior of terrorists. In Israel, the search for clues about Dr. al-Abub was closely monitored by David Kimche who had been deputy-director of Mossad before taking a senior position in the Israeli Foreign Ministry. Among other moves, Kimche mobilized the considerable resources of the country's two "terror laboratories" at the University of Tel Aviv, the Dayan Center and the Jaffee Center. The pooled wisdom of, among others, Aerial Merari, Director of Terrorist Studies at the Jaffee, a psychologist who had made a close study of the Shiite mentality, and the research of Martin Kramer, the Dayan's resident expert on Hezbollah, was on the way to Langley within hours.

Merari's data included a comprehensive review of how the Shiites fitted into the long and colorful chronology of the Muslim faith. Kramer's findings concentrated on the Hezbollah, showing how the organization was formed and why it believed it was now the chosen redeemer of Lebanon. He predicted the kidnapping of Buckley would be followed by others. Merari concurred, adding that there would soon come a clear-cut statement from Sheikh Fadlallah, the movement's spiritual leader, on the morality of kidnapping.

Other information about Dr. al-Abub was received from the Saudi Ambassador to the United Nations, Prince Bandar bin Sultan. The son of his country's Defense Minister, the gregarious high-living Arabian diplomat had also been an Agency informer for years. Bandar's tidbits were passed on to Casey. He fed them to Dr. Post who passed the information on to colleagues around the world. Thus were the links forged in the attempt to discover everything possible about Dr. al-Abub. But, a week after his kidnapping, there was still no news about Buckley.

Doctors at Langley continued to assess how Buckley would react to captivity. Working with the findings of Dr. Martin Symonds, a psychiatrist consultant to the New York Police Department — and recognized as probably having the widest experience within North America of how kidnap victims respond — the CIA specialists concluded Buckley's reactions would follow a predetermined pattern. It would make little difference that he was an intelligence officer trained to resist interrogation. Dr. Symonds posited that while Buckley was reeling from the blow from the briefcase, he would experience a feeling of disbelief, an instinctive denial that what was happening was actually occurring to him. That feeling may have remained until his arrival at the hiding place his captors had prepared.

Desperate denial — the only immediate psychological defense response open to him — would be replaced by a sudden and shattering reality. It was happening to him. At that point Buckley's reactions could have included "frozen fright" and, most disturbing of all a need to talk to his kidnappers — if only to try and convince them he should be freed. At that stage, Symonds said, kidnappers invariably uncovered valuable information about a hostage's background. For Buckley's captors that period was one of critical importance. They would begin to feed back information they had earlier gleaned from him, leading him to believe that they were all-knowing and therefore all-powerful and that to resist them would be pointless.

The CIA doctors produced a study of Buckley at that stage of his captivity: a man bowed down by despair, depleted physically and mentally, suddenly aged, his face haggard, his voice monotonous, every word and movement a fearful burden. He would feel constantly exhausted, and any sleep would leave him unrefreshed. He would become most depressed in the small hours and then be at his most vulnerable. Self-accusation would be at its most destructive and his despair insurmountable. Buckley's mental stress would very likely be accompanied by other symptoms: loss of appetite and constipation, followed by a growing feeling that the only solution for him was suicide. No one could guess how long that feeling would last. but at some point would come another shattering self-discovery. Not only was resistance manifestly impossible, but so was escape. That would be the point when he might contemplate cooperating with his captors. The doctors continued to make their cautious predictions. If his captors were sufficiently clever, they would recognize that Buckley's mood changes were part of "a continuously carving-out and refilling of that inner void created by his kidnapping," Dr. Post said. Under their manipulation, Buckley's guilt could be redirected away from himself so that he would come to believe that what was important was not so much what he had done — failed to avoid being kidnapped — but what he had been: a hated "Western Imperialist."

This condition was known as "logical dishonesty." It would manifest itself in a video of a contrite Buckley which Dr. Post predicted would soon be issued to the world's media.

Another technique was Remote In-Depth Analysis (RIDA). This was used by the behaviorists and was based upon feeding a computer with all that was known about Buckley's past behavior and assessing how that could influence his reaction to captivity.

A copy of the Mossad photograph of Dr. al-Abub, which the Beirut *katsa* had given Buckley, had been enlarged by CIA technicians and studied under microscopes for signs the physician had undergone plastic surgery. Spectacles and various shapes of beard were superimposed on his face to suggest how he might look in disguise. Computers aged him, using a software system known as Facial-Analysis Comparison and Elimination System (FACES). Based on forty-nine characteristics, each categorized on a 1 to 4 scale, FACES would make 15 million binary yes/no decisions in a second. As data continued to arrive about Dr. al-Abub, it was fed through other computers to try to understand the complex psychological forces that motivated him. The conclusion was that he was driven by "masked violence." This allowed him to equate his actions with his own concept of virtue; to feel he was doing no more than responding to a threat to his own culture, his own environment, his own people, his own life.

The psychology of Islamic fundamentalism came under intense study. Specialists looked for differences and similarities in the psychopathology of the Hezbollah and other Muslim terror organizations. The CIA researchers studied the theology which their clerics used to adapt holy writ to wage holy war. The messianic aspirations of Hezbollah bore a striking resemblance to impulses which launched the French Revolution and the upheavals in Russia and China. All justified terror as a way to create a new society.

On Monday morning, May 7, 1984, the United States embassy in Athens received a packet posted in the city and addressed to the ambassador. It was routinely passed through the bomb scanner in the mailroom. Once the staff was satisfied that the package contained only a video, the wrapping with its boldly printed name and address was carefully undone and placed to one side. The VHS tape was of cheap German make commonly available throughout the Middle East. The mail room manager inserted the cassette in a video player. What he saw made him stop the film and summon a senior diplomat. When they had watched for a few minutes, the ambassador was sent for, together with the CIA's Chief of Station. They reviewed the tape. The CIA officer called Casey. Hours later, the mail room manager used his diplomatic passport to avoid even the lackadaisical Greek security checks at Athens airport and boarded a flight to Washington. He was met on the tarmac by a government car, whose driver had clearance to bypass immigration and customs, and driven to Langley.

The tape was taken to Casey's office where he and his senior staff began to view the video. It showed Buckley undergoing torture. The absence of sound made it all the more shocking. The camera zoomed in and out of Buckley's nude and damaged body. He held before his genitalia a document marked "MOST SECRET." It was proof the burn-bag had failed. Casey later told the author: "I was close to tears. It was the most obscene thing I had ever witnessed. Bill was barely recognizable as the man I had known for years. They had done more than ruin his body. His eyes made it clear his mind had been played with. It was horrific, medieval and barbarous."

The tape was handed over to technicians who enlarged frames in an attempt to establish the background against which Buckley had been filmed. They decided it was rough-plastered stone, suggesting the filming had taken place in a cellar. The wrapping paper was the kind Mediterranean shopkeepers used to wrap groceries. The handwriting suggested the writer was semi-literate.

The Agency's pharmacologists took over. They concluded Buckley had been drugged; his eyes were dull, his lips slack. His gaze suggested he had been deprived of daylight for some time and so had difficulty in adjusting to the photo-flood used to illuminate him for filming, an indication Buckley had spent long periods being hooded. There were chafe marks on his wrists and neck suggesting he had been tethered with a rope or chain. A careful study of every inch of visible skin revealed puncture marks indicating he had been injected at various points.

A second video arrived twenty-three days later, this time posted to the United States Embassy on Via Veneto in Rome. The tape was couriered to Washington. Once more the wrapping yielded no clue except that a different hand had penned the address and the paper was of Italian manufacture, the sort used by the boutiques in the city. The video had been shot against a similar background as the first one and revealed that Buckley had continued to be horrifically treated. There was sound on this tape and Buckley's voice was slurred and his manner noticeably more abject. Any of a dozen drugs could have made him appear sedated and stupefied. He appeared often unable to shape words. His hands shook, and his legs beat a tattoo on the floor as he mumbled pathetic pleas to be exchanged under a guarantee the United States would remove "all of its influences" from Lebanon and would persuade Israel to do the same.

A transcript of the video circulated within the Agency. Copies were also sent to the White House and State Department, accompanied by a document written by a CIA analyst, Graham Fuller. He argued that while there should be no wholesale U.S. or Israeli withdrawal from Lebanon, it might be possible to obtain Buckley's freedom by using Iran as a broker — in return for secretly providing the regime with arms to wage war against Iraq. A deal would be "a positive sign" to moderate elements in Tehran. Secretary of State Schultz summoned the Israeli ambassador who said he would consult Tel Aviv. Within hours he was back. Israel would not object to the United States opening a dialogue with Iran even if that included providing Tehran with weapons. The seeds had been planted for what became known as Iran-Contra.

In Langley, specialists tried to decide how long Buckley could survive. His last Agency medical records showed he was physically fit and had a natural stoicism that should help. No one could be absolutely certain, however, how he would respond to anxiety attacks, nightmares and overwhelming feelings of helplessness, followed by bouts of rage and periods of black resignation. While drugs would have an enormous impact on Buckley's moods, they would leave no permanent damage if he were rescued soon enough. That gave added impetus to the plans beginning to take shape within the CIA, the Pentagon, the State Department and, ultimately, the White House for providing arms to Iran in return for Buckley's freedom. Casey repeatedly told colleagues they should see his release as the Agency's personal crusade: "It is partly a matter of esprit de corps — we look after our own," was the director's constant refrain.

Dr. al-Abub would not have to look far in West Beirut to find men ready to swear by Allah, the Beneficent and Merciful, that the treatment of Buckley was proof of what had been revealed to the Prophet at al-Madinah and set down in the Surah XIX. "O he who believe! Spy not!" In those weeks following the kidnapping, the rumors about Buck-lee had been many and varied. He had sent signals from his penthouse to the ships of the Great Satan. There was a transmitter in his apartment so powerful he could not only communicate with Tel Aviv, but also directly with the Great Satan in Washington. Men would pause on their way to prayers and exchange the latest news. Buck-lee had confessed to supplying Iraq with chemicals which burned the skins of their Shiite brothers-in-arms. A rocket had been found on Buck-lee's apartment roof which, when fired, would have been the signal for the Great Satan's ships to once more rain ruin from the air upon Beirut. There were many such fables.

During his first weeks in captivity, Buckley was hidden in a succession of cellars in West Beirut, each soon filled with the stench of his body waste, misery and, no doubt, fear. Dr. al-Abub used the techniques he had acquired in Moscow to ensure Buckley did as ordered. Few people in West Beirut could begin to understand the precise nature of his intervention: what injections he used, their quantity and strength. The contents of his black bag remained as mysterious to them as always.

On Friday, October 26, 1984, two hundred and twenty-four days after Buckley was kidnapped, a third video arrived at the CIA. The tape was even more harrowing than its predecessors. Buckley was practically gibbering. His words were often incoherent; he slobbered and drooled and, most unnerving of all, he would suddenly scream in terror, his eyes rolling helplessly and his body shaking. From time to time he held up documents which had been in his burn-bag. These he displayed to the camera. Then he delivered a pathetic defense of his captor's right to self-determination in Lebanon. Over several days, various specialists reviewed the tape to try and obtain further insights into Buckley's mind to decide whether he was already resigned to inevitable death.

The specialists noted Buckley's hands sometimes unconsciously moved across his private parts as he pleaded to live in exchange for the patently impossible demands of his captors. Was he displaying something more than modesty? The specialists knew a fear of castration was a common response in a male hostage; a deep concern about emasculation often surpassed fear of death. The specialists tried to estimate the level of anxiety in Buckley's voice. It became clear he could no longer confront the sheer terror of his situation. Its magnitude had overwhelmed him. For hours the specialists considered whether his words showed "true guilt" or "neurotic guilt." They used a language no layman could readily comprehend as they tried to make distinctions regarding how much "the human order of being is disturbed" and how far he might have experienced "existential guilt arising from a specific act," by revealing secrets to his captors. Finally they considered whether Buckley not only accepted but yearned for the inevitability of death.

CHAPTER TWENTY

The winter passed. Few knew where Buckley was. Sometimes his guards moved him two or three times a night. He would be driven at high speed, bundled from one car to another, to safe houses in the suburbs of Shatila or Sabra, where even an army could not have found him. At dawn, when the lookouts climbed to their vantage points and reported the sea remained empty of threat, Buckley would be driven, squashed on the floor, hooded and drugged, back to his prison cell deep under the ruins. It was known as the Beirut Hilton.

Throughout the spring of 1985, in Washington and elsewhere, the specialists continued their work. Case files on Nazi doctors were studied for further clues to Dr. al-Abub's personality. Was he like Josef Mengele who had found complete self-expression through what he had done in Auschwitz? Was he like one of those Soviet psychiatrists who saw themselves as not so much acting on orders from the KGB, but performing the normal functions of a doctor? The whole gamut of behavioral technology was surveyed. In the words of Dr. Post: "None of it helped us understand what Buckley was going through. It was a measure of the desperation we all felt to get answers to the seventh floor."

The window in Casey's office suite looked out over the tops of the trees. This gave the Agency's 216-acre site the appearance of being deep within a forest. There Casey unfailingly spent a portion of each day reviewing the dossier on Buckley. He called the specialists regularly, asking sharp questions, noting down the answers on one of the four-by-four cards he carried around with him, using the gold Tiffany pen his wife,

Sofia, had given him one Christmas. At every meeting with Casey, President Reagan would ask, "What's happening in that mess, Bill?" The director would shake his massive head and mumble "Everyone is on top of it."

Chuck Cogan, an agent who had been close to Buckley, reckoned Buckley was too steeped in *omerta* — the old Sicilian code of silence Agency veterans wore as a badge of pride — to have talked. The specialists were less certain. They knew that no one could ultimately withstand a skilled medical torturer; that the physiology of the human nervous system is the same in all people regardless of race, culture or profession. Nothing Buckley had been taught in spy tradecraft would have made it any easier for him to withstand electroshocks, beatings, prolonged hanging by the arms or feet, drugging, isolation and hooding. He was as vulnerable as anyone else — perhaps even more so because the basic will to resist would be that much greater in him and, therefore his surrender, when it came, would be all the more spectacular. Casey could not bring himself to accept such reports.

One day he sent for Dr. Gottlieb and spent an entire afternoon closeted with the former chief of the CIA's "dirty tricks department." He went over the time Buckley worked for Dr. Gottlieb. Had Buckley seemed like a man who would crack? In a dozen different ways Casey asked the same question. Dr. Gottlieb could not be certain.

Casey sent a CIA agent down to Farmer to interview Candace Hammond. She recalled her last conversation with Buckley. Close to tears she recounted his phone call: "Bill said he hoped to be coming home soon. I sensed he felt he was in some sort of danger. He never said as much, but the upset was there in his voice. He kept talking about going with me to antique shops and how much he would enjoy that. It was like he was going over the past because he did not want to think of the future." Casey pored over her words, over what Dr. Gottlieb had said, over Chuck Cogan's conviction that William Buckley would rather die than spill his secrets. But no one had been able to tell him that for certain.

After the third video there was nothing new to work on. No message. No demands. Only silence. It was likely that Buckley's captors had learned all he could from him. By now he could be dead. But again nobody could be certain. All the evidence suggested that Dr. al-Abub was alive and still in Beirut. A Mossad *katsa* had spotted him a few weeks before going into West Beirut. A Lebanese businessman, whom Oliver North was using to help put together the deal in which the foreign hostages still held by the Hezbollah in Beirut would be traded for arms, had recently seen Dr. al-Abub driving on the road to Damascus.

Once more Casey sent for Dr. Gottlieb and asked him to explain about the CIA's own mind-control experiments. Gottlieb insisted that it was all a long time ago, and he couldn't remember specific details. But he admitted Buckley acted as "a go-between" for the Agency and Dr. Ewen Cameron.

Casey decided Dr. al-Abub was motivated by a perverted moral certitude and a fanatical belief in his own rightness. Dr. Gottlieb and Dr. Cameron had been driven by the same forces. Were they cast from the same mold? The question continued to haunt the director as he studied those CIA files which had not been destroyed and whose contents Dr. Gottlieb had insisted he could not now recall. Although those experiments had taken place in Montreal, one of the most civilized cities in North America, the methods Dr. al-Abub was using were in many respects similar to the ones Dr. Cameron and Dr. Gottlieb had used on unsuspecting patients. The idea, Casey later recalled to the author, "chilled me."

Nonetheless, the director refused to abandon all hope. He had rejected the proposal made a year after the kidnapping that Buckley's name be officially added to the list of CIA agents killed or missing on duty. Their fate was commemorated by small stars carved into the marble walls in the CIA main lobby. Before Buckley vanished, there had been over fifty such stars, each representing an officer who had lost his or her life in the service of the Agency. Since then a further half dozen had been added. But Casey had mumbled it was too soon to include Buckley in the display.

His aides knew Casey stubbornly clung to the hope that Buckley might not, after all, be dead, but was being kept alive for a trade. The idea had taken root in his mind when the Israeli Ambassador in Washington told Casey that a number of Israel's own prisoners, who had been captured in various wars with its Arab neighbors, were being kept alive in Syria and Iran to barter in future exchanges. With this encouragement, Casey sat, often late into the night, at his desk going over all the reports on the hunt for Buckley. He paid particular attention to the bulky file on Dr. al-Abub. One report said the physician remained in Beirut. Was he still using his bag of chemicals to leach out the last of Buckley's spirit, ready for the day when he could finally be swapped? But what would the deal be? That was the rub of course. There really could not be one. President Reagan had made that clear; his Administration did not deal with terrorists.

Beirut remained the focus of the search. But reports from foreign diplomats in the city all said that while other hostages still clung to life in the bowels of the infamous "Beirut Hilton" — a series of cells scooped out deep beneath the rubble of West Beirut — there was not a whisper about Buckley. There had also been rumors Buckley had been transferred to a Hezbollah redoubt out in the Beka'a Valley, and a claim he had been secretly flown to Tehran for interrogation. Finally there were no more rumors to track down. Yet Casey remained convinced Buckley was worth more to his captors alive than dead. One day there would be a new administration in Washington, one perhaps more malleable and ready to trade than Reagan's.

Since his last meeting with Israel's ambassador, Casey had allowed an idea to germinate in his own mind. By April 1985, he became increasingly attracted to the idea of using Israel to recover William Buckley. Never a man to be rushed — a trait that others sometimes saw as a fault — Casey spent many hours considering the possibility of persuading Israel to swap a large number of its Arab prisoners in return for Buckley's freedom. It had been done before, notably after the 1956 Suez War. Mossad's chief, Meir Amit, had written to Egypt's then president, Gamal Abdul Nasser, asking him to exchange two Israeli spies in return for hundreds of Egyptian prisoners-of-war captured in the Six-Day War of 1967. Initially Nasser had refused. Amit had applied psychological pressure. He told the Egyptian POWs they were being held prisoner because Nasser refused to hand over the two Israelis. When the prisoners wrote this in letters home, Nasser was besieged by the prisoners' relatives, demanding he free the two Israelis. Meir Amit then wrote a personal letter to Nasser assuring him that if he freed the pair, Israel would ensure he received worldwide credit for recovering his soldiers, and there would be no mention of the exchange. Nasser had asked that the POWs be freed first. Meir Amit agreed. The Egyptians were taken by trucks to the edge of the Sinai Desert where they were transferred to Egyptian buses. Two days later the two Israeli spies were flown from Cairo to Geneva. From there they were brought to Tel Aviv.

Casey knew there had been other occasions when similar swaps had been organized by previous Mossad chiefs. And none of them was more astute than Mossad's present Director General, Nahum Admoni. While Casey knew that Admoni had a deep-seated suspicion of U.S. intentions in the Middle East, his own personal relationship with him was cordial, and they regularly communicated through the back-channel Allen Dulles had originally created as a means for the CIA to by-pass the government in dealing with Israeli intelligence.

On April 20, 1985, Casey flew to Tel Aviv via London. In London he met Dr. William Sargant. By now the psychiatrist had retired from his post as advisor to MI5 and MI6 and had given up his position as head of the department of psychological medicine at St.Thomas' Hospital. But he still kept a private practice in Harley Street, and it was in his consulting room that he received Casey.

They had first met at the British Embassy in Washington where Dr. Sargant was a house guest. Both men had formed an instant liking for each other, fuelled by a common belief that the growth of international terrorism was still largely controlled by the Soviet Union. Dr. Sargant recalled he had found ready agreement from Casey that "the Soviets will get badly burned trying to win over the Islamic fundamentalists."

Now, many years later, as they sipped tea in Dr. Sargant's consulting room seated in armchairs before an old-fashioned gas fire, the subject of Middle East terrorism once more preoccupied them. Dr. Sargant would remember that Casey wanted to know if it was possible for a man like Buckley to have survived over a year in that kind of captivity. Dr. Sargant recalled to the author: "I told Casey I could only offer a broad opinion. Buckley had seemed a well-integrated personality, but after a year in captivity under the conditions he was being held, that would count for little. While Buckley may physically have retained some of his strength, his mental faculties would have been seriously impaired if he had undergone the kind of treatment which Casey indicated had been used; lengthy periods of hooding, being bound for long periods, given a variety of drugs to make him more compliant. Casey wanted to know if Buckley would have received electroshock treatment and I said this would almost certainly not be the case. That kind of treatment would be counterproductive if the intention was to keep Buckley alive for some future swap. I also said such a swap was debatable. Buckley was being held by Islamic fundamentalists. For them any dealing at all with the West would be anathema. They would see it as a sign of weakness on their part. As it was clear there would be no strategic or political benefits to go with a swap from their standpoint, his captors would have no valid reason to free Buckley. Casey asked what then was the point of his captors keeping him alive. I said my opinion was that just not knowing if he was dead or alive gave his captors an advantage. His kidnapping would serve to create fear in others."

Casey then flew to Tel Aviv.

Admoni met Casey at the airport, and on the drive into the city they exchanged small talk about two men both knew well. Richard Helms, after a spell as U.S. ambassador to Iran, now served on President Reagan's Commission on Strategic Forces. More surprising, William Colby, who had once worked closely with Admoni in Paris and Ethiopia on covert operations, had joined the public debate on nuclear arms control on the side of the American Catholic bishops and the nuclear freeze movement. Colby had insisted that neither his strong religious views nor guilt had brought him to his present view. Admoni had snorted in derision, saying "If any guy has guilt in his soul, it is Bill Colby."

Once Casey settled into his Tel Aviv seafront hotel, he told Admoni the purpose of his visit: to see if Israel would go along with a deal to swap Buckley for Arab prisoners held in Israeli prisons. Casey recalled Admoni said that was "no go for a start. There would be protest marches if it emerged we exchanged a foreigner, Buckley, for Arab prisoners, when we had a number of our own people being held in terrible conditions by the Hezbollah and other terror groups."

With that avenue firmly closed, Casey asked if it was possible for Mossad to find out if Buckley was dead. Over the next few days, Admoni introduced Casey to some of the key Mossad operatives with up-to-date knowledge of Lebanon. They included David Kimche who until recently had been in charge of Mossad's 'Lebanese account.' He had no doubt: Buckley was dead. Rafi Eitan, a former Director of Operations for Mossad, held a similar view. So did Admoni.

"Buckley's over and done with," Admoni said as he drove Casey back to the airport to catch his flight back to Washington.

The news that Casey had gone on what had turned out to be a fruitless mission brought to the surface questions which had been simmering for some time in Langley. They had started in the heat of the hunt when Casey had been pushing everyone, trampling over egos and yelling at even his most senior staff that he wanted Buckley found — and he didn't care what it took. Everyone had accepted why all steps must be taken to try and recover Buckley. It was bad for morale every time an agent was lost and another star was added to the galaxy in the entrance hall. But the impression had gotten around that Casey appeared to be making Buckley his special case.

There were those who recalled that it had been the same when Dulles ran the CIA. In those days Buckley, gung-ho from the Korean War, had been treated like a favorite son by Dulles, given access that at the time even senior men had envied. Others remembered the way Buckley had been allowed to come and go more or less as he pleased and set his own agenda in Vietnam. In the end others in the CIA, men like Colby, had been badly burned over what America had done in that war. But Buckley had been held blameless despite his involvement in Operation Phoenix. It had been the same with the MK-ULTRA and MK-SEARCH projects. In the closed world of Langley, that alone was enough to raise eyebrows.

Certainly, a number of factors had contributed to the animus some felt toward Buckley. He understood better than anyone that to survive within the Agency you had to cope with the office politics, the battles for turf, the back-stabbing. His way of dealing with that was to fight back — hard. It had not made him popular, but then, as he used to say, "I'm not running for Miss Langley Pageant Queen." He had also acquired a record of success that was almost unmatched by any agent in the history of the Agency. That had led some people to envy him. Buckley was difficult, ruthless and at times short-tempered, and he made no apology for being so. Shortly before going to Beirut he had expressed his attitude succinctly: "I try and do my work well, but I also understand that gratitude is not part of doing it."

While the loss of Buckley was constantly in Casey's thoughts, there was much else to preoccupy him about biological and chemical warfare. What disturbed Casey, he later admitted, was that those weapons did not respect boundaries: "The further man seemed to probe the intricate system of life itself, the more scientists at Fort Detrick and elsewhere seemed intent on creating a weapon that could intervene in what God had created," he told the author.

Casey felt deep repugnance towards a proposal for what amounted to ethnic-related biochemicals, designed to affect only certain racial groups. The idea had been proposed by a scientist at Fort Belvoir, Virginia, an annex of Fort Detrick, who had written a paper that claimed: "It is theoretically possible to develop so called 'ethnic-chemical weapons;' to exploit naturally occurring genetic differences among specific population groups. Such weapons would be capable of killing a selected enemy population." The ethnic bomb would be programmed to attack the digestive systems of certain racial groups, "to make them unable to cope with the food of another group. Arabs, for instance, would be given a pork-related toxin." The bomb would also target different blood groups. Muslims in the Soviet Islamic republics had a high preponderance of type O blood. The ethnic bio-bomb would be targeted to infect that group. Casey had scribbled a note to the president: "This kind of thing must not be allowed."

But Casey foresaw a time, "probably by the twenty-first century, when the double-helix of DNA can be sufficiently tampered with to have its use in the biological warfare research. The most likely target would be to produce a new super germ that would make the human immune system more defenseless than ever before. Ultimately it could not only kill large populations but, if needs be, turn those who survived into mutants — monsters of man's own creation."

By late May 1985, William Casey had finally given up hope of getting Buckley back. Colonel Oliver North was the linchpin of a plan to recover all the U.S. hostages held in Lebanon. He was working closely with Amiram Nir, an Israeli counterterrorism expert. Nir said his own sources in Lebanon had told him that a decision had been taken by the Hezbollah leadership that Buckley must die in captivity. Nir's sources told him the decision had been made at a meeting of the Hezbollah leadership. Nir was certain Buckley was now dead.

No one knows for certain when William Buckley died. The likeliest date is sometime during the night of June 3, 1985, the 444th day of his captivity. David Jacobson, who had been the director of the Beirut University Hospital and had been kidnapped some months before and incarcerated in the "Beirut Hilton," believed Buckley was in a nearby cell on that night. When he was released some seventeen months later, Jacobson tried to recall what he had heard in the stifling darkness of that June night: "The man was an American. Of that I have no doubt. But he was in a very bad way, delirious and coughing. It was hard for me to make out what he was saying because I myself was hooded. Then, in the end there was just this long silence. After a while I heard the guards shouting in Arabic and then what sounded like a body being dragged away."

In October 1985, confirmation that Buckley was dead came in an announcement by the Hezbollah. Accompanying it was a photograph of the corpse, together with copies of the once secret documents from Buckley's burn bag. The announcement added that the corpse would not be handed over to the United States for burial. The Hezbollah refused to say what had been done with the body. Casey went to the White House to break the news to President Reagan. Afterwards the two men had sat for a while in silence in the Oval Office.

Finally the president said: "The sooner we get all those other hostages out of Beirut, the better. Do whatever it has to take, Bill." The arms-sales-for-hostages deal, which became known as Iran-Contra, went into overdrive.

Buckley's death had a profound effect on William Casey. He felt he had failed "a man I so admired, so trusted. He was truly a credit to the CIA and to the United States." On May 6, 1987, William Casey died of pneumonia following surgery to remove a brain tumour.

By late October of that year, CIA agents were back in Beirut. One of the first reports sent to Langley was that Dr. al-Abub had left Beirut for Tehran.

Bill Buckley had served the CIA for thirty years, joining at a time when the agency had been part of the American dream of creating a new world. He died at a time when the Agency had become increasingly a bureaucracy driven by a belief in technology and quantitative analysis: the twin gods who ruled over Langley. In that world Buckley had become an outsider. Like Ronald Reagan, one of the few presidents he admired, Buckley's vision of America was that its strength was in being different from the rest of the world. The America he wanted had largely disappeared: one of mid-western virtues and an all-embracing

Christianity. Despite being highly professional, his ideals were no longer those of his paymasters. He was like a medieval knight left alone on a modern-day battlefield. Ari Ben-Menashe, the former Israeli intelligence officer, who had briefly known Buckley, saw him "as someone who still clung to his sword while the rest of us were using laser guns. But he was a decent man who was a faithful servant of the Agency and his country."

It was a fitting epitaph.

In the years following the Hezbollah announcement, there were conflicting reports that Buckley's body had been burnt or had been buried under the foundations of one of the new hotels rising along Beirut's seafront. There were even claims that the corpse had been cut into pieces and taken out to sea and fed to the fish. When none of these reports could be verified, whispers ran through the alleys of West Beirut that the Americans would pay big money for Buckley's corpse. Soon gangs of teenagers could be seen digging in the rubble. But finding nothing, the hunters soon lost interest. By the end of the first year after his reported death, there were no grave diggers to be seen.

Then, early in January 2001, two young Arabs drove a battered van out of West Beirut heading for the Beka'a Valley. They reached the spot they were looking for some hours later. It was marked on a piece of paper, which had cost a substantial sum. The man who had sold them the paper boasted he had been one of the guards who had watched Buckley die and had brought him to this spot for burial. One using a pick, the other a shovel, the youths began to dig. By late afternoon they had excavated a sizeable hole but had not come across even a bone. When darkness came, they dug on using the headlights of the van. Finally they gave up, realizing they had been the victims of a con man.

Almost certainly, if he had been alive, that would have brought a smile to the lips of William Buckley.

NOTES ON THE INTERVIEWEES

Before I met Bill Buckley, I had come to know a number of members of the intelligence services who had expressed views concerning the CIA. Some envied its huge budget and access to the latest technology; others felt the Agency had been responsible for some of the greatest intelligence disasters since the end of World War Two. Bill Buckley helped to bring those divergent views into sharper focus for me. We developed a rapport that grew into a genuine friendship. As time passed, at the back of my mind was the thought that, when he retired, Bill would allow me to tell his story; it was certainly as enthralling as any of the memoirs of other agents I had read. His kidnapping and subsequent death put an end to those plans. Nevertheless, I still wanted to tell as much of his story as I could piece together from all he had told me and the notes he agreed I could write up from our conversations. Those formed the framework for this book. But to capture Bill as he really was, or at least how I saw him, I also needed to expand that framework to include the most dramatic episode of his career. Undoubtedly that was his involvement with the CIA's MK-ULTRA and MK-SEARCH projects. He had been an eyewitness to the work Ewen Cameron had done at the Allan Memorial Institute. Then he had himself become the victim of another medical torturer, Aziz al-Abub.

My research was intermittent and spread over several years. It included trips to Montreal and other parts of Canada, to Washington, Israel and finally to Beirut. At times I found the story so overwhelming that I was inclined to give it up. Indeed, on several occasions I put it aside to write other books. But in 1999 an old friend of mine, the film director and producer Kevan Barker, who has long been fascinated by the world of secret intelligence, encouraged me to return to the project — this time as a script for a motion picture.

I had not gotten far with the film treatment before I realized that the only way it would work for me was if I set out in book form the entire story of the CIA's mind control experiments, as seen largely through the eyes of Bill Buckley, and end with Bill's own death at the hands of Dr. al-Abub. From this I would then adapt a screenplay. It would not have the traditional Hollywood upbeat ending, but Kevan said that did not matter. In his words, he wanted the film to be "stark and dark, the way the intelligence world is." I went back to the research and produced what you have read in these pages. A number of people deserve special mention for the time and effort they put into helping me.

Bill, of course, gave of his time and friendship. His own analysis of intelligence issues was invaluable. Through his words I came to understand the Agency during the three decades he served it. What made his views so important to me was that he usually spoke without recrimination or regret. The only times he displayed those feelings were when talking about Sidney Gottlieb and Ewen Cameron. He made it clear that what they did was morally wrong and deserved to be exposed.

I owe a great debt to him for the way he was able to recall matters or check them in his own diaries; like many an intelligence officer (my late father-in-law, an MI6 officer, was another example), Bill Buckley kept copious notes. They enabled him to provide confirmation in the story of Frank Olson, among much else. The notes and his memories also provided valuable insights into the CIA's brainwashing programs and the Agency's work with Fort Detrick in biochemical weaponry. In many ways he is the prime source for this book. If there are errors in his recollection, then I accept responsibility on his behalf.

*   *   *

Dr. William Sargant was generous with his time. I had gotten to know him during my time as a television producer with the BBC in London. He was a consultant on a number of programs I produced. Afterwards we stayed in touch, and a bond of trust was created that allowed him to talk openly about Dr. Gottlieb, Dr. Cameron and the MK-ULTRA/MK-SEARCH programs and what he knew about germ warfare.

Over dinner one night at his home, Dr. Sargant insisted he saw nothing wrong in what he had done by informing his superiors in Britain's Secret Intelligence Service about Frank Olson's reactions after his trip to Germany and the need to deny him further access to sensitive research centers in Britain. Dr. Sargant said he had nevertheless been deeply shocked over what had happened to Olson. He blamed the murder on Dr. Gottlieb's "obsession with solving mind control. Anything or anybody who threatened that had to be removed," was how my host put it.

Shortly before his death Sargant gave me signed first editions of three of his books that he had privately printed for close friends: *Battle for the Mind*; *The Unquiet Mind*; and *The Mind Possessed*. For anyone wishing to understand more about various aspects of the mind under stress and mind control, they offer invaluable insights. In expressing his views, Dr. Sargant made it a condition I would not attribute such information to him during his lifetime. I agreed and we continued to remain in regular contact until his death in 1988.

In November 1988, I spoke to Sidney Gottlieb. I had been told he was already a sick man and in our conversation on the telephone he said he was unable to see me. He sounded weak-voiced and subdued.

A few weeks after my first telephone call to Dr. Gottlieb's home, I made another, in the hope he might have recovered sufficiently to answer at least some of my questions. The woman who answered the phone said that was not possible; she did not give her name. It was frustrating not to have properly interviewed the man who could have told his side of the story, especially as his shadow fell over so much of what I learned throughout my long investigation.

In one of the documents I uncovered — I had amassed a small library in the end — was the only official reprimand I ever found given to Dr. Gottlieb. It was dated February 10, 1954, and was signed by Allen Dulles, then Director of Central Intelligence. It is marked PERSONAL. Its tone is cold and to the point. In the note Dr. Gottlieb is told that Dulles had "personally reviewed the files from your office" (on Frank Olson's death). "You apparently did not give sufficient emphasis to the necessity for medical collaboration and for proper consideration of the rights of the individual to whom it was being administered. This is to inform you that in my opinion you exercised poor judgment in this case."

The note seems to reinforce my own conclusion, supported by Buckley's belief, that Dulles knew little, if anything, beforehand of Dr. Gottlieb and Richard Helm's plan to have Frank Olson murdered.

I wanted to ask Dr. Gottlieb about his meeting on February 17, 1970, with the then chief of the CIA's Chemistry Branch, Nathan Gordon. Gordon later said they had discussed what should be done with the considerable quantity of biological agents that the CIA stored at Fort Detrick. President Nixon had announced a few days before that the United States was ending its chemical-biological warfare program.

Gordon showed me a memo Dr. Gottlieb had drafted: "Contingency Plan for Stockpile of Biological Warfare Agents." The memo, dated February 18, 1970, was addressed to Richard Helms, then the CIA director. At the end of the month Dr. Gottlieb had a meeting with both Helms and Thomas H. Karamessines, then the CIA Deputy Director of Plans. Afterwards, Dr. Gottlieb ordered one of his men to go to Fort Detrick and immediately withdraw two one-gallon cans containing paralytic shellfish poisoning. The cans contained sufficient poison to kill up to 60,000 people. What did Dr. Gottlieb want to do with the poison? Why did he order the cans be kept in the CIA's biological storage unit at the U.S. Navy Bureau of Medicine and Surgery on 23rd Street in Washington? Now we will never know.

I wanted to ask him about his involvement in biological warfare during the Korean War. There was a tantalizing memo, written by U.S. Air Force Chief of Staff, General Hoyt Vanderberg, in February 1952. He had just returned from a visit to Korea and, in a "Most Secret" document seemingly never officially declassified, he wrote that "There is now great progress in biological warfare and certain offensive capabilities are rapidly materializing."

What part had Dr. Gottlieb played in that process? It would have been a key question to put to him. I also wanted to ask him about his briefing to Robert Lovett, then Secretary of Defense. Lovett's memo provides further evidence that the United States had used biological weapons. On February 25, 1952, days after Vanderberg's return from Korea, the Secretary had written to the Chiefs of Staff that there was a need to develop "a strong BW capability without delay [as part of] all effective means of waging war without regard to precedent to their use."

I wanted to explore with Dr. Gottlieb his moral position at the time and later, when he left the CIA. Had he changed his views? I did not want to trap him into admissions; I only wanted to understand what had made him what he was.

Still, my portrait of Dr. Gottlieb, as presented here, comes from a wide number of sources. They include documents obtained using the Freedom of Information Act (FOIA) in the

United States and Canada's Access to Information Act (AIA). Time and again I turned back to a clip of news footage. It shows Dr. Gottlieb coming out of an elevator. He is casually dressed and wearing a cap. He looks like a sports fan on the way to a game. The camera has caught him unawares. A reporter tries to question him. Dr. Gottlieb looks startled. His lips part in what may be the start of a grimace. His eyes blink. "That's all in the past," he manages to say. Then he is gone.

For Sidney Gottlieb it is now indeed in the past. But what he did will live on, not least because it continues.

I owe a very real debt to Eric Olson. He is a man I truly admire. For over forty years he relentlessly fought to make known the truth about the death of his father. He proved to be a valuable source for many details about the CIA.

An early version of the story of Frank Olson was carefully read by Eric. He provided me with detailed notes. He was very concerned that his long and careful pursuit of the truth about his father's death not be sentimentalized. On November 17, 2001, he wrote me a passage that provides a hint of the many fine qualities Eric possesses:

"My anger and bitterness, if that is what I have, is not about the loss of a father; it is about the fact that my father was murdered; that I have been consistently lied to about the nature of his death and that even when we (the family) received a Presidential apology for the death, that turned out to be based on a lie as well. The loss of a father when one is a young boy is one thing (certainly a painful and fateful thing); a father murdered by the State is quite a different thing. Let's not get mushy at the end and conflate everything in a big psycho babble stew here."

He went on to offer what he called "the key" to the story about his father: "Nobody has ever made any positive comments about what happened. The story is that there never was a story. Lashbrook sets the tone here with his assertion that he never saw what happened."

Over the years I had tried to help Eric as far as I could, using my own intelligence sources, including those in Mossad. In a note to me on November 20, 2001, Eric wrote: "It all accords perfectly that the technique of [my father's] murder was described in an assassination manual. We must be clear that this was murder. Next Wednesday, November 28, marks the 48th anniversary of my father's murder. Nearly half a century of struggling with this nightmare."

In March 1996, I arranged to meet William Colby, the former Director of Central Intelligence, in Washington. Physically he was the man Bill Buckley had described to me. He spoke of Buckley being an "outstanding person and an agent of the first rank." We touched upon a number of areas that were still clearly sensitive to Colby: Operation Phoenix, his public admission of the past sins of the Agency and his belief that in revealing them he had actually preserved the CIA from being destroyed by outsiders. Listening to him, it was hard to doubt his integrity.

A month later, April 27, 1996, Colby left his home near the Wincomico River in Virginia for a short solo canoe trip. He wore no life vest as he began to paddle into a wind stiff enough to kick up white caps. He never returned home. A week later his body was found on the shore of the Wincomico close to where it flows into the Potomac River south of Washington. No one knew what had prompted him to take to the water without a life vest in such dangerous conditions, as he was 76 years old. Among the items police later found in his study were the latest copy of Colby's faxed newsletter that offered "strategic weekly briefings" and a computer CD-ROM game about espionage and counterterrorism. Colby had created the disk with Oleg Kalugin, a former intelligence officer with the KGB.

For a brief time the media was filled with speculation that Colby had been the victim of foul play, killed because he had betrayed the CIA or for some other unspecified "dark secret in his past." But no hard evidence to support such allegations was ever produced.

I had several interviews with William Casey before and after his retirement from his post as Director of the Central Intelligence Agency. Our first meeting set a pattern for the others that followed and deserves to be described in some detail.

On that March afternoon in 1986, he cut a shambling figure despite his custom-made suit. His jowled face was pale and the rims of his eyes were red as we sat in a Washington club; five years of leading the CIA had clearly drained his vitality. Over a Perrier he confirmed the conditions for our meeting: no notes, no tape recordings.

He sat, watchful, waiting for my first question: what could he tell me about Bill Buckley, who, almost two years earlier to the day — on Friday, March 16, 1984 — had been kidnapped in Beirut? I wanted to know what efforts the CIA had made to save Bill's life. I had spent time in the Middle East, including Israel, trying to piece together the background.

"You speak to Admoni or any of his people?" Casey interrupted, then went on to describe Admoni as "a soft-spoken, intelligence bureaucrat who, when he became Mossad's chief, ran a tight ship. Socially gregarious, he had as keen an eye for women as for what's best for Israel."

His next words came in the same mumbling undertone: "Nobody can surprise like someone you took to be friendly disposed. By the time we realized Admoni was going to do nothing, Bill Buckley was dead. Remember what it was like at the time over there? There had been the massacre of almost a thousand Palestinians in those two Beirut refugee camps. The

Lebanese Christian forces did the killings; the Jews looked on in a kind of reversal of the Bible. Fact is, Admoni was in bed with that thug, Gemayel."

Bashir Gemayel had been head of the Phalangists and later became president of Lebanon.

"We ran Gemayel as well, but I never trusted the bastard. And Admoni worked with Gemayel all the time Buckley was being tortured. We had no idea where exactly in Beirut Bill was being held. We asked Admoni to find out. He said no problem. We waited and waited. Sent our best men to Tel Aviv to work with Mossad. We said money was not a problem. Admoni kept saying okay, understood."

Casey sipped more water, locked in his own time capsule. His next words came out flat, like a jury foreman handing down a verdict.

"Next thing, Admoni was selling us a bill of goods that the PLO was behind the kidnapping. We knew the Israelis were always ready to blame Yasir Arafat for anything, but Admoni was very plausible. He made a good case. By the time we figured it wasn't Arafat, it was long over for Buckley. What we didn't know was that Mossad had also been playing real dirty pool — supplying the Hezbollah with arms to kill the Christians while at the same time giving the Christians more guns to kill the Palestinians."

In other meetings, Casey's partial glimpse of what the CIA now believed had happened to Bill Buckley — that Mossad had deliberately done nothing to save him in the hope the PLO could be blamed and thus frustrate Arafat's hopes of gaining sympathy in Washington — provided a chilling insight into the relationship between two intelligence services supposedly friendly with each other. Casey revealed another side to the ties between the United States and Israel other than fund-raising and other manifestations of American-Jewish solidarity. At our final meeting, Casey had a last thought: "A nation creates the intelligence community it needs. America relies on technical expertise because we are concerned to discover, rather than secretly rule. The Israelis operate differently. Mossad, in particular, equates its actions with the country's survival."

Ellen Mercer at the American Psychiatric Association arranged for me to have full access to Dr. Cameron's papers which the Association has in its archives. They turned out to be a trove of information.

Dr. Robert Cleghorn, a sprightly 82-year-old when I interviewed him, took time off from his still busy daily schedule at Sunnybrook Hospital in Toronto to guide me through his own detailed, so-far unpublished account of working with Dr. Cameron. It is a truly remarkable document, filled with insight and penetrating analysis. Then Dr. Cleghorn allowed me to record still further impressions, updating his original impressions, trying to put his old chief in what he hoped was "a fair light."

Mrs. Peggy Edwards (née Mielke), spent a long time recalling her time at the Institute. Her testimony had the painful honesty of a woman still deeply troubled that she had been a part of what she readily acknowledged was "a bad business."

Dr. Edward Kingston, who had been one of Dr. Cameron's residents and, in 1987, was chairman of the Department of Psychiatry at McMaster University near Toronto, produced a compelling overview of his old chief. He always tried to balance his criticism with understanding, constantly saying, "You have to try and see it in the context of the day," and "He wasn't all bad, but not all good either, somewhere in between."

*   *   *

Dr. Allen Mann, Professor of Clinical Psychiatry at Montreal General Hospital, developed the same theme. Engaging and often witty, he made his points quickly and without hesitation. The Dr. Cameron who emerges from his taped reminiscences was altogether a kinder man than the person whom David Orlikov described to me a few days later in his office in the Parliament Buildings in Ottawa.

Orlikov provided full access to his wife's case notes. "Nobody wants to see their private lives washed in public, but it is a small thing to bear for the truth to come out." Over dinner in the Members dining room, he said: "Velma and the other patients can't remember many things. It is one of the great tragedies of this case that their memories were forever destroyed by Cameron." He didn't say it in anger, more in sadness. This dignified and courtly man seemed a long way from the description Dr. Cameron wrote of him in Velma's case file.

From Ottawa I traveled to Detroit to speak with Eddie Lacroix, Madeleine's husband. He had remarried and at first he was reluctant to meet me. "It's over. Madeleine's gone. So what's the point?" I told him about Velma Orlikov not being able to remember. He asked me to call him back in twenty-four hours. When I did, he agreed to meet me in a Detroit hotel. We sat and spoke from dinner until close to dawn — when he went off to work in an auto shop. Next evening he invited me home. There, in his den, he produced the documentation on Madeleine, including a copy of her case notes. He also agreed to a taped interview. I have used its transcript and her case notes to tell the story of Madeleine's life and death.

Dr. Peter Roper dipped deep into his quite remarkable memory. Not only could he recall minute details, but was able to explain how he felt they fitted into the broad picture. His enthusiasm for telling the story was infectious and meals were skipped as he talked on and on, and I kept changing tapes. Spotting my difficulty with getting a new tape into my recorder, he grinned and said, "You could do with that bounder Rubenstein."

In many ways I realized that I had a choice, to either set off in pursuit of Leonard Rubenstein or leave him out of the story. Dr. Roper convinced me. "You can't possibly tell the story without including him. Even if he doesn't speak to you, that's important. And speak to Zielinski."

The next stage of the trail took me back once again to Ottawa. There I spoke to Zielinski. He went from "I'm going to put the phone down now," to "Look, I'm only a Pole who doesn't want to make waves," to "No, it wasn't like that. I tried to help people. That's all. I tried to help." In between those statements, I kept on questioning him. Finally he agreed to meet. What he had to say was not only extraordinary, but also of considerable importance. He revealed the 'interrogation center' in the Institute basement and described fully what had gone on there. He ended his long interview by urging me to "go after Rubenstein."

I flew to London and telephoned Rubenstein. I explained to him in detail the purpose of my call. He finally said that he couldn't speak about what he had done. I asked him why. He said he was "just about to leave the country." I asked where he was going and if I could come along. "I'm going to be away for a long time." Throwing caution to the wind, I asked him if he could justify what he had done to people like Madeleine at the Institute. There was a lengthy pause before he spoke. "Yes, I can justify it. Dr. Cameron was a great man..."

For a good hour I scribbled furiously while he sought to explain himself. The voice in my ear was gentle and insistent. "Those were different times. Very different times." Then, as abruptly as he had begun, he stopped. "Got to go," and put down the phone. A few days later when I next called the number, the operator said it had been disconnected.

There were, inevitably, some refusals. Mrs. Cameron was unwilling to discuss her husband. Her son, Duncan, a Washington lawyer, was sympathetic to my quest but felt he too could not help. I spoke to Dr. Mary Morrow several times, running over with her various points in the lengthy deposition she had made to the CIA's lawyers. She was helpful but explained she was writing her own account of what had happened and so could not provide me with everything I hoped for. Nevertheless, she provided sufficient detail to ensure her place in the story. In all, in various parts of the world, I spoke to over a hundred persons.

One of them was Kathleen Sullivan. She introduced me to a number of men and women who, like her, had been caught up in CIA mind control programs. Though many had never met each other, they told the same numbing story of being used as human guinea pigs by scientists and doctors and intelligence officers whose obsession, like that of Sidney Gottlieb, drove them beyond all moral and ethical considerations.

In late summer of 2001, Kathleen arranged for me to receive five CD-ROM disks. They contained some 22,000 documents relating to MK-ULTRA and other CIA programs. To the best of my knowledge none of the documents has ever been published before. I am certain, given the sensitivity of the material on the discs, they could only have originated from a whistle-blower inside the Agency. He or she could have had several reasons for releasing this material: a desire for self-justification, perhaps the need for expiation, a sense of guilt long withheld. We shall probably never know. But no matter. The discs enabled me to fill in important gaps in the book and confirm much of what Bill

Buckley told me. In those CD-ROMs are thousands of memos between CIA officers that show only too well the deception and shocking cruelty that was at the core of their endeavors. It took many months to sift through the disks. But every hour was well spent in uncovering a story that until now has remained buried.

In my search to understand how widespread was the use of mind control, I was greatly helped by Dr. Anne White. She read an early version of this book and then revealed that Dr. William Sargant had actually duplicated some of Dr. Ewen Cameron's experiments on his own patients at St Thomas' Hospital in London. It was a revelation that deeply shocked me. In all the years I had known Dr. Sargant, he had never so much as given a hint that he had used such methods. At one time Dr. White had herself been a patient of Dr. Sargant's. Her story is an eerie echo of Mary Matilda Morrow's account in some respects.

On a bleak February day in 1970, Anne Margaret White, a mother of three small children, was admitted to one of the world's great teaching hospitals, St Thomas', in London, England. She was thirty-one years old and suffering from post-partum depression. Three months later Anne emerged from the hospital, physically and mentally so changed her father thought she was "a zombie."

The transformation had been achieved by Dr. Sargant. Long regarded as a ground-breaking physician, his clarion call could be heard through the hospital corridors: "An ounce of phenobarbitone, or some rather more modern tranquilizer, may be worth more than a hundred-weight of persuasive talk." When Anne White became his patient, Dr. Sargant had already been at the forefront of research into mind control for a quarter of a century.

By that February day, Dr. Sargant had made thirty-one flights to Washington. He had visited American research centers where secret experiments were being conducted. In Washington, Dr. Sargant was regularly invited to Allan Dulles' annual Christmas party.

At one Christmas party was a slim, diffident man. His name was Heinz Lehmann. Dr. Sargant's diary note of the meeting described "a man not frightened to be radical in his use of drugs. Lehmann's speciality was giving his patients Thorazine and Largactil in combinations. Sometimes with Nembutal, Seconal, Veronal and Phenergan."

These were some of the drugs of choice used in MK-ULTRA. Dr. Sargant became an enthusiastic prescriber. By 1970, MK-ULTRA had officially been disbanded. But Anne White was about to find out, as hundreds of patients before her had, that MK-ULTRA continued to thrive in the hands of Dr. Sargant and others like him.

Sargant continued to use the massive doses of electroshock and drugs as part of his behavioral modification regime. Using his highly placed connections to the American drug industry, Sargant's arsenal of mind-altering drugs was unequalled in Britain. He was the first to treat — depending on the definition of "treatment" — patients with Thorazine, Stelazine and Melaril; antidepressants like Elavil and Tofranil; antimaniacs like lithium carbonate. He gave them in combinations.

He scoured the psychiatric journals for news of new drugs. His files included an advertisement from the *Archives of General Psychiatry*. It showed a dark skinned, thick-lipped young man, fists clenched. Above the figure are the words "Assaultive and Belligerent?," beneath the figure is the message: "Cooperation often begins with Haldol (haloperidol). It acts to control assaultive, aggressive behavior."

Dr. Sargant worked closely with the Eli Lilly Company, Hoffman La-Roche and Geigy. Other drug houses that regarded him with favor were Merck, Sharon and Dohme, Parke-Davis and

Company, Smith Kline, French Laboratories, and Searle Laboratories. From them came drugs that did not necessarily free Dr. Sargant's patients from their demons, anxieties and psychoses. They were often no more than a means of control. Patients who did not respond were consigned to one of the asylums that still dotted the countryside of post-war England.

For a psychiatrist of lesser ambition, running a busy department would have sufficed. But Dr. Sargant, like Dr. Cameron, had a vision bordering on messianic zeal. He would lead psychiatry into a new world. He outlined his methods in his book, *Physical Methods of Treatment*. It became required reading for the growing number of his medical followers in Britain and America.

At the outset of the Cold War, Britain's two intelligence services, MI5 and MI6, had urgently looked for new ways to understand, combat and overcome the medical manipulations of Soviet and Chinese psychiatrists. In Dr. Sargant they found a willing tutor. From 1948, he ruled supreme over the Department of Psychological Medicine at St Thomas'. Once he agreed to work for Britain's intelligence services, money was no longer a problem and through the U.S. drug companies, he met like-minded psychiatrists.

But most disturbing of all, I discovered that Dr. Sargant knew and approved of the "terminal" experiments the CIA had conducted on German nationals in post-war Germany.

This was the doctor whose methods would turn Anne White, a woman desperately seeking his help, into that zombie-like figure her father saw when she emerged from his "care."

For Sargant, depression was a chemical event. The invisible, choking substance that leaches out the spirit, he would say, was the result of some electrolytic imbalance in the brain. While he would concede that all depressions, like flakes of snow, are not alike, "they are all formed on the template of past experience."

Tall and muscular, with a toothy smile, Dr. Sargant had an athlete's stride, a legacy of his days as a Cambridge University track athlete. His clipped speech and penetrating stare discouraged any challenge to his authority. His lodestar was that "insanity must be treated by primarily physical methods. Just as the heart can be stimulated by a physical shock and a tumour removed from the brain to give relief, so can mental illness be similarly treated."

His early medical career was remarkable in the way he gathered to himself powerful men in medicine, like Lord Moran (Winston Churchill's wartime physician) and Professor Edward Mapother. It was their encouragement that inspired his serious research into what eventually became mind control. His early subjects were the victims of "acute battle neurosis." These were men who had simply cracked under the strain of a long war. They were written off as "lacking moral fibre." But for Dr. Sargant they were ideal for his first steps into heavy sedation, drug-induced sleep, modified insulin treatment and barbiturate dosages.

Not everyone approved. The sight of young men lying comatose for long periods only to be awakened for food and electroshock treatments did not sit easily with Dr. Sargant's peers.

To discover all this was shocking for me. Not just for what he did, but because I had counted on Dr. Sargant as a friend. To learn he was a monster, who managed to hide the truth about his work even after MK-ULTRA had been exposed, was indeed painful.

Dr. Sargant told me over dinner in his London club and later, sipping coffee in his Harley Street apartment, how much he "hated what Cameron did. The chap was totally unethical." And yet, a few miles from where we sat in cozy companionship, on the other side of the Thames in St Thomas' Hospital, he was doing exactly what Dr. Cameron had done.

Sargant died on August 27, 1986. With his death I was freed of my undertaking and began to slowly explore his background. It was not easy; he still had powerful friends in the World Psychiatric Association he had helped to establish, and the Royal College of Psychiatrists. They tried to steer me away from his work to the medical papers he had written, along with best-selling books.

Then Anne White contacted me. She had read a story of mine relating to Frank Olson's death. It had contained a reference to William Sargant. That was the starting point.

Today Anne White can look back at a fulfilled career. She is an Examiner for the Medical Council of Canada and Assistant Clinical Professor of Medicine in the Department of Psychiatry at McMaster University Medical School in Ontario. Her area of expertise includes neurology and behavioral medicine. Her long list of awards and research grants are testimony to her work. A buoyant, vivacious woman, she shows no outward signs of what happened to her when she was admitted into St Thomas' Hospital under the overall "care" of Dr. Sargant.

Her medical history is not unusual. After the birth of each of her three children — two boys and a girl — she developed post-partum depression. She told me: "After each birth I felt tired all the time even after getting sleep; weepy; worthless as a mother; guilty that I wasn't doing a good job. Everything was an effort, including looking after the baby. I lost all pleasure in things I normally loved. I couldn't concentrate to read; I couldn't listen to and enjoy music. I was intermittently suicidal and nearly always thinking everyone would be better off without me; that I was a drag on my family. There was no light at the end of the tunnel.

"As soon as I was pregnant with the second child this situation resolved and, during the pregnancy, I felt good. I had my first two children 13 months apart, and then there was a gap of two years before the next one was born. I spent six weeks in hospital with my last pregnancy due to high blood pressure. The baby ended up in an incubator for a week. Again I became depressed. But as no one diagnosed the problem, it went untreated for two years."

At the time she was living in Zambia, a nation with limited medical facilities. Her then husband (they are now divorced) was a family doctor. After consulting with another doctor, it was decided that Anne should return with the children to her parents in England and be admitted to St Thomas'. She had no idea what to expect. But she had been assured that the hospital was at the cutting-edge of medicine. She would be taken good care of. She would get better. With that expectation, she became Dr. Sargant's trusting patient. He decided that the young mother was a suitable case for the Sleep Room.

Dr. Sargant's Sleep Room was modelled on the one Ewen Cameron had created in the Allan Memorial Institute as part of the MK-ULTRA program. It was at the back of Dr. Sargant's department; a dormitory with six single beds. Each was one foot from the next with a low-wattage bulb barely providing sufficient light for the nurses to see. At the Institute, Dr. Sargant had seen Dr. Cameron's patients "lying inert or sometimes whispering unintelligibly. When it was time to feed them they were spoon-fed. When it was time to go to the toilet they were placed on a commode and then lifted back into bed." Anne was injected with Largactil and Seconal to keep her in a drugged sleep. She also received doses of other drugs, Amitriptyline and Nardil. This was what life was like for her over the ensuing weeks.

"I don't ever remember being taken to a bathroom or lavatory, although that must have happened. Unfortunately, I was so drugged up that every time I stood, I passed out, because my blood pressure dropped into my boots. I don't remember talking to any patients. I could just see the next bed but no details. When I reached the point that the medication wouldn't keep me asleep, however much they gave me, I lay in the dark with virtually no auditory input. I think I remember listening to tapes. But I can't be sure and that may be something which is a false memory."

It was not a figment of her drugged mind. Dr. Sargant, like Dr. Cameron, had devised a system where all patients in the Sleep Room received endless instructions on a tape loop played through a recorder placed under each pillow. In between lying in the Sleep Room, Anne White was wheeled to a treatment room for electroshock. She later discovered she had been given 26 bi-lateral shock treatments. The recommended number is no more than six. The only protection against the *grand mal* seizure that followed was the muscle relaxant drug she received. When she awoke back in the Sleep Room, her head throbbed with pain. "My mind felt like a blurred, pounding emptiness." She began to feel like a zombie.

But the spirit of resistance still flickered in Anne's mind. She demanded a halt to the treatment. The nurses in the Sleep Room consulted with Dr. Sargant. Suddenly, Anne recalled: "I was placed in a small room by myself. I was left to my own devices while I went through a week of barbiturate withdrawal. The nurses hardly bothered with me. I was the one who had dared to challenge the system. I felt I was being punished." It was only years later, long after she had left St Thomas' Hospital, that Anne White, the "zombie-like creature" that so shocked her father, began to discover the truth about William Sargant.

Testifying at the trial of Patty Hearst in 1976, Sargant told the court that Hearst was "an unwilling victim of brainwashing." This judgement could just as well fit the case of Anne White. Her case notes disappeared from St Thomas' shortly after Dr. Sargant's death. Her efforts to find them have failed.

My own enquiries suggest they were taken by MI5 and shredded. The CIA did the same with the records of Dr. Cameron's work at the Allan Memorial Institute.

The story of Anne White, and all those like her, is ultimately a story of terror: the story of the familiar — a respected hospital — becoming a place of horror. Anne White believes to this day that the best defense against unethical behavior is public disclosure and awareness. The less disclosure and awareness there is, the closer we are to allowing the successors of Dr. Sargant, Dr. Cameron, Dr. Gottlieb, and all the other doctors who torture, to continue their work.

It would not have been possible to produce the background to Dr. Aziz al-Abub without the considerable help of a number of people in Beirut and elsewhere in the Middle East. Some have asked to remain anonymous; but a number of excellent Arab journalists gladly gave of their time and knowledge to assist me. One was Mohamad al-Awwam, then an editor with the widely respected *Asharq al-Awsat* newspaper. Dr. Mohammed Samir was also helpful in filling in gaps in the time al-Abub was in Lebanon.

Other contacts in Israel and Lebanon provided intriguing insights into that country. I owe a special debt to Meir Amit, the former director general of Mossad; to Rafi Eitan, former Deputy-Director of Mossad; and my Arab language publisher, Mohammed Maatouk, based in Beirut.

Grateful thanks are due to Ibraham al-Tafoli in Damascus who, for a year, monitored the Arab-language press on my behalf.

I thank Noel Walsh, former Professor of Clinical Psychiatry at St Vincent's Hospital, Dublin, Ireland, who patiently answered my questions about Ewen Cameron — Noel had worked at

McGill University. I feel there is still hope as long as there are men like him in medicine.

I am grateful to Kevan Barker, who was right. Writing this book was therapeutic.

And finally I owe a great debt to my assistant, Emer Lenehan. Her patience and eye for detail made this book all the more pleasant to write. She is truly that rare person: good-natured and with boundless energy. Thanks, Emer.

DEPOSITIONS

Velma Orlikov: Before Patricia Gaffney, Notary Public, in the U.S. Attorney's office, 555 4th Street, NW, Washington D.C., June 17, 1986.
Appearances: Joseph Rauh, Counsel for Plaintiff;
Scott T. Kragie, Counsel for Defendant, United States of America;
Page Moffett Office of General Counsel, Central Intelligence Agency, Counsel for Defendant.
155 pages, plus exhibits.

Mary Matilda Morrow, M.D.: Before Judith F. Richard, Notary Public, at Judiciary Center, 555 4th Street, NW, Washington D.C., June 19, 1986.
Appearances: James C. Turner, Counsel for Plaintiff;
Scott T. Kragie, Counsel for Defendant, United States of America;
Page Moffett and Barbara A. Rubino, Office of General Counsel, Central Intelligence Agency.
188 pages.

Jean Charles Page: Before the Consul General of the United States in Montreal, June 24, 1986.
Appearances: Scott T. Kragie, Counsel for Defendant, United States of America; . James C. Turner, Counsel for Plaintiff.
89 pages.

Moe Langleben: Before Patricia Mitchell, Verbatim Reporter, at 333 Constitution Avenue, NW, Washington, D.C., May 6, 1986.
Appearances: James C. Turner, Counsel for Deponent.
Scott T. Kragie, Counsel for Defendant, United States of America.

103 pages plus exhibits.

Rita Zimmerman: Before the Consul General of the United States in Montreal, June 26, 1986.
Appearances: James C. Turner, Counsel for Plaintiff.
Scott T. Kragie and Ms. Rebecca Ross, Counsel for Defendant, United States of America.
34 pages.

Jeannine Huard: Before the Consul General of the United States in Montreal, June 25, 1986.
Appearances: James C. Turner, Counsel for Plaintiff. Scott T. Kragie and Ms. Rebecca Ross, Counsel for Defendant, United States of America.
114 pages.

Louis Weinstein: Before the Consul General of the United States in Montreal, June 23, 1986.
Appearances: James C. Turner, Counsel for Plaintiff.
Scott T. Kragie and Ms. Rebecca Ross, Counsel for Defendant, United States of America.
112 pages.

Richard McGarrah Helms: Before Baleigh Milton, Notary Public, 1001 Connecticut Avenue, NW, Washington, D.C., on March 14, 1983.
Appearances: Joseph Rauh and James C. Turner for the Plaintiffs;
For Richard Helms, Robert M LaPrade and Philip Kinsberg, Counsel for Central Intelligence Agency;
For the Central Intelligence Agency, Steven Hermes;
For the United States of America, Les Strictland, Assistant U.S. Attorney.
268 pages.

AFFIDAVITS

Mrs. Alice W. Olson, widow of Frank Olson.
October 6, 1986.

Robert Jay Lifton, M.D. , Distinguished Professor of Psychiatry and Psychology, City University of New York, John Jay College of Criminal Justice.
October 24, 1986.

Harvey M. Weinstein, M.D., Clinical Associate Professor of Psychiatry, Stanford University of Medicine.
November 7, 1986.

Leon Salzman, M.D., Professor of Psychiatry, Georgetown University Medical School.
November 29, 1986.

Osmond M. Solandt, Ph.D., former Chairman, Canadian Defense Research Board.
October 6, 1986.

Jay Peterzell, Research Associate, Center for National Security Studies.
November 5, 1986.

Paul E. Termansen, M.D., FRCP(C), Clinical Associate Professor, Department of Psychiatry, University of British Columbia.
October 6, 1986.

Lloyd Hisey, M.D., former Registrar and Director, the Allan Memorial Institute.
February 20, 1983.

David J. Rothman, Ph.D., Bernard Shoenberg, Professor of Social Medicine and Director, Center for the Study of Society

and Medicine, College of Physicians and Surgeons, Columbia University.
October 15, 1986.

David I. Joseph, M.D., Faculty member, Saint Elizabeth Hospital and Associate Clinical Professor of Psychiatry and Behavioral Science, George Washington School of Medicine.
November 7, 1986.

Brian B. Doyle, M.D., Clinical Professor of Psychiatry and of Family and Community Medicine, Georgetown University School of Medicine.
November 3, 1986.

Senator Allan J. MacEachen, Former Canadian Member of Parliament and Secretary of State for External Affairs.
October 29, 1986.

Miss Eva H. Bothwell.
November 4, 1986.

Wayne Langleben.
August 26, 1986.

TRANSCRIPTIONS

Examination in chief by Maitre Alex Paterson; testimony of Dr. Allan Mann, taken May 5, 1981, before the Hon Mr. Justice Marcel Belleville, Superior Court, District of Montreal, Province of Quebec; in case no: 500-05-006872-788: Dame Velma Orlikov -v- Royal Victoria Hospital.

Direct Examination of Dr. Peter Roper by Mr. Sullivan, taken on February 5, 1981 as expert testimony in the case of Dr. Mary Matilda Morrow -v- Royal Victoria Hospital.

Plaintiffs' Statement of Genuine Issues in Civil Action No: 80-3163: detailed in following separate exhibits.

(a) The MK-ULTRA program was established to explore covert brain-washing techniques for both offensive and defensive use by the CIA (Def. No. 6-9).

(b) The central activity of the MK-ULTRA program was conducting and funding brain-washing experimentation with dangerous drugs and other techniques performed on persons who were not volunteers by CIA Technical Service Division employees, agents and contractors (Def. No. 10-17).

(c) CIA employees were negligent in killing Frank Olson in an MK-ULTRA experiment during November 1953, as related by his widow in her affidavit (Def. No. 18, 19).

(d) The CIA negligently failed to implement appropriate measures to curb Gottlieb and Lashbrook (Def. No. 20-23).

(e) The Society for the Investigation of Human Ecology (hereafter "Society") was established and operated by the CIA to conceal its role in conducting and financing brain-washing research (Def. No. 24-26).

(f) In January of 1956, an article by Dr. Ewen Cameron appeared in the *American Journal of Psychiatry* which described potentially injurious experimental procedures similar to Communist brain-washing methods (Def. No. 27, 28).

(g) John Gittinger and former Air Force brain-washing expert Col. James Monroe recruited Dr. Ewen Cameron to perform experiments with potentially injurious experimental procedures similar to Communist brain-washing methods (Def. No. 29-32).

(h) The application submitted to the Society by Dr. Ewen Cameron was a transparent proposal to conduct experiments with techniques extrapolated from the academic literature on brain-washing, which deviated from the standard and customary psychiatric therapies during the 1950s and which ran the gamut of brain-washing procedures including depatterning, experimental drugs, psychic driving, partial sensory isolation and continuous sleep. (Def. No. 33-38).

(i) Without investigation of any kind, Gottlieb, Lashbrook, Gittinger and their CIA colleagues approved MK-ULTRA Sub-Project 68 which provided some $60,000 over four years for the brain-washing experiments described in the application (Def. No. 39-48, 121-124, 127, 129).

(j) Gottlieb, Lashbrook, Gittinger and their CIA associates failed to take any steps to ensure that only volunteers were used in MK-ULTRA Sub-Project 68 or to protect the well-being of experimental subjects (Def. No. 39-48).

(k) During the time CIA provided funds for MK-ULTRA Sub-Project 68, Gottlieb, Lashbrook, Gittinger and their associates failed to supervise the MK-ULTRA Sub-Project 68 brain-washing experimentation in any way (Def. No. 39-48).

(l) Cameron was aware of CIA interest in the brain-washing experiments he conducted (Def. No. 29-31, 42-45, 48).

(m) MK-ULTRA Sub-Project 68 provided over $60,000 to support brain-washing experiments from 1956 through the early 60s (Def. No. 39-48).

(n) Plaintiffs never volunteered to participate in experiments (Def. No. 51, 68, 77, 92, 102).

(o) Each plaintiff was subjected to one or more of the experimental brain-washing techniques (depatterning with intensive electro shock or LSD and other drugs, psychic driving, partial sensory, isolation and continuous sleep experiments) described in the application and financed by MK-ULTRA Sub-Project 68, instead of standard therapies for their psychiatric conditions (Def. No. 49, 50, 52, 53, 56-58, 61-64, 67, 69, 70, 74-76, 82-85, 88-91, 95, 96, 99-101, 119, 120).

(p) The CIA concealed MK-ULTRA Sub-Project 68 and failed to notify plaintiffs that they had been unwitting subjects of those brain-washing experiments (Def. No. 78-81, 106-118).

(q) Defendant has admitted negligence in the CIA's MK-ULTRA brain-washing experiments (Def. No. 13-26, 121-29).

(r) Each plaintiff was injured by exposure to one or more of these brain-washing techniques of depatterning with intensive electro shock or LSD and other drugs, psychic driving, partial sensory isolation and continuous sleep experiments described in the application and financed by MK-ULTRA Sub-Project 68. (Def. No. 104, 124, 128).

(s) The brain-washing experiments financed by MK-ULTRA Sub-Project 68 were unethical and irresponsible violations of recognized standards governing research with human subjects. (Def. No. 123, 125-127).

(t) The CIA violated accepted standards governing research involving human subjects by financing brain-washing experiments upon non-volunteers in MK-ULTRA Sub-Project 68. (Def. No. 123, 125-127).

REPORTS ON TERRORIST GROUPS
AND
POLITICAL IDEOLOGY

The Ethiics of Terror. Professor Abraham Kaplan, Department of Philosophy, University of Haifa, Israel.

The Psychiatrist and the Terrorist. Professor John Gunn, Institute of Psychiatry, The Maudsley Hospital, London.

Ethics in Hostage Encounters. Professor Burr Eichelman, University of Wisconsin at Madison.

Victimization and Rehabilitative Treatment. Professor Martin Symonds, John Jay School of Law, Director of Psychological Studies, New York City Police Department.

Hostage Victims. Dr. Frank Ochberg, St Lawrence Hospital, Lansing, Michigan.

The Hostage Situation: Law Enforcement Options. Captain Frank Bolz, Chief Negotiator, Hostage Negotiation Team, New York City Police Department.

Preparing Law Enforcement Personnel for Terrorist Incidents. Conrad Hassell, Unit Chief, Special Operations and Research Unit, FBI Academy, Quantico, Virginia.

Law Enforcement and Psychiatry: Forging and Working Alliance. Professor David Soskis, Clinical Associate Professor of Psychiatry, Temple University, Philadelphia, Pennsylvania.

Research in Terrorism. Professor William Reid, Nebraska Psychiatric Institute, University of Nebraska College of Medicine, Omaha, Nebraska.

Areas of Consensus: Areas of Ignorance. Brian Jenkins, Program Director, Security/Subnational Conflicts. The Rand Corporation, Santa Monica, California.

Psychodynamic Theory of Terrorist Behavior. Professor Jerrold M Post, Department of Psychiatry and Behavioral Science, George Washington University.

Hizbollah: The Moral Logic of Extraordinary Means. Professor Martin Kramer, Dayan Center, University of Tel Aviv, Israel.

The Logic of Terrorism. Professor Martha Crenshaw, Department of Government, Wesleyan University.

Messianic Sanctions for Terror. Professor David C Rapport, Professor of Political Science, University of California, Los Angeles.

Ideology and Repentance: Terrorism in Italy. Professor Franco Ferracuti. Professor of Criminological Medicine and Forensic Psychiatry, University of Rome School of Medicine.

Nationalism, Sectarianism and Political Violence. Joseph Montville, Research Director, Center for the Study of Foreign Affairs, Foreign Service Institute, U.S. Department of State.

Ideology and Rebellion: Terrorism in West Germany. Konrad Kellen, The Rand Corporation.

The Problems and Challenges of Research on Terrorism. Dr. Jo Groebel. Postgraduate Program in Communication Psychology, Rheinland-Pfalz, West Germany.

Militant Islamic Movements in Lebanon: Origins, Social Basis and Ideology. Professor Marius Deeb, The Center for Contemporary Arab Studies, Georgetown University, Washington.

Revolutionary Iran: Challenge and Responses. Professor Shimon Shapira, University of Tel Aviv, Israel.

CHEMICAL-BIOLOGICAL WARFARE DOCUMENTS

US Government Documents:
Cochrane, Rexmond C. *History of the Chemical Warfare Service in World War II* (1 July 1940-15 August 1945). *Volume II: Biological Warfare Research in the United States.* U.S. Army Chemical Corps: Historical Section, November 1947.

Department of the Army. *U.S. Army Activity in the U.S. Biological Warfare Programs.* Volumes I and II. 24 February 1977. (Reprinted in U.S. Congress. Senate. Hearings before the Subcommittee on Health and Scientific Research of the Committee on Human Resources. *Biological Testing Involving Human Subjects by the Department of Defense, 1977.* 95th Congr., 1st sess., March 8 and May 23, 1977.

War Research Service. *Historical Report of War Research Service, November 1944-Final.* (1945) (Declassified top secret typescript; Archives, National Academy of Sciences).

Operational Suitability of a BW Munition. Dugway Proving Ground Report 134 (BW 16-52). Dugway Proving Ground, Utah, 29 January 1954.

Special Report No. 44: Munitions for Biological Warfare. Two volumes. Camp Detrick, Maryland: Technical Department, Munitions Division, June 1943-September 1945. (Unpublished, declassified top secret document. Ft. Belvoir, Virginia: Defense Technical Information Center: AD 310773 (Volume 1), AD310774 (Volume 11).

Report on Scientific Intelligence Survey in Japan, September and October 1945. Volume V. Biological Warfare. General Headquarters, United States Army Forces, Pacific: Scientific and Technical Advisory Section, 1 November 1945. (Declassified secret document; Office of the Command Historian, Headquarters, U.S. Army Garrison, Fort Detrick, Maryland).

Report on Japanese Biological Warfare (BW) Activities. Camp Detrick, Maryland: Army Service Forces, 31 May 1946. (Declassified secret document; Office of the Command Historian, Headquarters, U.S. Army Garrison, Fort Detrick, Maryland).

Summary of New Information about Japanese BW Activities. Camp Detrick, Maryland, 20 June 1947. (Declassified confidential document; Office of the Command Historian, Headquarters, U.S. Army Garrison, Fort Detrick, Maryland).

Summary Report on BW Investigations. Camp Detrick, Maryland, 12 December 1947. (Office of the Command Historian, Headquarters, U.S. Army Garrison, Fort Detrick, Maryland).

Report on Special BW Operations. Washington, D.C. : National Military Establishment, Research and Development Board, 5 October 1948.

A Study of the Vulnerability of Subway Passengers in New York City to Covert Attack with Biological Agents. Special Operations Division, Fort Detrick.

SELECT BIBLIOGRAPHY

Barnaby, Wendy, *The Plague Makers: The Secret World of Biological Warfare*. London: Vision Paperbacks, 1997.

Brown, J.R.C. *"Techniques of Persuasion: From Propaganda to Brainwashing."* London: Penguin Books, 1963.

Bryden, John. *Deadly Allies: Canada's Secret War 1937 – 1947*. Toronto: McClelland & Stewart 1989. (The story of the Canadian germ warfare project)

Colby, Kenneth Mark. *An Introduction to Psychoanalytic Research.*
New York: Basic Books, 1960.

Crowcroft, Andrew. *The Psychotic: Understanding Madness.*
London: Pelican Books, 1967.

Harris, Robert and Paxman, Jeremy. *A Higher Form of Killing: The Secret Story of Chemical and Biological Warfare*. New York: Hill and Wang, 1982.

Hersh, Seymour M. *Chemical and Biological Warfare: America's Hidden Arsenal*. Indianapolis and New York: Bobbs-Merrill, 1968.

Lifton, Robert Jay. *"The Nazi Doctors. Medical Killing and the Psychology of Genocide."* New York: Basic Books, 1987.

Marks, John. *The Search for the Manchurian Candidate: The CIA and Mind Control*. New York: Times Books, 1979.

McDermott, Jeanne. *The Killing Winds: The Menace of Biological Warfare*. New York: Arbor House, 1987.

INDEX

Index

Index

Hunt, Jim, 292–294
Hussein, Saddam, 7, 10
hypnosis/hypnotic suggestion, 3–4
   and Buckley's use of, 222–223, 239, 263–264
   and MK-ULTRA/MK-SEARCH, 214, 222–223, 264–265, 276–277
   and American POWs theory, 81

I
interrogation
   centers. *see* torture centers
   of interrogates, 3, 8
   methods/techniques, 2–4, 8
Iran-Contra Affair, 356, 368
Iraq
   and biochemical/germ warfare, 354, 355
   and Saddam Hussein, 7, 10
   and torture, 4, 7, 37
   Islamic
   fundamentalist(s)/fundamentalism, 7, 352, 364
   terrorism/terrorist group(s), 23, 316

J
Jacobson, David, 367
Japanese men, executed after questioning by CIA, 67
jihad/holy war, 316, 352
Journal of Tropical Medicine and Hygiene, 50
Journal of Psychiatry, 260
Johnson, Lyndon
   becomes President after Kennedy assassination, 267–268, 281
   and CIA, 274, 279, 309
   as Congressman, 62, 63
Journal of Tropical Medicine and Hygiene, 50
Justice Department. *see* U.S. Justice Department

K
Kellman, Dr. Frank, 181–182
Kennedy Administration, 209, 223
Kennedy, John F., 195–196, 208–209, 211, 216, 230, 250, 291
assassination of, 265–268, 279, 282
Kennedy, Robert, 150, 223
KGB, 18, 208, 210, 264, 357
   assassinations, 274

and biological weapons, 274–275
and Fidel Castro assassination attempt, 208, 224
and James Schlesinger, 303–304
officer used in CIA mind-control experiment, 95, 265
and psychic driving, 197
and Soviet dissidents, 274–275
and Yuri Nosenko, 281–286
Technical Operations Directorate, 274
and torture centers, 304
Khoklov, Nicholai, 274–275
Khomeini, Ayatollah Seyyed Ruhollah Musavi, 320–321, 331
Kimche, David, 349, 365
King Hussein (of Jordan), 323
King, J.C., 276
Korean War, 13, 18, 33, 40, 44–52, 55, 57, 64, 85, 113, 147–152, 195, 315, 365
and U.S. Air Force officers confess they had dropped biological weapons, 51, 58–59, 78

L
Lacroix, Madeline, 97, 99, 102–105, 110, 126–129, 184, 190, 192, 197, 210–214,
lobotomy of, 233–238
transferred to St. Jean de Dieu Hospital, 238
Lashbrook, Dr. Robert, 12, 158, 161–166, 170
Le May, Custis, 62–63
links between the CIA and the Mafia, 302
the "living dead", 203, 206, 256
lobotomy. *see* psychosurgery
LSD (d-lysergic acid diethylamide), 40–41, 67, 122, 145, 157, 161, 189, 203, 243, 257-258, 261, 283
   doctors use of, to drug themselves, 122
   used to drug
      Adventists, 85
      Glickman, 27–28
      Nosenko, 286
      Olson, 14, 41–42, 159–160, 282
      patients of Dr. Louis Lasagnar, 82
      patients of Cameron
         Rosemary Bonner, 203
         Velma Orlikov, 187, 260
      patients of West, 76, 309–310

evaluates the files the CIA held on the
American POWs, 71–72, 124–126
and the power of his personality, 68
and the Society for the Investigation of Human Ecology, 72, 81, 198, 267

Z
Zielinski, Jan, 174, 183–184, 190–192, 204,
211–213, 253–254, 272, 283